Using SQL

George T. Chou

CORPORATION

LEADING COMPUTER KNOWLEDGE

Using SQL

Library of Congress Catalog No.: 90-60373

ISBN 0-88022-507-6

93 92 91 90   8 7 6 5 4 3 2 1

Interpretation of the printing code: the rightmost double-digit number is the year of the book's printing; the rightmost single-digit number, the number of the book's printing. For example, a printing code of 90-1 shows that the first printing of the book occurred in 1990.

Using SQL covers the standard versions of SQL, with emphasis on Oracle's and dBASE IV's SQL.

Dedicated to
Harold (Hal) H. Morley and J. Thomas Morrow
my dear friends and associates
and
my wife, Jane-Wen
and our children
Doris, Tina, and Tom

Publishing Director

Lloyd J. Short

Acquisitions Editor

Karen A. Bluestein

Product Director

David Maguiness

Book Design and Production

Dan Armstrong
Bill Basham
Claudia Bell
Brad Chinn
Don Clemons
Sally Copenhaver
Tom Emrick
Dennis Hager
Corinne Harmon
Tami Hughes
Bill Hurley
Becky Imel
Jodi Jensen
David Kline
Larry Lynch
Lori A. Lyons
Jennifer Matthews
Cindy L. Phipps
Joe Ramon
Dennis Sheehan
Mae Louise Shinault
Bruce Steed
Mary Beth Wakefield
Jenny Watson
Nora Westlake

Production Editor

Jeannine Freudenberger

Editors

Sara Allaei
Daniel Schnake

Technical Editor

Rick Spear

Indexer

Joelynn Gifford

Composed in Garamond and OCRB
by Que Corporation

ABOUT THE AUTHOR

George Tsu-der Chou

George Tsu-der Chou of Lake Oswego, Oregon, is an Executive Vice President and Director of Morley Capital Management, Inc., a leading professional investment manager, where he also is in charge of the design and development of the company's comprehensive management information system. Before assuming his position at Morley, he was a consultant in the field of database design and development. He developed many database management systems, including analytical managerial database systems and administrative database management programs that deal with inventory and accounting functions.

The author earned his Ph.D. in Quantitative Methods, with supporting disciplines in Computer Science, Economics, and Econometrics, from the University of Washington at Seattle, Washington. He is currently a full professor at the University of Portland in Oregon. In the past twenty years, he has taught courses in business data processing and data management, quantitative methods, operations research, business forecasting, and other subjects. He also has taught computer programming in FORTRAN, COBOL, BASIC, and IBM Assembler.

Dr. Chou has written two college texts, *Computer Programming in BASIC* and *Microcomputer Programming in BASIC*, both published by Harper & Row. He is the author of *dBASE III Handbook*, *dBASE III Plus Handbook*, *dBASE IV Handbook*, and *Using Paradox*, all published by Que Corporation. The best-selling *dBASE III Plus Handbook* has been translated into several foreign languages.

CONTENTS AT A GLANCE

TABLE OF CONTENTS ▼

I   Introduction to Databases and SQL ▼

1   Introduction to Relational Databases 9

2   An Overview of SQL 29

III   Working with Data in Relational Databases

IV   Advanced Topics

10   Advanced Operations 309

ACKNOWLEDGMENTS

First, I would like to thank you for reading this book. If it were not for you, there would be no need for this book.

I would like to express my appreciation to Jeannine Freudenberger and the editorial staff at Que for the outstanding job they have done in editing the manuscript. As always, they are the best editors I have ever worked with. Special thanks to the technical editor, Rick Spear, for carefully checking all the examples in this book to ensure their accuracy and validity.

I also thank Lloyd J. Short, Publishing Director, for the confidence and guidance he has given me in pursuing this writing project. In addition, thanks to David Maguiness, Product Director, for his encouragement and support on the project.

Of course, most important of all, I am grateful to my wife and children for patiently putting up with my neglect during my work on this manuscript. Their love and understanding have made this writing project a great joy and pleasure.

TRADEMARK
ACKNOWLEDGMENTS

Que Corporation has made every effort to supply trademark information about company names, products, and services mentioned in this book. Trademarks indicated below were derived from various sources. Que Corporation cannot attest to the accuracy of this information.

COMPAQ DeskPro is a trademark of COMPAQ Computer Corporation.

dBASE is a registered trademark and dBASE IV is a trademark of Ashton-Tate Corporation.

HP is a registered trademark and LaserJet is a trademark of Hewlett-Packard Co.

IBM and PS/2 are registered trademarks of International Business Machines Corporation.

Informix is a registered trademark of Informix Software, Inc.

Lotus and 1-2-3 are registered trademarks of Lotus Development Corporation.

Microsoft is a registered trademark of Microsoft Corporation.

NEC MultiSync is a registered trademark of NEC Home Electronics (USA) Inc.

Paradox is a registered trademark of Borland/Ansa Software.

PICK is a registered trademark of Pick Systems.

R:base is a registered trademark of Microrim, Inc.

SQL*Plus, SQL*FormsDesigner, and SQL*ReportWriter are registered trademarks of Oracle Corporation.

WordPerfect is a registered trademark of WordPerfect Corporation.

Zenith is a registered trademark of Zenith Electronics Corp.

Introduction

Using SQL is a book about using the SQL language. The book deals with ways to use the SQL commands for efficiently managing your data in a relational database.

SQL is an acronym for Structured Query Language. It is designed for retrieving and manipulating data in a relational database. SQL is a simple yet powerful database language with a small set of commands. These commands are governed by a set of logical and flexible syntax rules. An SQL command consists of one or more clauses, each of which consists of reserved keywords and phrases. You have a great deal of flexibility in arranging these clauses in an SQL command. Because the semantic rules of SQL are similar to English semantics, the rules are understood easily by English-speaking people.

Although the language was not implemented on microcomputers until recently, SQL has been around for quite a while. In 1970, Dr. E. F. Codd introduced the concept of a relational data model. During the next few years, several research projects focused on the development and implementation of a number of relational languages for managing data in a relational data model. One such language was the Structured English Query Language, or SEQUEL, the early version of SQL. Since then, the language has gone through several stages of changes and enhancements. Different dialects of the language have been developed.

During the development and implementation of SQL, the American National Standards Institute (ANSI) chartered its Database Committee to develop a proposal for a standard relational language. In 1986, ANSI ratified a proposal that adopted the IBM dialect of SQL. The International Standards Organization (ISO) also accepted *SQL* as an international standard. This 1986 ANSI-ISO standard version of SQL has since become the official standard version of the language. Subsequently, several commercial vendors have announced different SQL-based products. Currently, more than fifty products on the market support some dialect of SQL.

1

Because the main focus of this book is on how to use SQL as a relational language for managing data in a relational database, every attempt is made to conform to the official standards. This book does not attempt to cover all the commands and features that are unique to all the different SQL implementations. However, I occasionally discuss some of these commands as a supplement to the standards. These discussions are noted accordingly.

How Do You Use This Book?

The primary objective of this book is to demonstrate, through a large collection of examples, the effective use of SQL commands to perform database management functions. SQL commands can be processed by entering them individually in an interactive mode or by embedding them in a program written in another database language or a general programming language. To help you understand the effects of these commands, most of the commands introduced in this book are executed interactively. In this mode, each command is issued at the SQL prompt so that the user can examine the command's results before issuing the next command. Because of the benefits of immediate feedback, the interactive mode is a preferred way for learning commands.

Because SQL has numerous versions, this book cannot discuss all the commands implemented beyond the official standards of the language. This book is not intended as a substitute for a reference manual for a specific version of the SQL language. Instead, *Using SQL* is a user's guide that goes beyond the basics presented in the manuals, showing you how to use the SQL commands correctly to manage your relational databases effectively and efficiently.

Although this book features Oracle's SQL*Plus and dBASE IV's SQL, discussions of the SQL commands are applicable to most SQL implementations. The SQL commands introduced in this book should be legal for most versions of SQL, except for minor variations in some of the commands' syntaxes. In order to find these minor variations, experiment with the commands in your version of SQL. Through these experiments, not only can you find the proper use of the commands, you also can discover additional features offered by that particular version of the language.

Who Should Use This Book?

This book is written mainly for users who want to learn about SQL. If you want to know how you can use the SQL commands for managing your data effectively and efficiently, this book is for you.

For those of you who are interested in learning how to design and implement relational databases, this book is also for you. SQL was developed as a relational database language. It gives you all the powerful tools you need for organizing your data in a relational data model. Through the use of SQL, you can gain a better understanding of the design and implementation of a relational database.

If you are a current user of a database management system, such as dBASE, R:base, or Paradox, this book gives you a new perspective on relational database management.

Just a few years ago, the power of database management could be enjoyed only by users of large, expensive computer systems. The introduction of microcomputer-based database programs revolutionized the way data was organized and managed. Consequently, information often is stored in various noncompatible database management systems, and sharing data among these systems is a difficult, if not impossible, task. The search for a suitable solution to the problem of information sharing has become increasingly urgent. From all the evidence seen recently, SQL undoubtedly will become a major link among various database management systems. The knowledge you gain from this book will prepare you for the next revolution of database management.

How Is This Book Organized?

This book is divided into four parts. The first part, consisting of the first two chapters, provides an overview of the concepts and practices of relational databases and the SQL language. Chapters 3 and 4 make up the second part, which covers the design and creation of relational databases. Next, Part III discusses the commands and procedures relating to operations of data retrieval and manipulations. This part includes Chapters 5 through 9. The last three chapters of the book deal with advanced topics and interfaces between SQL and other database management systems.

Chapter 1, "Introduction to Relational Databases," introduces the basic concepts and fundamentals of relational databases. This chapter presents the data models you can use to organize and manage your data. The focus of this chapter is on the basic elements and components of a relational database.

Chapter 2, "An Overview of SQL," presents an overall perspective of the SQL language. After a brief history of the language, the chapter covers the functions and syntax of various types of SQL commands. You also learn how these commands can be executed in different processing modes.

Chapter 3, "Designing Relational Databases," builds the important foundation from which the SQL commands can be applied effectively. This chapter deals with the proper design and structure of a good relational database. The material covers ways in which you can normalize your base tables so that you can maintain data integrity and avoid the problems of data redundancy.

Chapter 4, "Creating Tables and Entering Data," begins the process of building a relational database. The text shows you how to create base tables for organizing your data. In this chapter, you learn all the commands for creating the table structure and its contents.

Chapter 5, "Finding and Displaying Information," introduces the SQL commands for retrieving information from the data stored in the base tables. This chapter shows you how to use a data query command to find information. You learn how to use different logical operators and connectors to define a detailed filter condition for getting your results.

Chapter 6, "Modifying and Updating Databases," explains the important function of editing the contents of a base table. From the examples in this chapter, you learn how to modify the base table structure and the information stored in the tables. This chapter shows you how to add data to and delete data from an existing base table.

Chapter 7, "Sorting and Indexing Data," discusses an effective means for arranging your results by using the sorting operation. This chapter introduces the commands and keywords for sorting character strings and numeric values. This material also deals with the important function of indexing. By properly indexing your data, you can improve greatly the performance of your data query operations.

Chapter 8, "Summarizing and Grouping Data," covers the procedures and commands for producing summary statistics for the data elements in your database. These summary functions include count, total, average, and maximum and minimum values. The summary functions can be applied to all the data values in a column of the base table or to data grouped by certain criteria. In this chapter, you learn the commands and operations for grouping data.

Chapter 9, "Joining Data Tables," addresses the powerful function of linking base tables. With the commands introduced in this chapter, you can retrieve and manipulate data elements from several tables at the same time. The examples introduced in this chapter demonstrate the power of SQL. By using a simple command, you can link several tables and easily get the information you want from these tables.

Chapter 10, "Advanced Operations," discusses using subqueries and views. Subqueries are powerful SQL tools you can use for performing sophisticated data management operations. Subqueries are queries nested within other queries. Results from subqueries are used as data elements for the other queries. Views are means by which you can view your data in a flexible way without restructuring your tables. As a result, you can organize your data in a relational database logically by the data entities without concern about the size and number of base tables.

Chapter 11, "Data Security and Integrity," addresses two of the most important database management concerns: the issues of data security and data integrity. Data security deals mainly with the problem of confidentiality and with authorized data access. In this chapter, you learn how to solve the data security problem by granting the appropriate privileges to the authorized persons. The problem of data integrity involves ensuring the accuracy and validity of the data in your database. You learn procedures for maintaining the integrity of your data elements in this chapter.

Chapter 12, "Interfacing with Other Database Management Systems," introduces the links between SQL and other database management systems. For performing data query operations, SQL is a powerful database language. It lacks some commands for performing other database management functions, however. For example, you cannot design a custom data entry form with the standard set of SQL commands. As a result of these lacks, you need to supplement SQL commands with other mechanisms provided by other database management systems. This chapter shows you how you can cause SQL to interact with these systems. In addition, this chapter shows you how to embed your SQL commands in a program written in another database language, such as dBASE, or in a regular programming language like C.

This book contains three appendixes. Appendix A presents a summary of the data types supported by a number of commercial implementations of SQL. Appendix B shows the structure and contents of all the base tables and views created in this book. You should note, however, that the contents of these tables may look different in different parts of the book because the tables have been changed in some chapters. Appendix C lists all the SQL commands introduced in this book. Together with examples, this list provides a quick reference to these commands.

Conventions Used in This Book

In order to help you learn the material easily, a few simple conventions have been adopted in this book. For easy identification, all keywords are capitalized. All the data object identifiers, such as table names, column names, and view names, are in lowercase italic letters. Unless the example is showing a special feature that is unique for a given version of SQL, all SQL commands are represented without the SQL prompt.

On-screen results, whether shown in figures or within the text, are printed in a special typeface. Most of these screens are intended to be generic. Your version of SQL may produce slightly different results.

Material that the user types is printed in italic or set off in a line by itself.

I

Introduction to Databases and SQL

Includes

Introduction to Relational Databases
An Overview of SQL

1

Introduction to Relational Databases

The main topic of this book is how to use the Structured Query Language (SQL) to manage a relational database. SQL is a powerful query language that you can use to perform most data management operations. Effective use of the language, however, can be achieved only through a thorough understanding of the underlying concepts of database management systems in general and of a relational model in particular. In this chapter, you first learn the fundamentals of a database management system. In addition to the basic components of the system, this chapter discusses the main functions and characteristics of a relational database model. Knowledge you acquire in this chapter will build the necessary foundation so that you can design correct databases and create and maintain them effectively and efficiently with SQL.

What Is a Database?

A database is a collection of related data items that are organized and stored in a certain systematic way. Although this book focuses on computerized databases, they do not have to be computerized. For example, a telephone directory is a database that contains data elements consisting of names and their phone numbers. You can arrange the names and phone numbers in the telephone directory in many ways. For instance, you may store and organize each person's name and phone number on a separate line:

John J. Smith (206) 574-4568
Harry M. Nelson (503) 636-7890
Albert K. Zeller (503) 635-5555
Kirk D. Chapman (415) 697-1111
Larry A. Baker (206) 573-2345
Kathy T. Dixon (212) 235-6878

Robert F. Frazer (503) 283-7275
David G. King (503) 635-1212
Mike J. Wong (213) 567-8932
Cathy B. Duff (503) 636-4509

In this telephone directory, each line contains a number of items: a person's first name and middle initial, his or her last name, and a phone number that includes an area code and the phone number itself.

The way you organize your data items, or elements, plays an important role for later retrieving and extracting information from them. For example, if you store a person's full name and phone number, as shown in the preceding list, and you want to find a person by his or her last name, you need to scan the first and last names in every line in the directory until you find that person. Finding a name can be quite time-consuming. Similarly, if you need to find all the people who live in a city with a particular area code, you need to scan the person's name and area code in every line and retrieve the names whose area codes match the area code you want. This process also can be slow.

Therefore, anticipating your data search needs, you may want to store and organize your names and phone numbers differently. For example, if you intend to search for a person by his or her last name (or first name) and area code, you may want to store the last names and area codes as separate data items:

Smith, John J., 206, 574-4568
Nelson, Harry M., 503, 636-7890
Zeller, Albert K., 503, 635-5555
Chapman, Kirk D., 415, 697-1111
Baker, Larry A., 206, 573-2345
Dixon, Kathy T., 212, 235-6878
Frazer, Robert F., 503, 283-7275
King, David G., 503, 635-1212
Wong, Mike J., 213, 567-8932
Duff, Cathy B., 503, 636-4509

When you organize your data items in this manner, the data search process is greatly enhanced. For example, to find a person by his or her last name, you need to scan only the first items in each line. Similarly, to search for phone numbers by their area codes, you can skip the first two items—which are separated, or delimited, by commas—and go directly into the area codes themselves.

From these examples, you can see that a database design involves not only the data elements to be stored but, most important, the organization of the elements. These data elements should be organized so that your data manipulation operations can be carried out effectively.

Data Versus Information

Items stored in a database like the phone list represent a set of related data items. These data items are usually not very useful or meaningful on their own. However, they can be retrieved collectively in a manner that provides useful information for a user of the data. For example, from the telephone directory, you can obtain a list of individuals, alphabetized by last names, who live in the state of Oregon, just by listing phone numbers with the area code 503:

Duff, Cathy B. (503) 636-4509
Frazer, Robert F. (503) 283-7275
King, David G. (503) 635-1212
Nelson, Harry M. (503) 636-7890
Zeller, Albert K. (503) 635-5555

In this example, the information is obtained by retrieving the necessary data items from the database (the phone directory) by using a key item (the area code). Then the information is arranged by another key item (the last name). You can see that in order to produce useful information, the data items must be organized in such a way that you easily can identify and search for key items. That is, the key items, such as a person's last name and area code, must be stored as separate data items for easy reference. As a result, the way you store and organize your data items and the procedure and steps you choose in order to retrieve the appropriate data items play a vital part in how efficiently you can extract useful information from the database.

Database Management Systems and Functions

The term *database management system*, or *DBMS*, refers to the systematic organization and management of a large collection of related data. Even though you may have a manual system for organizing and managing your data, the term *DBMS* is used in this book mainly to refer to a collection of computer software programs that you use for storing, maintaining, and retrieving the data items from the databases you create for your data applications.

From the phone directory database example, you have seen that you can find a person's phone number by his or her last name. Similarly, you also can list all the people who live in a given city by searching the area codes in the directory.

The most important function of a good database management system is the capability to retrieve the needed information from the database quickly and with the least amount of effort. Such a data retrieval function can be achieved in a number of ways. The system may provide a user-friendly interface for specifying how and which data items are to be retrieved. The user-friendly interface may be in the form of a menu system from which a user specifies the data retrieval operations. The interface also may be in the form of data retrieval, or query, commands you issue to carry out the data retrieval functions. SQL provides all the commands you need to search for and extract information from the data stored in your databases.

Data search is only one of the functions a properly designed and maintained database provides. Another important function of a database management system is the capability of efficiently maintaining your data. An efficient data maintenance function includes the means for adding new data to the database, removing unwanted data from the database, and modifying the existing data after it has been created.

A properly designed database should attempt to avoid storing redundant data elements in order to minimize the efforts directed toward data maintenance. In addition, the database should provide a way to ensure the integrity of the data in the system. That is, when the values of any data items are changed, all data items related to the changed items must be modified accordingly.

Another useful function a database management system may provide is the capability of producing good summary reports from the data elements stored in the system. For example, if you store all the sale transactions as data elements in a database, with a report generator, you can produce a sales report that tallies all the sales and provides summary statistics, such as total, average, maximum and minimum sales, and so on.

Models of Database Management Systems

As mentioned in the preceding section, a main function of a database management system is to provide a systematic and logical means for storing and organizing your data items. You can choose from a number of database management models for organizing your data. Although the choice of a model depends largely on the nature of your data, you can structure your data to fit any of these models. The model you choose, however, determines the database management software you can use to manage your data, because most software is designed for a specific model.

Database management systems can be structured according to the way you want to organize and relate your data items within the database system. A number of data models have been developed for designing database structures. The three most commonly used data models are the hierarchical model, the network model, and the relational model. Because the focus of this book is on relational databases, only brief discussions of the other two data models are given. Nevertheless, because a good understanding of database structures is vital for ensuring proper design for your database system, you should know about these data models.

Data Relationships

One of the main considerations in choosing a data model depends significantly on how your data elements are related. Therefore, before learning about the different data models you can use to manage your data, you need to understand some of the relations that exist among most data items.

The relations among data items can be categorized as

- ❏ One-to-one relations
- ❏ One-to-many relations
- ❏ Many-to-many relations

One-to-One Relations

A *one-to-one (1:1) relation* is also called a *single-parent–single-child relation*. A single-parent–single-child relation means that a parent can have only one child and that the child belongs to (or is owned by) one parent. A one-to-one relation can be illustrated with a class assignment example in which one instructor can teach only one course and one course can be taught by only one instructor. For example, you assign Franklin to teach History, and therefore that course is taught only by Franklin. Similarly, the Philosophy course is assigned to Quine, and Quine teaches only Philosophy . These one-to-one relations can be represented with a single line linking the name of the teacher and the name of the course:

Teacher	*Course*
Franklin——————History
Quine——————Philosophy

In this one-to-one relation, you can say that Franklin is the parent of the course named History and that the course is the only child of the parent. Similarly, you can say that Quine owns the Philosophy course and the course belongs to (or is owned by) Quine.

One-to-Many Relations

A *one-to-many (1:m)* relation is also called a *single-parent–multiple-child relation*. A single-parent–multiple-child relation means that a parent can have multiple children, but a child can belong to (or be owned by) only a single parent. In the class assignment example, if you assume that a teacher can teach more than one class, the data elements can be viewed as one-to-many relations. For example, if Newton teaches both the Mathematics and Physics courses, you can say that Newton is the parent of two children. However, either course can be taught by only one teacher, Newton. In order to represent the one-to-many relation, two lines are drawn between Newton and the two courses:

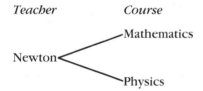

A one-to-one relation is a special case of a one-to-many relation. That is, a one-to-one relation is a one-to-many relation; but not all one-to-many relations are one-to-one relations.

Many-to-Many Relations

A *many-to-many (m:m) relation* is a *multiple-parent–multiple-child relation*, in which a parent can have a number of children and a child can belong to (or be owned by) a number of parents. For example, a course may have a number of students in it; each student may take more than one course:

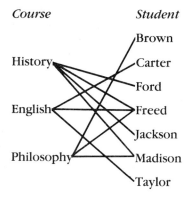

Looking at this example, you see that the History course is the parent for the students Ford, Freed, Jackson, and Madison. The student Freed belongs to the History, English, and Philosophy courses.

Many-to-many relations are the most complex form of relationships that can exist among data elements. Many-to-many relations encompass one-to-one and one-to-many relations. The one-to-one and one-to-many relations can be considered special cases of a many-to-many relation.

Hierarchical Data Model

A *hierarchical data model* organizes data items in a tree structure. It has a main trunk, and a number of branches can grow out from the main trunk. Each tree branch may, in turn, grow a number of sub-branches. At the end of a sub-branch, several leaves may grow out. Several levels of sub-branches may exist between the main trunk and the leaves. You can view the structure using a top-down approach, in which you look at the main trunk on the top and then go down to its branches, sub-branches, and leaves. Or you can use a bottom-up approach, in which you view your database structure from the bottom, or leaves, and then trace each leaf back to the top of the main trunk through levels of branches and sub-branches.

The most important characteristic of a hierarchical data model is that only one-to-one or one-to-many relations are allowed in the structure for describing the relationships among the data items.

In the tree structure analogy, a tree branch can have several sub-branches; but a sub-branch can belong to only one branch. Similarly, a sub-branch can have several leaves; but any one leaf can belong to only a single sub-branch. That is, you cannot have two sub-branches sharing the same leaf; nor can you have a leaf belonging to more than one sub-branch.

In order to see how a hierarchical data model is used to organize the data items, look at a relatively simple data structure that involves a set of classes to be taught by a number of teachers. Each class is taken by a number of students. The data items to be used in this sample data structure are as follows:

Five teachers: Franklin, Hemingway, Newton, Quine, Shaw

Five courses: English, History, Mathematics, Philosophy, Physics

Ten students: Austin, Brown, Carter, Ford, Freed, Gilmore, Jackson, Madison, Reed, Taylor

Depending on how you want to organize and view the data items, you can choose some of these data items as parents to which other data items, or children, belong. For example, you can organize and view the data items so that an instructor teaches one or more courses, each of which is taken by a number of students. More specifically, you can set these conditions:

1. Franklin teaches History, which is taken by Ford, Freed, Jackson, and Madison.

2. Hemingway and Shaw jointly teach English, which is taken by Carter, Freed, and Taylor.

3. Newton teaches Mathematics and Physics, where the former is taken by Austin, Brown, and Reed and the latter is taken by Carter, Gilmore, Madison, and Reed.

4. Quine teaches Philosophy, which is taken by Brown, Freed, and Madison.

As a result, the data items can be organized with a hierarchical structure, as shown in figure 1.1.

In examining the hierarchical structure in figure 1.1, you will notice that all the relationships among these data items are defined with one-to-one or one-to-many relations. An instructor can teach one or more courses; but a course can be taught by only one teacher. For example, Franklin teaches History, and History is taught by Franklin. Similarly, the History course has four students (Ford, Freed, Jackson, and Madison); each student belongs to the History course.

Also note that the English course is taught by Hemingway and Shaw. In a hierarchical model, you cannot represent English as belonging to both Hemingway and Shaw (as multiple parents). As a result, you repeat the English course in the structure: once as the child of the parent named Hemingway and again as the child of the parent named Shaw. Similarly, when a student is

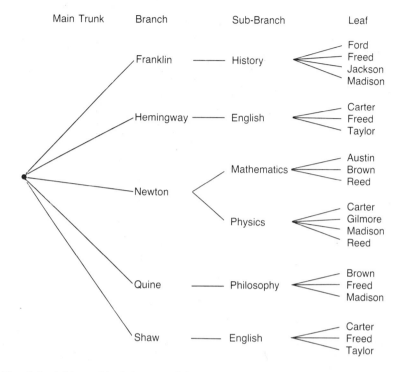

Fig. 1.1. *A hierarchical data model.*

taking more than one course, his or her name is viewed as a child for a number of single parents. For example, the student named Carter appears several times in the structure.

One advantage of using a hierarchical model to organize your data items is that the link between any two data items is defined simply, as illustrated in the structure. However, the model often requires a large number of redundant data items in the structure in order to represent all the data links in one-to-many relations.

Network Data Model

Like the hierarchical model, a *network data model* also can be viewed as a tree structure. In fact, a hierarchical structure is a special case of a network structure. That is, a hierarchical structure always conforms to a network structure, but not all network structures fit a hierarchical model. The main difference between the hierarchical and the network models is that the former uses only one-to-one (1:1) and one-to-many (1:m) relations in presenting the data links but the latter presents the data structure with many-to-many (m:m) relations.

One of the major advantages of a network model is that you can avoid the problem of data redundancy by allowing many-to-many relations in your data structure. For example, if you choose a network model to organize the data items presented in the preceding example, the structure looks like that shown in figure 1.2.

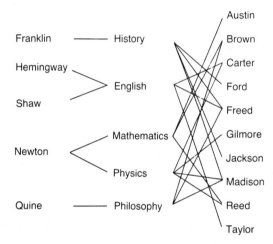

Fig. 1.2. *A network data model.*

Notice the complexity of a network model. Although each student and course appears only once in the structure, relations among these data items can be very complex.

In comparing the hierarchical and network models, you can see the tradeoffs between the simplicity of their data relations and the amount of data redundancy. Therefore, the choice of a data model should be made by weighing the extra amount of data storage required for holding the redundant data items against the additional time needed to retrieve your information in a more complex data structure.

Relational Data Model

Unlike the hierarchical and network models, a relational model does not organize its data items in a tree structure. Instead, a relational model organizes its data in a table format. A *table* is divided into vertical columns and horizontal rows. The intersection between a row and a column is a *data cell*, which is used for holding a *data value*. For example, in a relational data model, you may hold the personal data related to the teachers in a base table that looks like that in figure 1.3.

The teacher table:

TEACHER ID	TEACHER LAST NAME	TEACHER FIRST NAME	RANK	OFFICE	PHONE
T1	Franklin	Benjamin	Professor	West 103	235-1234
T2	Hemingway	Ernest M.	Professor	West 301	287-6666
T3	Newton	Isaac	Associate Prof.	East 150	635-1414
T4	Quine	Willard V.	Professor	East 250	636-2626
T5	Shaw	George B.	Assistant Prof.	West 104	235-7878

Fig. 1.3. *A base table in a relational data model.*

From figure 1.3, you will notice that the base table is divided into six columns and five rows. Each row holds information about a teacher. Each column is given a name and is used for storing a data element related to a given teacher.

When properly designed, a relational data structure can accommodate one-to-one, one-to-many, and many-to-many relations. The problem of data redundancy can be minimized or avoided with the correct database design. As a result, a relational model is the preferred model for managing data. Many database management systems are designed around a relational model.

A Relational Database

A *relational database* is a collection of tables that contain data items organized in accordance with a relational data model. A simple relational database can consist of only one table. But for most applications, you probably need a number of tables for holding related data items.

The main ingredients of a relational database are data elements, or data items. These elements are stored as data values in a collection of base tables. Depending on the nature of the information, you can store different types of data elements in base tables. Base tables also can be structured in accordance with their intended usages and so can be classified as association tables and relation tables. Other types of tables also can be created and set up during the process of data manipulation. Some of these tables may be in the form of temporary working tables created for holding the intermediate results, and others are set up by the database management systems for cataloging the contents of the database.

Data Elements

A *data element* is a piece of a data item and describes a single property of a data entity. A *data entity* is any distinguishable object; it can be something tangible, like a teacher or a student, or something intangible, such as a course, a rank, or a sale. A data entity has properties; for instance, a teacher may have a set of properties such as a last name, a first name, a rank, an office, and so on. A data element can be something like *Franklin*, which represents a single fact about a property (last name) of an entity (a teacher). Such a data element is called a *data value* in a database. A data value is usually stored in the intersection between a row and a column in a base table (again see the *teacher* table in fig. 1.3).

Data Types

You can store different types of data values in a base table. The *T1* in the *teacher id* column, for example, is called an alphanumeric or character string because the value can contain a combination of alphabetic and numeric characters. The types of data values are

❏ Alphanumeric or character values

❏ Numeric values

❏ Date and time values

❏ Logical values

Numeric data is used to represent values and quantities that are in the form of integers and decimal numbers. Arithmetic operations can be applied to numeric data. Monetary values and scientific floating-point values are special types of numeric data.

Dates and times, in forms like Jul-04-1990 12:00:00 p.m., are not treated the way character strings are, even though dates and times contain mainly alphabetic and numeric characters. The rules a database management system uses to sort dates and times are different from the rules used to arrange character strings. In addition, you often can perform arithmetic operations on dates and times. For example, you can calculate the number of days between two dates by subtracting.

Logical data is usually represented in the form of T/F (true/false) or Y/N (yes/ no) for the two possible logical states. This data type is an efficient way to group your data elements into the two logical groups.

Base Tables

Base tables are the backbones of a database system because all the data elements are stored and organized in a collection of base tables. A base table is divided into rows and columns. The intersection of a row and a column is called a cell and is used for holding a data element. The size of the table is immaterial. In a computerized database system, the number of rows and columns and the size of the data cells are limited by the database management software and available storage capacity.

Each base table also is identified by a name for storing the data elements that are related to a given entity. As seen in figure 1.3, the table called *teacher* is used for storing the data elements about the teachers.

Columns and Rows

Each column in a base table is identified by a name. These columns are used to store the data values for describing the properties of a data entity. The *teacher* table has six columns:

- ❏ TEACHER ID
- ❏ TEACHER LAST NAME
- ❏ TEACHER FIRST NAME
- ❏ RANK
- ❏ OFFICE
- ❏ PHONE

These columns are used to describe the properties associated with a teacher. These properties are called *column attributes* in a base table. For example, the data entity *teacher* has a set of properties: his or her identification number, last and first names, academic rank, office number, and phone. These properties are described with the set of column attributes (or column names) in the table.

The data values stored in a given column of a base table also are called characteristics for describing a specific property of the entity or a column attribute of the table. For example, the data value *Franklin* in the *teacher* base table is a characteristic describing a property (last name) of the data entity (teacher).

In summary, you can relate the term *data entity* and its components with the term *table* with its columns in this way:

Data entity ⟵⟶ Table
Properties ⟵⟶ Column attributes
Characteristics ⟵⟶ Data values

Each row in a base table is used to hold the data values for all the properties, or column attributes, associated with a data entity. A row is often called a *tuple*, meaning a set of ordered elements. In the *teacher* table, for example, each row holds the data values for all the properties associated with a given teacher. The number of rows a base table can contain is often limited by the available storage capacity.

Primary Keys

In order to distinguish the data elements stored in a row, often you need to assign a unique value to each row in a key column for identifying specific rows. If you look at the *teacher* table in figure 1.3, you can see that the first column of the table (named *teacher_id*) is set up for providing a unique identification for each row. The value T1 in the *teacher_id* column uniquely identifies the data elements associated with the row that belongs to the teacher named Franklin. Such a column is called a *primary key*. In addition to being used for identifying a specific row in the table, a primary key also is used for linking the table itself with other tables. (As explained later in this chapter, a primary key also may consist of more than one column.)

Relation Tables

Although all the data elements in a relational database system are organized and stored in the form of base tables, these tables may perform different functions depending on the tables' structures.

Most base tables are created for storing data values for the column attributes associated with an entity. Data values stored in these types of base tables can be used independently or linked with other tables to produce useful information. A base table, however, can be structured so that its main function is to provide links between different base tables. This type of table is called a *relation table* because data elements stored in these tables define the relations among different tables.

Foreign Keys

A main characteristic of a relation table is that it must contain one or more foreign keys in the table. Data values in the foreign-key columns provide the necessary links between different tables.

A *foreign key* usually is represented in a relation table by a column whose values match the data values of the primary key in some other table. Although data elements stored in a foreign key in a relation table may describe properties of the data entity, these same data elements also are used for relating data in the relation table with data elements stored in another table. An example of a foreign key can be seen in the *teacher_id* column in the *course* table presented in figure 1.4.

The course table:

COURSE ID	COURSE TITLE	COURSE DESCRIPTION	CREDIT HOURS	TEACHER ID
C1	ENGL 101	English Literature	3	T2
C2	ENGL 101	English Literature	3	T5
C3	HIST 100	American History	3	T1
C4	MATH 105	Calculus I	5	T3
C5	PHIL 101	Philosophy	3	T4
C6	PHYS 102	Physics I	5	T3

Fig. 1.4. *A relation table.*

If you examine the *course* table in figure 1.4, you will notice that the table looks like an ordinary base table. Each column stores data elements associated with a given course. The course is identified by the *course_id* as a primary key. However, the table contains a foreign-key column named *teacher_id*. In addition to describing the teacher who teaches the course, the data value in the foreign key provides the link between data elements in the *course* table and data elements in the *teacher* table. That is, with the data value stored in the foreign key in the *course* table, you can find those data values in the *teacher* table. For example, by knowing the data value of T2 in the foreign key in the *course* table, you can locate in the *teacher* table the information that is related to that teacher in the row with the same data value in its primary key (*teacher_id*) column.

Although a relation table often contains a primary key and one or more foreign keys for relating different tables, a relation table can contain only foreign keys. The main function of such a relation table is to provide the necessary links among other tables. For example, the *class* table shown in figure 1.5 is a relation table that contains only two columns, both of which are considered foreign keys.

In the *class* table, you can see that the table relates the data elements in the *course* table with the data elements in the *student* table by using the *course_id* and *student_id* columns as foreign keys. The *course_id* column refers to the course information in the *course* table, and *student_id* links the courses to the students in the *student* table. The content of the *student* table is shown in figure 1.6.

The class table:

COURSE ID	STUDENT ID
C1	S3
C1	S5
C1	S10
C2	S3
C2	S5
C2	S10
C3	S4
C3	S5
C3	S7
C3	S8
C4	S1
C4	S2
C4	S9
C5	S2
C5	S5
C5	S8
C6	S3
C6	S6
C6	S8
C6	S9

Fig. 1.5. *A relation table.*

In summary, the *course* and *student* tables are linked by using the information provided by the *class* relation table. The links among these three tables are depicted in figure 1.7.

The student table:

STUDENT ID	STUDENT LAST NAME	STUDENT FIRST NAME	BIRTH DATE	SEX	HIGH SCHOOL GPA
S1	Austin	Linda D.	03/08/71	F	3.98
S2	Brown	Nancy J.	05/14/70	F	3.35
S3	Carter	Jack F.	10/10/71	M	2.87
S4	Ford	Harvey P.	06/12/71	M	2.60
S5	Freed	Barbara J.	07/28/69	F	3.15
S6	Gilmore	Danny S.	11/01/70	M	3.86
S7	Jackson	Brad L.	04/15/71	M	2.75
S8	Madison	George G.	08/15/70	M	2.35
S9	Reed	Donna E.	09/26/69	F	2.96
S10	Taylor	Bob K.	02/14/71	M	3.14

Fig. 1.6. Another example of a base table.

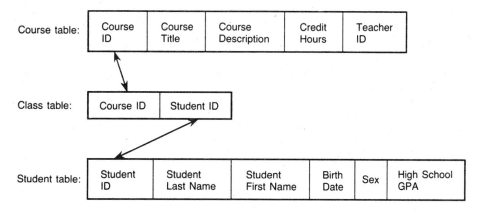

Fig. 1.7. Linking the course and student tables.

In the figure, you can see that the foreign key *course_id* in the *class* table is linked to the primary key with the same column name in the *course* table. Similarly, the primary key *student_id* in the *student* table is linked to the foreign key with the same column name in the *class* table.

Derived Tables

During data manipulations, in order to speed operations, it is often necessary or beneficial to extract portions of one or more base tables for performing certain data management functions. For example, if you have a table that contains a large number of columns and you do not need to use all these columns for generating your reports, you may want to select the needed columns and store them in a working table. This kind of working table is a form of a *derived table*. Most derived tables are temporary tables, meaning that they are not saved as permanent tables. They are deleted from the database after they have been used. Although you can save derived tables as base tables, this step is not recommended, because you will be saving redundant data items that can be extracted from other base tables as the items are needed.

Views

Views are often called *virtual tables*, meaning that views look like real tables but do not actually exist. Views are used mainly for viewing specific data elements that are stored in other base tables. For example, if you want to allow certain users of the database to view only certain columns of information in the *student* table, you can set up a view that includes only these columns. When you look at the contents of the view, you see all the data elements in the columns included. However, the view does not actually contain those elements. Items stored in the view are "pointers" to base table columns that actually contain the data elements.

Another useful function of views is generating computed values by performing arithmetic operations on data values in other base tables. For example, if you store employees' annual salaries in a base table, you can set up a view that specifies a formula for computing the monthly salaries by dividing the annual salaries by 12. After the view is set up, you can look at the monthly salary figures for the employees by displaying the contents of the view.

Views differ from derived tables in three important ways:

❏ Derived tables actually contain data elements in the columns, but views do not.

❏ Views are dynamic in nature whereas derived tables are static. This difference means that when you change the data elements in the underlying base tables composing the views, the views' data is changed accordingly. This relationship is not true for derived tables because the values in the derived tables remain unchanged even if the values in the base tables from which the derived tables were created have been changed. If you want to update the contents of the derived tables, you need to repeat the process for generating the derived tables.

❏ Views are permanent, whereas derived tables are temporary. Unlike derived tables, which are lost when you exit from the current database, views remain intact until you delete them.

Chapter Summary

In this chapter, you have been introduced to the fundamental concepts of database management. A number of data models are discussed. The data model you choose determines the database management system you use to manage your databases. Although database management software is available to handle hierarchical and network models, the emphasis of this chapter is on relational databases. The main ingredients of a relational database are the data elements and the base tables for storing the data elements. In this chapter, you have learned how data elements can be organized in these base tables. You learned how a base table can be structured as a relation table for linking data elements in different tables by using primary and foreign keys.

In this chapter, discussions are given about the important functions of a database management system. In the next chapter, you get an overview of the SQL language and learn how the language can be used to manage the database functions discussed.

2

An Overview of SQL

Although SQL can be considered a computer language in a broad sense, SQL differs from regular computer languages in a number of significant ways. These differences are one of the topics discussed in this chapter.

SQL is a database language that consists of a set of powerful commands for performing most of the database management functions in a relational data model. In this chapter, you get an overview of the use of SQL commands for performing these functions. SQL has two modes in which you can process commands. In one mode, you issue the commands interactively at the SQL prompt, and in the other mode, you embed your SQL commands in a computer program. You will see examples of both processing modes.

Because SQL was developed mainly as a query language, some of the commands for other data management operations are not included in the standard version of the language. For example, in order to produce sophisticated reports and data entry forms, you need to use the report generators and form generators implemented by other database management systems, or you have to write your own program in a regular computer language to supplement the SQL language. In this chapter, you see examples of how to interface SQL with other database management systems.

A Brief History of SQL

SQL is an acronym for Structured Query Language. It is a database "language" for performing most of the data manipulation operations in a relational database. The language SQL (pronounced "ess-cue-ell" or sometimes referred as to "sequel") has gone through a series of developmental changes and functional improvements since its inception in the early 1970s.

In 1970, Dr. E. F. Codd, at the IBM Research Laboratory, introduced the concept of a relational data model by publishing a definitive paper entitled "A Relational Model of Data for Large Shared Data Banks" (*Communications of*

29

the ACM, Vol. 13, No. 6, June 1970). During the next few years, several research projects focused on the development and implementation of a number of relational languages for managing the data in a relational model. One language was the Structured English Query Language (called SEQUEL). In 1974, this language was implemented as a prototype by IBM and referred to as SEQUEL-XRM.

A revised version of SEQUEL-XRM, called SEQUEL/2, was defined in 1977. This version went through several stages of change, and in 1981 IBM implemented the language as SQL/DS for running in the DOS/VSE environment. Again, different versions of SQL/DS were announced by IBM for the VM/CMS (SQL/DS) and MVS (DB2) environments. Since the early 1980s, several vendors have announced different SQL-based products, among them the following:

❑ ORACLE by Relational Software, Inc. (later renamed Oracle Corporation), in 1981

❑ INGRES by Relational Technology, Inc., in 1981

❑ DG/SQL by Data General Corporation, in 1984

❑ SYBASE by Sybase, Inc., in 1986

❑ dBASE IV SQL by Ashton-Tate Corporation, in 1989

Currently on the market are more than 50 products, each of which supports some dialect of SQL. Early versions of SQL were implemented in large mainframe computers, but recent implementations of the language allow microcomputers to benefit from the power of this relational language.

During the development and implementation of SQL, the American National Standards Institute (ANSI) chartered its Database Committee to develop a proposal for a standard relational language. In 1986, a proposal that basically adopted the IBM dialect of SQL was ratified by ANSI. This standard was soon accepted as an international standard by the International Standards Organization (ISO). The 1986 ANSI-ISO standard version of SQL has since become the official standard version of the language.

Because the main focus of this book is on how to use SQL as a relational language for managing your data, efforts have been made to conform as closely as possible to the language standards so that the commands introduced are legal in most commercial versions of the language. Occasionally, however, in taking advantage of the power of the added commands and features offered by some versions of the languages, some dialects are covered. When a dialect is included, these commands and features are noted clearly so that you can choose to experiment with them at your own discretion.

What Is SQL?

SQL is a relational language that consists of a set of commands for defining, manipulating, and controlling data in a relational database. Although SQL contains all the semantics and syntax usually associated with most computer programming languages, SQL differs from these languages in a number of important ways.

First, SQL is not a procedural language like BASIC, COBOL, Pascal, and others. To accomplish a task with a procedural language, you have to define each procedural step required for getting the task done. For example, if you need to sort a list of values, you must write a set of commands (a program) in the procedural language to specify the detailed steps required for arranging these values. With SQL, however, instead of defining the procedural steps, all you need to specify is the result you want; then you let SQL find the "best" procedure to achieve that result. For example, if you want to sort the data elements in a table, you need issue only an SQL command indicating the column or columns of data to be arranged and the order you desire, without specifying the detailed steps involved.

Because of its capability to find the best method for solving a problem without the user's direction, SQL is sometimes referred to as a "smart" language with a built-in intelligence. But SQL is not an expert system or an artificial intelligence language because SQL does not gain extra knowledge from users or experts.

SQL lacks some of the commands found in most computer programming languages. For example, SQL does not have the commands and procedures needed for generating detailed and sophisticated summary reports from the data elements stored in the database. As a result, some versions of SQL provide additional commands to supplement the report generation function. Similarly, SQL has no commands for developing sophisticated data entry forms. In order to design a custom data entry form, you need to use a form generator provided by a database management system as a supplement to the SQL language.

SQL does have a set of powerful commands for creating and maintaining relation tables in databases. These types of database management commands usually are not available in a regular computer programming language. In addition, SQL gives you a set of query commands that provide all the tools you need for effective data retrieval operations. Despite the lack of a report writer and a form generator, the power of SQL's data maintenance and data query commands makes SQL a superior language for managing your data in a relational database.

SQL Commands

An SQL command is a statement that defines the objects and results of a data management function. The object defined in the command may be a base table to be created, modified, or deleted. The results may be the information that is to be retrieved and extracted from a set of data stored in one or more base tables. In addition to the objects and results, some filter conditions may be specified for qualifying the data elements involved. These filter conditions tell SQL which rows in the tables are the subjects of the commands. Similarly, the columns to be affected also are specified in the command.

In order to understand the basic components of an SQL command, look at an example:

```
SELECT    l_name, f_name, title, salary
  FROM    employee
 WHERE    title = 'Manager'
ORDER BY  salary;
```

Basically, this command tells SQL to "select the data elements in the *l_name*, *f_name*, *title*, and *salary* columns from the *employee* base table for the rows having the value of Manager in the *title* column and to arrange the results by the *salary* values."

This command can be divided into three main parts:

1. A set of keywords: SELECT, FROM, WHERE, ORDER BY

2. Objects of the command: name of the base table (*employee*), names of the data columns (*l_name, f_name, title, salary*)

3. A filter condition for qualifying the rows: title = 'Manager'

Syntax Rules

The SQL language consists of a set of commands, each of which must conform to the syntax rules of the language. These syntax rules govern the form, or format, in which an SQL command can be composed. The syntax rules tell you whether you can capitalize the words in the command and how you can separate the clauses and phrases; syntax rules also tell you the importance of blank spaces in the command, the legitimate symbols you can use in the command, and so on. Unfortunately, these rules differ among various implementations of SQL. I have tried to discuss the rules that are common to most implementations.

Case

An SQL command is composed much like a sentence in English with a few exceptions. Like an English sentence, an SQL command can be composed of a number of clauses and phrases, which include the necessary SQL keywords and names for identifying the data objects involved. In an English sentence, you normally capitalize the first letter of the first word. However, case is not important in an SQL command. You may choose to capitalize any or all of the words in an SQL command without changing the meaning of the command. For example, you can issue the whole command in capital letters:

```
SELECT   L_NAME, F_NAME, TITLE, SALARY
   FROM   EMPLOYEE
  WHERE   TITLE = 'MANAGER';
ORDER BY   SALARY
```

Or you can define the command in all lowercase letters:

```
select   l_name, f_name, title, salary
  from   employee
 where   title = 'Manager';
order by   salary
```

An advantage of using all capital letters or all lowercase letters in an SQL command is that you do not have to switch between cases when you type the command. In this book, however, for easy identification, all the keywords are capitalized in all the commands. All the data object identifiers, such as table names and names of the data columns, are in lowercase letters. The indentation is insignificant. You can align the clauses in a way that is pleasing in appearance to you.

Spacing

Blank spaces do not play an important part in an SQL command as long as at least one blank separates every two words in the command. You can issue the command as one or more lines, and the blank spaces between these lines have no effect on the command. For example, the former command can be issued as follows:

```
SELECT   l_name, f_name, title, salary FROM employee
WHERE   title = 'Manager' ORDER BY salary;
```

Length

The total length of an SQL command is determined by the specific version of SQL you are using. For example, many versions allow you to have an SQL command up to 256 characters long. Furthermore, depending on the editor provided by your version of SQL, when you enter the command in multiple lines, a line number may be inserted automatically by the language for each command line. For example, if you enter the command in Oracle's SQL*Plus, the command may look like this:

```
SQL> SELECT l_name, f_name, title, salary
  2    FROM employee
  3  WHERE title='Manager' ORDER BY salary;
```

The **SQL>** is the symbol used by SQL*PLus as the SQL prompt for requesting the command. Other versions of SQL may use different prompts, such as **SQL.** (in dBASE IV's SQL) or **SQL:** (in SYBASE), and so on. In this book, unless the example is showing a special feature unique for a given version of SQL, all SQL commands are represented without the SQL prompt.

Punctuation Marks

In an English sentence, punctuation marks are used for separating parts of the sentence. For example, you always end a declarative sentence with a period (.), and you use commas (,) and semicolons (;) to separate the clauses and phrases in the sentence. However, symbols like periods, commas, and colons are used in an SQL command for purposes other than punctuation. More specifically,

❏ You do not always use a comma to separate the phrases or clauses in an SQL command.

❏ You must end an SQL command with a semicolon.

❏ Periods are used to separate data items, such as in *employee.l_name* for separating the table name (*employee*) and a column name (*l_name*).

❏ Underscores (_) are used (in this book) as a part of the name of a data object (the name of a column, *l_name*).

Single Quotation Marks

Single quotation marks are used to enclose a character string. For example, you can enclose the last name in a pair of quotation marks and enter it as a data value into the *employee* base table:

```
INSERT INTO    employee (l_name, f_name)
       VALUES    ('Smith', 'John J.');
```

The character string also can be used as the value for a filter condition:

```
SELECT   l_name, f_name, salary
  FROM   employee
 WHERE   l_name = 'Smith';
```

Although some versions of SQL allow you to use either single quotation marks or double quotation marks to enclose a character string, that liberty is not universal. Try to stay with using single quotation marks because many versions of SQL do not accept double quotation marks for enclosing character strings, but all versions accept single quotation marks.

Commas

Commas are used to separate some phrases or clauses in an SQL command. For example, these phrases may define the column attributes in a CREATE TABLE command:

```
CREATE TABLE employee
        (ss_no        CHAR(11),
         l_name       CHAR(7),
         f_name       CHAR(10),
         title        CHAR(10),
         dept         CHAR(10),
         salary       DECIMAL(8,2));
```

Commas are used to separate column names and data values, as seen in the following command:

```
INSERT INTO   employee (l_name, f_name, salary)
     VALUES   ('Smith', 'John J.', 89500);
```

You must not use commas to separate numeric digits in a value like 89,500.

Parentheses

Parentheses are required for defining column attributes, specifying a list of column names in some SQL commands. As you have seen, you need to enclose column definitions in the CREATE TABLE command in parentheses:

```
CREATE TABLE employee
        (ss_no        CHAR(11),
         l_name       CHAR(7),
         f_name       CHAR(10),
         title        CHAR(10),
         dept         CHAR(10),
         salary       DECIMAL(8,2));
```

You need to specify the column names in an INSERT INTO statement as

> INSERT INTO employee (l_name, f_name, salary)
>   VALUES ('Smith', 'John J.', 89500);

However, not all the column names are to be enclosed in parentheses. For example, you do not enclose the column names in a SELECT command:

> SELECT l_name, f_name, title, dept, salary
>   FROM employee;

You need to pay attention to the exact syntax of every SQL command.

Parentheses also can be used to indicate the order for evaluating an arithmetic expression or for interpreting a filter condition. For example, when you specify an arithmetic formula, you can use parentheses to indicate the order in which the formula is to be evaluated:

> $((value\_a + value\_b)/(value\_c + value\_d))*(value\_e/value\_f)$

When you express your formula this way, following the regular algebraic conventions, the expressions in the inner parentheses are evaluated first.

Similarly, you may use parentheses to define your filter condition clearly so that no ambiguity can arise:

> SELECT l_name, f_name, dept, salary
>   FROM employee
> WHERE (dept = 'Sales' OR dept = 'MIS')
>   OR (salary >= 20000 AND salary <= 30000);

Keywords

Keywords are special words reserved by SQL for performing specific functions; keywords cannot be used for other purposes, such as for naming a table or identifying a column. The set of SQL reserved keywords that conforms to the ANSI-ISO standards is given in table 2.1.

Each clause, or key phrase, in a command must begin with a keyword. For example, the phrase *FROM employee* defines the name of the base table from which the SELECT operation is to perform. Similarly, the phrase *WHERE title = 'Manager'* specifies the filter condition that determines which rows in the table are to be selected.

For each command, the syntax rules specify the proper order of all the key phrases allowed in that command. You may skip the optional phrases; but you must not switch their order.

Table 2.1
SQL Reserved Keywords

ALL	FETCH	ORDER
AND	FLOAT	PASCAL
ANY	FOR	PLI
AS	FORTRAN	PRECISION
ASC	FOUND	PRIVILEGES
AUTHORIZATION	FROM	PROCEDURE
AVG	GO	PUBLIC
BEGIN	GOTO	REAL
BETWEEN	GRANT	ROLLBACK
BY	GROUP	SCHEMA
CHAR	HAVING	SECTION
CHARACTER	IN	SELECT
CHECK	INDICATOR	SET
CLOSE	INSERT	SMALLINT
COBOL	INT	SOME
COMMIT	INTEGER	SQL
CONTINUE	INTO	SQLCODE
COUNT	IS	SQLERROR
CREATE	LANGUAGE	SUM
CURRENT	LIKE	TABLE
CURSOR	MAX	TO
DEC	MIN	UNION
DECIMAL	MODULE	UNIQUE
DECLARE	NOT	UPDATE
DELETE	NULL	USER
DESC	NUMERIC	VALUES
DISTINCT	OF	VIEW
DOUBLE	ON	WHENEVER
END	OPEN	WHERE
ESCAPE	OPTION	WITH
EXEC	OR	WORK
EXISTS		

The functions of a keyword in an SQL command may be

❏ Identifying the command itself

❏ Specifying the data management operation required

❏ Defining the results desired from the specified operation

❏ Identifying the data objects involved

❏ Defining the filter conditions for the data search process

For example, the keywords included in the SQL command mentioned in a previous section are SELECT, FROM, WHERE, and ORDER BY. The keyword SELECT is used to identify the command, indicating that it is a data selection, or data query, command. The keyword also specifies the data management operation; namely, selecting certain data elements from the data object, defined as a table name (*employee*) by the keyword FROM. The results from the data selection operation are defined as data values in the list of columns whose names are specified in the parentheses. The filter condition, title = 'Manager', defined by the keyword WHERE, determines which rows are to be the subject of the selection operation. The ORDER BY keyword specifies how the selected data elements are to be arranged.

The order in which these clauses and key phrases are specified in an SQL command is very important for some versions of the SQL. For example, you may not switch the phrase FROM employee with WHERE title = 'Manager' in the command, as

```
    SELECT   l_name, f_name, title, salary
    WHERE    title = 'Manager'
      FROM   employee
  ORDER BY   salary;
```

In addition to the standard SQL keywords, other keywords are reserved by different versions of SQL. For a list of these keywords, consult your language reference manual.

Types of SQL Commands

SQL is a simple data management language. It has a small set of powerful commands. These commands can be grouped into five basic categories: data definition, data query, data manipulation, transaction processing, and data control statements.

Data Definition Commands

The main functions of the data definition commands are

❑ Creating the structure of a new base table

❑ Modifying the structure of an existing base table

❑ Deleting a table from the database

❑ Creating a new view

❑ Deleting an existing view

❑ Creating an index

❑ Deleting an existing index

The respective data definition commands for performing these functions are CREATE TABLE, ALTER TABLE, DROP TABLE, CREATE VIEW, DROP VIEW, CREATE INDEX, and DROP INDEX.

Data Query Commands

The most powerful SQL command is the SELECT statement. SELECT is used for performing the data query function. With this command, you can retrieve and extract the desired information from the database by including the appropriate conditions for screening the data elements in the database.

Data Manipulation Commands

In the SQL language, you find a set of commands for manipulating the contents of the database. These commands are INSERT, UPDATE, and DELETE. The INSERT command enables you to add new data elements to a base table, and the UPDATE command provides a means for modifying the contents of a base table. The DELETE command can be used to remove some or all of the rows from a base table.

Transaction Processing Commands

In many versions of SQL, when you issue a data manipulating command for changing the contents of a database, the changes are tentative and are not made permanent until you reach a normal termination. If you want to make these changes permanent before normal termination, you can issue the COMMIT command. You also can issue the ROLLBACK command to undo all the tentative changes and return the database to its contents before the last COMMIT command. COMMIT and ROLLBACK are called transacting process commands.

Data Control Commands

SQL provides two data control commands for determining authority levels and access privileges for users. The granting of privileges is done by means of the GRANT command. The privileges you can grant a user have different levels. You can grant a user the authority for accessing an entire database, certain base tables, only selected columns in these tables, and so on. You can allow a user to issue only certain SQL commands. For instance, in order to protect data integrity, you may grant only data entry persons the privilege of using the UPDATE, INSERT, and DELETE commands. For other users, who need only to view the data, you grant the data query privileges of using the SELECT command. Any privileges granted can be canceled with the REVOKE command.

Notation Conventions

Although SQL provides a great deal of freedom for specifying an SQL statement, in order to avoid ambiguity and confusion, the following conventions have been adopted for describing the notations used in this book.

Uppercase Keywords

All SQL keywords in uppercase must be written exactly as shown. Names of tables and columns are shown in lowercase. Every SQL command must end with a semicolon (;):

```
   SELECT   ss_no, l_name, f_name, title, dept, salary
     FROM   employee
    WHERE   dept = 'Sales'
       OR   dept = 'MIS'
 ORDER BY   salary DESC;
```

In the preceding SQL statement, the keywords SELECT, FROM, WHERE, OR, ORDER BY, and DESC (for descending order), entered as uppercase letters, must be entered exactly as shown.

Angle Brackets (< >)

In describing the format of an SQL command, a description of an object may be given by a phrase enclosed in angle brackets (< >), <name of base table> or as a single word linked with underscores, as column_definition. For example, the format of a CREATE TABLE command is

```
   CREATE TABLE   <name of base table>
                  (column_definition ....);
```

These <> brackets are not part of the command and should not be typed. Following is an example of the CREATE TABLE command:

```
   CREATE TABLE   employee
                  (ss_no CHAR(11) ....);
```

Square Brackets ([])

Square brackets ([]) are used to indicate that the object enclosed in the brackets is optional and can be omitted. The brackets are not part of the command and should not be typed. Vertical bars (|) are used to separate alternatives. An asterisk is used to represent all the columns in a given table.

```
    SELECT    *|<column list>
      FROM    <name of base table>
   [WHERE     <filter condition>]
 [ORDER BY    <sorting key>];
```

Other examples of SELECT commands are the following:

```
    SELECT    *
      FROM    employee;
```

```
    SELECT    l_name, f_name
      FROM    employee
  ORDER BY    l_name;
```

```
    SELECT    l_name, f_name, salary
      FROM    employee
     WHERE    salary>30000;
```

```
    SELECT    l_name, f_name, salary
      FROM    employee
     WHERE    salary>3000
  ORDER BY    salary;
```

Ellipses (...)

Ellipses (...) indicate the continuation of a series or the repetition of a part of the command. For example, in describing the format of the CREATE TABLE command, the ellipses are used to show that the column definition portion may be repeated as often as desired:

```
CREATE TABLE    <name of base table>
                (column_definition [, column_definition] ... );
```

The ellipses in the parentheses mean that you can specify as many column definitions as desired. These column definitions are to be separated by commas:

```
CREATE TABLE  employee
              (ss_no        CHAR(11),
               l_name       CHAR(7),
               f_name       CHAR(10),
               title        CHAR(10),
               dept         CHAR(10),
               salary       DECIMAL(8,2));
```

Each phrase in the parentheses (for example, ss_no CHAR(11),) defines a column by specifying the name of the column (*ss_no*) and its data type and size (CHAR(11) indicating that the column is a character string containing up to 11 characters). The ellipsis (...) means that you can specify as many columns as desired in the parentheses.

SQL Functions

SQL is a database language that provides a set of commands for managing your data in a relational database. More specifically, these commands are used for performing the following data management functions:

❑ Creating the base tables for storing the data elements from which useful information can be retrieved and extracted

❑ Maintaining data in the base tables so that all changes are updated

❑ Finding and displaying the desired information from the database by using the data query operation

❑ Manipulating data in the database, including sorting and summarizing the data elements stored in the base tables, joining base tables, and creating view tables

Detailed discussions of all these functions are in the forthcoming chapters. To provide a quick overview about the language, however, examples of the SQL commands for performing these functions described in the following sections.

Storing Data

Before any other database management operations are carried out, you need to store the data elements in a set of base tables. The creation of a base table begins with identifying the table and defining the table structure by using the CREATE TABLE command as shown:

```
CREATE TABLE    employee
                (ss_no       CHAR(11),
                 l_name      CHAR(7),
                 f_name      CHAR(10),
                 title       CHAR(10),
                 dept        CHAR(10),
                 salary      DECIMAL(8,2));
```

The table creation operation involves assigning a name (*employee*) and defining the table structure. This process includes naming the columns (*ss_no*, *l_name*, *f_name*, and so on) and specifying the column attributes (CHAR(11), DECIMAL(8,2), and so on).

After a table structure is properly defined, you can put data elements into the table by using an INSERT statement:

```
INSERT INTO    employee
    VALUES     ('123-45-6789', 'Smith', 'James J.', 'President',
               'Corporate', 89500);
```

Because this statement inserts data values into all the columns in the table, you do not need to specify the column names. Otherwise, you have to list the column names if you want to insert data elements into selected columns.

Maintaining Data

Data maintenance is one of the important functions in a database management system. The function may involve

❑ Modifying, in existing tables, the data elements that require changes

❑ Adding new data elements to a table

❑ Removing data elements no longer needed

Modifying Data

The SQL command for changing data values in an existing table is the UPDATE statement. UPDATE enables you to change the value of a data element by setting the value to another value. For example, the following statement changes James J. Smith's title from the current value of President to a new value of CEO:

```
UPDATE   employee
   SET   title = 'CEO'
 WHERE   l_name = 'Smith'
   AND   f_name = 'James J.';
```

Adding New Data

The INSERT command can be used for appending a new data value to an existing table:

```
INSERT INTO   employee (ss_o, l_ame, f_ame, title)
   VALUES   ('909-10-8910', 'Parker', 'Susan C.', 'Trainee');
```

Deleting Data

The command to remove data from a database is DELETE. You can use this command to delete a specific row of data in a base table. To delete a row of data, you use the WHERE clause to define the row to be deleted:

```
DELETE FROM   employee
     WHERE   ss_no = '123-45-6789';
```

This command deletes the information about the employee whose social security number is 123-45-6789. You also can use the WHERE clause to delete a set of rows in the table. For example, the following command deletes all the rows for employees who belong to the Sales department:

```
DELETE FROM   employee
     WHERE   dept = 'Sales';
```

You can delete all the rows in a table with the DELETE command:

```
DELETE FROM employee;
```

This DELETE command removes all the data rows from the table but retains its structure so that you can insert new data rows into the table later. If you want to delete the complete contents (including the table structure and all the data elements in the table), you use the DROP TABLE command:

```
DROP TABLE employee;
```

Retrieving and Indexing Data

A data query operation enables you to find in the database the data elements that satisfy the qualifying, or filter, conditions you specify. The results from the query operation can be displayed or used to create another working table. The SQL command for a query operation is the SELECT statement. The simplest form of a SELECT statement is

```
SELECT   *
 FROM    employee;
```

This statement selects all (represented by the asterisk, *) the data elements in the *employee* table.

By adding the appropriate filter conditions, you can instruct SQL to retrieve data elements in the specified columns from selected rows (that satisfy the filter conditions):

```
SELECT    Lname, f_name, title, salary
 FROM     employee
WHERE     dept = 'Sales'
   OR     dept = 'MIS'
  AND     salary>30000;
```

This statement finds employees in both the Sales and MIS departments, who earn more than $30,000 annually.

To speed query operations, you can create quick indexes. These indexes are created by using the CREATE INDEX command:

```
CREATE INDEX    bylast
          ON    employee (Lname);
```

In this example, an index named *bylast* is created by using the data values in the *Lname* column of the *employee* table. The information stored in the index will be used for providing a quick reference to the data values in the column. As a result, when you perform a query operation that involves finding a specific value in that column, you can retrieve the value quickly by using the reference without the need of searching every value in the column.

Manipulating Data

A main reason for setting up a database is that you can extract or manipulate the data elements stored in the database and obtain meaningful information. For example, after data elements are stored in the base tables, you can sort them into a specified order to produce a meaningful report. Summary statistics also can be generated by using the data elements in the base tables.

Sorting Data

You can add the ORDER BY clause to a SELECT command to arrange the results from the data query into a specific order. The following SELECT command, for example, displays all the salaries of the employees in a descending order (from the largest to smallest):

```
    SELECT   l_name, f_name, title, salary
      FROM   employee
  ORDER BY   salary DESC;
```

Summarizing Data

SQL has a set of functions you can use to produce summary or aggregate statistics from lists of data values stored in the base tables. A function is specified as a clause in a SELECT statement. These summary, or aggregate, functions are given in table 2.2.

Table 2.2
SQL Aggregate Functions

Function	Description
AVG	Average of the values in the column
COUNT	Total count of data values in the column
MAX	The maximum value in the column
MIN	The minimum value in the column
SUM	Sum of all the values in the column

An example of a SELECT command with an SQL function clause is

```
  SELECT   MAX(salary), MIN(salary), AVG(salary)
    FROM   employee;
```

This statement computes and displays the maximum, minimum, and average salaries for all the employees in the firm.

Different instructions can be added to a SELECT command so that selected data elements can be grouped for producing the summary statistics:

```
    SELECT   dept, AVG(salary)
      FROM   employee
  GROUP BY   dept
    HAVING   AVG(salary)>35000;
```

This statement computes and displays the average salary for each department in which the average salary exceeds $35,000.

Linking Tables

With SQL's powerful commands, you can access data elements stored in more than one base table. This access is accomplished simply by naming all the data columns from the different base tables. The following SELECT command, for example, retrieves columns from the *parts* and *stock* tables:

```
SELECT   parts.stock_no, parts.parts.dscription,
         parts.unit_cost, stock.on_hand
  FROM   parts, stocks
 WHERE   parts.stock_no = stock.stock_no;
```

This command displays data from the *parts* and *stock* tables. The two tables are joined by using the *stock_no* column as the joining key.

In this command, the columns to be retrieved and displayed are identified by name with the names of the associated tables as prefixes (*parts.stock_no*).

Using Views

An SQL view is a so-called *virtual table*, meaning that the table can be "viewed," or considered a base table, but does not actually exist. A view table is usually the result of a data manipulation operation that has been performed on one or more base tables. For example, if you want to display an employee's monthly salary, you can use a formula to define the query result. The formula computes the monthly salary by dividing the annual salary by 12:

```
SELECT   l_name, f_name, salary/12
  FROM   employee;
```

If you issue this command frequently, you can create a view table named *monthpay* for saving the information needed to reproduce the same results. When you need to perform the SELECT operation again, as a shortcut, you can just view the "contents" of the view table instead of reissuing the SELECT command. The statement for creating the view table is

```
CREATE VIEW   monthpay
        AS   SELECT l_name, f_name, salary/12
             FROM    employee;
```

The view table can be treated like a base table for performing most (but not all) data manipulation operations. You view the "contents" of the table by using the following statement:

```
SELECT   *
  FROM   monthpay;
```

The results of this command are identical to the results of the original SELECT command:

```
SELECT   l_name, f_name, salary/12
  FROM   employee;
```

The view table named *monthpay* does not actually exist, however. It does not store the resulting data elements. Instead, *monthpay* contains only the information needed to produce the results. That is, in this example, the view table contains the column names (*l_name*, *f_name*) of the associated base table and the formula (*salary*/12).

Data Organization

SQL stores all the data elements in base tables. Some of these tables are base tables you create for holding the raw data elements. The *employee* table, shown previously, is such a base table. It is created for storing all the data values associated with the attributes about the data entity named *employee*. You set up other tables for holding results from data manipulation operations. These tables include the tables created by extracting selected data elements from base tables and view tables.

For cataloging contents of tables, SQL also creates and maintains system tables.

Understanding System Tables

Depending on the version you are using, SQL creates different types of system tables for keeping track of the contents of all the data tables. Basically, these tables are used to store names of your base tables, column definitions of all the base tables, names of all the existing indexes and views, and information about the access authority levels for these data objects. Names and contents of these system tables usually begin with *SYS* (see table 2.3).

Managing Disk Files

Those of you who are familiar with other database management systems—such as dBASE, R:base, Paradox, and others—may have learned that each data element stored in a table is stored and managed as an individual disk file.

Table 2.3
SQL System Tables

Table Name	Contents
DTAB	Description of views and tables in Oracle databases
SYSCOLAUTH (SYSCOLAU)	Column access privileges
SYSCOLUMNS (SYSCOLS)	Specifications of existing columns
SYSCOMMANDS	Precompiled commands for the C precompiler
SYSKEYS (INDEXES)	Existing index keys
SYSINDEXES (SYSIDXS)	Listing of existing indexes
SYSSYNONYMS (SYSSYNS, SYNONYMS)	Existing table and view synonyms
SYSTABAUTH	Table access privileges
SYSTABLES (SYSTABLS, SYSCATALOG)	Profiles of tables and views accessible to user
SYSUSERAUTH (SYSAUTH)	Users' passwords and authority levels
SYSVIEWS	Listing of views

Each table is assigned a unique name for identification. SQL does not manage its data elements in the same manner.

Although SQL organizes all its data elements in tables, each SQL table is not saved in a separate disk file. Data values in all the base tables are stored as a single data file, and summary information about these data values is cataloged and stored in some of the system tables. All the disk files associated with the same database are usually grouped and stored in a separate section of the storage media. In a microcomputer environment, the disk files associated with a database are usually stored in an individual subdirectory within the program. Nevertheless, because of the great differences among various versions of SQL, you need to consult the system manual for details about how disk files are organized in the databases.

Processing Modes

You can process SQL commands in one of two modes: interactive and embedded. You can enter your commands one at a time from the keyboard at the SQL prompt. You wait for the results to be returned before entering another SQL command. Or you can process a set of SQL commands by embedding the commands in a regular computer program written in a computer language, such as FORTRAN, COBOL, Pascal, or C.

Interactive Processing

The most convenient way to execute an SQL command is to issue the command at the SQL prompt. When you finish entering the command at the prompt, the command is executed, and the results are displayed (usually on the screen). This mode is an interactive mode of processing. The SQL prompt may be indicated by a short phrase such as SQL, SQL., or SQL>, depending on the version of SQL you are using. For example, if you want to enter a command in dBASE IV's SQL, you issue the command at the SQL. prompt:

```
SQL. SELECT * FROM employee;
```

The results may look figure 2.1.

SS_NO	L_NAME	F_NAME	TITLE	DEPT	SALARY
123-45-6789	Smith	James J.	President	Corporate	89500.00
634-56-7890	Nelson	Harry M.	Manager	Sales	65000.00
445-67-8801	Zeller	Albert K.	Salesman	Sales	48900.00
562-87-8800	Chapman	Kirk D.	Salesman	Sales	42500.00
404-22-4568	Baker	Larry A.	Clerk	Sales	30500.00
256-09-5555	Dixon	Kathy T.	Accountant	Accounting	45000.00
458-90-3456	Frazer	Robert F.	Bookkeeper	Accounting	28000.00
777-34-6543	King	David G.	Manager	Personnel	38000.00
100-45-8021	Wong	Mike J.	Manager	MIS	44000.00
303-25-7777	Duff	Cathy B.	Secretary	Personnel	26500.00
909-10-8910	Parker	Susan C.	Trainee		

Fig. 2.1. Results of issuing the SELECT command in dBASE IV.

The same command, when issued at the SQL prompt (indicated as SQL>) in Oracle's SQL*Plus, produces results similar to figure 2.2.

```
SQL> SELECT * FROM employee;

SS_NO          L_NAME    F_NAME      TITLE        DEPT         SALARY
------------   -------   ---------   ----------   ----------   ------
123-45-6789    Smith     James J.    President    Corporate    89500
634-56-7890    Nelson    Harry M.    Manager      Sales        65000
445-67-8801    Zeller    Albert K.   Salesman     Sales        48900
562-87-8800    Chapman   Kirk D.     Salesman     Sales        42500
404-22-4568    Baker     Larry A.    Clerk        Sales        30500
256-09-5555    Dixon     Kathy T.    Accountant   Accounting   45000
458-90-3456    Frazer    Robert F.   Bookkeeper   Accounting   28000
777-34-6543    King      David G.    Manager      Personnel    38000
100-45-8021    Wong      Mike J.     Manager      MIS          44000
303-25-7777    Duff      Cathy B.    Secretary    Personnel    26500
909-10-9010    Parker    Susan C.    Trainee

11 records selected.
```

Fig. 2.2. Results of issuing the SELECT command in SQL*Plus.

In looking at the results produced by these two versions of SQL, you may notice differences, such as the way numerical values are aligned. However, the format in which the results are displayed is not important for learning the principles of SQL. Therefore, as long as you are aware of the differences in the versions, you can treat the SQL commands as generic. You can issue the same command in most versions of SQL unless I have noted otherwise.

Embedded SQL Commands

Another mode of processing is embedding the SQL commands in a computer program that is written in a general programming language like FORTRAN, COBOL, Pascal, PL/I, or C. One advantage of using this mode of processing is that you can enter all the SQL commands at the same time and then execute them as a part of the program later without your intervention. This method has many uses. Because SQL lacks the commands for generating sophisticated reports, for example, you can write a set of the SQL commands for extracting the data elements needed for the reports. Later, you can produce the reports with commands provided by the general programming language. Similarly, you can design complex forms for your data entry process by using general computer programming commands, and you can insert the data values from the appropriate base tables by using embedded SQL commands.

When you incorporate SQL commands into a regular computer program, every embedded SQL statement must be preceded by the keywords EXEC SQL. The EXEC SQL command is terminated by a semicolon or some other terminator, depending on the host programming language. Here is the example of an embedded SQL command:

EXEC SQL UPDATE   employee

SET   title = 'CEO'
WHERE   title = 'President';

In this example, you include the SQL UPDATE command in a computer program written in a regular programming language. The SQL command changes the value in the *title* column.

When you embed SQL commands in a host program, you may be able to communicate between the host program and the SQL commands through a set of host variables. The purpose of these host variables is twofold:

❏ Host variables can hold the data values in the host program.

❏ Host variables can pass data values between the host program and the SQL commands.

Figure 2.3 shows a program segment written in C. This program segment illustrates how you can communicate between the host program written in C and the embedded SQL statements.

Experienced C programmers may think that this program is not written in a very elegant style and is not efficient for performing the data input operation. In order to illustrate the interface between the C program segment and the embedded SQL statement, however, the program is intentionally simplified so that most readers can understand the interface process. Because the C program is executed outside the database management system at the operating system prompt, the program needs a section of code for getting on the system. That section includes specifying the user name, password, and so on. Furthermore, depending on the versions of SQL and C you are using, some statements may be written differently.

The first segment of the program begins the data input process by entering data values into the six host variables: *essno, elname, efname, etitle, edept,* and *esalary*. Because the first five variables hold strings of characters, these variables are defined as character arrays with predetermined dimensions: *essno[11], elname[7], efname[10], etitle[10], edept[10]*. The numeric variable for storing the annual salary value is declared as *esalary*. Data values in the form of character strings are entered from the keyboard by using the *gets()* statement, which reads a string of characters until the Return key is

```
/* DATAFORM.C, Embedding SQL Commands in a C Program */

#include <stdio.h>
char     *essno[11];
char     *elname[7];
char     *efname[10];
char     *etitle[10];
char     *edept[10];
float    esalary;

main()
{
   /* Enter data from keyboard */
   clrscr();
   printf("Type employee's social security # ... ");
   gets(essno);
   printf("Type employee's last name ........... ");
   gets(elname);
   printf("Type employee's first name .......... ");
   gets(efname);
   printf("Type employee's title ............... ");
   gets(etitle);
   printf("Type department name  ............... ");
   gets(edept);
   printf("Type employee's annual salary ....... ");
   scanf("%f",&esalary);

/* Insert data elements into the base table */
EXEC SQL INSERT INTO employee
               VALUES (:essno, :elname, :efname,
                        :etitle, :edept, :esalary);

}
```

Fig. 2.3. *SQL commands embedded in a program written in C.*

pressed. The *scanf()* statement is used to input a numeric value into the *esalary* variable.

After all the data values have been entered into the host variables, the data values are passed to the embedded SQL statements by specifying these variables in place of column names in the INSERT INTO statement. In order to differentiate the host variables from the column names, colons are added in front of the variables.

This program segment can be used to enter a set of data values into the host variables and then insert the values into a row in the base table. If you need to enter additional rows of data into the base table, you can add the necessary program loops to repeat the input process.

Connecting with Other Database Programs

As stated, SQL is a powerful relational language that provides the necessary commands for performing most database management functions. Because of the lack of certain commands, however, certain database management functions cannot be performed effectively with standard SQL commands alone. As a result, you need to supplement the language with additional commands and procedures for accomplishing these functions.

As previously stated, one weakness of SQL is the lack of sufficient commands for producing sophisticated reports and designing complex data entry forms. One solution to this problem is to write a program in a regular computer language, as demonstrated in the preceding section. This program produces the reports or data entry forms, using data extracted from the base table by SQL commands embedded in the program. This technique is one method for interfacing SQL commands with another program written in a regular programming language.

You also can embed SQL commands in another database language. For example, you can incorporate your SQL commands into a dBASE program. The example in figure 2.4 embeds the SQL commands that are required for adding data to the existing table named *employee*. The data elements to be inserted into the table are entered from the keyboard and controlled by the commands written in the dBASE language.

Those of you who are familiar with dBASE can see that the data values are first read into the memory variables (*m_ssno, m_lname, m_fname, m_title, m_dept, m_salary*) by using a custom data entry form (see fig. 2.5). The data entry form is produced by the @...SAY...GET dBASE statements. In addition to labeling the data values to be entered, single- and double-line boxes also can be added to enhance the appearance of the data entry form. After data values have been entered into the memory variables, the data values are inserted into the *employee* base table by using the embedded SQL INSERT INTO statement by means of these memory variables. You may notice that you do not add the colons in front of the memory variables when they are used in place of the column names in the embedded INSERT INTO SQL command.

```
*****************************************************************
***  DATAFORM.PRS, a dBASE program with embedded SQL commands ***
*****************************************************************
SET TALK OFF
SET STATUS OFF
STORE 'Y' TO m_add_data
DO WHILE m_add_data='Y'
   * Initialize your memory variables
   STORE SPACE(11) TO m_ssno
   STORE SPACE(7) TO m_lname
   STORE SPACE(10) TO m_fname
   STORE SPACE(10) TO m_title
   STORE SPACE(10) TO m_dept
   STORE 0 TO m_salary
   * Clear the screen and read data values into variables
   CLEAR
   @1,5 to 22,75 DOUBLE
   @3,25 TO 5,52
   @4,27  SAY "EMPLOYEE DATA ENTRY FORM"
   @7,17  SAY "Employee's Social Security # " GET m_ssno
   @9,17  SAY "              Last Name " GET m_lname
   @11,17 SAY "             First Name " GET m_fname
   @13,17 SAY "                  Title " GET m_title
   @15,17 SAY "      Name of Department " GET m_dept
   @17,17 SAY "          Annual Salary " GET m_salary
   READ
   * Insert the data elements into the base table named employee
   INSERT INTO employee
        VALUES (m_ssno, m_lname, m_fname,
               m_title, m_dept, m_salary);
   @19,15 SAY "These data items have been added to the base table."
   @20,21 SAY "Would you like to add more data (Y/N) ?";
      GET m_add_data
   READ
   CLEAR GETS
ENDDO
RETURN
```

Fig. 2.4. A dBASE program with embedded SQL commands.

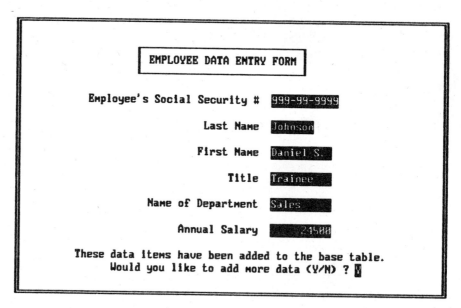

Fig. 2.5. *A custom data entry form.*

The dBASE program segment in figure 2.4 illustrates combining SQL state-ments with dBASE statements in the same program so that you can design the data entry form for the data input process. Similarly, you can extract data values from the base tables and then write a dBASE program segment to pro-duce the reports using these data values. This technique is another way to link SQL with another database management system.

An interface between SQL and other database management systems can be made in other ways, too. For example, when you are using dBASE IV's SQL, any base tables created with SQL commands can be accessed by dBASE IV commands. These dBASE IV commands can be issued in an interactive mode at the dot prompt or can be written as a program to be processed in batch mode. As a result, you can use the commands provided by dBASE to perform other data manipulation operations on the data tables created with SQL com-mands. You also can take advantage of the power of the data form and report generators provided by dBASE IV to facilitate your data input and reporting operations.

Similarly, if you are using Oracle's SQL*Plus, you can benefit from the many tools provided by SQL*Forms, SQL*Menu, and SQL*Report. You can use these tools to design and produce sophisticated data entry forms and com-plex reports with data stored in the SQL tables.

Chapter Summary

In this chapter, you have learned how you can use SQL commands to perform most data management functions on the data elements in a relational database. With the notation conventions introduced in this chapter, you can understand the syntax rules for the SQL commands to be discussed in later chapters. From the examples, you have seen how SQL commands can be executed in two processing modes. The interactive processing mode yields immediate results after processing the command at the SQL prompt, but by embedding your SQL commands in a program, you can perform a complete data management task more efficiently in batch mode.

Unlike a procedural language, SQL is a solution-oriented query language. You specify the results you want but do not need to define all the procedural steps required; SQL finds the best way to achieve the requested results. How fast the results can be produced depends significantly on how your data elements are organized in the relational model. As a result, if you want to manage your data efficiently, you must set up your tables properly. In the next chapter, you learn the important rules that govern the proper design of a good relational database.

II

Designing and Creating Databases

Includes

Designing Relational Databases
Creating Tables and Entering Data

3

Designing Relational Databases

The first chapter introduced you to the basic concepts of a relational data model. As discussed in that chapter, with a relational model, you organize and manage your data in a set of tables. Even more important than storing your data, you use some of these tables for defining the relations among the data elements. These base tables are the fundamental building blocks of relational databases. As a result, the efficiency and effectiveness of your databases depend significantly on how you structure and maintain these base tables.

Although a relational model outlines a set of properties for relational databases, it does not dictate how you organize your data in these tables.

Because of the significant differences in the nature of database management tasks, you cannot devise a single set of rules that guarantee a good database design for every application. But you need to understand and follow some important guidelines for designing databases if you want to avoid problems maintaining data integrity. Failure to follow these guidelines definitely reduces the efficiency of your data management.

Database design is not a pure science. Due to the flexibility of a relational model, simply following guidelines does not ensure a good database design or prevent a poor design. You can structure a good database only by acquiring sufficient knowledge of your data environment and extensive experience in database design. Therefore, the main focus of this chapter is to illustrate the task of designing a good relational database by using many examples.

Designing a relational database is a complex job. This statement is especially true if you are designing a large comprehensive database for a multiple-user system. If you are creating a small database for a single-user system, however, the designing task may not be so formidable. But regardless of the size and complexity of the databases, the principles of good relational database design are the same. Therefore, examples used in this chapter are designed around a single-user system. Although these examples are relatively small and simple, they demonstrate characteristics similar to the characteristics of a more complex system. What you learn from these examples about designing a good relational database should be applicable to other relational database applications.

Essential Properties of Relational Databases

Chapter 1 introduces several data models, one of which is the relational model. When the relational model was first proposed, a set of properties were outlined for relational databases. These properties govern how data is represented and organized in a relational database. Because SQL is designed for managing data in relational databases, your databases must possess these properties so that you can take full advantage of the power of the language.

These relational database properties can be summarized as follows:

❏ All the data elements in a relational database must be organized and viewed in a table form.

❏ All data elements must be atomic in nature.

❏ You must not allow duplicate rows in any table.

❏ The arrangement of columns in a table is immaterial.

Organizing Data in Tables

The basic unit of a relational database is a base table. All the data elements associated with a data entity can be organized in a base table. A data entity is any distinguishable data object. A data entity can be something tangible, like an employee, a teacher, or a student, or intangible, like an account, a course, or a class. For example, in a relational database, all the data associated with the employees in a firm can be organized in a base table named *employee* (see fig. 3.1).

A base table has many columns, each of which is identified by a name, or label. You use these columns for defining the attributes, or characteristics, of the data entity. In the *employee* table, for example, the columns describe the attributes (such as social security numbers, names, titles, and so on) for the employees. Although you can modify the structure of a base table later, at the time you create the base table, you must specify number of columns you think that you will need.

A base table can contain any number of rows. Each row holds data elements that belong to all the column attributes for an object of the data entity. For example, each row in the *employee* table holds the data elements associated with all the attributes of a given employee. You do not have to specify the number of rows you may need at the time you create the table. In some situations, you may have a table without any rows. You can reserve an empty table for maintaining data integrity and providing storage space for future data needs.

SS_NO	L_NAME	F_NAME	TITLE	DEPT	SALARY
123-45-6789	Smith	James J.	President	Corporate	89500.00
634-56-7890	Nelson	Harry M.	Manager	Sales	65000.00
445-67-8801	Zeller	Albert K.	Salesman	Sales	48900.00
562-87-8800	Chapman	Kirk D.	Salesman	Sales	42500.00
404-22-4568	Baker	Larry A.	Clerk	Sales	30500.00
256-09-5555	Dixon	Kathy T.	Accountant	Accounting	45000.00
458-90-3456	Frazer	Robert F.	Bookkeeper	Accounting	28000.00
777-34-6543	King	David G.	Manager	Personnel	38000.00
100-45-8021	Wong	Mike J.	Manager	MIS	44000.00
303-25-7777	Duff	Cathy B.	Secretary	Personnel	26500.00

Fig. 3.1. *The* employee *table of a relational database.*

Ensuring Atomic Data Elements

In a base table in a relational database, the intersection between a row and a column is called a data cell. Each data value must be *atomic*, meaning that each data cell in a relational table must be used to store only one piece of data. You cannot store multiple values in the cell. For example, if an employee, say Larry A. Baker, belongs to two departments—Sales and MIS —you cannot enter both department names in the same data cell:

SS_NO	L_NAME	F_NAME	TITLE	DEPT	SALARY
404-22-4568	Baker	Larry A.	Clerk	Sales MIS	30500.00

One way to represent Larry A. Baker in two different departments and still satisfy the data atomic rule is to use two rows for his data:

SS_NO	L_NAME	F_NAME	TITLE	DEPT	SALARY
404-22-4568	Baker	Larry A.	Clerk	Sales	30500.00
404-22-4568	Baker	Larry A.	Clerk	MIS	30500.00

In conforming to the data atomic rule, however, a problem arises because the table contains redundant information. The employee's social security number, name, title, and salary are duplicated in these rows. A solution to this problem is to split the contents of the *employee* table into two separate tables: *employee* and *dept* (see fig. 3.2).

Employee table:

SS_NO	L_NAME	F_NAME	TITLE	SALARY
123-45-6789	Smith	James J.	President	89500.00
634-56-7890	Nelson	Harry M.	Manager	65000.00
445-67-8801	Zeller	Albert K.	Salesman	48900.00
562-87-8800	Chapman	Kirk D.	Salesman	42500.00
404-22-4568	Baker	Larry A.	Clerk	30500.00
256-09-5555	Dixon	Kathy T.	Accountant	45000.00
458-90-3456	Frazer	Robert F.	Bookkeeper	28000.00
777-34-6543	King	David G.	Manager	38000.00
100-45-8021	Wong	Mike J.	Manager	44000.00
303-25-7777	Duff	Cathy B.	Secretary	26500.00

Dept table:

SS_NO	DEPT
123-45-6789	Corporate
634-56-7890	Sales
445-67-8801	Sales
562-87-8800	Sales
404-22-4568	Sales
404-22-4568	MIS
256-09-5555	Accounting
458-90-3456	Accounting
777-34-6543	Personnel
100-45-8021	MIS
303-25-7777	Personnel

Fig. 3.2. *Splitting a table into two tables to avoid data redundancy.*

If you look at the *dept* table, you will note that the names of the departments appear in more than one row. Two of these rows show Larry A. Baker's social security number (404-22-4568). Yet other information about Larry A. Baker appears in the *employee* table in only one row, without redundant data.

Avoiding Duplicate Rows

Another important property for a relational database is that you must not have duplicate rows in any base table. Storing duplicate rows of data wastes valuable storage space. At the same time, duplicate rows slow data retrieval because the table is too large. In addition, summary statistics generated from the table are distorted when you have duplicate rows in the table. Take the example of calculating the average salary for the employees in the firm. The computed average is inaccurate if duplicate values exist in the salary column.

In a relational model, each row in a table must be identifiable by a primary key. Duplicate rows violate this requirement. The primary key can be represented by a column in the table. For example, you can use the social security number (*ss_no*) column in the *employee* table as a primary key. The primary key allows you to identify each row in the table. By knowing an employee's social security number, you can find that row without a mistake.

A primary key does not have to be represented by a single column in the table, however. A primary key can be represented by a combination of columns. For example, in the *dept* table, neither of the two columns (*ss_no* and *dept*) by itself can be used as a primary key because data values in these columns are not unique. But if you combine the values of the two columns in the table, each pair of values is unique. Therefore, the primary key for the *dept* table is the combination of the two columns.

Determining Column Arrangement

As mentioned previously, a base table contains a fixed number of columns for describing the attributes of a data entity. How you arrange these columns in the table is not important as long as they contain the data elements needed. For example, the columns in the *employee* table shown in fig. 3.1 can be rearranged in the order shown in figure 3.3 without changing the meaning and usefulness of the table.

In this table, the columns *l_name* and *f_name* have been switched and the *dept* column moved to the left of the name columns. Because each column independently describes one attribute of the employees, how you arrange columns in the table is immaterial.

In the *employee* table, you store the name of an employee in two columns: *f_name* and *l_name*. The decision for splitting an employee's name into two parts is based on the anticipated uses of the data values in the two columns. By using two columns, you can find an employee by his or her first or last name. Otherwise, you may want to combine employees' first names and last names in a column called *full_name* (see fig. 3.4).

SS_NO	DEPT	F_NAME	L_NAME	TITLE	SALARY
123-45-6789	Corporate	James J.	Smith	President	89500.00
634-56-7890	Sales	Harry M.	Nelson	Manager	65000.00
445-67-8801	Sales	Albert K.	Zeller	Salesman	48900.00
562-87-8800	Sales	Kirk D.	Chapman	Salesman	42500.00
404-22-4568	Sales	Larry A.	Baker	Clerk	30500.00
256-09-5555	Accounting	Kathy T.	Dixon	Accountant	45000.00
458-90-3456	Accounting	Robert F.	Frazer	Bookkeeper	28000.00
777-34-6543	Personnel	David G.	King	Manager	38000.00
100-45-8021	MIS	Mike J.	Wong	Manager	44000.00
303-25-7777	Personnel	Cathy B.	Duff	Secretary	26500.00

Fig. 3.3. The employee *table with the columns rearranged.*

SS_NO	DEPT	FULL_NAME	TITLE	SALARY
123-45-6789	Corporate	James J. Smith	President	89500.00
634-56-7890	Sales	Harry M. Nelson	Manager	65000.00
445-67-8801	Sales	Albert K. Zeller	Salesman	48900.00
562-87-8800	Sales	Kirk D. Chapman	Salesman	42500.00
404-22-4568	Sales	Larry A. Baker	Clerk	30500.00
256-09-5555	Accounting	Kathy T. Dixon	Accountant	45000.00
458-90-3456	Accounting	Robert F. Frazer	Bookkeeper	28000.00
777-34-6543	Personnel	David G. King	Manager	38000.00
100-45-8021	MIS	Mike J. Wong	Manager	44000.00
303-25-7777	Personnel	Cathy B. Duff	Secretary	26500.00

Fig. 3.4. The employee *table with the names combined in one column.*

Other Characteristics of Good Relational Databases

The properties outlined in the preceding sections specify the essential characteristics to which your relational database must adhere strictly. Relational databases lacking these properties cannot be managed properly with SQL. However, databases that possess these properties are not necessarily good relational databases. A good relational database design has other desirable characteristics. Some of these characteristics are the following:

❑ Base tables are kept as simple as possible.

❑ Columns are grouped logically.

❑ Data integrity can be maintained easily.

❑ Data structure is flexible enough to accommodate all applications.

❑ Data redundancy is kept to a minimum.

❑ Tables are properly indexed.

Using Simple Base Tables

Except in a very simple case, most database applications require a set of base tables. The number of tables you use depends on several factors.

The nature of your data elements plays an important role in deciding how many base tables to create in the database. Usually, each data entity should be set up as a base table for storing data elements associated with that data entity. For example, in designing a school database, data elements may be stored in several base tables. Each table associates with a data entity, such as student, teacher, course, and so on.

Because each column in a base table describes an attribute of the data entity, your base table needs to contain many columns if the data entity has a large set of attributes. If the table has too many columns, you may want to split the base table into several smaller and simpler base tables. Small base tables are easy to understand and maintain because they contain less information. A small base table can be updated quickly if some data values need to be changed.

A good database design does not require that all the base tables be small. If the information you frequently need to retrieve is in many tables, the retrieval process is more time-consuming. Data retrieval is quicker if all the information is in fewer and larger base tables. But when you are working with large base tables, every time you need to change data values in the base table, updating takes longer because more columns of data are involved. Therefore, in designing your database, you must consider the trade-offs between the efforts required for data maintenance and the speed of data retrieval. You should try to maintain a proper balance between the number of base tables and their size.

Grouping Columns Logically

A good database design requires that your data columns be logically organized and grouped in an appropriate number of base tables. Although no rules can determine precisely how you should organize your data columns in the base table, some practical guidelines are available.

Before you decide to split a base table into several smaller tables, carefully study how your data elements are to be retrieved and maintained. Whenever possible, each table should hold the data elements related to a specific data entity. Each column then describes a characteristic of an attribute of that entity. For example, for keeping track of employee information, you may set up the base tables for storing data values associated with the following attributes:

- ❏ Employee's social security number
- ❏ Employee's name
- ❏ Employee's sex
- ❏ Employee's birth date
- ❏ Employee's title
- ❏ Department to which employee belongs
- ❏ Date employee is hired
- ❏ Name of employee's spouse
- ❏ Employee's permanent address
- ❏ Employee's current address
- ❏ Employee's home phone number
- ❏ Employee's annual salary
- ❏ Number of dependents
- ❏ Employee's income tax exemption number
- ❏ Amount of monthly standard deduction
- ❏ Date of last pay adjustment
- ❏ Amount of last pay adjustment

You can store all the data elements associated with these attributes about the employees in a single large base table or in several smaller tables. Both approaches have advantages and disadvantages, depending on how the data elements are related functionally and how you use them.

Storing all these attributes as columns in a single base table has two main advantages. First, you can retrieve your data more quickly if most columns are from the same table. SQL needs to search only one table for the information desired. Second, if you need to produce reports containing information in these columns, the reporting process can be simplified when all the columns are in the same table.

Working with a large table has some common problems, however. One problem occurs if the data queries you use often involve only a few columns in the table. SQL wastes processing time performing query operations on information that is irrelevant to the operations. Processing the query operations takes less time if you group frequently used columns in a separate table. You then save the less frequently used columns in another base table. For example, if you regularly need to retrieve the payroll information about the employees, store the payroll-related columns in one table and the other columns in another table.

Another possible problem with a large base table relates to the amount of time required for updating the large table if any data values change. For example, if you change an employee's address in the table, you need to update the whole table, which contains a large amount of information. Therefore, you may want to group columns that require frequent changes in a separate table and store columns containing permanent information in another table.

Maintaining Data Integrity

The term *data integrity* in a database management system concerns the correctness, timeliness, and relevance of the data elements stored in the base tables. Every effort should be made to ensure that all data elements are correct and current. They should be entered into the table as they become available; any changes should be incorporated immediately into all the tables.

When your database contains multiple base tables, to provide links between these tables, some columns may appear in more than one table as primary and foreign keys. For example, if you store employee information in several base tables, you may want to use the employee's identification number as a linking-key column. In this database design, the *ss_no* column appears in more than one table. When you change an employee's identification number in one table, your database design must provide a means by which the change can be updated easily in other tables that contain the same identification number. Similarly, your database design should ensure that deletion of a column or some of its values in one table does not damage the integrity of another table. One approach is to keep the user from changing the value in the primary key before all the corresponding values in the foreign keys have been changed. (You learn more about this issue, data integrity, in Chapter 11.)

Making Data Structure Flexible

When you design your database, you should structure your tables so that data elements in these tables can be extracted easily for future data applications. Data columns should be grouped in the base tables according to the columns' associations with the data entity. You should not create a table structure just for a special application and then have to revise the structure to satisfy the data needs for other applications.

A goal for designing a good database is to make its data structure independent of the applications. This goal does not mean that you can never change the structure after you have set it up. Instead, a good database should be designed with enough flexibility to accommodate structure changes when the entity associations are changed. However, you should avoid changing the data structure to fit different applications.

For example, suppose that you create a table for storing the names and addresses of your customers. How you decide to structure the table for storing these data elements is important. You can take one of two approaches in structuring the base table:

❏ You can store customers' full names in a column in the table

❏ You can split their names into two parts, first name and last name, each occupying a column.

The first approach allows you to search the table only by a customer's full name. With the second approach, you can refer to any customer by either first name or last name. With the first approach, breaking up a customer's full name into first and last names is difficult because each full name is treated as a single data element in the structure. Therefore, unless you are absolutely sure that you will never need to refer to a customer by only first name or last name, the second approach for structuring the base table is more desirable. In addition, with the second approach, you can combine the first name and last name columns and quickly generate a customer's full name if needed. Therefore, the second approach yields a more flexible data structure, which can fit all future applications.

Avoiding Data Redundancy

A good database design avoids storing the same data more than once in the base tables. An exception to this rule is for data elements you use as keys for joining base tables. As an example, look at the *course* table in figure 3.5.

Course table:

COURSE TITLE	COURSE DESCRIPTION	CREDIT HOURS	TEACHER FIRST NAME	TEACHER LAST NAME	TEACHER OFFICE
ENGL 101	English Literature	3	Ernest M.	Hemingway	West 301
ENGL 101	English Literature	3	George B.	Shaw	West 104
HIST 100	American History	3	Benjamin	Franklin	West 301
MATH 105	Calculus I	5	Isaac	Newton	East 105
PHIL 101	Philosophy	3	Willard V.	Quine	East 250
PHYS 102	Physics I	5	Isaac	Newton	East 105

Fig. 3.5. *Table containing redundant data.*

This table has a great deal of redundant data. For example, because the course ENGL 101 is taught by two teachers (Hemingway and Shaw), some information about the course (course title, course description, credit hours) appears twice in the table. Similarly, because Newton teaches both MATH 105 and PHYS 101, information about him appears in two rows.

Waste of storage is significant if a large amount of redundant data is stored in the table. Redundant data also slows the data query process and requires more effort to maintain data integrity. For example, when Newton moves to a different office, you need to change his office number in two rows of the base table. Failure to change all his office numbers in the table damages the integrity of the data.

A solution to the problem of data redundancy is to restructure the base tables. Except for the columns that provide the links between these tables, do not repeat data elements in any table. For example, the *course* table shown in figure 3.5 can be split into three tables, as shown in figure 3.6.

Assign (teaching assignment) table:

COURSE TITLE	TEACHER ID
ENGL 101	T2
ENGL 101	T5
HIST 100	T1
MATH 105	T3
PHIL 101	T4
PHYS 102	T3

Course table:

COURSE TITLE	COURSE DESCRIPTION	CREDIT HOURS
ENGL 101	English Literature	3
HIST 100	American History	3
MATH 105	Calculus I	5
PHIL 101	Philosophy	3
PHYS 102	Physics I	5

Teacher table:

TEACHER ID	TEACHER FIRST NAME	TEACHER LAST NAME	TEACHER OFFICE
T1	Benjamin	Franklin	West 301
T2	Ernest M.	Hemingway	West 301
T3	Isaac	Newton	East 105
T4	Willard V.	Quine	East 250
T5	George B.	Shaw	West 104

Fig. 3.6. *Splitting a table to avoid data redundancy.*

In this example, the *course* and *teacher* tables are used to store the data elements associated with the attributes about the data entities *course* and *teacher*, respectively. Note that no redundant data appears in either table. The *assign* table provides the links between the *course* and *teacher* tables. Each row in the *assign* table relates a course title to a teacher identified with a unique teacher's identification.

The process of splitting a single table into three tables is called *normalization*. A detailed discussion of the normalization process is forthcoming in this chapter.

Indexing Data Properly

As you know, a relational database is a collection of data elements organized according to a relational data model. An important characteristic of a well-designed database is that data elements are logically organized. From a well-designed database, you can find and retrieve any information quickly and easily.

In simple terms, conceptually, a database is like a telephone book or a merchandise catalog. A well-designed phone book organizes telephone numbers in a logical order. From a well-designed phone book, you easily and quickly find the phone number of a person or a business by using some kind of indexing scheme.

The index operation provides a quick reference for finding a specific piece of data in the database. For example, you may organize your personal phone numbers in a directory that lists your friends alphabetically by their last names. When you want to find an individual's phone number, you quickly find it by the last name. In this way, information can be retrieved efficiently by using the last name as an index.

Similarly, the yellow pages of a public telephone book arrange the listings by business types. If you want to find an entry for a particular type of business, you search the appropriate sections without scanning every entry in the phone book. In this case, business type provides a quick reference for your data query operation.

When you set up a base table in a relational database, you can speed data query operations by specifying the columns you want to use as indexes. When a column is indexed, the data elements in that column are arranged according to a specified order and then saved in a separate table. Information stored in the index table later is used for quickly finding any specific data element. Because an index table occupies memory space and needs to be updated as the data elements change, do not index every column in the table.

The choice of index columns depends on whether the columns will be involved in frequent query operations. Indexing the columns with which you intend to perform data query operations is always desirable. You should not index the columns you do not intend to use in any future query operation. For example, if you intend to find an employee's data by using his or her last name, the query operation will be greatly enhanced if you index the last name column. Similarly, if you want to group the information about your employees by their departments, you index the column that contains the department identification.

Therefore, before you decide to index a column, weigh the benefits from quick data query against the cost of maintaining the index. A good database design strikes a proper balance between too many and too few indexes. The database should allow query operations to be carried out quickly with the necessary indexes. At the same time, the database design should avoid maintaining unnecessary indexes. (See Chapter 7 for information about creating an index.)

Designing a Relational Database

Designing a good database can be a complex process. No simple rigid rules can prescribe how a good relational database is structured. Knowledge and experience play an important role in the designing process. An iterative process is usually useful in arriving at an acceptable and desirable design. That is, you try different designs until you find a satisfactory design.

The task of designing a relational database begins with gaining a clear understanding of the data environment involved. You need to study your data needs for all your anticipated future applications. You should try to find out what types of data elements you will keep in the database. You also need to determine the proper way to organize these data elements in the base tables.

Next, you need to decide the data entities involved in your database and identify the attributes, or characteristics, of these entities. You then need to structure base tables that logically organize the data elements related to the attributes in your base tables. To eliminate the problem of data redundancy and the difficulties in data maintenance, you need to make your tables conform to a normal form. The results of the normalization process are base tables that possess the essential properties of a relational database, outlined previously in this chapter.

The process of designing a relational database is often difficult to articulate. The process can be better explained with a simplified example. The example used to illustrate the steps involved in a database design is a *school* database.

Identifying Data Elements

The first step in designing your database begins with investigating and studying the data environment involved. You need to determine the relevant data elements and learn how to obtain and enter them into the database. You need to see what information is currently available and what information you need to acquire. After all, unless you have the data for describing certain attributes of the data entities you will later define, you cannot set up the base tables.

One way to begin the designing process is to list all the data elements that may be useful for future data applications. For example, the data elements involved in the *school* database, among others, include

- ❏ Teacher identification numbers
- ❏ Names of teachers
- ❏ Ranks of teachers
- ❏ Offices of teachers
- ❏ Phone numbers of teachers
- ❏ Student identification numbers
- ❏ Names of students
- ❏ Genders of students
- ❏ Students' birth dates
- ❏ Students' high school grade point averages (GPAs)
- ❏ Course identification numbers
- ❏ Course titles
- ❏ Course descriptions
- ❏ Credit hours of courses
- ❏ Class lists
- ❏ Teaching assignments

Grouping Data Elements

After you have identified the relevant data to be included in the database, you must decide how to organize these data items in your base tables.

Most of the data elements in the *school* database can grouped by their associations with three data entities (*teacher*, *student*, *course*), as listed in table 3.1.

Table 3.1
Grouping of Data Elements for School Database

Data Entity: Teacher

Teacher identification numbers
Names of teachers
Offices of teachers
Ranks of teachers
Phone numbers of teachers

Data Entity: Student

Student identification numbers
Names of students
Genders of students
Students' birth dates
Students' high school grade point averages (GPAs)

Data Entity: Course

Course identification numbers
Course titles
Course descriptions
Credit hours of courses

In examining the three data entities in table 3.1, you may notice that two data elements—class lists and teaching assignments— have not been grouped under any entity. A class list should identify the students who are taking a specific course, or the list should describe the courses a student takes. Similarly, information about teaching assignments relates who is teaching what courses, or the teaching assignments show what courses are being taught by which teachers. As a result, information about class lists and teaching assignments can be treated in several ways.

One way is to include these data elements in one of the three data entities. For example, teaching assignments can be included as an attribute of the *teacher* entity or as an attribute of the *course* entity. Another way is to set up teaching assignments as a separate entity. Like teaching assignments, you can handle the information about class lists by treating it as an attribute of the *student* entity, describing the courses a student takes. An alternative approach is to consider class list information as an attribute of the *course* entity, identifying all the students taking a given course. You also can choose to organize information about class lists as an individual data entity. These approaches are explored later.

Structuring Base Tables

Because you have grouped the data elements into separate data entities, a logical technique is to store in a separate base table the information associated with each entity. Therefore, you set up three base tables to organize the data in the *school* database. You name these tables *teacher*, *student*, and *course*.

Next, you define the columns (attributes) for the tables. This task involves naming the columns and deciding the type and amount of information to be stored in each column. For example, in the *teacher* table, you may want to use a column for storing all the names of the teachers in the school. To make the base table more flexible, you may want to split names of the teachers into two parts—first and last names—each name occupying a separate column. Similarly, you may store the first and last names of the students in separate columns. You may begin by structuring the three base tables as shown in table 3.2.

Table 3.2
Structure of Columns in Base Tables of School Database

Column Name	Description	Data Type	Column Size
Teacher table:			
T_ID	Teacher ID number	Character	2 characters
T_LNAME	Teacher's last name	Character	10 characters
T_FNAME	Teacher's first name	Character	10 characters
T_RANK	Teacher's rank	Character	15 characters
T_OFFICE	Office number	Character	8 characters
T_PHONE	Phone number	Character	8 characters
Student table:			
S_ID	Student ID number	Character	3 characters
S_LNAME	Student's last name	Character	10 characters
S_FNAME	Student's first name	Character	10 characters
S_SEX	Student's gender	Character	1 character
S_BDATE	Student's birth date	Date	
S_HSGPA	High school GPA	Numeric	
Course table:			
C_ID	Course ID number	Character	2 characters
C_TITLE	Course title	Character	8 characters
C_CREDITS	Credit hours	Numeric	
C_DESC	Course description	Character	20 characters

These base tables hold three types of data. A character data column contains strings of characters, and a numeric column holds a number. Dates are stored in a date column. Although the dates are specified in the form of a character string (03/08/71), they are treated differently.

Each table can be used for holding data elements that are associated with their attributes. Assume that you are using the data elements shown in the base tables in figure 3.7.

Teacher table:

T_ID	T_LNAME	_FNAME	T_RANK	T_OFFICE	T_PHONE
T1	Franklin	Benjamin	Professor	West 103	235-1234
T2	Hemingway	Ernest M.	Professor	West 301	287-6666
T3	Newton	Isaac	Associate Prof.	East 150	635-1414
T4	Quine	Willard V.	Professor	East 250	636-2626
T5	Shaw	George B.	Assistant Prof.	West 104	235-7878

Student table:

S_ID	S_LNAME	S_FNAME	S_BDATE	S_SEX	S_HSGPA
S1	Austin	Linda D.	03/08/71	F	3.98
S2	Brown	Nancy J.	05/14/70	F	3.35
S3	Carter	Jack F.	10/10/71	M	2.87
S4	Ford	Harvey P.	06/12/71	M	2.60
S5	Freed	Barbara J.	07/28/69	F	3.15
S6	Gilmore	Danny S.	11/01/70	M	3.86
S7	Jackson	Brad L.	04/15/71	M	2.75
S8	Madison	George G.	08/15/70	M	2.35
S9	Reed	Donna E.	09/26/69	F	2.96
S10	Taylor	Bob K.	02/14/71	M	3.14

Course table:

C_ID	C_TITLE	C_CREDITS	C_DESC
C1	ENGL 101	3	English Literature
C2	HIST 100	3	American History
C3	MATH 105	5	Calculus I
C4	PHIL 101	3	Philosophy
C5	PHYS 102	5	Physics I

Fig. 3.7. Base tables in the school database.

With the data elements stored in these three tables, you can issue an SQL command and quickly find information about any data entity. For example, if you want to know about a particular student, Madison (S8), you can display all the data elements associated with this student with the following SQL command:

```
SELECT *
  FROM  student
 WHERE  s_lname = 'Madison';
```

Results:

S_ID	S_LNAME	S_FNAME	S_BDATE	S_SEX	S_HSGPA
S8	Madison	George G.	08/15/70	M	2.35

Similarly, you can find information about a given course or a teacher with the SQL command:

```
SELECT *
  FROM  teacher
 WHERE  t_lname = 'Newton';
```

Results:

T_ID	T_LNAME	T_FNAME	T_RANK	T_OFFICE	T_PHONE
T3	Newton	Isaac	Associate Prof.	East 150	635-1414

You also can use the following command to learn about a single course:

```
SELECT *
  FROM  course
 WHERE  c_id = 'C3';
```

Results:

C_ID	C_TITLE	C_CREDITS	C_DESC
C3	MATH 105	5	Calculus I

Defining Relations

After you have set up the base tables for saving data elements associated with the attributes of the data entities, you are ready to define the relations among these tables. The defined relations enable you to combine information from these tables in a query operation. For example, if you need to know about a particular teacher, you can find that information from the *teacher* table by using the teacher's identification number or last name as a key. When you structure your base tables this way, however, you cannot find the courses taught by this instructor. That is, the relationships between teachers and courses have not been defined. Likewise, the three base tables do not contain any information that can be used to relate the students and the courses they are taking.

You have many ways to define relationships among data entities in a relational database, depending on the type of relationships existing. As explained in Chapter 1, relational databases include three types of relationships: one-to-one, one-to-many, and many-to-many.

One-to-One Relations

The simplest relationship between two data entities is a one-to-one relation. In the *school* database, one-to-one relations between teacher and course imply that one teacher teaches only one course and that any one course is taught by only one instructor:

```
Course                  Teacher

C2, HIST 100————————————T1, Franklin
C4, PHIL 101————————————T4, Quine
```

In this case, you can define the relationship between the teacher and course entities by adding to the *course* table the column of teachers' identification numbers (*t_id*):

```
Course table:

C_ID  C_TITLE   C_CREDITS  C_DESC             T_ID
----  --------  ---------  -----------------  ----
C2    HIST 100         3   American History   T1
C4    PHIL 101         3   Philosophy         T4
```

In this table, you can see that the course HIST 100 is taught by instructor T1, or Franklin (see the *teacher* table), and that Franklin teaches only that course. If you want to know who teaches a given course, you can find the teacher's identification number in the row associated with the course identification number. Similarly, you can find the course that is being taught by a given instructor from the same table by locating the course title in the row associated with the teacher's identification number.

By assuming one-to-one relations between course and student, you can add students' identification numbers as a column in the *course* table to define student-course relations.

One-to-Many Relations

If you do not limit the relationship between two data entities to one-to-one relations, you have different ways to handle the entities in the base tables. For example, by assuming that a given course can be taught by more than one instructor, you have one-to-many relations between the course and teacher entities:

Course   *Teacher*

                                  T2, Hemingway
C1, ENGL 101   T5, Shaw

In some database designs, you can enter multiple values in a data cell. The database management system named PICK is this type. However, you cannot store more than one data value in a data cell in a relational database. One way to handle the one-to-many relations in a relation table is to add extra columns for storing the multiple values for an attribute. For example, you can specify two columns named *t1_id* and *t2_id*, respectively, for accommodating up to two instructors for a given course:

```
Course table:

C_ID  C_TITLE   C_CREDITS  C_DESC               T1_ID  T2_ID
----  --------  ---------  -------------------  -----  -----
C1    ENGL 101       3     English Literature   T2     T5
C2    HIST 100       3     American History     T1
C4    PHIL 101       3     Philosophy           T4
```

This design, however, has problems:

❏ The structure is not flexible enough to handle other one-to-many relations. What happens if a course is taught by more than two instructors? You need to modify the structure to accommodate more instructors in the table.

❏ For the courses taught by only one instructor, you will have trouble assigning values to the *t2_id* column. Although you can store a missing, or null, value in that column, not every version of SQL can handle null values satisfactorily.

❏ In a query operation, you will have difficulty deciding how many columns are relevant to the instructors teaching a given course. Some designs may include another column in the table as a pointer indicating how many instructors are teaching a given course. However, SQL does not support a pointer operation efficiently.

Another way to handle the one-to-many relations in the base table is to use extra rows for accommodating the extra instructors who are teaching the same course:

Course table:

C_ID	C_TITLE	C_CREDITS	C_DESC	T_ID
C1	ENGL 101	3	English Literature	T2
C1	ENGL 101	3	English Literature	T5
C2	HIST 100	3	American History	T1
C4	PHIL 101	3	Philosophy	T4

This table is flexible enough to handle multiple instructors for any course. For each additional instructor assigned to the course, you simply add another row to the table. For example, two rows are used in the table to describe the two instructors (T2, T5) for the same course (ENGL 101).

When you set up the *course* table this way, you can easily find all the instructors who are teaching any specific course. All you have to do is list all the teacher identification numbers in the rows belonging to a given course. For example, to find all the teachers who are teaching the course T1 (ENGL 101), you issue the following SQL command:

```
SELECT  t_id
  FROM  course
 WHERE  c_id = 'C1';
```

Results:

```
T_ID
----
T2
T5
```

Other one-to-many relations may exist between teacher and course entities. That is, in your *school* database, an instructor may teach more than one course:

Course	Teacher
C3, MATH 105	
C5, PHYS 102	T3, Newton

These relations can be easily described in the *course* table in a manner similar to the method shown previously:

Course table:

C_ID	C_TITLE	C_CREDITS	C_DESC	T_ID
C1	ENGL 101	3	English Literature	T2
C1	ENGL 101	3	English Literature	T5
C2	HIST 100	3	American History	T1
C3	MATH 105	5	Calculus I	T3
C4	PHIL 101	3	Philosophy	T4
C5	PHYS 102	5	Physics I	T3

In the *course* table, note that the teacher identification number T3 appears in the *t_id* column twice, each time relating the teacher to a specific course. From this table, you can find all the courses a given instructor teaches. For example, you can issue the following SQL command for finding all the courses taught by T3 (Newton):

SELECT   c_title
  FROM   course
WHERE   t_id = 'T3';

Results:

C_TITLE

MATH 105
PHYS 102

Many-to-Many Relations

The most complex relationships between any two data entities can be represented by many-to-many relations. For example, in the *school* database, many-to-many relations may mean that a course can be taken by many students; each student can, in turn, be taking many different courses. Of the students who are taking a course, some may be taking another course. Two different courses can be taken by the same group of students. These many-to-many relations can be illustrated as shown in figure 3.8.

Lines between the courses and students identify who is taking a given course and which courses are being taken by a given student. For example, the course C1 (ENGL 101) is being taken by three students: S3 (Carter), S5 (Freed), and S10 (Taylor); and student S3 is taking two courses: C1 (ENGL 101) and C5 (PHYS 102).

One way to handle these many-to-many relations is to add to the *student* table a column describing the courses a student is taking. Each course taken by a student is stored in a row in the *student* table (see fig. 3.9).

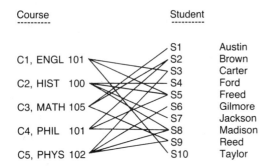

Course   Student

C1, ENGL 101   S1   Austin
                      S2   Brown
                      S3   Carter
C2, HIST 100   S4   Ford
                      S5   Freed
C3, MATH 105   S6   Gilmore
                      S7   Jackson
C4, PHIL 101   S8   Madison
                      S9   Reed
C5, PHYS 102   S10   Taylor

Fig. 3.8. *Many-to-many relations in the school database.*

Student table:

S_ID	S_LNAME	S_FNAME	S_BDATE	S_SEX	S_HSGPA	C_ID
S1	Austin	Linda D.	03/08/71	F	3.98	C3
S2	Brown	Nancy J.	05/14/70	F	3.35	C3
S2	Brown	Nancy J.	05/14/70	F	3.35	C4
S3	Carter	Jack F.	10/10/71	M	2.87	C1
S3	Carter	Jack F.	10/10/71	M	2.87	C5
S4	Ford	Harvey P.	06/12/71	M	2.60	C2
S5	Freed	Barbara J.	07/28/69	F	3.15	C1
S5	Freed	Barbara J.	07/28/69	F	3.15	C2
S5	Freed	Barbara J.	07/28/69	F	3.15	C4
S6	Gilmore	Danny S.	11/01/70	M	3.86	C5
S7	Jackson	Brad L.	04/15/71	M	2.75	C2
S8	Madison	George G.	08/15/70	M	2.35	C2
S8	Madison	George G.	08/15/70	M	2.35	C4
S8	Madison	George G.	08/15/70	M	2.35	C5
S9	Reed	Donna E.	09/26/69	F	2.96	C3
S9	Reed	Donna E.	09/26/69	F	2.96	C5
S10	Taylor	Bob K.	02/14/71	M	3.14	C1

Fig. 3.9. *One way to handle many-to-many relations in a base table.*

Although this table contains much redundant data, the table does allow you to organize the data elements in a logical way. From this table, for example, you can identify all the students who are taking a given course. You also can find all the courses taken by a given student. The SQL command for finding all the students who are taking course C1 (ENGL 101) can be issued as

```
SELECT  s_id
  FROM  student
 WHERE  c_id = 'C1';
```

Results:

```
S_ID
----
S3
S5
S10
```

If you want to list all the courses taken by a student, say S5 (Freed), you execute this SQL command:

```
SELECT  c_id
  FROM  student
 WHERE  s_id = 'S5';
```

Results:

```
C_ID
----
C1
C2
C4
```

When you structure the *course* and *student* tables this way, they possess the properties described earlier for a relational model:

❏ All the data elements are organized in tabular form.

❏ Each data cell in a base table contains only one data value.

❏ No duplicate rows exist in any base table.

If you examine these tables carefully, however, you will realize that they contain much redundant data. For example, most data values in the first two rows of the *course* table are the same, describing the identification number of a teacher. Similarly, the data takes three rows to repeat the information about student S8 (Madison) in order to show that this student is taking three courses (C2, C4, and C5).

The problem of redundant data can be significant when redundancy in a base table becomes as common as shown in the *student* table. Besides wasting memory, the redundant data drastically slows query operations. Therefore, the design requires additional work for making the design a good database design. One way to minimize data redundancy is through the process of table normalization, a later topic of this chapter.

Linking Tables

When saving data in different tables according to their associations with certain data entities, you often need to provide means for linking these tables in order to obtain useful information. For example, from the *student* table, you can find the courses taken by a given student. Because the *student* table contains only the course identification numbers, to produce a transcript for the student, you need to find the information in steps. First, you use the *student* table to find the course identification numbers. You then go to the *course* table to get detailed information about these courses. But you can accomplish the task in one step by using the course identification column as a linking key.

The *student* and *course* tables can be linked by using the course identification column as a common column in both tables. With this link, you can extract information from the two tables with a single SQL command. For example, if you want to know details about the courses taken by Madison (S8), you can issue the following SQL command:

```
SELECT   course.c_id, course.c_title, course.c_desc,
         course.c_credits, course.t_id
  FROM   course, student
 WHERE   course.c_id = student.c_id
   AND   student.s_lname = 'Madison';
```

This command is complex. If you find it confusing and difficult to understand, do not worry about the command now. You learn more about it in later chapters.

This command first locates from the *student* table the rows belonging to the student named Madison. From these rows, the command then finds all the course identification numbers from the *c_id* column. These course identification numbers are used to obtain detailed information about these courses. After SQL processes the command, the results may look like this:

```
C_ID  C_TITLE  C_DESC             C_CREDITS  T_ID
----  -------  -----------------  ---------  ----
C2    HIST 100 American History           3  T1
C4    PHIL 101 Philosophy                 3  T4
C5    PHYS 102 Physics I                  5  T3
```

In this example, the *course* and *student* tables are linked by using the common column *c_id* for identifying a course. This column represents a linking key serving two different purposes in the two tables. In the *course* table, you consider the *c_id* column a primary key (except for the minor violation of the duplication of the value C1). You use the primary key to identify the attributes associated with a given course. The same column appearing in the *student* table is considered a foreign key. With this column, you make reference to attributes associated with another table.

A primary key is any attribute or combination of attributes that uniquely identifies each row in a base table. In most cases, a primary key is represented by a single column in a base table. For example, the *t_id* column in the *teacher* table can be considered a primary key because *t_id* can be used to identify a particular teacher. For example, T1 in the *t_id* column of the *teacher* table uniquely identifies a specific row:

```
T_ID  T_LNAME   T_FNAME   T_RANK      T_OFFICE  T_PHONE
----  --------  --------  ----------  --------  --------
T1    Franklin  Benjamin  Professor   West 103  235-1234
```

Although having a single-column primary key is more desirable, a row cannot always be uniquely identified by using the value in only one column. Instead, a composite primary key, which uses a combination of attributes, or columns, is required. For example, not every row in the *course* table can be uniquely identified with the data value in the *c_id* column. Two rows in the table contain C1 in that column:

```
Course table:

C_ID  C_TITLE   C_CREDITS  C_DESC                T_ID
----  --------  ---------  --------------------  ----
C1    ENGL 101      3      English Literature    T2
C1    ENGL 101      3      English Literature    T5
```

To tell the two rows apart, you need to look at information in every column of the table. Besides the problem of redundant data, information organized in this way is confusing. Looking at these two rows, people can interpret the information in two ways. The rows may be considered two different sections of the course—each taught by a different teacher. In this case, the rows are treated as two different courses and should be assigned different course identification numbers. However, the rows also may be considered the same course jointly taught by two instructors. Appropriately, both rows should be assigned the same course identification number (C1).

One way to avoid the confusion and treat the *c_id* column as a primary key is to eliminate one of the C1 rows and to drop the *t_id* column:

Course table:

C_ID	C_TITLE	C_CREDITS	C_DESC
C1	ENGL 101	3	English Literature
C2	HIST 100	3	American History
C3	MATH 105	5	Calculus I
C4	PHIL 101	3	Philosophy
C5	PHYS 102	5	Physics I

In this table, no redundant data value is stored in the rows. Each row in the table now can be identified uniquely by the value in the primary key column, *c_id*.

For providing the links between the *course* table and the *teacher* table, you can create a relation table named *assign* (for teaching assignments):

Assign table:

C_ID	T_ID
C1	T2
C1	T5
C2	T1
C3	T3
C4	T4
C5	T3

In the *assign* table, each row is identified by a composite key, a combination of the values in the two columns.

Normalizing Your Tables

In database design, the relations among the data elements determine the appropriate structure of the database. These relations dictate how you structure the columns in the base tables so that you can organize your data logically.

As illustrated in previous examples, one way to minimize the problem of data redundancy is to split a base table into two or more tables. The amount of effort required for maintaining your database depends significantly on the number and size of these tables. Similarly, the way you choose to split the tables greatly affects the efficiency of the database. Good database design promotes a proper balance between the efficiency of data maintenance and the efficiency of data retrieval.

Several guidelines assist you in properly splitting a base table. These guidelines are a set of normal forms you can use for validating your tables. Tables that are not in the proper normal form may encounter significant problems during data maintenance. The process of making your tables conform to the normal form is called *normalization*. The normalization process provides another means for checking the tables for the essential properties of a relational database.

When Dr. Codd first proposed the relational data model, he outlined three normal forms (see Chapter 2). Most data maintenance problems can be avoided if your tables satisfy the rules of these three normal forms. To solve some of more obscure problems in data maintenance, additional normal forms have been developed.

Five normal forms are widely accepted. These normal forms progress from the first through the fifth and build on each other. To meet the requirement for the second normal form, for example, the table must already be in the first normal form. A table in the third normal form is automatically in the second and first normal forms.

First Normal Form

The first normal form requires that the table be flat, meaning that each attribute can contain only one data value per row. That is, each data cell (the intersection between the column and row) must hold one and only one value. This statement is equivalent to saying that each value in the data cell is atomic.

To understand the rules of the first normal form, look at the following table:

```
Course1 table:

C_ID   TITLE      CREDITS   DESCRIPTION           T_ID
----   --------   -------   --------------------  ----
C1     ENGL 101         3   English Literature    T2
C2     HIST 100         3   American History      T1
C3     MATH 105         5   Calculus I            T3
C4     PHIL 101         3   Philosophy            T4
C5     PHYS 102         5   Physics I             T3
```

This table is in the first normal form because each data cell contains only one value. For example, in the C1 row, only one teacher identification number (T2) is stored in the *t_id* column. The course ENGL 101 is taught by only one teacher, T2.

When you have one-to-one relations between course and teacher, you should not have any problem assigning your data values to the data cells. The *course1* table will always satisfy the rules of the first normal form. Because each row can be identified uniquely by the course identification number in the *c_id* column, you can designate the *c_id* column as the primary key.

But if you have one-to-many relations, you may have trouble storing the multiple values in a data cell. For example, if course C1 (ENGL 101) is taught by two teachers (T2, T5), you need to decide where to put their identification numbers. You may think that you can place the two identification numbers in the *t_id* column:

Course2 table:

C_ID	TITLE	CREDITS	DESCRIPTION	T_ID
C1	ENGL 101	3	English Literature	T2,T5
C2	HIST 100	3	American History	T1
C3	MATH 105	5	Calculus I	T3
C4	PHIL 101	3	Philosophy	T4
C5	PHYS 102	5	Physics I	T3

If you assign more than one value to any data cell in the table, the table is no longer in the first normal form. One problem with storing multiple values in a cell is that you will have difficulty deciding when and how to separate the values. One way to make the table conform to the first normal form involves using multiple rows for defining the one-to-many relations. For example, the *course3* table contains two rows for identifying the two teachers associated with the course ENGL 101:

Course3 table:

C_ID	TITLE	CREDITS	DESCRIPTION l	T_ID
C1	ENGL 101	3	English Literature	T2
C1	ENGL 101	3	English Literature	T5
C2	HIST 100	3	American History	T1
C3	MATH 105	5	Calculus I	T3
C4	PHIL 101	3	Philosophy	T4
C5	PHYS 102	5	Physics I	T3

Second Normal Form

The *course3* table is in the first normal form because each data cell in the table contains only one value. But you may notice the problem of data redundancy because the first four columns of the first two rows contain the same information. Besides wasting valuable memory, redundant data requires additional effort to maintain. For example, if you change the title of the course C1, you need to search the table and change all the rows associated with that course. To avoid data redundancy problems, your table must conform to rules beyond the first normal form.

The second normal form pertains to the rules governing composite primary keys. A composite key involves using more than one column as a primary key. For example, in the *course3* table, not every row can be uniquely identified with the *c_id* column alone. Instead, the composite primary key is the combination of the *c_id* and *t_id* columns.

The second normal form requires that every non-key column be functionally dependent on the entire composite primary key. Therefore, the table must not contain a non-key column that pertains to only part of the primary key. To satisfy the second normalization rule, every non-key column in the table must relate to all the attributes in the composite primary key.

Look again at the *course3* table and see whether it meets the requirement of the second normal form. In that table, the non-key columns are *title*, *description*, *credits*, *t_lname*, and *t_fname*. The first three columns describe the attributes associated with the course entity. They can be uniquely identified by a course identification number. That is, when you know the course identification number, you can identify its title, description, and credit hours. You do not need the value in the *t_id* column as part of the primary key.

Because not all non-key columns in the *course3* table are functionally dependent on the entire primary key, the table is not in the second form. Therefore, the second normalization rule requires that you split the *course3* table into two tables, one describing the courses and other defining teaching assignments (see fig. 3.10).

Course4 table:

C_ID	TITLE	CREDITS	DESCRIPTION
C1	ENGL 101	3	English Literature
C2	HIST 100	3	American History
C3	MATH 105	5	Calculus I
C4	PHIL 101	3	Philosophy
C5	PHYS 102	5	Physics I

Assign table:

C_ID	T_ID
C1	T2
C1	T5
C2	T1
C3	T3
C4	T4
C5	T3

Fig. 3.10. *Splitting a table to conform to the second normal form.*

The benefits of converting the *course3* table into two tables (*course4* and *assign*) are many. First, you can add a new course to the curriculum at any time, just by inserting a row into the *course4* table. You can insert the course before you know who will be teaching it. For example, if a new course, C6 (SPCH 107), has just been approved and you have not decided who is to teach it, you can insert a row into the *course4* table for describing the course:

Course4 table:

C_ID	TITLE	CREDITS	DESCRIPTION
C1	ENGL 101	3	English Literature
C2	HIST 100	3	American History
C3	MATH 105	5	Calculus I
C4	PHIL 101	3	Philosophy
C5	PHYS 102	5	Physics I
C6	SPCH 107	3	Speech I

You do not have to change the *assign* table until you have decided on the instructor for the new course. At that time, you can insert a new row into the *assign* table to describe the teaching assignment. For example, you add a new row to the *assign* table after you have decided that T2 will be teaching the new course (C6):

Assign table:

```
C_ID   T_ID
----   ----
C1     T2
C1     T5
C2     T1
C3     T3
C4     T4
C5     T3
C6     T2
```

But if you have not divided the *course3* table into two separate tables, you will encounter problems inserting the new data into the table. For example, before assigning an instructor to the new course, C6, you need to leave the *t_id* column blank when you insert a new row into the *course3* table:

Course3 table, after insertion:

```
C_ID   TITLE      CREDITS   DESCRIPTION          T_ID
----   --------   -------   -------------------  ----
C1     ENGL 101        3    English Literature   T2
C1     ENGL 101        3    English Literature   T5
C2     HIST 100        3    American History     T1
C3     MATH 105        5    Calculus I           T3
C4     PHIL 101        3    Philosophy           T4
C5     PHYS 102        5    Physics I            T3
C6     SPCH 107        3    Speech
```

You have two ways to handle the missing value in the *t_id* column. One is to enter a null value into the data cell, indicating a missing value:

Course3 table, after inserting the null value:

```
C_ID   TITLE      CREDITS   DESCRIPTION          T_ID
----   --------   -------   -------------------  ----
C1     ENGL 101        3    English Literature   T2
C1     ENGL 101        3    English Literature   T5
C2     HIST 100        3    American History     T1
C3     MATH 105        5    Calculus I           T3
C4     PHIL 101        3    Philosophy           T4
C5     PHYS 102        5    Physics I            T3
C6     SPCH 107        3    Speech               null
```

This solution is not satisfactory. Because the treatment of null values differs among various versions of SQL, you will get different results. Try to avoid using null values if possible.

Another way is to assign a fictitious, or dummy, value, such as TBA (to be announced) in the data cell:

```
Course3 table, after inserting a fictitious value:

C_ID   TITLE     CREDITS   DESCRIPTION           T_ID
----   --------   -------   -------------------   ----
C1     ENGL 101        3   English Literature    T2
C1     ENGL 101        3   English Literature    T5
C2     HIST 100        3   American History      T1
C3     MATH 105        5   Calculus I            T3
C4     PHIL 101        3   Philosophy            T4
C5     PHYS 102        5   Physics I             T3
C6     SPCH 107        3   Speech                TBA
```

One problem with using fictitious values is that they are not valid values. No teacher has TBA as an identification number. Besides, you will need to replace the fictitious values with the actual values when they are determined.

Another way to handle the data deletion problem is to use a null or fictitious (TBA) value for the identification number of the former instructor. This practice is not good for handling the data deletion operation because of the problems associated with null and fictitious values.

Besides insertion problems, you will encounter problems in deleting data if you do not split the *course3* table. For example, if instructor T3 decides to resign, you need to delete his identification from the database. You have two ways to handle the data deletion problem. One is to remove from the *course3* table the rows associated with that instructor:

```
Course3 table, after deletion:

C_ID   TITLE     CREDITS   DESCRIPTION           T_ID
----   --------   -------   -------------------   ----
C1     ENGL 101        3   English Literature    T2
C1     ENGL 101        3   English Literature    T5
C2     HIST 100        3   American History      T1
C4     PHIL 101        3   Philosophy            T4
```

The table no longer contains any information describing the courses (C3 and C5) that were taught by instructor T3. This solution is not satisfactory for the data deletion problem because the table gives misleading information about the courses offered. The courses C3 (MATH 105) and C5 (PHYS 102) should remain in the curriculum even though the instructor has resigned.

Finally, another advantage of splitting the *course3* table into *course4* and *assign* tables is the ease of data update (again, see fig. 3.10). For example, if you need to change a course description, you need to change information in only one row in the *course4* table. This statement is true even though many instructors are teaching that course. But with the *course3* table, you need to update information in multiple rows if several instructors teach the same course. For example, if you need to modify the information about the C1 course, you need to change information in the first two rows of the *course3* table. You have to change information in only the first row in the *course4* table because each course is always represented by one row.

Third Normal Form

Many people consider the third normal form the most important normal form for database designs because you avoid most problems associated with data maintenance if your tables are in this form. The third normal form requires that no non-key column depend on another non-key column. Every non-key column must be a fact about the primary key.

To understand the third normal form, look at the following table:

```
Course5 table:

C_ID  TITLE     CREDITS  DESCRIPTION          T_ID  T_LNAME    T_FNAME
----  --------  -------  -------------------- ----  ---------- ----------
C1    ENGL 101        3  English Literature   T2    Hemingway  Ernest M.
C2    HIST 100        3  American History     T1    Franklin   Benjamin
C3    MATH 105        5  Calculus I           T3    Newton     Isaac
C4    PHIL 101        3  Philosophy           T4    Quine      Willard V.
C5    PHYS 102        5  Physics I            T3    Newton     Isaac
```

Table *course5* is similar to *course3,* except that ENGL 101 is taught by only one instructor, T2, and two new columns, describing instructors' last and first names, have been added. When you first look at this table, the added information appears to make sense, because you can learn who is teaching a particular course. But many problems are associated with this table design.

The primary key for the table is the *c_id* column. Each row in the *course5* table can be uniquely identified by the value in the primary key. Every non-key column depends on the entire primary key. Therefore, *course5* is in the second normal form.

But the *course5* table is not in the third normal form because some non-key columns depend on other non-key columns. For example, the *t_lname* and *t_fname* columns depend on the *t_id* column. Information about instructor T3 appears in two rows. This redundancy is a consequence of the table's not being in the third normal form. To make the table conform to the third normal form, you split the *course5* table into three separate tables (see fig. 3.11).

Course6 table:

C_ID	TITLE	CREDITS	DESCRIPTION
C1	ENGL 101	3	English Literature
C2	HIST 100	3	American History
C3	MATH 105	5	Calculus I
C4	PHIL 101	3	Philosophy
C5	PHYS 102	5	Physics I

Teacher table:

T_ID	T_LNAME	T_FNAME
T1	Franklin	Benjamin
T2	Hemingway	Ernest M.
T3	Newton	Isaac
T4	Quine	Willard V.

Assign table:

C_ID	T_ID
C1	T2
C2	T1
C3	T3
C4	T4
C5	T3

Fig. 3.11. *Tables conforming to the third normal form.*

When you look at the tables in figure 3.11, you no longer notice any redundant data. For example, information about instructor T3 appears only once in the *teacher* table. Besides conserving valuable memory, information can be efficiently maintained in these separate tables.

Splitting the *course5* table into the three tables has other advantages. Adding a new course or a new instructor to the database is a simple task when you are using the *course6* and *teacher* tables. For example, to add a course, T6 (SPCH 107), you can append a new row to the *course6* table without knowing who is going to teach that course:

Course6 table, after insertion:

C_ID	TITLE	CREDITS	DESCRIPTION
C1	ENGL 101	3	English Literature
C2	HIST 100	3	American History
C3	MATH 105	5	Calculus I
C4	PHIL 101	3	Philosophy
C5	PHYS 102	5	Physics I
C6	SPCH 107	3	Speech

Similarly, you easily can delete a course or an instructor from the tables.

If you are using the *course5* table, you will have trouble filling in all the values before you know the instructor for the new course. As a solution to the missing values, you can enter null values for the attributes for the new course:

Course5 table, after inserting null values:

C_ID	TITLE	CREDITS	DESCRIPTION	T_ID	T_LNAME	T_FNAME
C1	ENGL 101	3	English Literature	T2	Hemingway	Ernest M.
C2	HIST 100	3	American History	T1	Franklin	Benjamin
C3	MATH 105	5	Calculus I	T3	Newton	Isaac
C4	PHIL 101	3	Philosophy	T4	Quine	Willard V.
C5	PHYS 102	5	Physics I	T3	Newton	Isaac
C6	SPCH 107	3	Speech	null	null	null

Another way to solve the problem of missing information is to place fictitious, or dummy, values in place of the null values:

Course5 table, after inserting fictitious values:

C_ID	TITLE	CREDITS	DESCRIPTION	T_ID	T_LNAME	T_FNAME
C1	ENGL 101	3	English Literature	T2	Hemingway	Ernest M.
C2	HIST 100	3	American History	T1	Franklin	Benjamin
C3	MATH 105	5	Calculus I	T3	Newton	Isaac
C4	PHIL 101	3	Philosophy	T4	Quine	Willard V.
C5	PHYS 102	5	Physics I	T3	Newton	Isaac
C6	SPCH 107	3	Speech	TBA	TBA	TBA

Both these approaches are unsatisfactory for handling the missing values. If you are using the *course6* table, however, you can add information about a new instructor before you know what courses he or she will be teaching. For example, when the new instructor George B. Shaw is hired, you can add his information by inserting a new row into the *teacher* table:

Teacher table, after insertion:

T_ID	T_LNAME	T_FNAME
T1	Franklin	Benjamin
T2	Hemingway	Ernest M.
T3	Newton	Isaac
T4	Quine	Willard V.
T5	Shaw	George B.

After you have decided what courses the new instructor will teach, you can define his teaching assignment by adding the appropriate rows to the *assign* table. For example, if you assign Shaw to teach the course C1 (ENGL 101), you insert the new row into the *assign* table, as follows:

Assign table, after insertion:

C_ID	T_ID
C1	T2
C2	T1
C3	T3
C4	T4
C5	T3
C1	T5

From the *assign* table, you may notice that the course C1 is taught jointly by two instructors (T2 and T5). The *assign* table allows one-to-many relations, meaning that a course can be taught by more than one instructor.

If you do not split the *course5* table into three tables, you may have trouble saving the information about the new teacher in that table before you make the teaching assignment. One solution to the problem is to use null values or fictitious values in the table:

Course5 table:

C_ID	TITLE	CREDITS	DESCRIPTION	T_ID	T_LNAME	T_FNAME
C1	ENGL 101	3	English Literature	T2	Hemingway	Ernest M.
C2	HIST 100	3	American History	T1	Franklin	Benjamin
C3	MATH 105	5	Calculus I	T3	Newton	Isaac
C4	PHIL 101	3	Philosophy	T4	Quine	Willard V.
C5	PHYS 102	5	Physics I	T3	Newton	Isaac
null	null	null	null	T5	Shaw	George B.

After you decide to assign C1 (ENGL 101) to an instructor, say T5, you can replace all the null values with the actual values:

Course5 table:

C_ID	TITLE	CREDITS	DESCRIPTION	T_ID	T_LNAME	T_FNAME
C1	ENGL 101	3	English Literature	T2	Hemingway	Ernest M.
C2	HIST 100	3	American History	T1	Franklin	Benjamin
C3	MATH 105	5	Calculus I	T3	Newton	Isaac
C4	PHIL 101	3	Philosophy	T4	Quine	Willard V.
C5	PHYS 102	5	Physics I	T3	Newton	Isaac
C1	ENGL 101	3	English Literature	T5	Shaw	George B.

This method brings up another problem with the table. This table is no longer in the second normal form because each row cannot be identified by a single primary key. You need to use a combination of the *c_id* and *t_id* columns as a composite primary key. As a result, some non-key columns no longer depend on the entire primary key. For example, the *title* value depends only on *c_id*, and *t_lname* depends only on *t_id*.

Another problem associated with the *course5* table is the difficulty you encounter when you delete information about a course or an instructor. For example, if you decide not to offer the C2 course, you may need to delete the second row from the table:

Course5, after deleting C2:

C_ID	TITLE	CREDITS	DESCRIPTION	T_ID	T_LNAME	T_FNAME
C1	ENGL 101	3	English Literature	T2	Hemingway	Ernest M.
C3	MATH 105	5	Calculus I	T3	Newton	Isaac
C4	PHIL 101	3	Philosophy	T4	Quine	Willard V.
C5	PHYS 102	5	Physics I	T3	Newton	Isaac

As a result, you lose all the information about instructor T1 (Benjamin Franklin). Similar problems occur if you remove information about any instructor from the table. If you delete information about an instructor, you lose all the information about the course that instructor teaches. But if you split the *course5* table into three tables, you will not have this problem. For example, if instructor T1 resigns, all you have to do is remove from the *teacher* table the row associated with that instructor, without changing anything in the *course6* table:

Teacher table, after deleting T1:

T_ID	T_LNAME	T_FNAME
T2	Hemingway	Ernest M.
T3	Newton	Isaac
T4	Quine	Willard V.
T5	Shaw	George B.

To delete the teaching assignment for the former instructor, you can delete the rows that pertain to him. For example, you remove the second row from the *assign* table:

Assign table, after deletion:

C_ID	T_ID
C1	T2
C3	T3
C4	T4
C5	T3

Note that after deleting all the information about the former instructor, you still maintain information about all the courses offered in the curriculum.

The third normal form also solves most of the data redundancy problems associated with many-to-many relations. For example, the *student* table shown in figure 3.12 identifies the courses the students take.

The table in figure 3.12 describes a set of many-to-many relations between students and courses. In this table, you can see that a student can take several courses and that a course can be taken by many students. This table is not in the second normal form and consequently not in the third form.

The primary key for this table is the combination of the *s_id* and *c_id* columns. Some non-key columns are not dependent on the entire primary key. A solution to the problem is to split the *student* table into three separate tables (see fig. 3.13).

Student table:

S_ID	S_LNAME	S_FNAME	C_ID	TITLE
S1	Austin	Linda D.	C3	MATH 105
S2	Brown	Nancy J.	C3	MATH 105
S2	Brown	Nancy J.	C4	PHIL 101
S3	Carter	Jack F.	C1	ENGL 101
S3	Carter	Jack F.	C5	PHYS 102
S4	Ford	Harvey P.	C2	HIST 100
S5	Freed	Barbara J.	C1	ENGL 101
S5	Freed	Barbara J.	C2	HIST 100
S5	Freed	Barbara J.	C4	PHIL 101
S6	Gilmore	Danny S.	C5	PHYS 102
S7	Jackson	Brad L.	C2	HIST 100
S8	Madison	George G.	C2	HIST 100
S8	Madison	George G.	C4	PHIL 101
S8	Madison	George G.	C5	PHYS 102
S9	Reed	Donna E.	C3	MATH 105
S9	Reed	Donna E.	C5	PHYS 102
S10	Taylor	Bob K.	C1	ENGL 101

Fig. 3.12. The student *table, showing many-to-many relations.*

These tables are now in the third normal form. All the redundant data elements have been eliminated from the tables.

Fourth Normal Form

The fourth normal form pertains to tables involving multiple independent many-to-many relations. As stated earlier in this chapter, if possible, you should organize your data elements so that a table stores information associated with only one data entity. Unless the data entities are related, you should not combine them in the same table. Do not store in the same table information relating to two or more independent entities when many-to-many relations exist among these entities. The fourth normal form is designed to address this problem.

Student1 table:

S_ID	S_LNAME	S_FNAME
S1	Austin	Linda D.
S2	Brown	Nancy J.
S3	Carter	Jack F.
S4	Ford	Harvey P.
S5	Freed	Barbara
S6	Gilmore	Danny S.
S7	Jackson	Brad L.
S8	Madison	George G
S9	Reed	Donna E.
S10	Taylor	Bob K.

Course table:

C_ID	TITLE
C1	ENGL 101
C2	HIST 100
C3	MATH 105
C4	PHIL 101
C5	PHYS 102

Class table:

S_ID	C_ID
S1	C3
S2	C3
S2	C4
S3	C1
S3	C5
S4	C2
S5	C1
S5	C2
S5	C4
S6	C5
S7	C2
S8	C2
S8	C4
S8	C5
S9	C3
S9	C5
S10	C1

Fig. 3.13. *Table split to conform to the third normal form.*

To understand the fourth normal form, look at another example—a relational database containing information about the following three entities: employee, department, and vehicle. Many-to-many relations exist between employee and department. That is, an employee can work in many departments, and a department can have many employees. Similarly, many-to-many relations exist between employees and vehicles. An employee can own one or more vehicles, and a vehicle can be jointly owned by several employees. These relations can be described as follows:

Employee	*Department*	*Employee*	*Vehicle*
E1	D1	E1	V1
E2	D2	E2	V2
E3	D3	E3	V3

These relations can be described as follows:

- ❏ E1 belongs to D1 and D3, E2 belongs to D1 and D2, and E3 belongs to D3.

- ❏ D1 has two employees, E1 and E2; D2 has only one employee, E2; and D3 has two employees, E1 and E3.

- ❏ E1 owns V1 and V2, E2 owns V2, E3 owns V1 and V3.

- ❏ V1 is owned jointly by employees E1 and E3, V2 is owned jointly by employees E1 and E2, and V3 is owned by employee E3.

Departments and vehicles are two independent data entities. No relation describes a direct link between a department and a vehicle. If you use a single table to store information about these three entities, you will encounter several problems. For example, you can organize your data elements in several ways, one of which may look like the following table:

Company table:

E_ID	D_ID	V_ID
E1	D1	V1
E1	D1	V2
E1	D3	V1
E1	D3	V2
E2	D1	V2
E2	D2	V2
E3	D3	V1
E3	D3	V3

This table design will have a great deal of redundant data if you include more attributes for each data entity. For example, besides the employee identification number, if you add other attributes, such as name and address for each employee, the table will have much duplicate information. Besides redundant data, this table contains confusing information. It implies some association between the two independent entities: department and vehicle. Does the table mean that department D1 owns V1 and V2 and department D3 owns all three vehicles? Does the table mean that department D2 owns only one vehicle, V2?

One way to avoid the confusion may be to use null values in the table so that department entity is independent of the vehicle entity:

```
Company1 table:

E_ID  D_ID  V_ID
----  ----  ----
E1    D1    null
E1    D3    null
E1    null  V1
E1    null  V2
E2    D1    null
E2    D2    null
E2    null  V2
E3    D3    null
E3    null  V1
E3    null  V3
```

This design is not satisfactory because of the extensive use of null values. Besides, with this table, you will encounter problems when you need to add new entries to any of the three data entities. For example, if you need to add a new employee, say E4, to the table, you need to use null values to represent the missing information before the employee is assigned to a department:

```
Company1 table:

E_ID  D_ID  V_ID
----  ----  ----
E1    D1    null
E1    D3    null
E1    null  V1
E1    null  V2
E2    D1    null
E2    D2    null
E2    null  V2
E3    D3    null
E3    null  V1
E3    null  V3
E4    null  null
```

If the new employee does not intend to own a vehicle, a null value in the data cell for the *v_id* column is incorrect. A null value does not mean a blank. You plan to replace a null value with the actual value later.

These problems occur mainly because you are including in the same table attributes associated with two or more independent entities. The fourth normal form deals with this problem. A solution to the problem is to organize the information about the data elements in the following two tables:

```
Dept table:

E_ID   D_ID
----   ----
E1     D1
E1     D3
E2     D1
E2     D2
E3     D3

Vehicle table:

E_ID   V_ID
----   ----
E1     V1
E2     V2
E2     V2
E3     V1
E3     V3
```

Fifth Normal Form

From the examples you have seen in this chapter, you have learned important advantages of splitting a table into several tables. Besides eliminating redundant data, you can easily maintain data integrity if you split a table properly through normalization. But when you normalize your tables, you generally are sacrificing retrieval speed to prevent data maintenance difficulties. More important, unless you can get from the split tables the same information that was in the original table, your tables are not flexible and useful. Therefore, the fifth normal form requires that if you split a table into several tables, you must be able to reconstruct the original table by joining these tables. The operations of joining tables are discussed in Chapter 9. In that chapter, you will see how to join several tables with the appropriate SQL commands.

Chapter Summary

Because of its flexibility, a relational model does not impose many rigid rules in its implementations. Although the model outlines certain basic guidelines for designing your database, following the model does not prevent you from designing a poor database. This chapter introduces you to several characteristics that are generally associated with a good relational database.

In designing a relational database, you always have to consider the trade-offs between two factors: speed of data retrieval and efficiency of data maintenance. These factors depend on both the number and size of the tables you use to organize your data. This chapter discusses five generally accepted guidelines for splitting a table into several smaller tables. These guidelines are expressed in five normal forms. Tables that conform to these normal forms enable you to avoid many problems in data maintenance.

After you have structured your database according to the guidelines outlined in this chapter, you will be ready to begin creating your base tables for organizing your data. In the next chapter, you learn how to create your base tables.

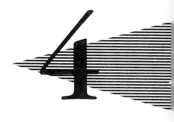

Creating Tables and Entering Data

This chapter explains the SQL commands and procedures you use to create a base table. You begin by defining a table structure that describes the attributes—type, name, and size—associated with the data columns to be included in the table. In this chapter, you also learn about the various types of data columns you can use to save different kinds of information.

After you have learned how to set up a base table, you learn the appropriate commands for entering the data rows into the table, where they are saved as a group in your database. Depending on the version of SQL you are using, you can create one or more databases within the program. This chapter begins by showing you how to set up and use a database.

Creating a Database

In Chapter 3, you learned that the base table is the basic unit of a database in a relational database design. In order to store the information related to a database application, you need to create a number of base tables; to manipulate this data, you need to set up and maintain additional related tables. For example, to speed the search process, you can create index files based on the values in the base table.

The SQL administrator automatically sets up a number of system files in order to organize your tables effectively. These system files are used to catalog information in the related tables. For instance, the system file SYSTABLS (SYSTABLE) contains the names of the tables and their creators. (Refer again to table 2.3 for a list of system tables.) Information about the names and types of all the columns is stored in the system table SYSCOLS (SYSCOLUMNS). Information about the indexes created is maintained in the SYSIDXS (SYSINDEXES) system file. SQL organizes these tables and system files quite differently from other database management systems that save information about a table as an independent disk file.

107

In most cases, SQL tables and system files are stored in a certain portion of the storage space. The actual physical storage device for storing these tables and system files may vary depending on your computer system. A microcomputer system commonly sets up an SQL database as a subdirectory on a hard disk. As a result, if you want to create a new database using some commercial versions of SQL (for example, Ingres's SQL or Oracle's SQL*Plus), you need to set up the database at the operating system level. In other words, you need to issue the appropriate commands at the DOS (Disk Operating System) prompt to specify the name and memory requirement of the database to be created.

However, with other versions of SQL, such as dBASE IV, you can create a new database by issuing an SQL command such as CREATE DATABASE (in dBASE IV, DB2, SYBASE) or CREATEDB (in INFORMIX). When you issue one of these two commands, you specify the name of the database after the key phrase CREATE DATABASE or the keyword CREATEDB as follows:

CREATE DATABASE <name of database>

CREATEDB <name of database>

In some versions of SQL, in the CREATE command, you also can specify the actual data storage device (such as a disk volume and subdirectory) and the memory size of the database.

Naming a Database

The first step in creating a new database is to assign it a name. The database name enables you to identify the groups of tables you can access. Although the various dialects of the SQL language have minor differences, the following rules for naming a database apply to most versions of SQL:

❏ A database name consists of a string of characters, including letters (A–Z) and numerals (0–9). For example, EMPLOYEE and BUDGET89 are possible database names.

❏ A database name may not include blanks. (For example, MY DBASE is not acceptable.)

❏ Avoid using asterisks (*) or periods (.) in a database name (NEW.ACCT, PHONES*) because these symbols are reserved for special uses.

The maximum number of characters allowed in a database name varies among different versions of SQL. However, a database name generally can be up to eight characters long. Although you cannot include blanks in a database name, you can use underscores (_) in place of blanks to separate parts of a name (for example, MY_DBASE).

In most versions of SQL, case is significant. Thus, a database named *EMPLOYEE* is different from one named *Employee*. However, some SQL versions do not distinguish between upper- and lowercase in a database name.

When you create a new database in a single-user system, the database normally belongs to you. In other words, you are the author and owner of the database, and other users must be granted permission to access the data stored in your database. In this case, you have complete freedom to name the database and determine the storage requirements as you wish. If you are using a multiuser system, however, you may not have the authority to assign a database to yourself because you need to work with the system operator or database manager to create the database at the system level.

Selecting a Database

After you have set up a database, you need to select it, or move into it, before you can create the necessary base tables. The commands and procedures required to select the database with which you want to work vary among the different versions of SQL. In some versions, you select the database at the operating system level by issuing the appropriate commands at the DOS prompt. In other versions of SQL, you can enter at the SQL prompt an SQL command, such as

START DATABASE   <name of database>

USE   <name of database>

DATABASE   <name of database>

For information on how to select a database in your system, consult the system manual for the version of SQL you are using.

Creating a Base Table

After you have selected your database, you are ready to create the base tables you need. The process of creating a new base table involves three steps:

1. Assigning a unique name to the base table

2. Defining the table structure

3. Filling the table with data

The table name is used to identify the base table. The table structure specifies the attributes of the data table, including the name, the type, and sometimes the size of each column.

The SQL command for creating a base table follows this syntax rule:

    CREATE TABLE   <name of base table>
                    (definition of table structure)

Notice that the angle brackets (<>) shown in the command syntax are used to indicate the base table name; you do not include these brackets when you enter the actual command. Information describing the table structure is enclosed in parentheses, which must be included as part of the command.

The following is an example:

    CREATE TABLE employee
                (ss_no   CHAR(11),
                 Lname   CHAR(7),
                 f_name   CHAR(10),
                 title   CHAR(10),
                 dept   CHAR(10),
                 salary   DECIMAL(8,2));

In this example, the new base table is identified by the name *employee*. Although you have a great deal of freedom in naming a base table, some important basic rules are given in the next section, followed by instructions for defining the table structure.

Naming a Base Table

Like a database name, a base table name can include up to a certain number of characters, which may be a combination of letters, numeric digits, and underscores (_). No blank spaces can be included in a table name. Minor differences exist among different SQL versions in the maximum and minimum number of characters allowed in a base table name, but a length of eight characters is quite safe. Here are some legitimate table names:

    employee
    ACCOUNTS
    ItemSold
    PhoneLst

Avoid using asterisks (*) or periods (.) in a table name because in most versions of SQL, these characters are reserved for performing special functions. Similarly, do not use the pound sign (#) to create a name such as PHONE# because the pound sign is not allowed in many versions of SQL.

Note: In many versions of SQL, case is significant in assigning a table name. If you assign *employee* as the table name when you create a table, you cannot find the table if you use the table name *Employee*. Therefore, although a table name such as *ItemSold* may be neat, you should standardize your table names in all upper- or lowercase letters (for example, *ITEMSOLD* or *itemsold*) so that you do not have to remember the exact form of a table name. In this book, all the table names are in lowercase letters.

Defining the Table Structure

In a relational database model, a base table is divided into a number of columns and rows. Figure 4.1 shows a sample *employee* table.

SS_NO	L_NAME	F_NAME	TITLE	DEPT	SALARY
123-45-6789	Smith	James J.	President	Corporate	89500.00
634-56-7890	Nelson	Harry M.	Manager	Sales	65000.00
445-67-8801	Zeller	Albert K.	Salesman	Sales	48900.00
562-87-8800	Chapman	Kirk D.	Salesman	Sales	42500.00
404-22-4568	Baker	Larry A.	Clerk	Sales	30500.00
256-09-5555	Dixon	Kathy T.	Accountant	Accounting	45000.00
458-90-3456	Frazer	Robert F.	Bookkeeper	Accounting	28000.00
777-34-6543	King	David G.	Manager	Personnel	38000.00
100-45-8021	Wong	Mike J.	Manager	MIS	44000.00
303-25-7777	Duff	Cathy B.	Secretary	Personnel	26500.00

Fig. 4.1. The employee *base table.*

In the *employee* table shown in figure 4.1, you can see that the table is divided into six columns and ten rows. Each column, which contains a particular type of data, is identified by a column heading, or column name, as follows:

Column Name	Description
ss_no	Employee's identification number
l_name	Employee's last name
f_name	Employee's first name and middle initial
title	Employee's job title in the firm
dept	Employee's department
salary	Employee's annual salary

The *l_name* column is reserved for an employee's last name, which is represented by a string of characters, such as *Smith*. Each row stores the information pertaining to one employee.

After you assign a table name, you must define the table structure by assigning each column a name and specifying the type of data to be stored in that column. With certain types of data, you also need to specify the amount of storage space required to hold the anticipated data value. With this information, the program can set up the base table and reserve the appropriate amount of storage space in the database for handling your data needs.

You set up the table structure by describing the structure inside the parentheses of the CREATE TABLE command:

CREATE TABLE   <name of base table>
        (column_definition [,column_definition] ...);

A *column_definition* is defined with a column name followed by its data type and, if necessary, a parameter keyword such as NULL or NOT NULL. If you remember the syntax rules for an SQL command, described in Chapter 3, you notice that the square brackets in the CREATE TABLE command enclose an optional column definition. The ellipsis (...) indicates that you can repeat the optional item as many times as desired. Many commercial versions of SQL require that you end each SQL command with a semicolon (;). The following SQL command creates the *employee* table shown in figure 4.1.

```
CREATE TABLE    employee
                (ss_no      CHAR(11),
                 l_name     CHAR(7),
                 f_name     CHAR(10),
                 title      CHAR(10),
                 dept       CHAR(10),
                 salary     DECIMAL(8,2));
```

With the CREATE TABLE command, each column is identified by name, data type, and column size if needed. For example, the first column of the *employee* table is identified by the column name *ss_no* (social security number) followed by the data type CHAR, indicating that only a string of characters (a combination of letters, digits, and acceptable symbols) is allowed. The value, specified in the data type keyword CHAR(11) instructs the program to reserve enough storage space to store up to 11 characters of data in that column. All the information defining the table structure is enclosed in parentheses.

You can choose data types other than character to be stored in a column. Other sections in this chapter explain how to set up these types of data columns.

Assigning Column Names

Like a table name, a column name consists of a string of standard characters that can include letters, digits, and underscores (_). Blank spaces cannot be embedded in a column name, and you should never use a period (.). Although some versions of SQL allow you to use some special symbols, you should use only the standard characters if you want your database to be compatible with different versions of the language. Minor differences also exist in the maximum column-name length allowed by different SQL versions. However, in most versions you can have a column name up to 10 characters long. Here are examples of some acceptable table names:

    ACCOUNT_NO
    last_name
    staff_id
    PartNo
    Birth_Date
    QTY_SOLD

As with table names, case is important in assigning column names for many versions of SQL. Following a format convention in naming columns—using all uppercase or all lowercase letters—is recommended. To help you distinguish the table and column names from the SQL command keywords, which are in capital letters, this book uses all lowercase letters for column names.

Specifying Data Type

In almost every version of SQL, you can store data in a column in one of two basic types:

    Character, or text
    Numeric values

You use a character column for text that includes letters, numeric digits, and all the normal symbols on a typewriter keyboard. For example, to store an employee's last name in the *Lname* column, you can choose a character string, such as *Smith*, as the value for the column. The following SQL command places the character string in the *Lname* column in the *employee* table:

    INSERT INTO employee (Lname)
         VALUES ('Smith');

Similarly, you can store a numerical value (for example, $89,500) for an employee's annual salary in the *salary* column by using an SQL command such as

```
UPDATE   employee
   SET   salary = 89500
WHERE    Lname = 'Smith';
```

If you don't understand these commands, don't worry. You learn more about them later in this chapter and in subsequent chapters.

When you store a character string in a character column, you can define the column as fixed length or variable length. The main difference between a fixed-length and a variable-length column lies in the way SQL reserves storage space for a character string. For example, the last name of an employee, such as Smith, can be stored in a fixed-length or a variable-length column. In a fixed-length column, no matter how long the character string, the system always reserves the same amount of storage space for the string, measured by the number of characters specified in the table structure (for example, CHAR(7)). On the other hand, if you save a character string in a variable-length column, the system uses only the exact amount of storage space (in characters) needed to hold the string. For example, if you define the column as VARCHAR(7) and the string contains only three characters, the string occupies only three characters in memory. This subject is discussed further in the section about variable-length character strings.

Numbers are stored in columns defined as containing numeric values. Depending on the degree of precision required and the presentation format desired, you may define a numeric column as integer (whole number), regular decimal value, or floating decimal value.

In addition to these two basic data types, some versions of SQL enable you to specify time, date, and logical as legitimate data types. Time and date columns hold time and date values, respectively, in a given format (such as JAN-01-1990, 01/01/90). A logical column is similar to a single-character string; a logical column can store the logical values of T (True) and F (False). A summary of data types used by several versions of SQL is given in Appendix A.

Fixed-Length Character Strings

A fixed-length character string holds a string of a predetermined number of characters in the form of numeric digits (0–9), letters (a–z, A–Z), and other valid symbols. The character string is enclosed in single quotation marks (for example, 'Smith, John J.', '123-45-6789').

The SQL keyword for defining a fixed-length character string is

CHAR(n)

where *n*, an argument value, indicates the length of the string in number of characters. For example, if you define the data type as CHAR(7) for a column named *Lname*, a fixed length of up to seven characters is expected for the data value. If you store in that column a string that is shorter than the specified length, blank spaces are added to make up the specified string length. For example, if you store the string *JOHN* in the *Lname* column, three blank characters are added to the end of the string. If the character string is longer than the column width, the string usually is truncated—with or without a warning message, depending on the SQL version.

Fixed-length character columns are easy to set up and maintain. They are also simple to format in a report because you can display each data value neatly in a fixed column width. The one major disadvantage of using fixed-length character strings in a table is that the storage space taken up by the padded blank spaces cannot be used. Nevertheless, if the character strings to be stored in the column are relatively uniform in length, a fixed-length character column is your best option.

Variable-Length Character Strings

A variable-length character column stores character strings of different lengths as data values, without adding blank spaces to the strings. When defining a variable-length character column, you specify the maximum anticipated length of the string, but only the storage space for the actual string length is allocated when the string is stored. Variable-length character columns use your memory resources economically.

The SQL keyword for defining a variable character column is

VARCHAR(n)

where the argument value *n* specifies the maximum number of characters that can be stored in the data column. For example, if you define the *Lname* column as VARCHAR(10) and the data value you store in that column contains five characters (such as *Smith*), only five characters are stored in the column; no blank spaces are added to the string. However, some implementations of SQL use a different data type to represent a variable-length character column (refer to Appendix A for details).

Numeric Values

Two basic types of numeric values exist: integers (whole numbers) and decimals. Depending on the maximum number of digits required to represent a whole number, you can define an integer as regular or small. Similarly, you can define different types of decimal numbers depending on the number of digits and decimal places needed to represent the value and the form in which the value is to be represented.

Regular Integers

A regular integer contains up to a maximum number of significant (or precision) digits plus a sign (+ or −). The maximum number of digits allowed in a regular integer varies among commercial versions of SQL. Some allow up to 10 significant digits (for example, dBASE IV SQL), whereas others enable you to define an integer up to 40 significant digits (for example, Oracle). For practical purposes, you should not have any trouble using a regular integer to store a whole number with a specified number of significant digits.

The common SQL keyword for defining a regular integer in a data definition command is INTEGER, as the following command illustrates. Notice that the *on_hand* and *reorder* columns are set up as regular integers to hold the on-hand quantity and the reorder point, respectively.

```
CREATE   TABLE stock
         (stock_no        CHAR(5),
          on_hand         INTEGER,
          reorder         INTEGER,
          vendor_id       CHAR(2));
```

Some commercial versions of SQL use keywords like NUMBER or INT for defining a regular integer. For a summary of these key words in different versions of SQL, refer to Appendix A.

Small Integers

If you plan to work with only small whole numbers in your database, you may choose to define the data column as small integer in order to conserve memory space. For example, if you need to store the number of exemptions for income tax purposes in a payroll table, you may want to define the column as a small integer column. Other examples of small integers may include quantity on-hand in an inventory table, number of units sold in a sales table, and so on.

A small integer column enables you to store a whole number with a small number of significant digits and so conserves memory. The maximum number of digits allowed in a small integer column varies among commercial versions of SQL. However, a maximum of five to ten significant digits is generally acceptable.

The common SQL keyword for defining a small integer is

```
SMALLINT
```

For example, the *on_hand* and *reorder* columns in the *stock* table can be defined as small integers:

```
CREATE TABLE    stock
                (stock_no    CHAR(5),
                 on_hand     SMALLINT,
                 reorder     SMALLINT,
                 vendor_id   CHAR(2));
```

Unless the on-hand and reorder quantities are very large, small integer columns are the most efficient way to store these values.

Small integers conserve storage space, but because the size of the numbers is fixed, a small integer column still may be too large for some of your data values. In this case, some versions of SQL provide you with a very small integer type such as TINYINT (for tiny integer in SYBASE) or enable you to specify fewer digits (such as I2 for a two-byte integer in Ingres's SQL).

To provide the greatest flexibility, some versions of SQL, such as Oracle's SQL*Plus, enable you to specify the exact number of digits in an integer. The keyword is NUMBER(n). In these versions, you can define a small integer by using a small argument value in the keyword, for example, NUMBER(4).

Decimal Numbers

A decimal value contains a number of digits and decimal places in addition to a sign. Each of the following values is a decimal number:

$$2579.95$$
$$-245.00$$
$$-12.345$$
$$0.2456$$
$$-1234500000.00$$
$$0.000006789$$

The first two decimal numbers are monetary values; the last two are "long" decimals.

The common SQL keyword for defining a decimal number is

DECIMAL(m,n)

where *m* specifies the total number of digits (including the sign) required by the decimal number and *n* specifies the number of decimal places used to represent the number. For example, by using the keyword DECIMAL(8,2) in the data definition command, you can define a decimal value that has up to eight digits (including the sign), with two digits to the right of the decimal point.

The following command creates a sample table, named *parts*, which contains a decimal value column, *unit_cost*:

```
CREATE TABLE    parts
                (stock_no       CHAR(5),
                 part_type      CHAR(11),
                 dscription     CHAR(25),
                 unit_cost      DECIMAL(8,2));
```

Because business database applications involve extensive use of monetary values, some commercial SQL versions provide a MONEY data type that automatically assumes a decimal value with two decimal places (see Appendix A). In such versions, the *unit_cost* column is defined as a MONEY data type, as the following command illustrates:

```
CREATE TABLE    parts
                (stock_no       CHAR(5) NOT NULL,
                 part_type      CHAR(11),
                 dscription     CHAR(25),
                 unit_cost      MONEY));
```

Floating-Point Numbers

A floating-point number is a decimal value, but it usually represents a very small or very large value. For example, in many financial calculations involving complex formulas, a floating-point number can be used to provide the high level of accuracy (for example, a large number of significant digits) that is required to represent the answer.

The two decimal numbers shown earlier, -1234500000.00 and 0.000006789—are usually defined as floating decimal values. A concise way to represent the value is to use an exponential (E) or scientific format, representing the value in the form of a power (exponent) of ten. For example, the value -123450000 can be represented in any of these ways:

$$-12345 \times 100000$$
$$-12345 \times 10^5$$
$$-12345E+05$$

You also can represent the same value as $-1.2345E+09$ because it is equivalent to

$$-1.2345 \times 10^9$$

Similarly, the value -0.000006789 can be represented in any of these ways:

6789×0.000000001
6789×10^{-9}
$6789E-09$
$6.789E-06$

The SQL keyword for defining a floating-point number is

FLOAT

Floating values may look like

-351.276
1682.02
-45.0345
0.45678

The maximum size of a floating-point number varies depending on the commercial version of SQL. Because most commercial database applications do not use floating-point values, this data type is not crucial for learning the SQL language.

Date and Time Values

Some versions of SQL enable you to define a DATE data type as follows:

```
CREATE TABLE    student
                (s_id        CHAR(3) NOT NULL,
                 s_lname     CHAR(7),
                 s_fname     CHAR(10),
                 s_bdate     DATE,
                 s_sex       CHAR(1),
                 s_hsgpa     DECIMAL(6,2));
```

The type of data that can be stored in a date column varies among the different SQL versions. In most cases, a date value represents a valid date in one of many formats named DATE, such as dd/mm/yy (04/07/90), mm/dd/yy (07/04/90), dd-MON-yy (04-JUL-90), or dd-MON-yyyy (04-JUL-1990). In some versions, you also can store a time value in a date column, expressed in the form "8:30:10 am" or as a time interval, such as "5 years 10 months 3 days 50 minutes."

Date and time values can play an important role in some database applications. For example, by storing in a date column the birth dates for a group of students, you can arrange the students by age. Similarly, if you have stored the check-in and checkout times for your workers in a date and time column, you easily can compute the length of time they have worked.

Although date and time values may look like character strings, they are treated differently in SQL. In most versions that provide the DATE data type, you can calculate the time period between two DATE values. This feature is important if your application requires that algebraic operations be performed on dates.

Logical Values

Another data type offered by some versions of SQL is the logical value, which is usually represented by a single character of T or F or Y or N. This data type is treated much like a character string. Because you can achieve the effect of a logical value with a single-character string, a logical data type is not so important. However, in some versions of SQL (such as dBASE IV's SQL), a logical column in a base table provides more compatibility for importing data from a dBASE table.

Null Values

A frequent problem with data entry is incomplete information. For example, when you add information about a new employee to the *employee* table, you may not have decided on the job title and salary at the time you enter the data, so you want to leave the *title* and *salary* columns as empty, or unknown, to be filled in at a later date. In this case, you store a null value in those columns.

In many versions of SQL, null values are displayed with the word null or NULL. Other SQL implementations show null values as blank, but a null value is different from a blank column because a null value indicates that no information about an employee's title is available; null does not mean that the employee's title is a string of blank spaces. A null value in a numeric column does not represent zero.

In designing a base table, you often need to allow null values in certain columns. However, some key columns must not be allowed to have any null value. For example, in the *employee* table, you should not allow a null value in the employee's identification (*ss_no*) column because this information identifies an employee and is often used as a key column for linking information in this table with information in other tables. A null value in a key column causes problems with data linking and other operations.

The use of null values is controversial. Some users believe that you need to represent missing or unknown data values and therefore may allow null values in data columns. Many other people recommend that you not allow any null values in a table because they are treated quite differently by various versions of SQL. You may get different results when you process the null values with different versions of SQL.

One way to represent a missing value without using a null value is to use a specially coded value; for example, you can enter *NA* (not available, not applicable) or *TBA* (to be added later) into the column when the value is not available at the time of data entry. For numeric values, you can enter a dummy value such as −9999.99 (or some other "strange" value) to represent a null value. Using alternate values does not have the same effect as using null values, and you can achieve similar results with the appropriate SQL commands. These "strange" values, however, will bias the summary statistics (such as average, total, and so on) when these values are included in the computation.

If you do not want to allow null values in a column, you must specify the keyword NOT NULL in the CREATE TABLE command following the data type:

```
CREATE TABLE   employee
               (ss_no       CHAR(11) NOT NULL,
                ........
                ........ );
```

Some versions (such as dBASE IV's SQL) do not allow this keyword in the CREATE TABLE command. In this case, be careful not to leave the key column empty if you need to use it for linking tables.

Entering Data into the Table

After you have set up the structure for a new base table, you are ready to add data to the table. To enter data into a base table, you insert or append data one row at a time to the end of the table. The SQL command for adding a row of data to an existing base table is

```
INSERT INTO    <name of base table>
     VALUES    (data values for the columns);
```

Entering Data into All Columns

The most common way of adding data to a row is to insert values into every column. You specify a value for each column in the parentheses that follow the keyword VALUES. For example, if you want to add a row of values to the *employee* table shown in figure 4.1, you enter the values as follows:

```
INSERT INTO    employee
     VALUES    ('123-45-6789', 'Smith', 'James J.', 'President',
               'Corporate', 89500.00);
```

You need to separate the data values with commas and enclose all character strings in single quotation marks. For numeric values, do not include a dollar sign or commas. Numeric values are not enclosed in quotation marks.

To fill all the rows in the *employee* table, you issue the INSERT command for each row. If this process seems too tedious, you can embed the command in a program written in a programming language, such as C or COBOL, so that you can enter the data values from the keyboard without issuing the command for each row. Chapter 12 gives an example of such a program.

To practice setting up and filling a base table, you may want to set up the *employee* table and fill in all the data in the table by issuing the appropriate INSERT commands.

Entering Data into Selected Columns

Although the practice of filling only some columns in a particular row is not universal, you may choose to insert data values into only certain columns in a row of the table. You specify in the INSERT command the columns into which you want to insert data:

```
INSERT INTO    <name of base table>
               (column list)
      VALUES   (data values for the columns);
```

You enclose the list of columns in parentheses. The order in which you list the columns may differ from the actual order in the table structure you have defined, but the data values must be in the same order as the column list. The following is an example:

```
INSERT INTO    employee
               (ss_no, f_name, Lname, title)
      VALUES   ('909-10-8910', 'Susan C.', 'Parker', 'Trainee');
```

This command adds these data values to the four columns specified in the last row of the table, leaving the *dept* and *salary* columns empty (see fig. 4.2).

SS_NO	L_NAME	F_NAME	TITLE	DEPT	SALARY
100-45-8021	Wong	Mike J.	Manager	MIS	44000.00
303-25-7777	Duff	Cathy B.	Secretary	Personnel	26500.00
909-10-8910	Parker	Susan C.	Trainee		

Fig. 4.2. Filling data in selected columns.

The *salary* and *dept* columns contain null values, not blanks or zeros, an important distinction. The absence of values in these columns does not mean that the salary of Susan C. Parker is zero or that she does not work in any department in the firm. Therefore, you cannot enter a null value into a row with the INSERT command in the following manner:

```
INSERT INTO   employee
                (ss_no, f_name, l_name, title, dept, salary)
        VALUES   ('909-10-8910', 'Susan C.', 'Parker', 'Trainee', ' ', 0 );
```

The character string ' ' and the value 0 in this INSERT command are legitimate values for the *dept* and *salary* columns, respectively. Therefore, if you need to enter null values, you must enter them by default, as shown in the previous example, by filling in only those columns for which you have data and leaving the other columns unspecified. Of course, if you do not want to have null values in the *title* and *salary* columns in that row, you can enter the dummy values NA and -9999.99 in the INSERT command, as follows:

```
INSERT INTO   employee
                (ss_no, f_name, l_name, title, dept, salary)
        VALUES   ('909-10-8910', 'Susan C.', 'Parker', 'Trainee',
                'NA',-9999.99);
```

When you insert a row into a base table, the row always appears at the end of the table. You cannot insert a row into the middle of the table without performing a more complex data manipulation operation. The actual location of a row in a table is immaterial, however. You can rearrange the order of the rows in any way you choose with an SQL command (see Chapter 7 for more information).

Verifying Entered Data

After you have entered all the data into the table, you can display the contents of the table by using the SELECT command, one of the most important commands in SQL, if not the most important. You use various forms of this command to retrieve, manipulate, and display data stored in base tables. In Chapter 5, you learn how to issue the SELECT command with the appropriate qualifiers to retrieve and display your data in the desired format.

To display all the data rows in a base table, you issue the SELECT command in the following format:

```
SELECT   *
  FROM   <table name>
```

The asterisk (*), often called a wild card, instructs the program to include every column of the table in the select operation. Because no filter conditions are specified in the command to screen the rows, the command selects and displays the data in all the columns and rows.

For example, assuming that you have entered 10 rows of data (from fig. 4.1) into the *employee* table, you can view the data by issuing the following command:

```
SELECT   *
  FROM   employee;
```

Figure 4.3 shows the results of this command. Depending on the version of SQL you are using, the actual layout of the results may be slightly different from this figure. For example, some versions of SQL display the column headings in uppercase letters; others display them in lowercase. In addition, some versions provide a summary note indicating the number of rows displayed or affected.

SS_NO	L_NAME	F_NAME	TITLE	DEPT	SALARY
123-45-6789	Smith	James J.	President	Corporate	89500.00
634-56-7890	Nelson	Harry M.	Manager	Sales	65000.00
445-67-8801	Zeller	Albert K.	Salesman	Sales	48900.00
562-87-8800	Chapman	Kirk D.	Salesman	Sales	42500.00
404-22-4568	Baker	Larry A.	Clerk	Sales	30500.00
256-09-5555	Dixon	Kathy T.	Accountant	Accounting	45000.00
458-90-3456	Frazer	Robert F.	Bookkeeper	Accounting	28000.00
777-34-6543	King	David G.	Manager	Personnel	38000.00
100-45-8021	Wong	Mike J.	Manager	MIS	44000.00
303-25-7777	Duff	Cathy B.	Secretary	Personnel	26500.00

Fig. 4.3. *Contents of the* employee *table.*

Creating a Table from Other Tables

You may have learned in other database management systems how to define a new table structure by borrowing or copying the structure from an existing table. For example, in Paradox, you can choose the Borrow Structure menu option when you are creating a new table structure. You then can use the borrowed structure to append records to your table, or you can modify the structure before adding data. Unfortunately, SQL has no simple command to accomplish this function, but you can create a new table by using data stored in all or some of the columns and rows in one or more existing tables.

In some versions of SQL, you can save the CREATE TABLE statement in a command file and recall the statement by retrieving the file. This technique is one way to borrow an existing table structure.

You can use several methods to copy data from one table to another. Most of these methods require the knowledge of query operations and the use of filter conditions. You learn these methods in Chapter 6, which discusses modifying and updating data. Chapter 6 also explains how to create a new table by merging data from multiple tables.

Chapter Summary

In this chapter, you have learned how to set up a base table structure. In addition to learning the types of data columns you can include in a base table, you have learned how column attributes are defined with the CREATE TABLE command. After a table structure is set up, the INSERT INTO command is used to add the necessary data rows to the table.

This chapter also shows how to use the SELECT * command to display and verify the data rows you have placed in the table. The SELECT * command is a special form of the general SELECT command, one of the most important commands provided by SQL for performing data query operations. The command is used mainly to find, retrieve, and display the data in the base tables. By adding the appropriate keywords and clauses to the command, you easily can manipulate the contents of the tables. The next chapter introduces you to the tremendous power of the SELECT command.

III

Working with Data in Relational Databases

Includes

Finding and Displaying Information
Modifying and Updating Databases
Sorting and Indexing Data
Summarizing and Grouping Data
Joining Data Tables

Finding and
Displaying Information

In Chapter 4, you learned how to define the procedures and commands for structuring a new base table and adding rows of data to it. This chapter, in addition to showing you how to list the databases and base tables you have created, introduces you to the data query operation. A data query operation searches the contents of one or more base tables to retrieve the data elements you have identified through the SELECT command. In this chapter, you learn the appropriate keywords and filter conditions, including logical operators and connectors, that you use in the SELECT command.

Listing Databases

Using the procedure you learned in Chapter 4, you should be able to create as many base tables as you need for your database application. Unless you switch to a different database during the process, all the tables you create are saved in the database into which you first moved. Depending on the version of SQL you are using, you can set up more than one database. In this case, you may want to get a list of existing databases that are accessible.

To get this listing, you need to know how these databases were created. If your databases were set up at the operating system level, chances are that you need to use a DOS command to view the databases. Because of the significant variations in the operating system commands, you should consult your system manual for details. If you created a database at the SQL prompt with an SQL command, such as CREATE DATABASE, you may be able to issue an SQL command to list your databases. For example, if you are using dBASE IV'S SQL, you can issue the SHOW DATABASE command at the SQL prompt to get a database list:

```
SQL. SHOW DATABASE;
Existing databases are:
NAME      CREATOR    CREATED  PATH

SAMPLES   SYSTEM     11/28/88 C:\DBASE\SAMPLES
 ....
 ....
SQLBOOK              09/15/89 C:\DBASE\SQLBOOK
```

The SHOW DATABASE command is not supported by every SQL version. For example, SHOW DATABASE is not accepted at the SQL prompt in Oracle's SQL*Plus because this version, like some other versions of SQL, does not allow you create more than one database; therefore, you have no need to get a list of databases. In other cases, if you are using SQL in a multiuser environment, only the system operators are able to view all the databases. Such situations, however, are not important for learning the principles of SQL discussed in this chapter.

Listing Tables

As mentioned in Chapter 4, when you create a table, information about the table is saved (with information about other tables within the same database) in various system or catalog tables. For example, the names and types of all the tables in a given database usually are saved in a table such as SYSTABLS (in dBASE IV's SQL), SYSTABLES (in DB2), CATALOG, TAB, or DTAB (in Oracle's SQL*Plus). Although these system tables are used to store information about SQL tables, they are base tables in nature; that is, system tables are organized in rows and columns. Each row holds information about an SQL table, and each column defines an attribute of the table. These attributes may be labeled table name, name of creator, number of columns, creation date, update date, and so on.

Chapter 4 introduces the SELECT * command, used to display all the information stored in a particular table. The SELECT * command, when used without any qualifiers or filter conditions, enables you to retrieve all the data stored in a table. You can use the same command to get a list of the SQL tables stored in a database. For example, when you are in a database, you can issue the SELECT * command as follows to display the contents of a system table, such as SYSTABLS (in dBASE IV's SQL):

```
SQL. SELECT  *
     FROM  systabls;
```

The result of this command is a listing of all the SQL tables in the database (including other system tables, the base tables, and their related tables). Figure 5.1 shows a sample listing of these tables.

TBNAME	CREATOR	TBTYPE	COLCOUNT	CLUSTERRID	IDXCOUNT	CREATED	UPDATED	CARD	NPAGES
SYSTABLS	SYSTEM	T	10	10	0	01/01/88	11/28/89	17	1
SYSCOLS	SYSTEM	T	12	75	0	01/01/88	11/28/89	115	5
SYSIDXS	SYSTEM	T	12	0	0	01/01/88	11/28/89	0	0
SYSVIEWS	SYSTEM	T	7	0	0	01/01/88	11/28/89	0	0
SYSVDEPS	SYSTEM	T	4	0	0	01/01/88	11/28/89	0	0
SYSSYNS	SYSTEM	T	4	0	0	01/01/88	11/28/89	0	0
SYSAUTH	SYSTEM	T	11	10	0	01/01/88	11/28/89	0	1
SYSCOLAU	SYSTEM	T	6	0	0	01/01/88	11/28/89	0	0
SYSTIMES	SYSTEM	T	3	11	0	01/01/88	11/28/89	42	0
EMPLOYEE		T	6	0	0	11/28/89	/ /	13	0
STOCK		T	4	0	0	11/28/89	/ /	27	0
PARTS		T	4	0	0	11/28/89	/ /	11	1

....
....

Fig. 5.1. *A sample listing of SQL tables.*

If you are using Oracle's SQL*Plus, you can use the SELECT * FROM DTAB command to view the contents of the data dictionary. A data dictionary is a group of system tables and other objects related to the database. When you issue the following command, you get the listing of tables and objects shown in figures 5.2 and 5.3.

```
SQL>  SELECT  *
   2     FROM  DTAB;
```

```
TNAME           REMARKS
--------------- ----------------------------------------------------------------
Reference Date  ORACLE catalog as of 10-Oct-85, installed on 30-OCT-88 00:38:23.
AUDIT_ACCESS    Audit entries for accesses to user's tables/views (DBA sees all)
AUDIT_ACTIONS   Maps auditing action numbers to action names
AUDIT_CONNECT   Audit trail entries for user log-on/log-off (DBA sees all users)
AUDIT_DBA       Audit trail entries for DBA activities -- for DBA use only
AUDIT_EXISTS    Audit trail entries for objects which do NOT EXIST -- DBAs only
AUDIT_TRAIL     Audit trail entries relevant to the user (DBA sees all)
CATALOG         Tables and views accessible to user (excluding data dictionary)
CLUSTERS        Clusters and their tables (either must be accessible to user)
CLUSTERCOLUMNS  Maps cluster columns to clustered table columns
COL             Specifications of columns in tables created by the user
COLUMNS         Columns in tables accessible to user (excluding data dictionary)
DEFAULT_AUDIT   Default table auditing options
DTAB            Description of tables and views in Oracle Data Dictionary
EXTENTS         Data structure of extents within tables
INDEXES         Indexes created by user and indexes on tables created by user
PARTITIONS      File structure of files within partitions -- for DBA use only
PRIVATESYN      Private synonyms created by the user
PUBLICSYN       Public synonyms
SESSIONS        Audit trail entries for the user's sessions (DBA sees all)
SPACES          Selection of space definitions for creating tables and clusters
STORAGE         Data and Index storage allocation for user's own tables
```

Fig. 5.2. *A sample view of the contents of a data dictionary obtained using the
SELECT * FROM DTAB command.*

The TNAME (table name) column of DTAB gives a list of all the system
tables stored in the data dictionary. In this list, for example, the CATALOG
table holds the tables and views that are accessible to a given user.

If you want to get a list of the tables in the CATALOG table, you can issue
the following command at the SQL prompt in Oracle's SQL*Plus:

```
SELECT   tname, creator, tabletype
  FROM   catalog;
```

Figure 5.4 shows a sample list obtained by using this command. From these
results, you can see that to display the names, creators, and the type of tables
stored in the CATALOG table, you specify in the SELECT command the
names of the columns—*tname* (table name), *creator* (author of the table),
and *tabletype* (the type of table or object).

```
TNAME             REMARKS
----------------  ------------------------------------------------------------
SYNONYMS          Synonyms, private and public
SYSAUDIT_TRAIL    Synonym for sys.audit_trail -- for DBA use only
SYSCATALOG        Profile of tables and views accessible to the user
SYSCOLAUTH        Directory of column update access granted by or to the user
SYSCOLUMNS        Specifications of columns in accessible tables and views
SYSEXTENTS        Data structure of tables throughout system -- for DBA use only
SYSINDEXES        List of indexes, underlying columns, creator, and options
SYSPROGS          List of programs precompiled by user
SYSSTORAGE        Summary of all database storage -- for DBA use only
SYSTABALLOC       Data and index space allocations for all tables -- for DBAs
SYSTABAUTH        Directory of access authorization granted by or to the user
SYSTEM_AUDIT      System auditing options -- for DBA use only
SYSUSERAUTH       Master list of Oracle users -- for DBA use only
SYSUSERLIST       List of Oracle users
SYSVIEWS          List of accessible views
TAB               List of tables, views, clusters, and synonyms created by the user
TABALLOC          Data and index space allocations for all user's tables
TABQUOTAS         Table allocation (space) parameters for tables created by user
TABLE_AUDIT       Auditing options of user's tables and views (DBA sees all)
VIEWS             Defining SQL statements for views created by the user
DBLINKS           Public and private links to external databases
SYSDBLINKS        All links to external databases -- for DBA use only

44 records selected.
```

Fig. 5.3. *A continuation of the contents of the data dictionary shown in fig. 5.2.*

```
TNAME      CREATOR  TABLETY
--------   -------  -------
EMPLOYEE   CHOU     TABLE
PARTS      CHOU     TABLE
STOCK      CHOU     TABLE
STUDENT    CHOU     TABLE
  .....
  .....
```

Fig. 5.4. *A sample list of tables created by the user.*

If the version of SQL you are using enables you to set up multiple databases, you can get a list of the tables stored in a given database by selecting or moving into that database before issuing the SELECT * command. You may remember from Chapter 4 that you move into a database by using the appropriate command at the operating system level or by issuing an SQL command, such as START DATABASE or USE.

Displaying Data in Tables

You have learned how to display data stored in a base table by using the SELECT * command. As explained in Chapter 4, the SELECT command is one of SQL's most important tools for finding, retrieving, and displaying data. This command can take many different forms depending on the function you need to carry out. The simplest form, SELECT *, which does not specify a selection scope or any filter conditions, displays the data stored in every row and column of a table. By specifying a table list in the command, however, you can display data from more than one table. You also can display selected rows and columns from one or more tables by adding the necessary scope and filter conditions to the command.

Displaying Data in a Single Table

Before introducing more complex forms of the SELECT command, I will review the inclusive SELECT * command to display the contents of the *employee* table created in Chapter 4:

```
SELECT   *
  FROM   employee;
```

The appearance of the results may differ depending on the version of SQL you are using. The column labels may be displayed in upper- or lowercase letters with or without underlines. The numerical values may be displayed with or without zeros after the decimal point, and so on.

For example, figure 5.5 shows how the display appears if you issue the command at the SQL prompt in dBASE IV's SQL.

Figure 5.6 shows the results obtained by issuing the same command at the SQL prompt in Oracle's SQL*Plus.

```
SQL. SELECT * FROM employee;
```

SS_NO	L_NAME	F_NAME	TITLE	DEPT	SALARY
123-45-6789	Smith	James J.	President	Corporate	89500.00
634-56-7890	Nelson	Harry M.	Manager	Sales	65000.00
445-67-8801	Zeller	Albert K.	Salesman	Sales	48900.00
562-87-8800	Chapman	Kirk D.	Salesman	Sales	42500.00
404-22-4568	Baker	Larry A.	Clerk	Sales	30500.00
256-09-5555	Dixon	Kathy T.	Accountant	Accounting	45000.00
458-90-3456	Frazer	Robert F.	Bookkeeper	Accounting	28000.00
777-34-6543	King	David G.	Manager	Personnel	38000.00
100-45-8021	Wong	Mike J.	Manager	MIS	44000.00
303-25-7777	Duff	Cathy B.	Secretary	Personnel	26500.00
909-10-8910	Parker	Susan C.	Trainee		

Fig. 5.5. *The* employee *table displayed using the SELECT * command in dBASE IV's SQL.*

```
SQL> SELECT *
  2     FROM employee;
```

SS_NO	L_NAME	F_NAME	TITLE	DEPT	SALARY
123-45-6789	Smith	James J.	President	Corporate	89500
634-56-7890	Nelson	Harry M.	Manager	Sales	65000
445-67-8801	Zeller	Albert K.	Salesman	Sales	48900
562-87-8800	Chapman	Kirk D.	Salesman	Sales	42500
404-22-4568	Baker	Larry A.	Clerk	Sales	30500
256-09-5555	Dixon	Kathy T.	Accountant	Accounting	45000
458-90-3456	Frazer	Robert F.	Bookkeeper	Accounting	28000
777-34-6543	King	David G.	Manager	Personnel	38000
100-45-8021	Wong	Mike J.	Manager	MIS	44000
303-25-7777	Duff	Cathy B.	Secretary	Personnel	26500
909-10-9010	Parker	Susan C.	Trainee		

```
11 records selected.
```

Fig. 5.6. *The* employee *table displayed using the SELECT * command in Oracle's SQL*Plus.*

From figures 5.5 and 5.6, you can note that the numeric columns are displayed differently. One shows two decimal places, and the other shows only integers. The column labels also are treated differently.

The actual format in which the results are displayed is not important for learning the principles of SQL. Therefore, as long as you are aware of the differences in the appearance of the results, you can treat the SELECT * command as generic, usable in any SQL version unless noted otherwise. Therefore, in this book, all the results from SELECT are shown in a standardized layout, in which two decimal places are used to represent values; columns are labeled with their column names underlined with a broken line.

Note that the SELECT * command displays the columns in the *employee* table in the order in which they were specified in the table structure; rows are arranged in the sequence they were entered. You can easily change the column order and row sequence. As you learn in Chapter 7, you can rearrange the rows by performing the sorting operation. If you want to display the columns in a different order, you simply specify the new order in the SELECT command. In addition, you can select only the columns you want to view by identifying those columns in a column list in the SELECT command.

The SELECT command often is used for other data manipulation operations besides displaying the contents of a table. In general, you use the SELECT command for a query operation that finds data satisfying certain filter conditions. The data produced by the query operation can be displayed as shown in earlier examples or be used as input for other data manipulation operations. You are introduced to the different uses of data query operations in later chapters.

Selecting Columns for Display

To identify the columns to be displayed, you list the column names in the SELECT command as follows:

```
SELECT  <column list>
    FROM  <name of table>;
```

For example, if you want to produce a list showing the names of the employees and their salaries, you issue the following command:

```
SELECT f_name, l_name, salary
```

Figure 5.7 shows the results of this command. Note that only three columns of the *employee* table are displayed, and the columns are shown in the order specified in the command, not the order in which they appear in the table structure. You can arrange the appearance of all the selected columns in this way.

F_NAME	L_NAME	SALARY
James J.	Smith	89500.00
Harry M.	Nelson	65000.00
Albert K.	Zeller	48900.00
Kirk D.	Chapman	42500.00
Larry A.	Baker	30500.00
Kathy T.	Dixon	45000.00
Robert F.	Frazer	28000.00
David G.	King	38000.00
Mike J.	Wong	44000.00
Cathy B.	Duff	26500.00
Susan C.	Parker	

Fig. 5.7. *Selected columns displayed from the* employee *table.*

Specifying Column Headings

When displaying the results of a SELECT command, most versions of SQL use the selected column names for the column headings. However, some versions (such as Oracle's SQL*Plus) limit the column names to the column size defined in the table structure. As a result, if the column size is smaller than the length of the column name, the name is cut off to fit the column width. For example, if you define CHAR(3) as the size of the *student_id* column in the *student* table, only the first three characters of the column name, *stu*, are displayed as the heading for the column.

This limited length of a column name may result in short cryptic headings. Therefore, some versions of SQL (for example, Oracle's SQL*Plus) enable you to use a column alias to display a more descriptive column label, which may differ from the column name or expression. A column alias is specified after the name of the column in the column list, as follows:

```
SELECT    Lname Last_Name, fname First_Name,
          salary/12 Monthly_Salary
   FROM    employee;
```

Figure 5.8 shows the results of this command. Note that the alias for the *Lname* column is not displayed in full because the column was defined as CHAR(7) in the table structure. In some versions of SQL, you can display the complete alias by specifying the column width to accommodate the alias. This technique is explained later in this chapter.

```
LAST_NA   FIRST_NAME   MONTHLY_SALARY
-------   ----------   --------------
Smith     James J.            7458.33
Nelson    Harry M.            5416.67
Zeller    Albert K.              4075
Chapman   Kirk D.             3541.67
Baker     Harry A.            2541.67
Dixon     Kathy T.               3750
Frazer    Robert F.           2333.33
King      David G.            3166.67
Wong      Mike J.             3666.67
Duff      Cathy B.            2208.33
Parker    Susan C.

11 records selected.
```

Fig. 5.8. *Using aliases as column headings.*

Like a column name, a column alias cannot contain blanks. Therefore, you need to use underscores (_) to separate different parts of an alias (for example, *Last_Name*). An alias may not be enclosed in quotation marks. The following SELECT commands are unacceptable:

    SELECT Lname Last Name, f_name First Name, ...

    SELECT Lname 'Last Name', f_name 'First Name', ...

Some versions of SQL (such as Oracle's SQL*Plus) enable you to label a column heading with a character string enclosed in quotation marks. The column label is defined by using the COLUMN heading command. In the command, you also can specify the format, or a template, for displaying the data value. The following command is an example:

    COLUMN   Lname HEADING 'Last Name' FORMAT A12;
    COLUMN   f_name HEADING 'First Name' FORMAT A12;
    COLUMN   salary/12 HEADING 'Monthly|Salary' FORMAT $9,999.99;
    SELECT   Lname, f_name, salary/12
      FROM   employee;

In the COLUMN heading commands, *A12* specifies an alphanumeric, or character, string of 12 characters for displaying an employee's last and first names. For displaying the values of the *salary/12* column, a template in the form of $9,999.99 is used to display all the salary figures in a conventional business format (for example, $7,458.33). Vertical bars (|) are used to place column labels on separate lines. Figure 5.9 shows how the results produced by these COLUMN and SELECT commands may appear.

```
                                Monthly
       Last Name    First Name   Salary
       -----------  -----------  ---------

       Smith        James J.     $7,458.33
       Nelson       Harry M.     $5,416.67
       Zeller       Albert K.    $4,075.00
       Chapman      Kirk D.      $3,541.67
       Baker        Larry A.     $2,541.67
       Dixon        Kathy T.     $3,750.00
       Frazer       Robert F.    $2,333.33
       King         David G.     $3,166.67
       Wong         Mike J.      $3,666.67
       Duff         Cathy B.     $2,208.33
       Parker       Susan C.

       11 records selected.
```

Fig. 5.9. *Results obtained from the COLUMN HEADING command.*

The column heading defined by the COLUMN command remains effective until you clear it. To clear a previously defined column heading, you issue the following command:

COLUMN <column name> CLEAR;

For example, if you want to reverse the column heading for the *Lname* column, you issue the following command:

COLUMN Lname CLEAR;

Performing Arithmetic Operations on Numeric Columns

In addition to displaying the contents of a numeric column, you also can perform an arithmetic operation on the values and display the results. You specify the operation as an arithmetic expression in the column list of the SELECT command. An arithmetic expression consists of one or more columns with one or more of the following arithmetic operators:

Operator	Operation
+	Addition
−	Subtraction`
*	Multiplication
/	Division
**, ^	Exponent (not available on all SQL versions)

For example, if you want to show monthly salaries for the employees, you specify *salary/12* in the column list when you issue the SELECT command, as follows:

    SELECT   Lname, f_name, salary/12
      FROM   employee;

Figure 5.10 illustrates the results of this command. As you can see, the third column shows the results of the arithmetic operation *salary/12*, the monthly salaries of all the employees. The heading of the calculated column may be different depending on your version of SQL. For example, some SQL versions use EXP1, EXP2, EXP3, and so on, to describe the results of the first, second, and third arithmetic expressions in the command, respectively. Others (such as Oracle's SQL*Plus) label the column as it is specified in the column list, in this case, SALARY/12. Other versions of SQL enable you to display a column alias as the column label.

L_NAME	F_NAME	EXP1
Smith	James J.	7458.33
Nelson	Harry M.	5416.67
Zeller	Albert K.	4075.00
Chapman	Kirk D.	3541.67
Baker	Larry A.	2541.67
Dixon	Kathy T.	3750.00
Frazer	Robert F.	2333.33
King	David G.	3166.67
Wong	Mike J.	3666.67
Duff	Cathy B.	2208.33
Parker	Susan C.	0.00

Fig. 5.10. *Monthly salaries displayed as the result of an arithmetic operation.*

Performing Arithmetic Operations on Character Columns

Although you rarely need to perform arithmetic operations on character strings, you may want to combine two or more strings to form a new string. (Some versions of SQL, such as Oracle's SQL*Plus, do not allow you to combine two character strings.) For example, if an employee's name is stored as two character strings, one for the first name (*f_name*) and the other for the last name (*L_name*), you can display the full name by adding the two strings together in the following manner:

SELECT f_name + L_name
 FROM employee;

Figure 5.11 shows the display that results from this operation. Note that extra blanks appear between some first and last names because the names are stored as fixed-length character strings. These extra blanks were padded at the time of data entry so that every character string in that column holds 10 characters, as defined in the table structure (CHAR(10)).

```
EXP1
-------------------
James J.  Smith
Harry M.  Nelson
Albert K. Zeller
Kirk D.   Chapman
Larry A.  Baker
Kathy T.  Dixon
Robert F. Frazer
David G.  King
Mike J.   Wong
Cathy B.  Duff
Susan C.  Parker
```

Fig. 5.11. *Combining character columns.*

Some versions of SQL display the expression as a column heading, for example, F_NAME + L_NAME. If you want to display a full name without the blanks, you can trim them from the end of the string with a built-in function provided by SQL. For example, if you are using dBASE IV's SQL, you use the TRIM function to do the job, as follows:

TRIM(f_name)

After trimming the blank spaces, you can add a blank space, as the following command illustrates, between *f_name* and *L_name*, so that the two character strings are separated with a single space. Figure 5.12 shows the command and the results of using this trimming function.

```
SQL. SELECT TRIM(f_name)+' '+l_name
        FROM employee;
```

```
EXP1
-----------------
James J. Smith
Harry M. Nelson
Albert K. Zeller
Kirk D. Chapman
Larry A. Baker
Kathy T. Dixon
Robert F. Frazer
David G. King
Mike J. Wong
Cathy B. Duff
Susan C. Parker
```

Fig. 5.12. Using the TRIM function to eliminate padded blank spaces.

Selecting Rows for Display

In a relational data table, each row contains a value for each column defined in the structure. As a result, you can use any one of the values in a column to filter, or group, the data in the table. For example, you can use information stored in the *title* column of the *employee* table to screen the rows so that certain types of values in that column are grouped and displayed together. You accomplish this screening operation by defining the appropriate filter conditions in the SELECT command.

Defining Filter Conditions

You define a filter condition by using the keyword WHERE in a SELECT command to identify the condition under which rows in the specified columns are to be selected. The format of a filter condition is as follows:

```
SELECT   <column list>
  FROM   <table name>
 WHERE   <filter conditions>
```

For example, if you want to find the information about the president of the firm, you specify title = 'President' as the filter condition in the SELECT command (see fig. 5.13).

```
SELECT *
  FROM employee
 WHERE title='President';
```

SS_NO	L_NAME	F_NAME	TITLE	DEPT	SALARY
123-45-6789	Smith	James J.	President	Corporate	89500.00

Fig. 5.13. *Information about the president selected from the* employee *table.*

You also can use a filter condition to display a group of rows whose column values meet the condition specified. For instance, if you want to display the names of the managers in various departments of the firm, you specify title = 'Manager' as the filter condition in the SELECT command (see fig. 5.14).

```
SELECT l_name, f_name, title, dept
  FROM employee
 WHERE title='Manager';
```

L_NAME	F_NAME	TITLE	DEPT
Nelson	Harry M.	Manager	Sales
King	David G.	Manager	Personnel
Wong	Mike J.	Manager	MIS

Fig. 5.14. *Department managers selected from the* employee *table.*

These two examples illustrate that a simple filter condition consists of a column name, such as *title*; a logical operator, such as the equal sign (=); and a filtering value, such as 'Manager'. When the command is executed, the value in the column is compared, character by character, with the filtering value. Therefore, case is important when you specify the filtering value. If you specify the condition as WHERE title = 'manager' you will not locate the managers in the *employee* table.

Using Logical Operators

Table 5.1 lists the logical operators that you use in a filter condition. This section explains how to use these operators.

Table 5.1
SQL Logical Operators

Logical Operator	Meaning
=	Equal
<>, !=, ^=	Not equal to
>	Greater than
>=	Greater than or equal to
<	Less than
<=	Less than or equal to
BETWEEN ... AND	Between two values inclusively
LIKE	Match a certain character pattern
IS NULL	A null value
IN	In the value list
ANY	Any value in the value list

Some versions of SQL support a number of other logical operators, such as ALL, EXISTS, and so on. Many of these operators are redundant, however. Queries using these operators often can be formulated by using one of the operators listed in table 5.1.

The logical operators >, >=, <, and <= enable you to define the minimum or maximum values required for a column value when you are searching the rows with a SELECT command. For example, the SELECT command shown in figure 5.15 displays the employees who earn $30,000 or more a year.

You also can use the logical operators to filter character strings. That is, you can specify a filter condition such as

WHERE Lname >= 'N'

When used in a SELECT command, this filter condition displays all the last names in the *Lname* column that begin with the capital letters N through Z. Figure 5.16 shows the command and its results.

When the logical conditions in a SELECT command involve numeric values, the conditions are evaluated in accordance with conventional number theory (3 is greater than 2, and so on). When the conditions are specified with character strings, however (for example, WHERE Lname>= 'N'), a spe-

```
SELECT l_name, f_name, salary
  FROM employee
WHERE salary>=30000;
```

L_NAME	F_NAME	SALARY
Smith	James J.	89500.00
Nelson	Harry M.	65000.00
Zeller	Albert K.	48900.00
Chapman	Kirk D.	42500.00
Baker	Larry A.	30500.00
Dixon	Kathy T.	45000.00
King	David G.	38000.00
Wong	Mike J.	44000.00

Fig. 5.15. Selecting employees according to salary.

```
SELECT l_name, f_name
  FROM employee
WHERE l_name>='N';
```

L_NAME	F_NAME
Smith	James J.
Nelson	Harry M.
Zeller	Albert K.
Wong	Mike J.
Parker	Susan C.

Fig. 5.16. Using a logical operator to select character strings.

cial set of rules is necessary to evaluate the filter conditions. The set of rules that govern the order of a character string is specified by the American Standard Code for Information Interchange (ASCII).

If the character string contains only one character, the order simply follows the order given in the ASCII table. If the string contains more than one character, the order of the string is determined similarly to the way words are alphabetized in dictionaries. Case is important in determining the order or "value" of a character. From the ASCII table, you see that lowercase letters are greater than uppercase letters and that alphabetic letters are greater than numeric digits. For instance, each of the following filter conditions is considered true:

```
'B'>'A'
'A'>'9'
'$'>'#'
'z'>'a'
'a'>'Z'
'JOHNSON'>'JOHN'
'GOOD'>'BAD'
'bad'>'Good'
'Small'>'Large'
```

If you change the filtering value from an uppercase N to a lowercase n in the condition in the last SELECT command, you cannot find in the Lname column any last names that satisfy the filter condition because every last name begins with an uppercase letter.

The BETWEEN...AND logical operator enables you to specify a desired range for the column values you are looking for. For example, to display the employees whose salaries range between $30,000 and $50,000 inclusively, you can issue the command shown in figure 5.17.

```
SELECT l_name, f_name, salary
   FROM employee
 WHERE salary BETWEEN 30000 AND 50000;


L_NAME    F_NAME        SALARY
-------   ----------    --------
Zeller    Albert K.    48900.00
Chapman   Kirk D.      42500.00
Baker     Larry A.     30500.00
Dixon     Kathy T.     45000.00
King      David G.     38000.00
Wong      Mike J.      44000.00
```

Fig. 5.17. Numeric values selected by using the BETWEEN...AND operator.

You also can use the logical operator BETWEEN to define a specific range for a character string. For example, if you want to find all the employees whose last names begin with the letters A through D, you issue the command shown in figure 5.18.

```
SELECT l_name, f_name
   FROM employee;
WHERE l_name BETWEEN 'A' AND 'D';


L_NAME    F_NAME
-------   ---------
Baker     Larry
Chapman   Kirk
Dixon     Kathy T.
Duff      Cathy B.
```

Fig. 5.18. Character strings selected by using the BETWEEN logical operator.

Some versions of SQL may produce different results. You can issue this command to see how your SQL version may differ. To find the last names beginning with D, change the filter condition to

WHERE Lname BETWEEN 'D' AND 'D'

If you use the equality logical operator (=) in the filter condition to search for a character string, you need to know exactly how the character string looks; otherwise, you will not be able to find the string. For example, if you want to find an employee by last name, you need to know exactly how the last name is spelled. Sometimes, however, you may not know the exact spelling of the last name; you may know only that it ends with *er*, for example. In this situation, you cannot use the equality logical operator in the filter condition. To solve such a problem, most versions of SQL provide the powerful logical operator LIKE. The LIKE operator enables you to specify a filtering value with a particular character pattern.

A character pattern may consist of any legitimate characters (letters, digits, symbols, and so forth) and one of two special symbols: the percent sign (%) and the underscore (_). When used with the LIKE operator, the percent sign denotes any sequence of zero or more characters. For example, if you want to find all the last names that end with *er*, you can specify '%er' as the filtering value (see fig. 5.19).

```
SELECT l_name, f_name
  FROM employee
 WHERE l_name LIKE '%er';
```

L_NAME	F_NAME
Zeller	Albert K.
Baker	Larry A.
Frazer	Robert F.
Parker	Susan C.

Fig. 5.19. *Employees selected by using the LIKE operator.*

You use the underscore (_) to represent any single character. For example, if you want to find the social security numbers in the *ss_no* column that contain 45 in the middle of the number, you can use a character pattern of '___45%' with the LIKE operator. Figure 5.20 shows the command and the social security numbers displayed as a result of using this character pattern.

```
SELECT  ss_no, l_name
  FROM  employee
 WHERE  ss_no LIKE '____45%';
```

SS_NO	L_NAME
123-45-6789	Smith
100-45-8021	Wong

Fig. 5.20. *Social security numbers selected by using the LIKE operator with underscores.*

Note that the four underscores specified in the character pattern denote exactly four characters in front of the two characters 45. Therefore, the character pattern '___45%' yields different results from the character pattern %45%, as figure 5.21 illustrates.

Another powerful tool you can use in a filter condition to display selected rows of data is the IN logical operator. The IN operator enables you to compare a column value with the values in a predefined value list. If the column value belongs to the list, the filter condition is considered satisfied. The format of a SELECT command with the IN logical operator in the filter condition is as follows:

```
SELECT ss_no, l_name
  FROM employee
WHERE ss_no LIKE '%45%';
```

```
SS_NO          L_NAME
-----------    ------
123-45-6789    Smith
445-67-8801    Zeller
404-22-4568    Baker
458-90-3456    Frazer
100-45-8021    Wong
```

Fig. 5.21. *Social security numbers selected by using the LIKE operator with the percent sign.*

```
SELECT   <column list>
  FROM   <table name>
 WHERE   <column name> IN (value list);
```

For example, if you want to display the names of the employees who work in the Sales, Accounting, and Personnel departments, you issue the command shown in figure 5.22.

```
SELECT l_name, f_name, title, dept
  FROM employee
WHERE dept IN ('Accounting', 'Sales', 'Personnel');
```

L_NAME	F_NAME	TITLE	DEPT
Nelson	Harry M.	Manager	Sales
Zeller	Albert K.	Salesman	Sales
Chapman	Kirk D.	Salesman	Sales
Baker	Larry A.	Salesman	Sales
Dixon	Kathy T.	Accountant	Accounting
Frazer	Robert F.	Bookkeeper	Accounting
King	David G.	Manager	Personnel
Duff	Cathy B.	Secretary	Personnel

Fig. 5.22. *Employees selected according to department by using the IN operator.*

When the filter condition is evaluated, the value in the *dept* column is compared with the values in the value list. A row is selected when the column value matches one of the values in the list. In figure 5.22, you may have noticed that the order specified with the IN operator has no effect on the order in which the rows are displayed; they are displayed in the order in which they were entered unless the data in the table has been sorted. In some versions of SQL, however, the order specified in the IN clause determines the order in which the values are displayed.

You also can use the IN and NOT IN logical operators with a subquery to define a filter condition. A subquery is a query within a query defined by a SELECT command in the following format:

```
SELECT  <column list>
  FROM  <table name>
WHERE  <column name> IN (<a subquery>);
```

The data selected by the subquery is used to compare the column value specified in the filter condition of the main query. Subqueries are discussed in detail in Chapter 10, but figure 5.23 shows an example of a simple subquery.

```
SELECT ss_no, l_name, f_name, title
  FROM employee
 WHERE f_name IN (SELECT f_name
                    FROM female);

SS_NO         L_NAME   F_NAME    TITLE
-----------   ------   --------  ----------
256-09-5555   Dixon    Kathy T.  Accountant
303-25-7777   Duff     Cathy B.  Secretary
909-10-8910   Parker   Susan C.  Trainee
```

Fig. 5.23. *Data selected by using a subquery with the IN operator.*

In this command, the subquery is the inner SELECT command, which is enclosed in parentheses following the IN logical operator; the main query is defined by the outer SELECT command. When the filter condition is evaluated, the values returned by the subquery (SELECT f_name FROM female) form the list of values to be compared with the value of the *f_name* in the *employee* table, as defined in the WHERE clause. For example, assume that the *female* table contains a list of first names of the female employees; the list can be displayed by using the SELECT * command (see fig. 5.24).

```
SELECT *
  FROM female;

F_NAME      L_NAME
----------  ------
Kathy T.    Dixon
Cathy B.    Duff
Susan C.    Parker
```

Fig. 5.24. *Female employees displayed from the* female *table.*

Therefore, when the inner subquery is evaluated, the values in the *f_name* column of the *female* table are returned (in this case, Kathy T., Cathy B., and Susan C.). These returned values are placed in the list to be evaluated by the IN logical operator in the WHERE filter condition of the main query. At this point, the main query is equivalent to the following:

```
SELECT  ss_no, L_name, f_name, title
  FROM    employee
  WHERE   f_name IN ('Kathy T.', 'Cathy B.', 'Susan C.');
```

The ANY operator works in the same way as the IN operator, but ANY can be used only with a subquery, whereas the IN operator can be used with a list of specified values or with a subquery. The following is the format of a SELECT command containing a filter condition with an ANY operator:

```
SELECT  <column list>
  FROM    <name of table>
  WHERE   <column name> <arithmetic operator> ANY(<a subquery>);
```

An arithmetic operator is a logical operator used to define an arithmetic relation such as $=$, $!=$ or $<>$, $>$, $>=$, $<$, $<=$, $!>$, or $!<$. For example, the SELECT command given previously, using the IN operator with a subquery, can be written as follows with an ANY operator:

```
SELECT  ss_no, L_name, f_name, title
  FROM    employee
  WHERE   f_name = ANY(SELECT  f_name
                         FROM   female);
```

By comparing figure 5.25 with figure 5.23, you can see that the results of these two commands are identical. The latter command uses the $=$ operator to define the arithmetic relation between the value of the *f_name* column and the ANY operator.

SS_NO	L_NAME	F_NAME	TITLE
256-09-5555	Dixon	Kathy T.	Accountant
303-25-7777	Duff	Cathy B.	Secretary
909-10-8910	Parker	Susan C.	Trainee

Fig. 5.25. *Data selected by using a subquery with the ANY operator.*

You can use any arithmetic operator in the filter condition. The following example uses the not equal (! =) operator:

```
SELECT   ss_no, l_name, f_name, title
  FROM   employee
 WHERE   f_name! = ANY(SELECT  f_name
                        FROM  female);
```

Figure 5.26 shows the results of this command. Note that none of the female names contained in the *female* table are selected by the main query.

SS_NO	L_NAME	F_NAME	TITLE
123-45-6789	Smith	James J.	President
634-56-7890	Nelson	Harry M.	Manager
445-67-8801	Zeller	Albert K.	Salesman
562-87-8800	Chapman	Kirk D.	Salesman
404-22-4568	Baker	Larry A.	Salesman
458-90-3456	Frazer	Robert F.	Bookkeeper
777-34-6543	King	David G.	Manager
100-45-8021	Wong	Mike J.	Manager

Fig. 5.26. *Data selected by using the arithmetic operator != with the ANY operator.*

Using Logical Connectors

When defining a filter condition, you sometimes need to use more than one logical operator. For example, you may want to display information about employees who are managers working in a particular department, such as Sales. To accomplish this, your filter condition must specify more than one logical relation (title = 'Manager' and dept = 'Sales'), using one or more logical connectors to link these logical operators. You can use the following three logical connectors for this purpose:

Logical Connector	*Usage*
NOT	To reverse a logical relation
AND	To satisfy both logical relations
OR	To satisfy one or the other logical relation

You use the NOT logical connector to work with one or more logical operators in a filter condition to screen data. When used with a logical operator, NOT reverses the relation. For example, you can use the NOT connector with the BETWEEN...AND operator to select the values outside the range defined by the operator (see fig. 5.27).

```
SELECT l_name, f_name, salary
   FROM employee
 WHERE salary NOT BETWEEN 30000 AND 50000;
```

L_NAME	F_NAME	SALARY
Smith	James J.	89500.00
Nelson	Harry M.	65000.00
Frazer	Robert F.	28000.00
Duff	Cathy B.	26500.00
Parker	Susan C.	0.00

Fig. 5.27. *Data selected by using the NOT logical connector.*

You can see that this command selects all the salaries outside the range between $30,000 and $50,000. You may wonder why Susan C. Parker's salary is selected by the command when her salary is displayed as zero in the *salary* column. In some versions of SQL, such as dBASE IV's SQL, null values are selected regardless of the range specified by the BETWEEN clause. However, in other systems (for example, Oracle's SQL*Plus), null values are not included in the range.

Previous examples show how you can choose a set of character strings by using a character pattern with the LIKE operator. With a little modification of these commands, you also can avoid a set of character strings by using the same character pattern and adding the NOT logical connector before the LIKE operator (see fig. 5.28).

```
SELECT ss_no, l_name
  FROM employee
 WHERE ss_no NOT LIKE '%45%';


SS_NO          L_NAME
-----------    -------
634-56-7890    Nelson
562-87-8800    Chapman
256-09-5555    Dixon
777-34-6543    King
303-25-7777    Duff
909-10-8910    Parker
```

Fig. 5.28. *Data selected by using the NOT logical connector with the LIKE logical operator.*

To reverse the logical relation of the IN operator, you can use the NOT IN operator in a filter condition to exclude every row whose column value matches a value specified in the value list. For example, if you want to list the employees who do not work in the MIS, Accounting, or Sales departments, you can issue the command shown in figure 5.29.

```
SELECT l_name, f_name, title, dept
  FROM employee
 WHERE dept NOT IN ('MIS', 'Accounting', 'Sales');


L_NAME  F_NAME      TITLE       DEPT
------  ---------   ---------   ---------
Smith   James J.    President   Corporate
King    David G.    Manager     Personnel
Duff    Cathy B.    Secretary   Personnel
```

Fig. 5.29. *Data selected by using the NOT IN operator.*

The previous examples have shown that you can screen data in a table with a simple filter condition using only one logical operator. Sometimes, however, you need a more complex data screening operation requiring more than one logical operator in the filter condition. Then, you need to use one or more logical connectors to link the logical operators and form the appropriate filter condition. For example, if you want to search for all the employees who are managers earning more than $40,000, you need to specify two conditions: "managers" and "earn more than $35,000." In this case, you need the

AND logical connector to tie the two conditions together, as figure 5.30 shows.

```
SELECT l_name, f_name, title, dept, salary
  FROM employee
 WHERE title='Manager' AND salary>40000;
```

L_NAME	F_NAME	TITLE	DEPT	SALARY
Nelson	Harry M.	Manager	Sales	65000.00
Wong	Mike J.	Manager	MIS	44000.00

Fig. 5.30. Data selected by using the AND connector.

In order for a data row to be selected when the AND connector is used, both conditions must be satisfied. You may use more than one AND logical connector to join the logical operators in the filter condition. For example, the SELECT command in figure 5.31 finds and displays the employees who are "not managers" AND "not in the Sales department" AND "earning more than $35,000."

```
SELECT l_name, f_name, title, dept, salary
  FROM employee
 WHERE title<>'Manager'
   AND dept<>'Sales'
   AND salary>35000;
```

L_NAME	F_NAME	TITLE	DEPT	SALARY
Smith	James J.	President	Corporate	89500.00
Dixon	Kathy T.	Accountant	Accounting	45000.00

Fig. 5.31. Data selected by using two AND connectors.

In addition to NOT and AND, you can use the OR logical connector in a filter condition to join two or more logical operators. The OR connector enables you to select data rows when either logical condition is satisfied. For example, if you want to find the employees who are managers or who earn $50,000 or more in salary, you can use the OR logical connector to join the logical conditions title = 'Manager' and salary> = 50000. Figure 5.32 shows the command and the results.

```
SELECT l_name, f_name, title, dept, salary
  FROM employee
 WHERE title='Manager' OR salary>50000;
```

L_NAME	F_NAME	TITLE	DEPT	SALARY
Smith	James J.	President	Corporate	89500.00
Nelson	Harry M.	Manager	Sales	65000.00
King	David G.	Manager	Personnel	38000.00
Wong	Mike J.	Manager	MIS	44000.00

Fig. 5.32. *Data selected by using the OR connector.*

You can use more than one OR logical connector to join the logical operations in a SELECT command. In fact, the number of logical operators and connectors you can specify in a WHERE clause is unlimited as long as the total number of characters in a command is within the length limit imposed by the version of SQL you are using. The command in figure 5.33 uses two OR logical connectors to link three filter conditions.

This SELECT command displays all the employees in the three departments specified in the WHERE clause. You can see that using several OR logical connectors with multiple filter conditions enables you to display employees from various departments.

```
SELECT l_name, f_name, dept
  FROM employee
 WHERE dept='Sales'
    OR dept='MIS'
    OR dept='Personnel';
```

L_NAME	F_NAME	DEPT
Nelson	Harry M.	Sales
Zeller	Albert K.	Sales
Chapman	Kirk D.	Sales
Baker	Larry A.	Sales
King	David G.	Personnel
Wong	Mike J.	MIS
Duff	Cathy B.	Personnel

Fig. 5.33. *Data selected by using two OR connectors.*

To find the employees that do not belong to these departments, you can add the NOT connector to the command (see fig. 5.34).

```
SELECT l_name, f_name, dept
   FROM employee
 WHERE NOT (dept='Sales'
            OR dept='MIS'
            OR dept='Personnel');
```

L_NAME	F_NAME	DEPT
Smith	James J.	Corporate
Dixon	Kathy T.	Accounting
Frazer	Robert F.	Accounting

Fig. 5.34. *Data selected by using the NOT connector with two OR connectors.*

You also can mix OR and AND logical connectors in several logical operations to produce the desired data. For example, if you want to find the employees in the Accounting and MIS departments who earn $40,000 or more, you can issue the SELECT command using an OR and an AND logical connector (see fig. 5.35).

```
SELECT l_name, f_name, dept, salary
   FROM employee
 WHERE (dept='Accounting' AND salary>=40000)
    OR (dept='MIS' AND salary>=40000);
```

L_NAME	F_NAME	DEPT	SALARY
Dixon	Kathy T.	Accounting	45000.00
Wong	Mike J.	MIS	44000.00

Fig. 5.35. *Data selected by using combined AND and OR logical connectors.*

The filter conditions that appear in parentheses are evaluated first; then the results are evaluated with the OR logical connector. In this example, the SELECT command finds the employees in the Accounting department who earn $40,000 or more, or those in MIS who earn $40,000 or more. You can obtain the same results by issuing the command shown in figure 5.36.

```
SELECT l_name, f_name, dept, salary
  FROM employee
 WHERE (dept='Accounting' OR dept='MIS')
   AND salary>=40000;
```

L_NAME	F_NAME	DEPT	SALARY
Dixon	Kathy T.	Accounting	45000.00
Wong	Mike J.	MIS	44000.00

Fig. 5.36. *The same data selected by using a different combination of AND and OR logical connectors.*

In this case, the SELECT command first finds the data rows having Accounting or MIS in the *dept* column and then selects the rows that contain a value greater than or equal to 40000 in the *salary* column.

Note: Parentheses play a significant role in defining the filter conditions in a SELECT command. Depending on where the parentheses are placed, you get quite different results. For example, if the parentheses are placed around the last two filter conditions in the preceding command, different data rows are selected, as figure 5.37 illustrates.

```
SELECT l_name, f_name, dept, salary
  FROM employee
 WHERE dept='Accounting'
    OR (dept='MIS' AND salary>=40000);
```

L_NAME	F_NAME	DEPT	SALARY
Dixon	Kathy T.	Accounting	45000.00
Frazer	Robert F.	Accounting	28000.00
Wong	Mike J.	MIS	44000.00

Fig. 5.37. *Different data selected as a result of the location of the parentheses.*

In this case, no restrictions were placed on the employees to be selected from the Accounting department; only those in MIS are subject to the salary requirement ($40,000 or more).

The example in figure 5.38 also uses multiple logical connectors in a SELECT command.

```
SELECT l_name, f_name, salary
  FROM employee
 WHERE (salary>38000 AND salary<44000)
    OR (salary>65000 AND salary<90000);


L_NAME    F_NAME        SALARY
-------   ----------    --------
Smith     James J.      89500.00
Chapman   Kirk D.       42500.00
```

Fig. 5.38. *Data selected by using multiple logical connectors.*

Figure 5.38 shows that this SELECT command displays two groups of employees, each group with salary values within a specified range. Note that each of the two salary ranges is defined with a less than (<) and a greater than (>) condition. You cannot define the salary range with a filter condition by using a BETWEEN...AND operator, such as BETWEEN 38000 AND 44000, because this filter condition is equivalent to salary> = 38000 AND salary< = 44000 and produces the results shown in figure 5.39.

```
SELECT l_name, f_name, salary
  FROM employee
 WHERE (salary BETWEEN 38000 AND 44000)
    OR (salary BETWEEN 65000 AND 90000);


L_NAME    F_NAME        SALARY
-------   ----------    --------
Smith     James J.      89500.00
Nelson    Harry M.      65000.00
Chapman   Kirk D.       42500.00
King      David G.      38000.00
Wong      Mike J.       44000.00
```

Fig. 5.39. *Data selected by using the BETWEEN operator with the OR connector.*

Displaying Data from Multiple Tables

SQL is a powerful database management language, enabling you to display data from more than one table. The following examples use three base tables —*parts*, *stock*, and *vendors*—to illustrate how you can display data from multiple tables. These table structures are defined with the following CREATE TABLE commands:

```
CREATE TABLE parts
              (stock_no      CHAR(5),
               part_type     CHAR(11),
               dscription    CHAR(25),
               unit_cost     DECIMAL(8,2));

CREATE TABLE stock
              (stock_no      CHAR(5)
               on_hand       SMALLINT,
               reorder       SMALLINT,
               vendor_id     CHAR(2));

CREATE TABLE vendors
              (vendor_id     CHAR(2),
               name          CHAR(10),
               address       CHAR(13),
               city          CHAR(8),
               state         CHAR(2),
               zip           CHAR(5),
               phone_no      CHAR(12));
```

For later reference, the SELECT * command displays the contents of these tables. Figure 5.40, 5.41, and 5.42, respectively, show the contents of the *parts*, *stock*, and *vendors* tables.

```
SELECT *
  FROM parts;
```

STOCK_NO	PART_TYPE	DSCRIPTION	UNIT_COST
HW101	Printer	Epson LQ-1050 printer	628.50
HW102	Printer	HP LaserJet II printer	1435.00
HW201	Monitor	NEC MultiSync monitor	459.00
HW301	V. board	Paradise VGA board	230.00
HW401	Computer	IBM PS/2 Model 70/60MB	3250.00
HW402	Computer	COMPAQ 386S DeskPro/40MB	2600.00
HW403	Computer	Zenith Supersport 286/20	2975.00
SW101	Spreadsheet	Lotus 1-2-3 Version 2.01	250.00
SW201	WP	WordPerfect 5.0	195.00
SW202	WP	Microsoft Word 5.0	183.50
SW301	Database	Paradox 3.0	385.75
SW302	Database	dBASE IV Version 1.0	360.00

Fig. 5.40. The parts *table.*

```
SELECT *
  FROM stock;

STOCK_NO  ON_HAND  REORDER  VENDOR_ID
--------  -------  -------  ---------
HW101         8        3    V1
HW102         2        1    V1
HW201         4        2    V2
HW301         6        3    V2
HW401         3        2    V3
HW402         4        5    V3
HW403         3        1    V3
SW101        10        3    V4
SW201         7        4    V4
SW202         5        2    V4
SW301         2        3    V5
SW302         3        1    V5
```

Fig. 5.41. The stock *table.*

```
SELECT *
  FROM vendors;

VENDOR_ID  NAME       ADDRESS        CITY       STATE  ZIP    PHONE_NO
---------  ---------  -------------  --------   -----  -----  ------------
V1         Micromart  100 Main St    Seattle    WA     98105  800-123-4567
V2         CompuPlus  2120 Oak Ave   Portland   OR     97202  503-555-9999
V3         PC Ware    750 Grand Ave  Austin     TX     78727  800-666-4444
V4         CompuSoft  101 Fifth Ave  New York   NY     10120  212-333-5555
V5         PC Source  200 Front St   San Jose   CA     94930  415-777-8888
```

Fig. 5.42. The vendors *table.*

The *parts* table contains information about parts, and the *stock* table holds inventory information. The *vendors* table stores the names and addresses for the parts vendors. Note that the *stock* and *parts* tables share a common column, *stock_no*. Similarly, the *vendor_id* column in the *stock* and *vendors* tables provides the necessary connection between these two tables.

If you want to display data from two tables simultaneously, the tables must be joined with a common column. You can join multiple tables in many different ways, depending on the data manipulation operation you are using.

(Chapter 9 provides a detailed discussion on joining data tables.) In this section, you learn the joining operation you use to display information from columns stored in more than one base table.

For example, if you want to display an inventory list giving a description of the part, the inventory level, and the unit cost, you need to use information from the *parts* and the *stock* tables. To accomplish this, you do the following:

1. Select information about the part number, part description, and unit cost from the *parts* table.

2. Select information about the inventory level (on-hand quantity) from the *stock* table.

3. Specify the names of the tables involved.

4. Define the column that connects the two tables (in this case, the common column is *stock_no*).

Because you are selecting columns from two different tables, you need to identify the table to which each column belongs. One way of identifying the table is to precede the column name with the name of the table and a period (.). For example, when you select the *stock_no* column from the *parts* table, you define the column name as *parts.stock_no*. Therefore, the SELECT command can be defined as shown in figure 5.43.

The column labels have been modified in order to fit the text to the page. The actual column headings when you issue the command in dBASE IV SQL may differ slightly.

When you are displaying data from more than one table, you must provide the linking columns. In the preceding example, the *stock_no* column, which appears in the *parts* and *stock* tables, links the two tables. If you display the contents of multiple tables without identifying the linking columns, the program produces all the possible matches among the data rows. For example, if you display the contents of the *parts* and *stock* tables without specifying the linking columns, each row in the stock table is matched with each row in the *parts* table. Figure 5.44 shows the results of a command that does not specify the linking columns. Your sequence of the displayed data rows may be different from figure 5.44, depending on the version of SQL you use.

```
SELECT parts.stock_no, parts.dscription,
       parts.unit_cost, stock.on_hand
  FROM parts, stock
 WHERE parts.stock_no=stock.stock_no;
```

PARTS. STOCK_NO	PARTS. DSCRIPTION	PARTS. UNIT_COST	STOCK. ON_HAND
HW101	Epson LQ-1050 printer	628.50	8
HW102	HP LaserJet II printer	1435.00	2
HW201	NEC MultiSync monitor	459.00	4
HW301	Paradise VGA board	230.00	6
HW401	IBM PS/2 Model 70/60MB	3250.00	3
HW402	COMPAQ 386S DeskPro/40MB	2600.00	4
HW403	Zenith Supersport 286/20	2975.00	3
SW101	Lotus 1-2-3 Version 2.01	250.00	10
SW201	WordPerfect 5.0	195.00	7
SW202	Microsoft Word 5.0	183.50	5
SW301	Paradox 3.0	385.75	2
SW302	dBASE IV Version 1.0	360.00	3

Fig. 5.43. *An inventory list derived from two base tables.*

```
SELECT parts.stock_no, parts.dscription,
       parts.unit_cost, stock.on_hand
  FROM parts, stock
```

PARTS. STOCK_NO	PARTS. DSCRIPTION	PARTS. UNIT_COST	STOCK. ON_HAND
HW101	Epson LQ-1050 printer	628.50	8
HW102	HP LaserJet II printer	1435.00	8
HW201	NEC MultiSync monitor	459.00	8
HW301	Paradise VGA board	230.00	8
HW401	IBM PS/2 Model 70/60MB	3250.00	8
HW402	COMPAQ 386S DeskPro/40MB	2600.00	8
HW403	Zenith Supersport 286/20	2975.00	8
SW101	Lotus 1-2-3 Version 2.01	250.00	8
SW201	Word Perfect 5.0	195.00	8
SW202	Microsoft Word 5.0	183.50	8
SW301	Paradox 3.0	385.75	8
SW302	dBASE IV Version 1.0	360.00	8

(continued)

HW101	Epson LQ-1050 printer	628.50	2
HW102	HP LaserJet II printer	1435.00	2
HW201	NEC MultiSync monitor	459.00	2
HW301	Paradise VGA board	230.00	2
HW401	IBM PS/2 Model 70/60MB	3250.00	2
HW402	COMPAQ 386S DeskPro/40MB	2600.00	2
HW403	Zenith Supersport 286/20	2975.00	2
SW101	Lotus 1-2-3 Version 2.01	250.00	2
SW201	WordPerfect 5.0	195.00	2
SW202	Microsoft Word 5.0	183.50	2
SW301	Paradox 3.0	385.75	2
SW302	dBASE IV Version 1.0	360.00	2
HW101	Epson LQ-1050 printer	628.50	4
HW102	HP LaserJet II printer	1435.00	4
HW201	NEC MultiSync monitor	459.00	4
HW301	Paradise VGA board	230.00	4
HW401	IBM PS/2 Model 70/60MB	3250.00	4
HW402	COMPAQ 386S DeskPro/40MB	2600.00	4
HW403	Zenith Supersport 286/20	2975.00	4
SW101	Lotus 1-2-3 Version 2.01	250.00	4
SW201	WordPerfect 5.0	195.00	4
SW202	Microsoft Word 5.0	183.50	4
SW301	Paradox 3.0	385.75	4
SW302	dBASE IV Version 1.0	360.00	4
.....			
.....			

Fig. 5.44. Data displayed when linking columns are not specified.

Note that each value in the *on_hand* column in the *stock* table is matched with each value in the *stock_no*, *dscription*, and *unit_cost* columns in the *parts* table. Be sure to specify the linking columns when you want to display data from multiple tables; otherwise, your results will be quite surprising.

Preceding the column name with the name of the table enables you to identify quickly where the column comes from. However, you can save some typing in two ways, one of which is to use a shorter table alias in place of the table name. You may recall from previous examples that you can use a column alias to display a more descriptive column heading in place of the actual column name, which may be too short and cryptic. Similarly, you can use a table alias in place of a regular table name, attaching the alias to the front of a column name.

As a table alias, you can use any string of characters (within the length accepted by your version of SQL) to represent a table name as long as you do not use any reserved words. For example, if you are using dBASE IV's SQL, do not use the single letters A through J as table aliases because these letters are reserved names for working areas in dBASE IV.

A table alias is defined in the FROM clause immediately after the table name (without a comma). For example, the SELECT command shown in figure 5.44 can be issued with table aliases as follows:

```
SELECT. p.stock_no, p.dscription,
        s.unit_cost, s.on_hand
  FROM   parts p, stock s
 WHERE   p.stock_no = s.stock_no;
```

Note that when a table alias (for example, *p* or *s*) is defined in the FROM clause, the alias replaces the actual table name (*parts* or *stock*) in the command.

The second way to save typing is to omit the table name in front of column names that belong to only one of the tables specified in the command. For example, the preceding SELECT command can be issued as follows to obtain the same results:

```
SELECT   parts.stock_no, dscription, unit_cost, on_hand
  FROM   parts, stock
 WHERE   parts.stock_no = stock.stock_no;
```

Of course, you can use table aliases to shorten the column list further:

```
SELECT   p.stock_no, dscription, unit_cost, on_hand
  FROM   parts p, stock s
 WHERE   p.stock_no = s.stock_no;
```

The program is smart enough to know where to find these columns from the tables listed in the FROM clause of the command, as long as the column names listed without table names or aliases are unique.

You also can apply arithmetic operators to any of the column values selected from these tables. Figure 5.45 shows the results of a command that includes an arithmetic operator.

```
SELECT p.stock_no, p.dscription, p.unit_cost,
       s.on_hand, p.unit_cost*s.on_hand
  FROM parts p, stock s
 WHERE p.stock_no=s.stock_no;
```

P.STOCK_NO	P.DSCRIPTION	P.UNIT_COST	S.ON_HAND	EXP1
HW101	Epson LQ-1050 printer	628.50	8	5028.00
HW102	HP LaserJet II printer	1435.00	2	2870.00
HW201	NEC MultiSync monitor	459.00	4	1836.00
HW301	Paradise VGA board	230.00	6	1380.00
HW401	IBM PS/2 Model 70/60MB	3250.00	3	9750.00
HW402	COMPAQ 386S DeskPro/40MB	2600.00	4	10400.00
HW403	Zenith Supersport 286/20	2975.00	3	8925.00
SW101	Lotus 1-2-3 Version 2.01	250.00	10	2500.00
SW201	WordPerfect 5.0	195.00	7	1365.00
SW202	Microsoft Word 5.0	183.50	5	917.50
SW301	Paradox 3.0	385.75	2	771.50
SW302	dBASE IV Version 1.0	360.00	3	1080.00

Fig. 5.45. *Data selected with a command using an arithmetic operator.*

Note that the last column displays the total inventory value for each stock item, calculated by multiplying each value in the *unit_cost* column in the *parts* table by the corresponding value in the *on_hand* column of the *stock* table. Also note that the column headings used in this version of SQL (dBASE IV's SQL) are the column names plus the table names or aliases, or an expression (for example, EXP1), and the headings appear rather long and messy. In some versions of SQL (such as Oracle's SQL*Plus), you can replace these column headings with more descriptive column aliases or column labels, as discussed previously in this chapter.

You also can specify filter conditions to screen the columns selected from the tables involved. The example in figure 5.46 displays the inventory values for the hardware items in stock.

Because all the hardware items are identified with stock numbers beginning with HW, the character pattern 'HW%' is used with the LIKE logical operator to find these items.

Of course, you can display data from more than two tables in a SELECT statement in the same manner as illustrated in the preceding example. The example in figure 5.47 displays data from the *parts*, *stock*, and *vendors* tables.

```
SELECT p.stock_no, p.dscription, p.unit_cost,
       s.on_hand, p.unit_cost*s.on_hand
  FROM parts p, stock s
 WHERE p.stock_no=s.stock_no;
   AND p.stock_no LIKE 'HW%';
```

P.STOCK_NO	P.DSCRIPTION	P.UNIT_COST	S.ON_HAND	EXP1
HW101	Epson LQ-1050 printer	628.50	8	5028.00
HW102	HP LaserJet II printer	1435.00	2	2870.00
HW201	NEC MultiSync monitor	459.00	4	1836.00
HW301	Paradise VGA board	230.00	6	1380.00
HW401	IBM PS/2 Model 70/60MB	3250.00	3	9750.00
HW402	COMPAQ 386S DeskPro/40MB	2600.00	4	10400.00
HW403	Zenith Supersport 286/20	2975.00	3	8925.00

Fig. 5.46. *A display of inventory values for hardware items in stock.*

```
SELECT s.stock_no, p.dscription,
       s.reorder-s.on_hand,
       v.name, v.phone_no
  FROM stock s, parts p, vendors v
 WHERE s.on_hand < s.reorder
   AND s.stock_no = p.stock_no
   AND s.vendor_id=v.vendor_id;
```

S.STOCK_NO	P.DSCRIPTION	EXP	V.NAME	V.PHONE_NO
HW402	COMPAQ 386S DeskPro/40MB	1	PC Ware	800-666-4444
SW301	Paradox 3.0	1	PC Source	415-777-8888

Fig. 5.47. *Data selected from more than two tables.*

In this example, the SELECT command finds the parts that need to be reordered (when on-hand quantity is less than the reorder level) by comparing the values in the *on_hand* and *reorder* columns in the *stock* table. Information about these items is taken from the *stock*, *parts*, and *vendors* tables; the first table provides the part number, the second table the part description, and the third table the names and phone numbers of the vendors. The *stock* and *parts* tables are linked by the *stock_no* column; the *vendor_id* column connects the *stock* and *vendors* tables.

Chapter Summary

In this chapter, you have added to the concepts you mastered in Chapter 4 by learning how to display the contents of databases and base tables. Going beyond the simple SELECT * command, you have learned how to use the SELECT command to display selected rows from one or more tables by adding the necessary filter conditions. To perform a more complex query on the data, you learned to use logical operators and connectors to link multiple logical conditions. Other important concepts presented in this chapter included using arithmetic operations on the columns to be displayed and defining column headings with column aliases and other special formatting commands.

After you have created the necessary base tables for an application, you must maintain the data in these tables so that their contents are always updated to reflect changes. You learn how to update your base tables in the next chapter.

6

Modifying and Updating Databases

After you create a database, you often need to modify its contents to respond to changing data requirements. For example, you may need to add tables or remove them. You may need to change a few of the columns in a table structure. SQL has no direct command for adding columns to an existing table, but you can add columns with some of the features introduced in this chapter. You also may need to edit and update values in the rows.

In the last chapter, you learned how you can use the SELECT command for displaying the contents of a database and a base table. This chapter shows you how to edit the information stored in the database.

Manipulating and Modifying Databases

As you have seen, a database can be viewed as a portion of disk space that stores information in the form of tables. In many versions of SQL, you can create a number of databases with different names. You can store all the tables that are related to a given application in the same database with a descriptive name. For example, all the data tables in this book are saved in a database named *sqlbook*. The name and contents of a database can be modified with the appropriate commands. You also can delete a database or copy its contents to another database.

Dropping a Database

If your version of SQL can create multiple databases, you can delete a database after you have finished using it. You delete a database by issuing a DOS command or an SQL command, depending on the version of SQL you are using. If your SQL deletes databases with the operating system (SQL*Plus,

INGRES), follow the steps prescribed by your operating system. If your SQL enables you to delete databases at the program level, you can remove the database by issuing an SQL command such as DROP DATABASE (DB2, INFORMIX, SYBASE, dBASE IV's SQL) or DROP DBSPACE (SQL/DS). For example, if you are using dBASE IV's SQL, the command format is this:

DROP DATABASE <database name>;

Before you delete a database, you may want to get a listing of the existing databases by using the SHOW DATABASE command. Figure 6.1 shows an example of the results of this command:

```
NAME       CREATOR    CREATED     PATH
-------    ---------  ----------  ------------------
SAMPLES    SYSTEM     11/28/88    C:\DBASE\SAMPLE
SQLBOOK    CHOU       08/22/89    C:\DBASE\SQLBOOK
OLDBASE    CHOU       09/25/89    C:\DBASE\OLDBASE
```

Fig. 6.1. *Display resulting from the SHOW DATABASE command.*

If you are sure that the database is unnecessary, you can go ahead and drop it.

You cannot drop an open database (the database you are in). Only closed databases can be deleted. To close the database, you need to move into another database. No simple command, such as CLOSE DATABASE, exists. For example, if you are in the *oldbase* database and you want to drop it, you can move to the *sqlbook* database and close the *oldbase* database by issuing the following command:

START DATABASE sqlbook;

After that, you can issue the DROP DATABASE command:

DROP DATABASE oldbase;

You get a message warning you that the tables in the databases will be deleted if you choose to continue. To abort the operation, press Esc.

The DROP DATABASE command deletes the tables in the database, but the database name remains in the same subdirectory of the disk volume. You can remove the name by issuing the appropriate DOS command. In some systems, the system files remain after you have issued the DROP DATABASE command. In this case, you need to delete these system files before removing the subdirectory.

Warning: The results from the DROP DATABASE command are irreversible. Extreme care must be taken not to drop the wrong database, because you cannot bring back a database.

Copying a Database

If your version of SQL enables you to copy the contents of a database to another database at the operating system level, you need to follow the procedure prescribed by your operating system. If you are using a version of SQL that enables you to create a database at the program level, you can copy a database by following these steps:

1. Create a new database with the new name.

2. Copy all the files from the current database to the new database.

In dBASE IV's SQL, for example, to copy the *sqlbook* database and rename it *testdb*, you follow these steps:

1. Create the new database by issuing the following command at the SQL prompt:

   CREATE DATABASE testdb;

   When you see the message `Database TESTDB created`, you know that a database and subdirectory named *testdb* are in the system.

2. Exit from dBASE IV's SQL to the DOS prompt by issuing the QUIT command.

3. Copy all the files in the subdirectory with the first database name (*sqlbook*) to the new subdirectory (*testdb*). The DOS command is this:

   COPY C:\DBASE\SQLBOOK*.* C:\DBASE\TESTDB

4. Return to the dBASE IV's SQL and examine the new database. When you are at the SQL prompt, move into the renamed database by issuing the following command:

   START DATABASE testdb;

   To verify the contents of the database, try to issue a SELECT command to view a table. Because the *testdb* database is identical to *sqlbook*, you can verify its contents by issuing the following command:

   SELECT   *
     FROM   employee;

Renaming a Database

Changing the name of a database can be a tedious and risky process, depending on a number of factors. If the database is created at the operating system level, you need to issue the system commands at the DOS prompt to rename the database. Because a database is often represented by a subdirectory in the disk volume, you need to use a utility program (such as Norton Commander) to rename the subdirectory. When you rename it, you must update the information in the catalog or system file that keeps track of the database information. You must follow the instructions given by your version of SQL to rename a database.

If your database is created by issuing a command like CREATE DATABASE at the SQL prompt, you may be able to rename the database within SQL.

The procedure for renaming a database involves two steps:

1. Make a copy of the database to be renamed with a new name.

2. Drop the old database.

You may be able to rename the database with the following steps. (Of course, depending on the version of SQL you are using, these steps may vary. These instructions work for dBASE IV's SQL.) To rename the database from *testdb* to *backup*, this is what you need to do:

1. Create a database named *backup* with this command at the SQL prompt:

    CREATE DATABASE backup;

2. Exit to DOS from SQL. When you are at the DOS prompt, copy all the files in the *testdb* subdirectory to the *backup* subdirectory with the DOS command:

    COPY C:\DBASE\TESTDB*.* C:\DBASE\BACKUP

3. Return to the dBASE IV's SQL and move into the new database:

    START DATABASE BACKUP;

4. Issue the DROP DATABASE command to delete the old database:

    DROP DATABASE TESTDB;

Adding New Tables to a Database

When you are in a database, any table you create is automatically added to that database. For SQLs that support multiple databases, you cannot add a table to a database other than the database you are in. To add tables, you must switch to the database in which the new table will reside. Typical SQL commands to switch databases include

dBASE IV SQL: START DATABASE <database name>;

SYBASE: USE <database name>

Informix-SQL: DATABASE <database name>

Some versions of SQL (Oracle's SQL*Plus, Ingres, and others) require that you select the database by issuing a command at the DOS level.

Removing Tables from a Database

To remove a table from the current database, almost every version of SQL uses the DROP TABLE command in the following format:

DROP TABLE <table name>;

For example, if you want to delete the *temptble* table from the *sqlbook* database, you issue the following command when you are in the *sqlbook* database:

DROP TABLE temptble;

Be careful not to drop the wrong table. Tables cannot be recovered easily without using a disk file recovery utility program.

Copying Tables

During data manipulation you often need to copy a table. The copy may serve as a backup or may be used for experimenting with different data manipulation operations. If you mistakenly erase or corrupt the data, you can always go back to the original data and start over again.

The procedure for copying a table varies depending on the version of SQL. Some SQLs (but not dBASE IV's SQL) provide a simple command for creating a new table by using the structure and contents of a table. An example is the CREATE TABLE...AS command of Oracle's SQL*Plus:

```
CREATE TABLE   <target table name>
     AS SELECT  *
          FROM   <source table name>;
```

The command creates a target table whose structure is identical to that of the source table; then the command copies the data from the source table to the target table. For example, to create a *staff* table identical to the *employee* table, you can issue the following command:

```
CREATE TABLE  staff
      AS SELECT  *
          FROM  employee;
```

After the command is executed, the target table named *staff* contains the same information that is stored in the *employee* table. Both tables have the same structure and same data rows. The CREATE TABLE...AS command is a powerful tool for managing your tables, because in one step, the command copies the table structure and all the data in the rows.

Unfortunately, many versions of SQL do not support this command. If you are using one of these versions, you can accomplish the same task in two steps: Copy the structure of the source table when you create the target table; then copy the data from the source table to the target table. The following example creates a table named *staff* with the same structure as the *employee* table:

```
CREATE TABLE  staff
              (ss_no      CHAR(11),
               Lname      CHAR(7),
               f_name     CHAR(10),
               title      CHAR(10),
               dept       CHAR(10),
               salary     DECIMAL(8,2));
```

After creating the target table structure, you can issue the INSERT command to copy data from the source table to the target table in this command format:

```
INSERT INTO  <new table name>
      SELECT  *
        FROM  <old table name>
```

For example, you can copy data from the *employee* table and insert it into the *staff* table with this command:

```
INSERT INTO  staff
      SELECT  *
        FROM  employee;
```

When this INSERT command is executed, the message 11 row(s) inserted appears, indicating the amount of data inserted. The contents of the *staff* table can be viewed by using the SELECT * command (see fig. 6.2).

```
SELECT *
  FROM staff;
SS_NO          L_NAME   F_NAME      TITLE        DEPT         SALARY
-----------    -------  ---------   ----------   ----------   --------
123-45-6789    Smith    James J.    President    Corporate    89500.00
634-56-7890    Nelson   Harry M.    Manager      Sales        65000.00
445-67-8801    Zeller   Albert K.   Salesman     Sales        48900.00
562-87-8800    Chapman  Kirk D.     Salesman     Sales        42500.00
404-22-4568    Baker    Larry A.    Clerk        Sales        30500.00
256-09-5555    Dixon    Kathy T.    Accountant   Accounting   45000.00
458-90-3456    Frazer   Robert F.   Bookkeeper   Accounting   28000.00
777-34-6543    King     David G.    Manager      Personnel    38000.00
100-45-8021    Wong     Mike J.     Manager      MIS          44000.00
303-25-7777    Duff     Cathy B.    Secretary    Personnel    26500.00
909-10-8910    Parker   Susan C.    Trainee                       0.00
```

Fig. 6.2. Viewing the contents of a table after inserting data rows.

Notice that the INSERT command put a zero *salary* value in the last row of the *staff* table, even though the *employee* table has a null value (a blank) there. Some versions of SQL leave a null value instead of a zero because they treat a zero differently from a null value.

In Chapter 4, the INSERT command is used for adding one row of data values to the table where the data values are specified in the VALUES clause:

```
INSERT INTO  employee
      VALUES  ('123-45-6789', 'Smith', 'James J.',
                'President', 'Corporate', 89500.00);
```

When you replace the VALUES clause with a query defined with the SELECT * FROM phrase, all the data in the rows returned by the SELECT statement are added as rows in the new table. All the rows from the source table are added because the SELECT * statement selects all the rows.

Copying Selected Columns

In the preceding example, you see how to make a copy of a table with the identical structure and data rows. With a similar procedure, you can copy partial contents of a source table to a target table. If the CREATE TABLE...AS command is supported in your SQL, you can specify the target table columns whose values are to be supplied by the source table:

```
CREATE TABLE   <target table name> (column list)
     AS SELECT   <column list>
          FROM   <source table name>;
```

For example, if you want to copy the *ss_no*, *l_name* and *f_name* columns from the *employee* table to a new table named *payroll* (with columns named *ss_no*, *first_name*, *last_name* and *salary*, with others to be added later), you issue the following CREATE TABLE...AS command:

```
CREATE TABLE   payroll (ss_no, first_name, last_name, salary)
     AS SELECT   ss_no, f_name, l_name, salary
         FROM   employee;
```

If your version of SQL does not support the CREATE TABLE...AS command, you can accomplish the same task with the CREATE TABLE and INSERT commands:

```
CREATE TABLE   payroll
               (ss_no        CHAR(11),
                first_name   CHAR(10),
                last_name    CHAR(7),
                salary       DECIMAL(8,2));


INSERT INTO   payroll (ss_no, first_name, last_name, salary)
     SELECT   ss_no, f_name, l_name, salary
       FROM   employee;
```

The resulting *payroll* table contains the data shown in figure 6.3.

```
SELECT *
  FROM payroll;
```

SS_NO	FIRST_NAME	LAST_NAME	SALARY
123-45-6789	James J.	Smith	89500.00
634-56-7890	Harry M.	Nelson	65000.00
445-67-8801	Albert K.	Zeller	48900.00
562-87-8800	Kirk D.	Chapman	42500.00
404-22-4568	Larry A.	Baker	30500.00
256-09-5555	Kathy T.	Dixon	45000.00
458-90-3456	Robert F.	Frazer	28000.00
777-34-6543	David G.	King	38000.00
100-45-8021	Mike J.	Wong	44000.00
303-25-7777	Cathy B.	Duff	26500.00
909-10-8910	Susan C.	Parker	0.00

Fig. 6.3. *A table composed of columns copied from another table.*

When you are creating the structure for the target table, you need to make sure that the columns of the target table are wide enough to hold the data inserted from the source table; otherwise, the copying operation does not finish. If you make a mistake creating the target table structure, drop the target table and create a new one.

The columns of the target table are filled in the order specified in the column lists for the target and source tables. In the example, entries in the *ss_no, f_name, l_name.* and *salary* columns of the *employee* table are inserted into the *ss_no, first_name, last_name,* and *salary* columns, respectively.

If you are filling every column of the target table with data from some or all columns of the source table, however, you can omit the column names in the target table. In the example, you are filling all four columns of the *payroll* table with the four columns (*ss_no, f_name, l_name,* and *salary*) of the *employee* table, so you do not need to specify the column list for the *payroll* table:

```
INSERT INTO   payroll
      SELECT  ss_no, f_name, l_name, salary
        FROM  employee;
```

Copying Data from Multiple Tables

You also can copy information from more than one source table into a target table. Use a query with the SELECT command to find the columns you want to copy from the source tables and then insert those columns into the target table.

If your SQL has the CREATE TABLE...AS command, you can use it to create the *invvalue* (inventory value) target table and copy several columns from the *parts* and *stock* source tables:

```
CREATE TABLE   invvalue (stock_no, units, unit_value)
   AS SELECT   p.stock_no, s.on_hand, p.unit_cost
       FROM    parts p, stock s
       WHERE   p.stock_no = s.stock_no;
```

The CREATE TABLE...AS command sets the column attributes (column width, type, and so on) of the *invvalue* target table to match the columns from the source tables. If you want, you can redefine the column attributes by specifying the column widths with a column list, such as

```
CREATE TABLE    invvalue
                (stock_no    CHAR(5),
                units        SMALLINT,
                unit_value   DECIMAL(8,2))
   AS SELECT    p.stock_no, s.on_hand, p.unit_cost
      FROM      parts p, stock s
      WHERE     p.stock_no = s.stock_no;
```

If your version of SQL does not support the CREATE TABLE...AS command, you still can accomplish the same tasks by issuing the CREATE TABLE and INSERT commands in two steps:

```
CREATE TABLE    invvalue
                (stock_no    CHAR(5),
                units        SMALLINT,
                unit_value   DECIMAL(8,2));
  INSERT INTO   invvalue
      SELECT    p.stock_no, s.on_hand, p.unit_cost
      FROM      parts p, stock s
      WHERE     p.stock_no = s.stock_no;
```

The resulting *invvalue* table can be viewed with a simple SELECT command (see fig. 6.4).

```
SELECT *
  FROM invvalue;
STOCK_NO  UNITS  UNIT_VALUE
--------  -----  ----------
HW101       8        628.50
HW102       2       1435.00
HW201       4        459.00
HW301       6        230.00
HW401       3       3250.00
HW402       4       2600.00
HW403       3       2975.00
SW101      10        250.00
SW201       7        195.00
SW202       5        183.50
SW301       2        385.75
SW302       3        360.00
```

Fig. 6.4. *A table with columns copied from two other tables.*

Copying Selected Rows

In the previous examples, you have seen how you can copy all or some of the columns from one or more source tables to a target table. With the SELECT phrase of the CREATE TABLE...AS or INSERT command, you can add a filtering WHERE condition to copy selected rows from the source tables to the target table. For example, you can create a *manager* table that contains information about the managers (getting the information from the *employee* table) with the CREATE TABLE...AS command:

```
CREATE TABLE    manager
    AS SELECT   *
        FROM    employee
        WHERE   title = 'Manager';
```

Or you can issue the CREATE TABLE and INSERT commands in two steps to accomplish the same task if the CREATE TABLE...AS command is not available to you:

```
CREATE TABLE    manager
        (ss_no      CHAR(11),
        l_name      CHAR(7),
        f_name      CHAR(10),
        title       CHAR(10),
        dept        CHAR(10),
        salary      DECIMAL(8,2));

INSERT INTO     manager
    SELECT      *
        FROM    employee
        WHERE   title = 'Manager';
```

After these commands are executed, the contents of the *manager* table look like figure 6.5.

```
SELECT *
  FROM manager;
SS_NO         L_NAME  F_NAME     TITLE     DEPT        SALARY
-----------   ------  ---------  --------  ---------   --------
634-56-7890   Nelson  Harry M.   Manager   Sales       65000.00
777-34-6543   King    David G.   Manager   Personnel   38000.00
100-45-8021   Wong    Mike J.    Manager   MIS         44000.00
```

Fig. 6.5. A table composed of selected rows copied from another table.

Of course, you can copy selected rows from multiple source tables into target tables with a similar filter condition. Here is an example:

```
CREATE TABLE   hwstock
               (stock_no    CHAR(5),
                item        CHAR(25)
                qty         SMALLINT,
                unit_cost   DECIMAL(8,2));

  INSERT INTO  hwstock
      SELECT   p.stock_no, p.dscription,
               s.on_hand, p.unit_cost
        FROM   parts p, stock s
       WHERE   p.stock_no LIKE 'HW%'
         AND   p.stock_no = s.stock_no;
```

By executing these two commands, you create a table for storing information about the hardware stock by copying certain rows from the *parts* and *stock* tables. The WHERE x.stock_no LIKE 'HW%' clause selects the rows whose stock numbers begin with HW (for hardware items). To see the contents, enter the SELECT command (see fig. 6.6).

```
SELECT *
  FROM hwstock;
STOCK_NO  ITEM                       QTY  UNIT_COST
--------  -------------------------  ---  ----------
HW101     Epson LQ-1050 printer       8      628.50
HW102     HP LaserJet II printer      2     1435.00
HW201     NEC MultiSync monitor       4      459.00
HW301     Paradise VGA board          6      230.00
HW401     IBM PS/2 Model 70/60MB      3     3250.00
HW402     COMPAQ 386S DeskPro/40MB    4     2600.00
HW403     Zenith Supersport 286/20    3     2975.00
```

Fig. 6.6. *A table consisting of selected rows copied from two other tables.*

Of course, you can replace these two commands with the CREATE TABLE...AS command if your version of SQL supports the command:

```
CREATE TABLE   hwstock (stock_no, item, qty, unit_cost)
   AS SELECT   p.stock_no, p.dscription,
               s.on_hand, p.unit_cost
        FROM   parts p, stock s
       WHERE   p.stock_no LIKE 'HW%'
         AND   p.stock_no = s.stock_no;
```

Modifying a Table

After you have set up a table structure and inserted the necessary data rows, you can change any part of its contents as you want. For example, you may want to change the name of a table, add columns, delete columns, or redefine column attributes. As your data requirements change, you may want to add more data rows to the table, remove rows you no longer need, or update values in the tables to reflect new information.

Renaming a Table

Most versions of SQL lack a simple command for renaming a table. To rename a table in these SQLs, you must copy the structure and contents of the table to another table and then drop the old table. For example, to rename the *manager* table to a new table named *managers*, follow these steps:

1. Make a copy of the *manager* table and name the copy *managers*.

2. Drop the *manager* table.

The procedure also can be done by using the CREATE TABLE...AS and the DROP TABLE commands:

```
CREATE TABLE   managers
      AS SELECT   *
          FROM   manager;

   DROP TABLE   manager;
```

If your version of SQL does not support the CREATE TABLE...AS command, use the CREATE TABLE, INSERT, and DROP TABLE commands:

```
CREATE TABLE   managers
               (ss_no       CHAR(11),
                l_name      CHAR(7),
                f_name      CHAR(10),
                title       CHAR(10),
                dept        CHAR(10),
                salary      DECIMAL(8,2));

INSERT INTO   managers
     SELECT   *
       FROM   manager;

  DROP TABLE   manager;
```

The contents of the new *managers* table are shown in figure 6.7.

```
SELECT *
  FROM managers;
SS_NO         L_NAME  F_NAME     TITLE    DEPT        SALARY
------------  ------  ---------  -------  ----------  --------
634-56-7890   Nelson  Harry M.   Manager  Sales       65000.00
777-34-6543   King    David G.   Manager  Personnel   38000.00
100-45-8021   Wong    Mike J.    Manager  MIS         44000.00
```

Fig. 6.7. The renamed table.

Redefining a Table Structure

As your data needs change, you often need to modify the structure of your base table—changing the column names, adding columns, deleting columns, and modifying the column attributes (column size, type, and so on).

Most versions of SQL provide a command you can use to add a column to a table, but unfortunately, no simple commands exist to delete a column, change the column name, or change the attributes of a column.

Adding Columns

The command supported by most versions of SQL for adding a new column to a table is the ALTER TABLE command in the following format:

    ALTER TABLE   <table name>
          ADD   (definition for new columns);

For example, to add two columns, *month_pay* and *exemptions* (for monthly salary and number of exemptions claimed) to the *payroll* table, you issue the following command:

    ALTER TABLE   payroll
          ADD   (month_pay   DECIMAL(8,2),
                exemptions   SMALLINT);

After the command is executed, you see that two new columns are in the table when you view the table (see fig. 6.8).

```
SELECT *
  FROM payroll;
SS_NO         FIRST_NAME   LAST_NAME    SALARY   MONTH_PAY   EXEMPTIONS
-----------   ----------   ---------    -------- ----------  ----------
123-45-6789   James J.     Smith       89500.00
634-56-7890   Harry M.     Nelson      65000.00
445-67-8801   Albert K.    Zeller      48900.00
562-87-8800   Kirk D.      Chapman     42500.00
404-22-4568   Larry A.     Baker       30500.00
256-09-5555   Kathy T.     Dixon       45000.00
458-90-3456   Robert F.    Frazer      28000.00
777-34-6543   David G.     King        38000.00
100-45-8021   Mike J.      Wong        44000.00
303-25-7777   Cathy B.     Duff        26500.00
909-10-8910   Susan C.     Parker          0.00
```

Fig. 6.8. *The* payroll *table with two new columns added.*

Note that no values are in the new columns. Later, you will learn how to fill them with the appropriate values.

Changing Column Attributes

In most SQL implementations, the ALTER command you have just seen can only add new columns to a table; the ALTER command cannot delete columns or change their attributes. To delete a column in a table, you need to create a new table with a different structure and then copy the information from the old table. After that, you need to rename the table, following the procedure explained previously.

Suppose that you want to modify the structure of the *managers* table in the following ways:

1. Delete the *ss_no* column.

2. Rename the *l_name* column to *last_name*, and increase its width from CHAR(7) to CHAR(10).

3. Rename the *f_name* column to *first_name*.

4. Rename the *dept* column to *department* column and move it to the first column.

You can issue the following command to set up a *temptble* table for temporarily holding the revised structure:

```
CREATE TABLE   temptble
               (department   CHAR(10),
                last_name    CHAR(10),
                first_name   CHAR(10),
                salary       DECIMAL(8,2));
```

Then insert these rows from the *managers* table:

```
INSERT INTO   temptble
      SELECT   dept, Lname, f_name, salary
        FROM   managers;
```

To see the *temptble* table, issue the SELECT command, as shown in figure 6.9.

```
SELECT *
  FROM temptble;
DEPARTMENT   LAST_NAME   FIRST_NAME    SALARY
----------   ---------   ----------   --------

Sales        Nelson      Harry M.     65000.00
Personnel    King        David G.     38000.00
MIS          Wong        Mike J.      44000.00
```

Fig. 6.9. *The restructured* temptble *table.*

Now the *temptble* table holds the information of the *managers* table. You then can delete the *managers* table by issuing the following command:

```
DROP TABLE   managers;
```

Finally, rename the *temptble* table as *managers* with these steps:

```
CREATE TABLE   managers
               (department   CHAR(10),
                last_name    CHAR(10),
                first_name   CHAR(10),
                salary       DECIMAL(8,2));

INSERT INTO   managers
     SELECT   *
       FROM   temptble;

DROP TABLE   temptble;
```

After these commands are executed, the revised *managers* table has the new structure with the data of the original *managers* table. To see the revised *managers* table, enter the command shown in figure 6.10.

```
SELECT *
  FROM managers;
DEPARTMENT   LAST_NAME   FIRST_NAME    SALARY
----------   ---------   ----------   --------
Sales        Nelson      Harry M.     65000.00
Personnel    King        David G.     38000.00
MIS          Wong        Mike J.      44000.00
```

Fig. 6.10. *The revised* managers *table.*

Changing Column Width

In most versions of SQL, you can use the ALTER TABLE command only to add a new column with the ADD clause. However, some SQLs (such as Oracle's SQL*Plus) enable you to change the width of a column by adding the MODIFY clause to the ALTER TABLE command. This is the format:

```
ALTER TABLE   <table name>
      MODIFY  ( <existing column name> <new definition> );
```

For example, to change the column definition from DECIMAL(8,2) to DECIMAL(10,2) for the salary, you can issue the following command:

```
ALTER TABLE   employee
      MODIFY  (salary DECIMAL(10,2));
```

By using this command, you can expand the width of a column. Remember that if you narrow the column width, you risk losing the data that is already stored in the column. Try not to change data type with this command. Depending on the type of data involved, you may not be able to change data type. For example, you cannot change a character column to a numeric column with this command. In Oracle's SQL, you can decrease size only if the table contains no columns with null values.

Replacing Null Values

When you enter or insert data into a table, you may need to fill one or more columns with null values, because the needed values may not be available. Suppose that you had a new employee named Susan C. Parker to put into the *employee* table, but you did not know which department she worked in or what her salary was when the data was entered. As a result, the values in the *dept* and *salary* columns were left blank (a null value). Now you have values for these two columns. To enter these values, you can use the UPDATE command in the following format:

```
UPDATE   <table name>
    SET  (setting column values)
  WHERE  <filter condition>;
```

The SET clause in the command enables you to specify a new value for each column named in the clause. The WHERE clause defines the filter condition that determines the rows subject to the updating operation. If you leave out the filter condition, all the rows in the table are affected. For example, if you want to replace the null value in the *dept* column for the row that belongs to employee Parker with the value of MIS, you issue the following UPDATE command:

```
UPDATE   employee
    SET  dept = 'MIS'
  WHERE  Lname = 'Parker';
```

You can change the values in more than one column at a time by specifying the values for the columns involved in the SET clause. For example, to replace the null values in the *dept* and *salary* columns in the row that belongs to employee Susan C. Parker with the new data values of MIS and 28000, you issue the following command:

```
UPDATE   employee
    SET  dept = 'MIS', salary = 28000
  WHERE  Lname = 'Parker';
```

You can specify as many update values for the columns in the SET clause as you want. You separate these values with commas.

The contents of the updated *employee* table can be viewed after executing the command shown in figure 6.11.

```
SELECT *
  FROM employee;
SS_NO          L_NAME    F_NAME      TITLE        DEPT         SALARY
-----------    -------   ---------   ----------   ----------   --------
123-45-6789    Smith     James J.    President    Corporate    89500.00
634-56-7890    Nelson    Harry M.    Manager      Sales        65000.00
445-67-8801    Zeller    Albert K.   Salesman     Sales        48900.00
562-87-8800    Chapman   Kirk D.     Salesman     Sales        42500.00
404-22-4568    Baker     Larry A.    Clerk        Sales        30500.00
256-09-5555    Dixon     Kathy T.    Accountant   Accounting   45000.00
458-90-3456    Frazer    Robert F.   Bookkeeper   Accounting   28000.00
777-34-6543    King      David G.    Manager      Personnel    38000.00
100-45-8021    Wong      Mike J.     Manager      MIS          44000.00
303-25-7777    Duff      Cathy B.    Secretary    Personnel    26500.00
909-10-8910    Parker    Susan C.    Trainee      MIS          28000.00
```

Fig. 6.11. *The* updated *employee* table.

You can see that the null values in the *dept* and *salary* columns of the last row in the table have been replaced with new data values MIS and 28000.

Because the *payroll* table also contains salary information about the employees, you need to replace the null values in the *dept* and *salary* columns in the row that belongs to employee Parker. Use the UPDATE command like this:

```
UPDATE   payroll
   SET   salary = 28000
 WHERE   last_name = 'Parker';
```

In addition to the salary values, null values in the *exemptions* column of the *payroll* table also need to be filled. Because each employee may have a different value for the *exemptions* column, you need to replace each null value in the column by using an individual UPDATE command. For example, to replace the null value for the employee Smith in the *exemptions* column, issue the following command:

```
UPDATE   payroll
   SET   exemptions = 3
 WHERE   last_name = 'Smith';
```

To see the payroll, enter this command:

```
SELECT   *
  FROM   payroll;
```

After you issue the necessary UPDATE commands for filling in the values in the *exemptions* column, the contents of the *payroll* table become like those shown in figure 6.12.

SS_NO	FIRST_NAME	LAST_NAME	SALARY	MONTH_PAY	EXEMPTIONS
123-45-6789	James J.	Smith	89500.00		3
634-56-7890	Harry M.	Nelson	65000.00		2
445-67-8801	Albert K.	Zeller	48900.00		4
562-87-8800	Kirk D.	Chapman	42500.00		2
404-22-4568	Larry A.	Baker	30500.00		1
256-09-5555	Kathy T.	Dixon	45000.00		3
458-90-3456	Robert F.	Frazer	28000.00		3
777-34-6543	David G.	King	38000.00		2
100-45-8021	Mike J.	Wong	44000.00		2
303-25-7777	Cathy B.	Duff	26500.00		2
909-10-8910	Susan C.	Parker	28000.00		1

Fig. 6.12. *The updated* payroll *table.*

In the *payroll* table shown in figure 6.12, you can see that null values still appear in the *month_pay* column, because no values have been assigned to it. Because the *month_pay* column is set up for storing the monthly salaries for the employees, instead of entering each salary figure with an UPDATE command, you can use a formula for updating every value in the column at once. The formula, month_pay = salary/12, defines the column values in the UPDATE command. Because the updating operation is intended for every row, you need not specify the filter condition:

> UPDATE   payroll
>   SET   month_pay = salary/12;

Because no filter condition with a WHERE clause is specified, every row of the table is subject to the updating operation. Consequently, every value in the *month_pay* column is assigned the computed value.

After the updating operation, the contents of the *payroll* table look like figure 6.13.

SS_NO	FIRST_NAME	LAST_NAME	SALARY	MONTH_PAY	EXEMPTIONS
123-45-6789	James J.	Smith	89500.00	7458.33	3
634-56-7890	Harry M.	Nelson	65000.00	5416.67	2
445-67-8801	Albert K.	Zeller	48900.00	4075.00	4
562-87-8800	Kirk D.	Chapman	42500.00	3541.67	2
404-22-4568	Larry A.	Baker	30500.00	2541.67	1
256-09-5555	Kathy T.	Dixon	45000.00	3750.00	3
458-90-3456	Robert F.	Frazer	28000.00	2333.33	3
777-34-6543	David G.	King	38000.00	3166.67	2
100-45-8021	Mike J.	Wong	44000.00	3666.67	2
303-25-7777	Cathy B.	Duff	26500.00	2208.33	2
909-10-8910	Susan C.	Parker	28000.00	2333.33	1

Fig. 6.13. *Updating a table with a formula.*

Changing Data in a Table

In the preceding examples, the UPDATE command is used for filling in null values in the columns of a table. The same command can be used for changing the values in columns.

If you need to change any values in one or more columns in a table, you can specify the new values for the columns in the SET clause of the UPDATE command, as illustrated earlier. For example, if the employee Larry A. Baker has been promoted from a clerk to a salesman with a new salary of $33,500 (increased from $30,500), you can change the values in the *title* and *salary* columns with the following command:

```
UPDATE   employee
    SET   title = 'Salesman',
          salary = 33500
  WHERE   Lname = 'Baker';
```

To see the revised contents of the *employee* table, enter the command shown in figure 6.14.

```
SELECT *
  FROM employee;
SS_NO          L_NAME    F_NAME      TITLE        DEPT         SALARY
-----------    -------   ----------  ----------   ----------   --------
123-45-6789    Smith     James J.    President    Corporate    89500.00
634-56-7890    Nelson    Harry M.    Manager      Sales        65000.00
445-67-8801    Zeller    Albert K.   Salesman     Sales        48900.00
562-87-8800    Chapman   Kirk D.     Salesman     Sales        42500.00
404-22-4568    Baker     Larry A.    Salesman     Sales        33500.00
256-09-5555    Dixon     Kathy T.    Accountant   Accounting   45000.00
458-90-3456    Frazer    Robert F.   Bookkeeper   Accounting   28000.00
777-34-6543    King      David G.    Manager      Personnel    38000.00
100-45-8021    Wong      Mike J.     Manager      MIS          44000.00
303-25-7777    Duff      Cathy B.    Secretary    Personnel    26500.00
909-10-8910    Parker    Susan C.    Trainee      MIS          28000.00
```

Fig. 6.14. *The* employee *table with updates for Larry A. Baker.*

Using the IN Logical Predicate

If you need to change values in multiple selected rows, you can use the IN logical predicate in the filter condition to identify the rows involved. For example, if you want to give a five percent pay raise (salary = salary*1.05) to certain employees (Zeller, Frazer, and Duff), you can specify their last names in the IN predicate:

UPDATE   employee
    SET   salary = salary*1.05
  WHERE   Lname IN ('Zeller', 'Frazer', 'Duff');

You must enclose multiple values for columns in parentheses. The number of values you can specify is unlimited.

The revised contents of the *employee* table after the updating operation can be viewed as shown in figure 6.15. Notice that the salaries for the three employees (Zeller, Frazer, and Duff) have been increased by five percent.

```
SELECT *
  FROM employee;
SS_NO          L_NAME    F_NAME      TITLE        DEPT         SALARY
-----------    -------   ---------   ----------   ----------   --------
123-45-6789    Smith     James J.    President    Corporate    89500.00
634-56-7890    Nelson    Harry M.    Manager      Sales        65000.00
445-67-8801    Zeller    Albert K.   Salesman     Sales        51345.00
562-87-8800    Chapman   Kirk D.     Salesman     Sales        42500.00
404-22-4568    Baker     Larry A.    Salesman     Sales        33500.00
256-09-5555    Dixon     Kathy T.    Accountant   Accounting   45000.00
458-90-3456    Frazer    Robert F.   Bookkeeper   Accounting   29400.00
777-34-6543    King      David G.    Manager      Personnel    38000.00
100-45-8021    Wong      Mike J.     Manager      MIS          44000.00
303-25-7777    Duff      Cathy B.    Secretary    Personnel    27825.00
909-10-8910    Parker    Susan C.    Trainee      MIS          28000.00
```

Fig. 6.15. Table updated with the IN logical predicate.

To maintain data integrity, you need to update the *payroll* table to reflect the salary changes. Issue the following command:

UPDATE   payroll
    SET   salary = salary*1.05,
          month_pay = month_pay*1.05
  WHERE   last_name IN ('Zeller', 'Frazer', 'Duff');

In the SET clause, each value in the *salary* and *month_pay* columns is reassigned with a new value computed by the formula. Because the value of the *month_pay* column is related to the value of the *salary* column (month_pay = salary/12), you can rewrite the UPDATE command to update both columns:

UPDATE   payroll
    SET   salary = salary*1.05,
          month_pay = salary/12
  WHERE   last_name IN ('Zeller', 'Frazer', 'Duff');

Because the first formula (salary = salary*1.05) in the SET clause updates the *salary* column, the second formula (month_pay = salary/12) reflects the updated salary value.

For verification purposes, after the updating operation, the contents of the *payroll* table are displayed with the SELECT command (see fig. 6.16).

```
SELECT *
  FROM payroll;
  SS_NO          FIRST_NAME   LAST_NAME     SALARY   MONTH_PAY   EXEMPTIONS
  -----------    ----------   ---------    --------  ----------  ----------
  123-45-6789    James J.     Smith        89500.00   7458.33            3
  634-56-7890    Harry M.     Nelson       65000.00   5416.67            2
  445-67-8801    Albert K.    Zeller       51345.00   4278.75            4
  562-87-8800    Kirk D.      Chapman      42500.00   3541.67            2
  404-22-4568    Larry A.     Baker        30500.00   2541.67            1
  256-09-5555    Kathy T.     Dixon        45000.00   3750.00            3
  458-90-3456    Robert F.    Frazer       29400.00   2450.00            3
  777-34-6543    David G.     King         38000.00   3166.67            2
  100-45-8021    Mike J.      Wong         44000.00   3666.67            2
  303-25-7777    Cathy B.     Duff         27825.00   2318.75            2
  909-10-8910    Susan C.     Parker       28000.00   2333.33            1
```

Fig. 6.16. The payroll *table updated with the IN logical predicate.*

Using a Query in the Filter Condition

Another way to specify selected rows for updating—without listing all the values in the parentheses for the IN predicate— is to use the data values returned by a SELECT statement. The following UPDATE command accomplishes the same updating operation illustrated earlier:

```
UPDATE   payroll
   SET   salary = salary*1.05,
         month_pay = month_pay*1.05
 WHERE   last_name IN (SELECT  Lname
                         FROM  bonus);
```

Instead of listing the last names (such as 'Zeller', 'Frazer', 'Duff') for the IN predicate, the *SELECT Lname FROM bonus* query provides the values for the *last_name* column. (This UPDATE command duplicates the operation of the earlier UPDATE command.) The *bonus* table serves as a lookup table that contains the last names to be used in the IN predicate. Each value in the table specifies an acceptable value for the filter condition in the IN predicate. Enter this command to see the contents of the *bonus* table:

```
SELECT  *
  FROM  bonus;
```

You can assume that the contents of the *bonus* table look like this:

```
L_NAME
------
Zeller
Frazer
Duff
```

The SELECT command query in the parentheses is executed before the WHERE *last_name* filter condition. The results from the query ('Zeller', 'Frazer', 'Duff') are used by the IN predicate to evaluate the filter condition. Therefore, the filter condition is equivalent to that shown earlier:

WHERE last_name IN ('Zeller', 'Frazer', 'Duff').

You can use the *bonus* table for displaying selected rows of data from the *payroll* table (see fig. 6.17).

```
SELECT *
  FROM payroll
 WHERE last_name IN (SELECT l_name
                     FROM bonus);
```

SS_NO	FIRST_NAME	LAST_NAME	SALARY	MONTH_PAY	EXEMPTIONS
445-67-8801	Albert K.	Zeller	51345.00	4278.75	4
458-90-3456	Robert F.	Frazer	29400.00	2450.00	3
303-25-7777	Cathy B.	Duff	27825.00	2318.75	2

Fig. 6.17. *Using a lookup table to view selected rows of the* payroll *table.*

Using a table for selecting rows can be effective for assigning filter values. This method can simplify the UPDATE command, and you easily can change the values for the filter condition by modifying the values in the lookup table.

Because the *employee* table also contains the salary information, you need to update the salaries for Zeller, Frazer, and Duff:

```
UPDATE  employee
   SET  salary = salary*1.05
 WHERE  Lname IN (SELECT  Lname
                  FROM  bonus);
```

Changing Data in Multiple Tables

The UPDATE command can be used to change values in only one table at a time; you cannot update values in multiple tables. For example, the following command is not legal:

```
UPDATE    parts, stock
    SET    parts.unit_cost = 650.90,
           stock.on_hand = 7
  WHERE    parts.stock = 'HW101'
    AND    parts.stock_no = stock.stock_no;
```

You must change the values in one table at a time. For example, if you want to accomplish the updating operation intended by the preceding illegal UPDATE command, you must issue two UPDATE commands:

```
UPDATE    parts
    SET    unit_cost = 650.90
  WHERE    stock_no = 'HW101';
```

The second command is this:

```
UPDATE    stock
    SET    on_hand = 7
  WHERE    stock_no = 'HW101';
```

Adding Data to a Table

If you need to add data to a table, you can use the INSERT command. In Chapter 4, you learned how to use the INSERT command with the VALUES clause in order to add a row of data to a table:

```
INSERT INTO   employee
    VALUES   ('123-45-6789', 'Smith', 'James J.',
             'President', 'Corporate', 89500);
```

The same INSERT command can be used to add one or more columns to one or more rows by specifying the values in the command or by copying values from other tables.

The standard format for an INSERT command is this:

```
INSERT INTO   <table name> [<column list>]
    VALUES   (data values for the columns);
```

The column list is optional. If you omit the column list, every column is subjected to the inserting operation. However, by specifying the names of only the columns into which you want to insert data, you can add partial data to the new row while leaving other columns with null values. An example of such an INSERT command is

INSERT INTO   employee (ss_no, l_name, f_name, title)
       VALUES   ('909-10-8910', 'Parker', 'Susan C.', 'Trainee');

Because you omit the *dept* and *salary* columns, null values are inserted into these columns in the new row.

Several methods exist to insert multiple rows of data into a table. One method is to write all the data entry commands and embed them in a computer program written in a language like C or COBOL (see Chapter 12).

To insert multiple rows of data into a table by using data copied from other tables, use the INSERT command with a query in the place of the VALUES clause:

INSERT INTO   <table name> [<column list>]
       <a query>;

For example, if you want to copy data from the *employee* table to the *staff* table, issue the command shown in figure 6.18.

```
INSERT INTO staff
     SELECT *
       FROM employee
      WHERE dept='Sales';
```

SS_NO	L_NAME	F_NAME	TITLE	DEPT	SALARY
123-45-6789	Smith	James J.	President	Corporate	89500.00
634-56-7890	Nelson	Harry M.	Manager	Sales	65000.00
445-67-8801	Zeller	Albert K.	Salesman	Sales	48900.00
562-87-8800	Chapman	Kirk D.	Salesman	Sales	42500.00
404-22-4568	Baker	Larry A.	Clerk	Sales	30500.00
256-09-5555	Dixon	Kathy T.	Accountant	Accounting	45000.00
458-90-3456	Frazer	Robert F.	Bookkeeper	Accounting	28000.00
777-34-6543	King	David G.	Manager	Personnel	38000.00
100-45-8021	Wong	Mike J.	Manager	MIS	44000.00
303-25-7777	Duff	Cathy B.	Secretary	Personnel	26500.00
909-10-8910	Parker	Susan C.	Trainee	MIS	28000.00
634-56-7890	Nelson	Harry M.	Manager	Sales	65000.00
445-67-8801	Zeller	Albert K.	Salesman	Sales	51345.00
562-87-8800	Chapman	Kirk D.	Salesman	Sales	42500.00
404-22-4568	Baker	Larry A.	Clerk	Sales	33500.00

Fig. 6.18. Inserting multiple rows into a table.

The added rows are placed at the end of the table. Notice that the operation does not check for duplicate rows. You need to filter out the duplicate rows with other operations, to be discussed later.

By using a query in the INSERT command, you can insert data copied from multiple tables into a single table, such as

```
INSERT INTO   tablez (column_a, column_b)
     SELECT   tablex.column_c, tabley.column_d
       FROM   tablex, tabley
      WHERE   tablex.ss_no = tabley.ss_no;
```

In this example, multiple rows of data from *tablex* and *tabley* are copied and inserted into *tablez*. Specifically, the values of *column_c* in *tablex* are inserted into *column_a* of *tablez*; the values of *column_d* in *tabley* are inserted into *column_b* of *tablez*.

Deleting Data from a Table

The DROP TABLE command enables you to remove a table from the database. DROP TABLE erases the data structure and all the data rows in the table. If you want to erase selected rows of data or if you want to erase the table's contents without erasing its structure, you need to use the DELETE command.

If you intend to remove selected rows from a table, you can use the DELETE command and include a filter condition for identifying the rows to be deleted:

```
DELETE FROM   <table name>
      WHERE   <filter condition>;
```

Here is an example:

```
DELETE FROM   staff
      WHERE   dept = 'Sales'
         OR   dept = 'Accounting';
```

The filter conditions specified in the WHERE clause instruct the program to delete all the rows whose values in the *dept* columns equal Sales or Accounting. The contents of the *staff* table then look like figure 6.19.

SS_NO	L_NAME	F_NAME	TITLE	DEPT	SALARY
123-45-6789	Smith	James J.	President	Corporate	89500.00
777-34-6543	King	David G.	Manager	Personnel	38000.00
100-45-8021	Wong	Mike J.	Manager	MIS	44000.00
303-25-7777	Duff	Cathy B.	Secretary	Personnel	26500.00
909-10-8910	Parker	Susan C.	Trainee	MIS	28000.00

Fig. 6.19. *Deleting rows from a table.*

If you want to erase the contents of a table—but save the table structure—issue the DELETE command without specifying a filter condition. For example, if you want to empty the *staff* table, issue this command:

DELETE FROM staff;

Be careful. In some versions of SQL, deleted data cannot be recovered. However, some versions of SQL do provide a ROLLBACK command for reversing changes to a table.

Saving Changes

In earlier sections, you learned how to use the INSERT, UPDATE, and DELETE commands to change the contents of a table. Although data appears to change after you execute these commands (viewed with a SELECT command), the actual data stored on the disk may not have been updated.

When you are manipulating data at the SQL prompt with the appropriate commands, the contents of the tables affected are usually copied from the disk files and held in temporary storage space until you exit the SQL program. Depending on the version of SQL you are using, when you make changes to the table contents, these changes may or may not affect the table contents in the disk files before you leave SQL. The only way you can be sure that these changes are permanent is to leave the program.

As a result, in most versions of SQL, if you accidentally turn off the computer before properly exiting from the program, all the changes you have made are lost. In order to safeguard against such a loss of data, some versions of SQL (such as Oracle's SQL*Plus) enable you to save these changes to the disk file at any time by issuing the COMMIT command:

COMMIT;

You should issue the COMMIT command periodically to save the changes you have made.

Reversing Changes

Some versions of SQL keep track of changes. These changes are saved to the disk file when you exit the program or issue one of the following commands:

    COMMIT
    ALTER
    CREATE
    DROP

Before you switch to another table, you can reverse the changes you have made since you issued the last COMMIT command. The ROLLBACK command is a simple one:

    ROLLBACK;

The ROLLBACK command has the same effect as the undo function found in many other programs—the data changes back to its form just after the last COMMIT command.

Chapter Summary

In this chapter, you have learned the procedures for modifying the contents of your databases. The INSERT command enables you to add new data to a table. By using the UPDATE command, you can modify the values in the columns of the tables. With the CREATE TABLE...AS command provided by some versions of SQL, you can easily copy a table. If your version of SQL does not support this command, you still can copy all or part of a table by using the CREATE TABLE, INSERT, and DROP TABLE commands. If you need to remove some of or all the rows in a table, you use the DELETE command.

One of the most common ways of manipulating data is sorting. In the next chapter, you see how you can rearrange the character strings and rank numeric values with the appropriate SQL commands.

Sorting and Indexing Data

This chapter explains how to arrange your data so that you can manage it efficiently. You learn to use two important operations: sorting and indexing.

Sorting is one of the most important functions in a database management application. With the sorting function, you can rearrange the information in the order best suited for your application. In this chapter, you learn all the SQL commands and procedures for arranging lists of character strings and for ranking sets of numeric values.

Indexing, although not directly used in SQL for arranging data to be displayed, enhances data queries by providing a quick reference to the data. Indexing plays a vital part in data manipulation by speeding data retrieval. In this chapter, you learn why and when you should use the indexing operation.

Organizing Data in a Table

The contents of a base table are organized by columns and rows. The structure of the base table is specified when the table is created. As you enter data into the table, the data is stored sequentially, row by row. The actual layout and the physical location of these rows in a disk file, however, may not follow the input sequence. The rows may be scattered around on the disk—depending on where the disk has unused space. Nevertheless, you need not be concerned with disk location of data, because the location has no role in your data manipulation operations.

For practical purposes, you can imagine that the data rows are organized in the order of entry. Unless specified otherwise, entry order is the order in which the rows are displayed by a SELECT command. For example, the 11 rows of data in the *employee* table are organized in the order in which the rows were entered and appended (see fig. 7.1).

```
SELECT *
  FROM employee;
```

SS_NO	L_NAME	F_NAME	TITLE	DEPT	SALARY
123-45-6789	Smith	James J.	President	Corporate	89500.00
634-56-7890	Nelson	Harry M.	Manager	Sales	65000.00
445-67-8801	Zeller	Albert K.	Salesman	Sales	51345.00
562-87-8800	Chapman	Kirk D.	Salesman	Sales	42500.00
404-22-4568	Baker	Larry A.	Salesman	Sales	33500.00
256-09-5555	Dixon	Kathy T.	Accountant	Accounting	45000.00
458-90-3456	Frazer	Robert F.	Bookkeeper	Accounting	29400.00
777-34-6543	King	David G.	Manager	Personnel	38000.00
100-45-8021	Wong	Mike J.	Manager	MIS	44000.00
303-25-7777	Duff	Cathy B.	Secretary	Personnel	27825.00
909-10-8910	Parker	Susan C.	Trainee	MIS	28000.00

Fig. 7.1. The employee *table.*

Notice that data rows organized in this way may not be suitable for your needs. Because these rows are not arranged alphabetically, a listing of the rows in the *employee* table does not produce a satisfactory employee roster. Similarly, if you want to rank the employees by their salaries, you need to order the rows according to the *salary* values. As you can see, data rows often are rearranged when they are retrieved or displayed.

As already mentioned, two ordering operations exist: sorting and indexing. The sorting operation, using the ORDER BY command, can be used to determine the order in which the rows in a table are displayed. The sort is based on the values of one or more columns in the table. The major function of an index is for speeding the query process. The indexing operation sets up an index that tells the program where to find a given data value in the table. An *index* is a sorted list of values.

The sorting operation is carried out when you issue a command that includes an ORDER BY clause. As a result, the data rows are arranged in the order specified by the command.

On the other hand, the index information you create for a table may or may not be used by SQL in carrying out your query or display operations. SQL is often called a smart language because it finds the best (usually the quickest) way to produce the results you want and decides whether to use an index. In the latter part of this chapter, you learn how an index works and when to create an index.

Sorting Data in a Single Table

You can use a sorting operation to arrange data rows in ascending or descending order according to the contents of one or more specified columns—called *key columns*. The keyword for rearranging the data rows in a specific order is ORDER BY. This command is often used with a SELECT command in the following format:

```
   SELECT   <column list>
     FROM   <table names>
  [WHERE    <filter condition>]
 ORDER BY   <sorting keys>;
```

The sorting key specified in the ORDER BY clause of the SELECT command usually consists of one or more columns in the table. You can use one or more character columns as the sorting key. You also can use an expression (a formula) that consists of one or more numeric columns for specifying the order of the data rows.

Sorting Character Strings

In many data manipulation operations, you want to alphabetize a set of character strings, which may represent names of employees, titles of books, names of authors, and so forth. Depending on the level of cross-reference desired, you may want to arrange your rows with a simple sorting key (for one column) or with a nested sorting key (for several columns). For example, in sorting a phone list, you may want to sort the phone numbers first by their area codes and within each area code arrange the phone numbers by their prefixes. In this case, you need to specify multiple columns as your sorting key.

Sorting with a Single Key

The simplest sorting key in the ORDER BY clause is a character column in the table. For example, if you want to display the contents of the *employee* table in alphabetical order by the employees' last names, you can use the *L_name* column as a sorting key column in the ORDER BY clause. As you can see in figure 7.2, the command results in an alphabetical ordering of the values in the *L_name* column in the *employee* table.

```
   SELECT *
     FROM employee
ORDER BY l_name;
```

SS_NO	L_NAME	F_NAME	TITLE	DEPT	SALARY
404-22-4568	Baker	Larry A.	Salesman	Sales	33500.00
562-87-8800	Chapman	Kirk D.	Salesman	Sales	42500.00
256-09-5555	Dixon	Kathy T.	Accountant	Accounting	45000.00
303-25-7777	Duff	Cathy B.	Secretary	Personnel	27825.00
458-90-3456	Frazer	Robert F.	Bookkeeper	Accounting	29400.00
777-34-6543	King	David G.	Manager	Personnel	38000.00
634-56-7890	Nelson	Harry M.	Manager	Sales	65000.00
909-10-8910	Parker	Susan C.	Trainee	MIS	28000.00
123-45-6789	Smith	James J.	President	Corporate	89500.00
100-45-8021	Wong	Mike J.	Manager	MIS	44000.00
445-67-8801	Zeller	Albert K.	Salesman	Sales	51345.00

Fig. 7.2. Table sorted in alphabetical order.

When you sort your data rows with the ORDER BY clause, the rows appear rearranged, but the actual order in which the data rows are stored in the table remains unchanged. If you issue another SELECT command without the ORDER BY clause, the rows of the table are displayed in their original order.

If you want to display the contents of selected columns in a desired order according the values of the sorting key, you can specify the names of these columns in the SELECT command (see fig. 7.3). The SELECT command displays the values in the *l_name*, *f_name*, and *title* columns in the *employee* table; and the values are arranged alphabetically by the employees' last names.

```
   SELECT  l_name, f_name, title
     FROM  employee
 ORDER BY  l_name;

 L_NAME    F_NAME      TITLE
 -------   ----------  ----------
 Baker     Larry A.    Salesman
 Chapman   Kirk D.     Salesman
 Dixon     Kathy T.    Accountant
 Duff      Cathy B.    Secretary
 Frazer    Robert F.   Bookkeeper
 King      David G.    Manager
 Nelson    Harry M.    Manager
 Parker    Susan C.    Trainee
 Smith     James J.    President
 Wong      Mike J.     Manager
 Zeller    Albert K.   Salesman
```

Fig. 7.3. *Selecting and sorting columns with the SELECT command.*

In many versions of SQL, the sorting key must be included in the column list in order to be displayed in the SELECT command. That is, because the data rows are to be sorted by the values in the *l_name* key column, the *l_name* column must appear in the column list in the SELECT command. The following command may not be legal in these versions of SQL:

```
    SELECT   f_name, title
      FROM   employee
  ORDER BY   l_name;
```

Nevertheless, this command is acceptable in Oracle's SQL*Plus.

For screening data, you can add the filter conditions with the optional WHERE clause. The command selects only the data rows that satisfy the conditions and then applies the sorting operations. The command shown in figure 7.4, for example, displays a roster of the nonmanagers, which consists of the rows whose values are not equal to (!=) Manager.

```
   SELECT  f_name, l_name, title, dept
     FROM  employee
    WHERE  title!='Manager'
 ORDER BY  l_name;


 F_NAME      L_NAME    TITLE        DEPT
 ---------   -------   ----------   ----------
 Larry A.    Baker     Salesman     Sales
 Kirk D.     Chapman   Salesman     Sales
 Kathy T.    Dixon     Accountant   Accounting
 Cathy B.    Duff      Secretary    Personnel
 Robert F.   Frazer    Bookkeeper   Accounting
 Susan C.    Parker    Trainee      MIS
 James J.    Smith     President    Corporate
 Albert K.   Zeller    Salesman     Sales
```

Fig. 7.4. Screening data with the WHERE clause.

The filter condition title! = 'Manager' in the WHERE clause screens out the data rows that do not meet the condition. As a result, the sorting operation is applied to only the data rows that meet the filter condition. Therefore, the WHERE clause must be specified before the ORDER BY clause in the SELECT command. If you mistakenly put the WHERE clause after the ORDER BY clause, you get a syntax error message like SQL command not properly ended or something similar.

Sorting Data in Descending Order

When you are using the ORDER BY clause in a SELECT command, the data rows are displayed in an ascending (ASC) order, the default order. In display-ing character strings, an ascending order is the same as the order found in a dictionary (from A to Z). However, you can reverse this order and display your character strings in descending order (from Z to A) by adding the optional DESC keyword in the ORDER BY clause. Figure 7.5 shows an exam-ple of descending order.

```
    SELECT  l_name, f_name
      FROM  employee
  ORDER BY  l_name DESC;


  L_NAME    F_NAME
  -------   ---------
  Zeller    Albert K.
  Wong      Mike J.
  Smith     James J.
  Parker    Susan C.
  Nelson    Harry M.
  King      David G.
  Frazer    Robert F.
  Duff      Cathy B.
  Dixon     Kathy T.
  Chapman   Kirk D.
  Baker     Larry A.
```

Fig. 7.5. *Using the DESC keyword in an ORDER BY clause.*

Sorting Groups of Data

In addition to alphabetizing a list of character strings, the sorting operation also can group data—if values in one of the columns in the table can be used to identify the data. For example, because the values in the *dept* column in the *employee* table identify the departments to which the employees belong, the *dept* column can be used as a sorting key for grouping the data in the table. The SELECT command in figure 7.6 displays the names of the employees and the departments to which they belong.

```
    SELECT l_name, f_name, dept
       FROM employee
ORDER BY dept;

L_NAME     F_NAME       DEPT
-------    ---------    ----------

Dixon      Kathy T.     Accounting
Frazer     Robert F.    Accounting
Smith      James J.     Corporate
Wong       Mike J.      MIS
Parker     Susan C.     MIS
King       David G.     Personnel
Duff       Cathy B.     Personnel
Nelson     Harry M.     Sales
Zeller     Albert K.    Sales
Chapman    Kirk D.      Sales
Baker      Larry A.     Sales
```

Fig. 7.6. *Using the* dept *column as a sorting key.*

Notice that the rows are grouped by the values in the *dept* column. The *dept* column also shows the names of all the departments in the firm. If you want to display a list of these department names, you can use the SELECT command shown in figure 7.7.

```
    SELECT dept
       FROM employee
ORDER BY dept;

DEPT
----------
Accounting
Accounting
Corporate
MIS
MIS
Personnel
Personnel
Sales
Sales
Sales
Sales
```

Fig. 7.7. *Showing the departments.*

Sorting for Distinct Values

Notice that the department list contains redundant department names because the command listed the department names for each employee in the table. You may want to eliminate the duplicate values and produce a list of unique values by adding the necessary keyword in the SELECT command.

Use the DISTINCT keyword to select the unique values in the sorting key and eliminate duplicate values:

```
SELECT DISTINCT  <column list>
          FROM  <table name>
        [WHERE  <filter condition>]
      ORDER BY  <sorting keys>;
```

The DISTINCT keyword examines each value in the sorting key before selecting the values to be displayed. If one or more rows contain duplicate values, only the first of these values is selected and displayed. For example, if you want to produce a list of unique department names contained in the *dept* column of the *employee* table, issue the command shown in figure 7.8.

```
SELECT DISTINCT  dept
          FROM  employee
      ORDER BY  dept;

DEPT
----------
Accounting
Corporate
MIS
Personnel
Sales
```

Fig. 7.8. Using the DISTINCT keyword.

Sorting Numeric Values

Like character strings, numeric values in a sorting key can be arranged in ascending or descending order with the ORDER BY clause in the SELECT command. For example, you can rank the salaries of the employees by using the *salary* column as the sorting key in the SELECT command (see figure 7.9).

```
  SELECT  l_name, f_name, salary
    FROM  employee
ORDER BY  salary;


L_NAME    F_NAME       SALARY
-------   ---------   ---------

Duff      Cathy B.    27825.00
Parker    Susan C.    28000.00
Frazer    Robert F.   29400.00
Baker     Larry A.    33500.00
King      David G.    38000.00
Chapman   Kirk D.     42500.00
Wong      Mike J.     44000.00
Dixon     Kathy T.    45000.00
Zeller    Albert K.   51345.00
Nelson    Harry M.    65000.00
Smith     James J.    89500.00
```

Fig. 7.9. *Using the ORDER BY clause on numeric data.*

You can see that the values in the *salary* column are arranged in ascending order; that is, they are displayed from smallest to largest. This order is the default order assumed by the ORDER BY operation. If you want to produce a ranked salary list in which the name of the employee with the highest pay appears on top, add the DESC (descending) keyword to the end of the ORDER BY clause (see fig. 7.10).

```
  SELECT  l_name, f_name, title, salary
    FROM  employee
ORDER BY  salary DESC;


L_NAME    F_NAME      TITLE         SALARY
-------   ---------   ----------   ---------

Smith     James J.    President    89500.00
Nelson    Harry M.    Manager      65000.00
Zeller    Albert K.   Salesman     51345.00
Dixon     Kathy T.    Accountant   45000.00
Wong      Mike J.     Manager      44000.00
Chapman   Kirk D.     Salesman     42500.00
King      David G.    Manager      38000.00
Baker     Larry A.    Salesman     33500.00
Frazer    Robert F.   Bookkeeper   29400.00
Parker    Susan C.    Trainee      28000.00
Duff      Cathy B.    Secretary    27825.00
```

Fig. 7.10. *Arranging numeric values in descending order.*

Of course, you can add a filter condition to screen the data before applying the order operation (see fig. 7.11).

```
SELECT  l_name, f_name, title, salary
   FROM  employee
  WHERE  title='Manager'
ORDER BY  salary DESC;
```

```
L_NAME   F_NAME    TITLE     SALARY
------   --------   -------   --------
Nelson   Harry M.   Manager   65000.00
Wong     Mike J.    Manager   44000.00
King     David G.   Manager   38000.00
```

Fig. 7.11. Filtering out nonmanagers.

Sorting Dates and Times

Some versions of SQL offer a date and time date type. Although date value formats like mm-dd-yy (07-04-90) or day-month-year (15-Jun-1989) resemble character values, date sorting does not follow the rules for ordering character strings. If dates are treated as character strings, the dates would be arranged into an ascending numeric order like

05-Dec-1989
15-Jul-1985
20-Jan-1986
30-Apr-1981
30-Mar-1981

Because the dates in the example are treated as character strings, the list of dates does not follow chronological order. If the dates are treated as date values, however, they are sorted in chronological order.

30-Mar-1981
30-Apr-1981
15-Jul-1985
20-Jan-1986
05-Dec-1989

If your SQL does not enable you to use date values in a table, you cannot enter dates in the form of day-month-year (30-Mar-1981) as character strings. However, you can solve the problem by coding your dates in the form of yy/mm/dd (81/03/30). This yy/mm/dd format, sorted as a character string, arranges in chronological order:

81/03/30
81/04/30
85/07/15
86/01/20
89/12/05

When you code your dates in this form, be sure to place a zero in front of a single-digit day or month; for example, May is 05. Otherwise, the dates cannot be sorted properly. The following set of dates is arranged in ascending order if the dates are treated as character strings:

86/05/03
86/05/15
86/10/15
87/08/06
87/08/20

If your version of SQL supports a date type of data column, you do not have to worry about which date format to use (see fig. 7.12).

```
SELECT *
  FROM student
ORDER BY s_bdate;
```

S_ID	S_LNAME	S_FNAME	S_BDATE	S_SEX	S_HSGPA
S5	Freed	Barbara J.	07/28/69	F	3.15
S9	Reed	Donna E.	09/26/69	F	2.96
S2	Brown	Nancy J.	05/14/70	F	3.35
S8	Madison	George G.	08/15/70	M	2.35
S6	Gilmore	Danny S.	11/01/70	M	3.86
S10	Taylor	Bob K.	02/14/71	M	3.14
S1	Austin	Linda D.	03/08/71	F	3.98
S7	Jackson	Brad L.	04/15/71	M	2.75
S4	Ford	Harvey P.	06/12/71	M	2.60
S3	Carter	Jack F.	10/10/71	M	2.87

Fig. 7.12. Ordering by birth date.

In figure 7.12, you can see that the rows of the *student* table are displayed in ascending order according to the values in the *s_bdate* (student birth date) column, which has been specified as a date column. If you want to display dates in descending order (most recent to earliest), you can specify DESC in the ORDER BY clause (see fig. 7.13).

```
SELECT *
   FROM student
ORDER BY s_bdate DESC;
```

S_ID	S_LNAME	S_FNAME	S_BDATE	S_SEX	S_HSGPA
S3	Carter	Jack F.	10/10/71	M	2.87
S4	Ford	Harvey P.	06/12/71	M	2.60
S7	Jackson	Brad L.	04/15/71	M	2.75
S1	Austin	Linda D.	03/08/71	F	3.98
S10	Taylor	Bob K.	02/14/71	M	3.14
S6	Gilmore	Danny S.	11/01/70	M	3.86
S8	Madison	George G.	08/15/70	M	2.35
S2	Brown	Nancy J.	05/14/70	F	3.35
S9	Reed	Donna E.	09/26/69	F	2.96
S5	Freed	Barbara J.	07/28/69	F	3.15

Fig. 7.13. *Descending order by birth date.*

Sorting Null Values

Null values are treated differently in the sorting operation—depending on the version of SQL you are using. In some versions, the null values are treated as less than any non-null values, but other versions of SQL consider all null values greater than non-null values. The same rules apply for sorting null values in a numeric column. That is, when you rearrange values in a character column that contains some null values in the rows, these null values may be displayed on the top or the bottom of the display list, depending on the version of SQL.

Sorting with Multiple Keys

In the preceding examples, you see how to sort data in a table by using a single column as the sorting key. The rows in the *employee* table are sorted according to the character strings in the *l_name* column or the numeric values in the *salary* column. This sort is a *single-level sort*.

In many data management applications, you need to arrange your data with a multiple-level sort operation. For example, you may want to sort a list of phone numbers by area codes and then, within each area code, sort the phone numbers according to their prefixes. Or you may want to produce a salary report that groups the employees by the departments they belong to and then ranks the employees within each department by their salaries. These multiple-level sorts involve nested sorting operations—one sort is nested within another sort.

To create a nested sorting operation, you specify multiple keys in the ORDER BY clause of the SELECT command, as in the example in figure 7.14.

```
   SELECT  dept, l_name, f_name, title
     FROM  employee
 ORDER BY  dept, l_name;
 DEPT          L_NAME    F_NAME      TITLE
 ----------    -------   ---------   ----------
 Accounting    Dixon     Kathy T.    Accountant
 Accounting    Frazer    Robert F.   Bookkeeper
 Corporate     Smith     James J.    President
 MIS           Parker    Susan C.    Trainee
 MIS           Wong      Mike J.     Manager
 Personnel     Duff      Cathy B.    Secretary
 Personnel     King      David G.    Manager
 Sales         Baker     Larry A.    Salesman
 Sales         Chapman   Kirk D.     Salesman
 Sales         Nelson    Harry M.    Manager
 Sales         Zeller    Albert K.   Salesman
```

Fig. 7.14. A nested sort using dept *and* Lname *as the sorting keys.*

The sorting keys used in this command are the *dept* and *Lname* columns. The order in which these key columns are specified determines the sorting sequence. First, the data rows are sorted according to the values in the the first key column in the table; that is, the names and titles of the employees are arranged by the departments to which they belong. Then, within each department, the employees are arranged according to their last names.

Notice that the sorting order determines how the data is arranged and displayed. In the preceding example, the sorting order was specified as *ORDER BY dept, Lname*. If you reverse the sorting order to *ORDER BY Lname, dept*, the list is quite different, as shown in figure 7.15.

```
   SELECT dept, l_name, f_name, title
     FROM  employee
 ORDER BY l_name, dept;


 DEPT          L_NAME   F_NAME      TITLE
 ----------    ------   ---------   ----------
 Sales         Baker    Larry A.    Salesman
 Sales         Chapman  Kirk D.     Salesman
 Accounting    Dixon    Kathy T.    Accountant
 Personnel     Duff     Cathy B.    Secretary
 Accounting    Frazer   Robert F.   Bookkeeper
 Personnel     King     David G.    Manager
 Sales         Nelson   Harry M.    Manager
 MIS           Parker   Susan C.    Trainee
 Corporate     Smith    James J.    President
 MIS           Wong     Mike J.     Manager
 Sales         Zeller   Albert K.   Salesman
```

Fig. 7.15. *Changing the order in a nested sort.*

The last names are first arranged alphabetically before they are grouped into the departments.

In this example, the default ascending order is used in sorting data rows according to the values in the *dept* and *l_name* key columns. You can choose a descending order for arranging the data rows by the values in one or both of these key columns (see fig. 7.16).

```
   SELECT dept, l_name, f_name, title
     FROM  employee
 ORDER BY dept DESC, l_name;


 DEPT          L_NAME   F_NAME      TITLE
 ----------    -------  ---------   ---------
 Sales         Baker    Larry A.    Salesman
 Sales         Chapman  Kirk D.     Salesman
 Sales         Nelson   Harry M.    Manager
 Sales         Zeller   Albert K.   Salesman
 Personnel     Duff     Cathy B.    Secretary
 Personnel     King     David G.    Manager
 MIS           Parker   Susan C.    Trainee
 MIS           Wong     Mike J.     Manager
 Corporate     Smith    James J.    President
 Accounting    Dixon    Kathy T.    Accountant
 Accounting    Frazer   Robert F.   Bookkeeper
```

Fig. 7.16. *A table sorted in descending order by* dept.

The departments are displayed in descending order (from Z to A) because the DESC was add to the first sorting key, the *dept* column.

Using a nested sorting operation, you may include several columns as the sorting keys. These keys may be character columns, numeric columns, or a combination of both. Figure 7.17 shows a character column and a number column as the sorting keys.

```
SELECT dept, l_name, f_name, salary
  FROM employee
 WHERE dept='Sales'
    OR dept='Accounting'
ORDER BY dept, salary DESC;
```

DEPT	L_NAME	F_NAME	SALARY
Accounting	Dixon	Kathy T.	45000.00
Accounting	Frazer	Robert F.	29400.00
Sales	Nelson	Harry M.	65000.00
Sales	Zeller	Albert K.	51345.00
Sales	Chapman	Kirk D.	42500.00
Sales	Baker	Larry A.	33500.00

Fig. 7.17. *Using both* sales *and* salary *as sort keys.*

Notice that the data rows are first arranged by *dept* values in an ascending order (from A to Z) and then arranged by the *salary* values in a descending order (from highest to lowest). The filter conditions in the WHERE...OR clause select only employees who belong to the Accounting or Sales department.

Using Arithmetic Expressions with Numeric Columns

If a sorting key has values computed with an arithmetic operation that involves more than one column, the sorting key must be defined as an arithmetic expression. Suppose that you have a *sales* table which contains information on the unit prices and unit costs, and you want to order these units according to their unit profits. To compute the profit, you take the difference between the unit price and the unit cost as the sorting key in the ORDER BY clause:

```
SELECT   stock_no, unit_price, unit_cost
  FROM   sales
ORDER BY   unit_price-unit_cost;
```

This command appears to be quite logical. However, this command is not legal for most versions of SQL because the sorting key must appear in the list of columns to be displayed by the SELECT command. Therefore, you have to specify the arithmetic expression as a column in the column list. Then, in the ORDER BY clause, you refer to the expression by the item number from the SELECT list, as shown in figure 7.18. In the SELECT command, you note that the arithmetic expression is specified as the fourth item (or column) in the list of columns to be displayed. As a result, in the ORDER BY clause the sorting key refers to the fourth column in the column list of the SELECT clause.

```
   SELECT stock_no, unit_price, unit_cost,
          unit_price-unit_cost
     FROM sales
 ORDER BY 4;
```

STOCK_NO	UNIT_PRICE	UNIT_COST	UNIT_PRICE-UNIT_COST
HW301	295.00	230.00	65.00
SW202	250.00	183.50	66.50
SW201	275.00	195.00	80.00
SW101	350.00	250.00	100.00
SW302	490.00	360.00	130.00
HW201	590.00	459.00	131.00
SW301	520.00	385.75	134.25
HW101	850.50	650.90	199.60
HW102	1795.00	1435.00	360.00
HW402	3250.00	2600.00	650.00
HW403	3725.00	2975.00	750.00
HW401	4070.00	3250.00	820.00

Fig. 7.18. *Ordering by an arithmetic expression.*

You can add the DESC (descending) to the ORDER BY clause to rank unit profits from the largest to the smallest (see fig. 7.19).

```
    SELECT stock_no, unit_price, unit_cost,
           unit_price-unit_cost
      FROM sales
  ORDER BY 4 DESC;
```

STOCK_NO	UNIT_PRICE	UNIT_COST	UNIT_PRICE-UNIT_COST
HW401	4070.00	3250.00	820.00
HW403	3725.00	2975.00	750.00
HW402	3250.00	2600.00	650.00
HW102	1795.00	1435.00	360.00
HW101	850.50	650.90	199.60
SW301	520.00	385.75	134.25
HW201	590.00	459.00	131.00
SW302	490.00	360.00	130.00
SW101	350.00	250.00	100.00
SW201	275.00	195.00	80.00
SW202	250.00	183.50	66.50
HW301	295.00	230.00	65.00

Fig. 7.19. *Showing unit profits in descending order.*

Using Arithmetic Expressions with Character Columns

An arithmetic expression also can be used to combine multiple character columns as a sorting key for arranging character strings. For example, you may want to display and sort the employees' full names, the results of adding the values in the *l_name* and *f_name* columns. For this operation, you need to specify the full names as an arithmetic expression, *f_name + l_name*, in the ORDER BY clause in the SELECT command (see fig. 7.20).

Some versions of SQL (such as Oracle's SQL*Plus), however, do not enable you to combine character columns in an arithmetic expression. In this situation, you may be able to replace this command with the command in figure 7.21 and obtain the same results.

```
    SELECT  f_name+l_name
      FROM  employee
ORDER BY  1;

F_NAME+L_NAME
------------------
Albert K. Zeller
Cathy B.  Duff
David G.  King
Harry M.  Nelson
James J.  Smith
Kathy T.  Dixon
Kirk D.   Chapman
Larry A.  Baker
Mike J.   Wong
Robert F. Frazer
Susan C.  Parker
```

Fig. 7.20. Combining character columns as a sorting key.

```
    SELECT  f_name, l_name
      FROM  employee
ORDER BY  f_name, l_name

F_NAME       L_NAME
------------------
Albert K.    Zeller
Cathy B.     Duff
David G.     King
Harry M.     Nelson
James J.     Smith
Kathy T.     Dixon
Kirk D.      Chapman
Larry A.     Baker
Mike J.      Wong
Robert F.    Frazer
Susan C.     Parker
```

Fig. 7.21. A substitute for combining character columns.

Note that the results in the two sorting operations are identical because the sorting key used in the first command (*f_name + l_name*) is equivalent to that used in the second command (*f_name, l_name*).

If you want to eliminate the blank spaces between the first names and last names, use the TRIM function (if available) to trim off the trailing blanks (see fig. 7.22).

```
SELECT TRIM (f_name)+' '+l_name
       FROM employee
   ORDER BY 1;

EXP1
------------------
Albert K. Zeller
Cathy B. Duff
David G. King
Harry M. Nelson
James J. Smith
Kathy T. Dixon
Kirk D. Chapman
Larry A. Baker
Mike J. Wong
Robert F. Frazer
Susan C. Parker
```

Fig. 7.22. *Trimming trailing blanks.*

The TRIM function removes the trailing blanks in the *f_name* column so that only one space (the ' ') remains between the first and last names.

You can use an arithmetic expression as a sorting key, but you cannot mix character and numeric columns in an arithmetic expression. If you need to combine character and numeric columns in an arithmetic expression, you must convert the columns so that they are the same type. But you may specify multiple arithmetic expressions as sorting keys.

Sorting Data in Multiple Tables

To sort data from multiple tables, add the ORDER BY clause at the end of the SELECT command that finds the columns from the tables. For example, you can sort the data values in the *stock_no*, *part_type*, and *on_hand* columns from the *parts* and *stock* tables according to the values in the *on_hand* column (see fig. 7.23).

```
    SELECT p.stock_no, p.item_type, s.on_hand
      FROM parts p, stock s
     WHERE p.stock_no=s.stock_no
  ORDER BY p.item_type, s.on_hand;
```

P.STOCK_NO	P.ITEM_TYPE	S.ON_HAND
HW403	Computer	3
HW401	Computer	3
HW402	Computer	4
SW301	Database	2
SW302	Database	3
HW201	Monitor	4
HW102	Printer	2
HW101	Printer	8
SW101	Spreadsheet	10
HW301	V. board	6
SW202	WP	5
SW201	WP	7

Fig. 7.23. Sorting data from multiple tables.

You can see that the items are arranged first by type and then by the quantity on-hand.

Saving Ordered Data

Good databases are designed so that anticipated data needs can be satisfied without saving unnecessary duplicated data. In most cases, therefore, you do not need to save sorted data rows if they can be rearranged when they are needed. As a result, most versions of SQL provide no commands for saving sorted data into a table. For example, you cannot use the CREATE TABLE...AS command to save the data rows produced by the SELECT command with the ORDER BY clause. The following command is illegal:

```
CREATE TABLE    roster
           AS  (SELECT    f_name, L_name
                  FROM    employee
              ORDER BY    L_name);
```

Nor can you insert ordered data rows into a table with a command like the following:

```
INSERT INTO  roster
            SELECT   f_name, L_name
              FROM   employee
         ORDER BY   L_name;
```

Indexing Data

In a way, indexing involves sorting data in a table, but indexing is not used to display ordered data, as is the ORDER BY clause in a SELECT command. The major function of an indexing operation is to speed the query operation rather than to display data in a specific order.

The Power of Indexing

Those of you who have used a database management program that uses an index for arranging data elements may know how an index operation works. For example, in dBASE III Plus or dBASE IV, you can create an index file and then use the file to arrange and display data records in a given order (see fig. 7.24).

```
. USE EMPLOYEE
. INDEX ON L_NAME TO BYLAST
  100% indexed           11 Records indexed
. LIST
Record#   SS_NO       L_NAME    F_NAME     TITLE       DEPT        SALARY
      5   404-22-4568 Baker     Larry A.   Salesman    Sales       33500.00
      4   562-87-8800 Chapman   Kirk D.    Salesman    Sales       42500.00
      6   256-09-5555 Dixon     Kathy T.   Accountant  Accounting  45000.00
     10   303-25-7777 Duff      Cathy B.   Secretary   Personnel   27825.00
      7   458-90-3456 Frazer    Robert F.  Bookkeeper  Accounting  29400.00
      8   777-34-6543 King      David G.   Manager     Personnel   38000.00
      2   634-56-7890 Nelson    Harry M.   Manager     Sales       65000.00
     11   909-10-8910 Parker    Susan C.   Trainee     MIS         28000.00
      1   123-45-6789 Smith     James J.   President   Corporate   89500.00
      9   100-45-8021 Wong      Mike J.    Manager     MIS         44000.00
      3   445-67-8801 Zeller    Albert K.  Salesman    Sales       51345.00
```

Fig. 7.24. A dBASE index.

In this example, an index file named BYLAST is created by using the values in the *Lname* field (or column) of the *employee* database file (or table). After the index file is created, information in the index file is used to arrange the data in the table. As a result, when you issue the LIST command, the records (rows) in the table are displayed in the order of the indexed values.

Although SQL handles indexing differently than dBASE III Plus and other database programs handle it, the logic of the operation is the same. An index file tells the program where to find a specific item in the original table. Suppose that the contents of the index file *bylast* consist of two columns: one holds the list of last names in alphabetical order, and the other shows the record numbers:

Record#	L_NAME
5	Baker
4	Chapman
6	Dixon
10	Duff
7	Frazer
8	King
2	Nelson
11	Parker
1	Smith
9	Wong
3	Zeller

A record number is the sequential number assigned to a specific row of data in the table when the data is entered. In this index file, the key values (the last names of the employees) are shown in the *Lname* column, and the record numbers tell the program where each key value can be found in the original database file. For example, the last name King can be found in the eighth record in the database file.

An index file (table) is like an index to a book—all the subject keywords are listed alphabetically with their corresponding page numbers. If you need to find a specific keyword in the index, you can go directly to the page of the book. This method is how SQL uses an index for speeding the query operations.

To understand how an indexing operation can enhance the speed of data retrieval, examine this simple data query:

```
SELECT   *
  FROM   employee
 WHERE   Lname = 'Frazer';
```

Without the assistance of an indexing operation, the program searches each row in the *Lname* column of the *employee* table in order to find the rows whose values match the character string *Frazer*. The matching rows are displayed. If the table contains a large number of rows, this process is time-consuming.

With an index table like the *bylast* file shown earlier, however, the program quickly finds the specific rows. If the program has the reference record, or row number, the program can go directly to that record, or row, to search for the character string.

Creating an Index

An index can be set up in SQL as an index table. An index table resembles a base table. An index table contains the values of the indexed items and the information that provides a quick reference to data in the base table. You create an index by using an index key, which can be represented by one or more columns from one or more base tables. Each index should be assigned a unique name. Like a table name, an index name consists of a certain number of characters (determined by the version of SQL). The name can be letters or a combination of letters and numbers.

The SQL command for setting up an index conforms to the following format:

    CREATE INDEX   <index name>
          ON   <table name> (<index key>);

You need to know some basic rules when you are creating indexes:

❏ You can create several indexes from one table.

❏ You cannot create an index from more than one table.

❏ You can use multiple columns as an index key, but these columns must be from the same base table.

❏ You cannot use an arithmetic expression (such as *salary/12* or *Lname+f_name*) as an index key.

Indexing on a Single Column

The simplest index key involves using a single column in the base table. For example, if you want to set up an index named *bylast* for arranging the last names in the *Lname* column in the *employee* table, issue the following CREATE INDEX command:

    CREATE INDEX   bylast
          ON   employee (Lname);

All the values in the *Lname* column of the *employee* table are arranged alphabetically and saved to an index table named *bylast*. From now on, whenever you need to search the contents of the *employee* table in the *Lname* column, the program can use information in the index table to aid the search.

Because the information contained in the index table is used mainly by SQL for speeding the data search and retrieval operations, the information has little value to you. As a result, you may not be able to view the contents of an index table by using a SELECT command like

```
SELECT  *
 FROM   bylast;
```

Similarly, most SQL version provide no command to show the indexes you have created—except viewing the contents of one of the system tables such as SYSIDXS (in dBASE IV's SQL):

```
SELECT  ixname, tbname, colcount
  FROM  SYSIDXS;
```

IXNAME	TBNAME	COLCOUNT
BYLAST	EMPLOYEE	1

The names of the indexes are listed in the *ixname* column in the *sysidxs* table system, together with the names of the base tables involved. The *colcount* column shows the number of columns used in creating the index. In most SQL versions, however, the name of the column used as the index key is not saved in the system table. Therefore, you must keep track of the index keys as the indexes are created so that you remember which columns in the base tables are indexed.

You can arrange the data in descending order by adding the DESC keyword in the index command:

```
CREATE INDEX  bylast
          ON  employee (Lname DESC);
```

The decision between an ascending order index or a descending order index depends on the order you want to search and the data in the table.

Similarly, you can create an index using a numeric column as the key for arranging the data values. The index can be set up in the default ascending order like

```
CREATE INDEX  bycost
          ON  parts (unit_cost);
```

The preceding command sets up the *bycost* index that contains the ordered values in the *unit_cost* column. Therefore, when you issue the SELECT command to query the values in that column, the information in the *bycost* index may be used for speeding the data search.

Indexing on Multiple Columns

Chapter 5 explains how you can search the contents of a base table with a filter condition that involves multiple columns from the table. One data query example looks like

```
SELECT   Lname, f_name, title, dept, salary
  FROM   employee
 WHERE   title = 'Manager'
   AND   salary>35000;
```

In anticipation of this data query, you can set up an index that presorts the data rows in the *title* and *salary* columns of the *employee* table so that the query is faster. Because this query operation involves searching the values in the *title* and *salary* columns, you can create an index that uses these two columns as an index key:

```
CREATE INDEX   manager
          ON   employee (title, salary);
```

Note that you can specify multiple columns as an index key, as long as the column names are separated by commas.

Creating a Unique Index

Besides using an index to speed the data query and retrieval, you can set up a unique index for validating the values in a column. For example, in the *ss_no* column of the *employee* table, you store the social security numbers of the employees. Each number should be unique; therefore, you may want to design a data table so that no duplicate values are possible.

The format for creating a unique index is the following:

```
CREATE UNIQUE INDEX   <index name>
                 ON   <table name> (<index key>);
```

Here is an example of a unique index command:

```
CREATE UNIQUE INDEX   byssno
                 ON   employee (ss_no);
```

A unique index works much like a regular index, except that the unique index excludes all duplicate values. For example, when you issue the preceding command, the *byssno* index is set up, containing the social security numbers of the employees. From then on, each time you enter a new social security number in the *ss_no* column of the *employee* table, the new social security number is checked against old numbers. If the number is a duplicate, the program does not enter it into the table. Similarly, you cannot create a unique index on a column whose values are not unique. An attempt to do so results in an error message, such as INDEX failed – key is not DISTINCT.

A unique index is one way to validate the data to be inserted into a table when duplicate values are undesirable. This method is an effective approach to ensure the integrity of the data.

Deleting an Index

If you want to get rid of an index, you can delete it by using the DROP INDEX command:

    DROP INDEX <name of index>;

When Do You Use Indexes?

Because an index provides a quick reference to the data in the base table, the speed of data query and retrieval operations can be greatly enhanced by using a properly set up index. However, costs are associated with the index operation.

One of the costs is the disk storage required for holding the indexes. The amount of disk storage required is significant when the indexed columns are numerous and the number of data rows is large.

Another cost associated with an index is the time required to keep its contents current. When you create an index on a table, data values in the index columns are used to set up the index. When you add new values to the table or modify the values in the index columns, the values in the index must be changed accordingly.

Create only indexes you know that you will use. Otherwise, you are wasting memory resources and slowing data entry and data modifying processes. Following are some other guidelines you should consider in determining whether you should use an indexing operation:

❑ Index the columns that may be used in a filter condition in the WHERE clause of a SELECT command. For example, if you intend to search the data in the *employee* table by the employee's title, index the *title* column with

CREATE INDEX   bytitle
           ON   employee (title);

❑ If you need to validate the values in a column, set up a unique index on that column so that no duplicate values are mistakenly entered.

❑ If you intend to display and retrieve data from multiple tables that require the use of a linking key column, index the key column to speed the data search. For example, if you want to carry out the following command:

SELECT   p.stock_no, p.dscription, p.unit_cost, s.on_hand
  FROM   parts p, stock s
WHERE   p.stock_no = s.stock_no

Index the *stock_no* column in the *parts* and *stock* tables with the following two commands:

CREATE INDEX   pstockno
           ON   parts (stock_no);

CREATE INDEX   sstockno
           ON   stock (stock_no);

After the *pstockno* and *sstockno* indexes are created, values in the *stock_no* columns in the tables are arranged in ascending order and held in the indexes. When you execute the SELECT command, information from these two indexes is used to aid the data search.

❑ If a column contains few distinct values, do not index that column because the data query speed is not increased. For example, the values in the *s_sex* column in the *student* table are M or F—an index of these values is not effective.

Chapter Summary

In this chapter, the concepts of sorting and indexing are discussed. Sorting plays a vital part in database management because sorting enables you to arrange your information for a given application. Data in the form of character strings or numerical values can be arranged in ascending or descending order with the ORDER BY clause in a SELECT command. The sorting key for ordering data can consist of one or more columns in one or more tables. An arithmetic expression that involves multiple columns of the same type also can be used as a sorting key.

Indexing differs significantly from sorting. The main function of indexing is to set up a quick reference for the values in the indexed columns so that these values can be located quickly in a data query operation. In addition to the commands for creating and deleting indexes, this chapter gives important guidelines for determining when to use an index.

The next chapter discusses another important data manipulation operation: generating summary statistics for the data values stored in a table. These statistics may be in the form of average, total, row count, and so on.

Summarizing and Grouping Data

Chapter 7 discusses the SQL commands and procedures you use to arrange your data elements. In this chapter, you learn how to produce summary statistics from the data values in the database by using the SQL aggregate functions, which include COUNT(), SUM(), AVG(), MAX(), and MIN(). The examples in this chapter show you how to obtain summary values by applying these functions to selected rows in one or more tables. You select the rows to be summarized by adding the appropriate filter conditions to the SQL SELECT command or by using the grouping operation, also introduced in this chapter.

Using Aggregate Functions

An aggregate function produces summary information about a group of rows in a specified column. The following aggregate functions are supported by most SQL implementations:

Name of Function	Summary Information Returned
COUNT(), COUNT(*)	Number of data entries counted
SUM()	Sum of values in the specified column
AVG()	Average value in the specified column
MAX()	Largest value in the specified column
MIN()	Smallest value in the specified column

Also called built-in functions, aggregate functions are similar to the mathematical functions used in other programming languages. You include aggregate functions in a data query operation with the SELECT command, expressing the function in two parts: the name of the function and its argument. The argument, expressed in parentheses, is the object of the function. In most cases, the argument for an aggregate function is the name of a specified column; for example, in the statement *SUM(salary)*, the argument is

229

salary, the column whose values you want to summarize. A special case is the function COUNT(*), which has an asterisk as its argument. You also can add the keyword DISTINCT to the argument to specify distinct values for the function; COUNT(DISTINCT *dept*) is an example. The following sections explain in detail how to use these aggregate functions.

Using the COUNT( ) Function

The COUNT( ) function enables you to determine the number of data entries in a specified column. The standard format for the function is

    COUNT([DISTINCT] column_name)

The function can be a data object in a SELECT command as follows:

    SELECT   COUNT(L_name)
      FROM   employee;

The COUNT( ) function returns a single value. Unless you have qualified selected rows with filter conditions, the function counts every valid (non-null) entry in the specified column. For example, the preceding SELECT command returns a value representing the total number of data entries in the *L_name* column of the *employee* table. The returned value may be labeled differently, depending on the version of SQL you are using. If you process the command with Oracle's SQL*Plus, the results are labeled with the aggregate function as follows:

    COUNT(L_NAME)

               11

However, dBASE IV's SQL uses a less descriptive label to describe the result:

    COUNT1
         11

This chapter uses the more descriptive labels to describe the returned values, but the actual label for the returned value is not important. To determine how your SQL version labels the results, issue the command at your SQL prompt.

You can include more than one COUNT( ) function in the same SELECT command. For example, the following command uses two COUNT( ) functions to count the data entries in the *L_name* and *dept* columns:

```
SELECT  COUNT(l_name), COUNT(title)
   FROM employee;

COUNT(L_NAME)  COUNT(TITLE)
-------------  ------------
          11            10
```

To verify the count, you can list all the last names in the *Lname* column with the following simple SELECT command:

```
SELECT  Lname, title
   FROM  employee;
```

Figure 8.1 shows the results of this command.

```
L_NAME    TITLE
-------   ---------
Smith     President
Nelson    Manager
Zeller    Salesman
Chapman   Salesman
Baker     Salesman
Dixon     Accountant
Frazer    Bookkeeper
King      Manager
Wong      Manager
Duff      Secretary
Parker    Trainee
```

Fig. 8.1. *Verifying the results of the COUNT() function by using a simple SELECT command.*

Counting Null Values

Different versions of SQL count null values differently. Some versions count null values as valid values, and other implementations ignore null values. You need to experiment with the COUNT( ) function to determine how your SQL counts null values. If you want to count every value, null and non-null, you can use the COUNT(*) function as follows:

```
SELECT  COUNT(*)
   FROM employee;

COUNT(*)
--------
      11
```

Because COUNT(*) counts every row in the table, you can use this function to determine the number of rows in a table. You do not specify a column name for the COUNT(*) function because every column contains the same number of rows.

Excluding Duplicate Values

The COUNT() and COUNT(*) functions do not recognize duplicate values in the specified column. For example, if you want to find out how many different job titles you have in the firm, you can issue the following command:

```
SELECT COUNT(title)
   FROM employee;


COUNT(TITLE)
------------
          11
```

The results indicate that the *employee* table has 11 job titles. This title count is misleading, however, because it does not consider the duplicate entries, which you can see when you list all the entries in the title column. Figure 8.2 shows that the column contains several duplicate entries.

```
SELECT title
   FROM employee;

TITLE
----------
President
Manager
Salesman
Salesman
Salesman
Accountant
Bookkeeper
Manager
Manager
Secretary
Trainee
```

Fig. 8.2. A list of titles from the employee *table.*

To exclude these duplicate entries, you add the keyword DISTINCT to the COUNT argument as follows:

```
SELECT COUNT(DISTINCT title)
  FROM employee;


COUNT(DISTINCT TITLE)
---------------------
                    7
```

You can verify the result by listing the seven unique titles in the *title* column. Figure 8.3 shows the results of this command. Note that the titles are arranged alphabetically. When you add the keyword DISTINCT to the SELECT command, all rows are sorted before the counting operation takes place, so the resulting display is in alphabetical order.

```
SELECT DISTINCT title
  FROM employee;


TITLE
----------
Accountant
Bookkeeper
Manager
President
Salesman
Secretary
Trainee
```

Fig. 8.3. Verifying the results of using the COUNT(DISTINCT) function.

In some versions of SQL (such as dBASE IV's SQL), you cannot issue in the same command more than one COUNT( ) function with the DISTINCT keyword. The following command is acceptable in Oracle's SQL*Plus but not in dBASE IV's SQL:

```
SELECT  COUNT(DISTINCT title), COUNT(DISTINCT dept)
  FROM  employee;
```

In most SQL implementations, all null values are treated as duplicate values. However, you need to verify this treatment with your version of SQL.

Counting Selected Rows

When you apply the COUNT() or COUNT(*) function to a column, every row in that column is counted. If you want to limit the counting operation to a set of selected rows, you can include filter conditions in the command. For example, to determine the number of employees working in the Sales department, you can issue the following command:

```
SELECT  COUNT(l_name)
   FROM  employee
  WHERE  dept='Sales';


COUNT(L_NAME)
--------------
            4
```

To get more information about these four employees, you can issue the command shown in figure 8.4.

```
SELECT  ss_no, l_name, f_name, title
   FROM  employee
  WHERE  dept='Sales';


SS_NO          L_NAME    F_NAME      TITLE
------------   -------   ----------  --------
634-56-7890    Nelson    Harry M.    Manager
445-67-8801    Zeller    Albert K.   Salesman
562-87-8800    Chapman   Kirk D.     Salesman
404-22-4568    Baker     Larry A.    Salesman
```

Fig. 8.4. Information about employees in the Sales department.

You cannot use the same SELECT command to count the number of employees in the Sales department and display their names. Commands like the following are unacceptable:

```
SELECT   ss_no, Lname, f_name, title, COUNT(dept)
   FROM   employee
  WHERE   dept = 'Sales';
```

The COUNT() function is also useful for constructing a frequency table that divides a set of values into classes or groups. For example, the COUNT() function enables you to count the number of employees in a particular salary bracket. You can find the number of employees earning an annual salary from $20,000 to $30,000 by issuing the following command:

```
SELECT  COUNT(salary)
   FROM  employee
  WHERE  salary BETWEEN 20000 AND 30000;

COUNT(SALARY)
-------------
            3
```

The object of the counting operation is usually a column in a given table. However, the column also can be a returned value from a query operation that joins two or more tables. The *class* and *course* tables displayed in figures 8.5 and 8.6, respectively, help illustrate how this feature works.

```
C_ID  S_ID
----  ----
C1    S3
C1    S5
C1    S10
C2    S4
C2    S5
C2    S7
C2    S8
C3    S1
C3    S2
C3    S9
C4    S2
C4    S5
C4    S8
C5    S3
C5    S6
C5    S8
C5    S9
```

Fig. 8.5. The class *table.*

```
C_ID  C_TITLE   C_CREDITS  C_DESC
----  --------  ---------  --------------------
C1    ENGL 101          3  English Literature
C2    HIST 100          3  American History
C3    MATH 105          5  Calculus I
C4    PHIL 101          3  Philosophy
C5    PHYS 102          5  Physics I
```

Fig. 8.6. The course *table.*

The *class* table contains information about the classes. Each row in this table relates a course identification number with a student identification number. For example, students S3, S5, and S10 are taking course C1, as the following command verifies:

```
SELECT  s_id
  FROM  class
 WHERE  c_id='C1';


S_ID
----
S3
S5
S10
```

If you want to find the number of students taking the C1 course, you can issue the following simple command:

```
SELECT  COUNT(s_id)
  FROM  class
 WHERE  c_id='C1';


COUNT(S_ID)
-----------
          3
```

With this command, you need to know the course identification number in order to count the students in that course. What if you know the course only by its name, ENGL 101? In this case, you first must find the course identification number from the *course* table. After finding the identification number associated with the course, you can determine the number of students taking the course from the *class* table.

To find out who is taking ENGL 101, you issue the following command:

```
SELECT  x.s_id
  FROM  class x, course y
 WHERE  y.c_title = 'ENGL 101'
   AND  x.c_id = y.c_id;
```

Remember that the table aliases *x* and *y* can be used as a shortcut to refer to the *class* and *course* tables, respectively. This command returns the following student identification numbers:

```
S3
S5
S10
```

Finally, you can count the returned data entries by using the COUNT() function in the SELECT command as follows:

```
SELECT COUNT(x.s_id)
   FROM class x, course y
  WHERE y.c_title='ENGL 101'
    AND x.c_id=y.c_id;

COUNT(X.S_ID)
-------------
            3
```

Grouping Rows

You can divide rows into several groups and then count data entries in each of these groups by using the GROUP BY clause in the SELECT command. The GROUP BY clause sorts all the data entries in a column into various groups according to the grouping criteria you specify. For example, if you want to find the number of departments in the *employee* table, you can issue the following command:

```
SELECT  dept
    FROM  employee
GROUP BY  dept;
```

This command is equivalent to

```
SELECT  (DISTINCT dept)
   FROM  employee
```

The grouping criteria in this command are unique, or distinct, values in the *dept* column; in other words, each distinct value in that column constitutes a unique group. Therefore, the result of the command is a listing of department names arranged alphabetically:

```
Accounting
Corporate
MIS
Personnel
Sales
```

When you use the GROUP BY clause in a SELECT command, the grouping criterion you specify in the clause also must be a data object to be selected. For example, the following command will not be processed because the grouping criterion, the *dept* column, is not the object of the SELECT clause. Therefore, the command will not list the last and first names of the employees by department.

```
    SELECT  L_name, f_name
      FROM  employee
  GROUP BY  dept;
```

The GROUP BY clause is useful for producing summary statistics. When you include it in a SELECT command with a COUNT() function, you can count data entries in various groups. For example, if you want to know the number of employees in each department, you can issue the following command:

```
    SELECT  dept, COUNT(L_name)
      FROM  employee
  GROUP BY  dept;
```

This command first sorts the last names in the *L_name* column into groups by department. The command then counts the number of entries in each group. Figure 8.7 shows the results.

DEPT	COUNT(L_NAME)
Accounting	2
Corporate	1
MIS	2
Personnel	2
Sales	4

Fig. 8.7. *A count of last names grouped by department.*

Note that *MIS* has replaced the null value in the *dept* column for the employee named Susan Parker. No null values remain in the column. The current *employee* table is shown in figure 8.8.

SS_NO	L_NAME	F_NAME	TITLE	DEPT	SALARY
123-45-6789	Smith	James J.	President	Corporate	89500.00
634-56-7890	Nelson	Harry M.	Manager	Sales	65000.00
445-67-8801	Zeller	Albert K.	Salesman	Sales	48900.00
562-87-8800	Chapman	Kirk D.	Salesman	Sales	42500.00
404-22-4568	Baker	Larry A.	Clerk	Sales	30500.00
256-09-5555	Dixon	Kathy T.	Accountant	Accounting	45000.00
458-90-3456	Frazer	Robert F.	Bookkeeper	Accounting	28000.00
777-34-6543	King	David G.	Manager	Personnel	38000.00
100-45-8021	Wong	Mike J.	Manager	MIS	44000.00
303-25-7777	Duff	Cathy B.	Secretary	Personnel	26500.00
909-10-8910	Parker	Susan C.	Trainee	MIS	28000.00

Fig. 8.8. *The updated* employee *table.*

The GROUP BY clause is discussed in more detail later in this chapter.

Using the SUM() Function

When you need to total a set of values in a column, you use the SUM() function. This function operates on numerical values only; in other words, the argument of the function must be a numeric expression. You cannot specify a non-numeric column in the argument because a character column cannot be totaled mathematically. The format of a SUM() function is

SUM([DISTINCT] <a numeric expression>)

A numeric expression is a formula that includes one or more numeric columns and arithmetic operators (+, −, *, /) or a formula that includes only a numeric column. Numeric columns can be integer or floating columns. The following example includes only a numeric column:

SELECT   SUM(salary)
  FROM   employee;

This command totals all the values in the *salary* column of the *employee* table and returns the sum. The results, the total salary values, may appear as follows:

```
SUM(SALARY)
-----------
  494070.00
```

The SUM() function totals all values. whether they are duplicate or not. You can compute the sum of only the distinct values in the column by adding the keyword DISTINCT to the function argument as follows:

SELECT   SUM(DISTINCT salary)
  FROM   employee;

With some versions of SQL (such as dBASE IV's SQL), you can use the keyword DISTINCT when you specify a column name in the argument, but you cannot use DISTINCT when the argument is a numeric expression unless the expression consists of only one column.

The SUM() function treats null values differently, depending on the version of SQL. Most versions ignore null values or treat them as zeros when computing the sum, but you need to determine how your version handles null values. This varied treatment of null values in different versions of SQL is one reason that you should avoid using null values in your database if you want to produce results consistent among different SQL implementations.

You also can define a numeric expression as an argument of the SUM() function. For example, if you want to find the total monthly salaries paid to employees, you can issue the following command:

```
SELECT SUM(salary), SUM(salary/12)
   FROM employee;


SUM(SALARY)   SUM(SALARY/12)
-----------   --------------
  494070.00         41172.50
```

This command illustrates that you can include more than one SUM() function in the same SELECT command. The second SUM() function in this command totals the values and then divides this value (the annual salary) by 12.

You also can use the result of the function as part of a numeric expression. For example, if you decide to give your employees a bonus of five percent of their monthly salaries, you can issue the following command to determine the total amount of the bonus:

```
SELECT (SUM(salary)/12)*0.05
   FROM employee;


(SUM(SALARY)/12)*0.05
---------------------
              2058.63
```

By adding the appropriate filter conditions, you can produce a subtotal from the set of values in the specified column. For example, for budgeting purposes, you may need to know the total salaries paid to Sales department personnel. To find this figure, you can use the dept = 'Sales' filter condition in the command, as follows:

```
SELECT SUM(salary)
   FROM employee
 WHERE dept='Sales';


SUM(SALARY)
-----------
  192345.00
```

If you want to produce subtotals for more than one group, you can use the GROUP BY clause to divide your data entries into appropriate groups. For example, if you want to know the total salaries for each department in the firm, you can issue the following command:

```
    SELECT  dept, SUM(salary)
       FROM  employee
  GROUP BY  dept;
```

Figure 8.9 shows the results of this command, which first divides all the values into five groups according to the distinct values in the *dept* column. The command then totals the values in each group and returns the subtotals.

```
DEPT          SUM(SALARY)
-----------   -----------
Accounting      74400.00
Corporate       89500.00
MIS             72000.00
Personnel       65825.00
Sales          192345.00
```

Fig. 8.9. *Subtotals of salaries displayed according to department.*

Using the AVG() Function

The AVG() function returns the average of a set of values in a specified numeric expression. Like the SUM() function, the AVG() function must have a numeric expression as its argument. Of course, a numeric column is the simplest form of a numeric expression. The format of the AVG() function is

AVG([DISTINCT] <a numeric expression>)

For example, if you want to find the average salary for the employees in the firm, you issue the following command using the AVG() function:

```
SELECT  AVG(salary)
   FROM  employee;


AVG(SALARY)
-----------
   44915.45
```

If you need to compute the average for a set of values from selected rows of data, you can use the appropriate filter condition to screen the data. For example, to find the average salary for the managers in the firm, you issue the following command:

```
SELECT  AVG(salary)
   FROM  employee
  WHERE  title='Manager';


AVG(SALARY)
-----------
   49000.00
```

You also can compute averages for groups of data by using the GROUP BY clause in the command. For example, you can display the average salary of employees according to department (see fig. 8.10).

```
    SELECT dept, AVG(salary)
       FROM employee
  GROUP BY dept;


  DEPT         AVG(SALARY)
  ----------   ------------
  Accounting     37200.00
  Corporate      89500.00
  MIS            36000.00
  Personnel      32912.50
  Sales          48086.25
```

Fig. 8.10. Average salaries displayed according to department.

This command produces group averages for every department in the *employee* table. If you want to find the average salaries in certain departments, you can add a filter condition to select the departments (see fig. 8.11).

```
    SELECT dept, AVG(salary)
       FROM employee
      WHERE dept='Accounting' OR dept='Sales'
  GROUP BY dept;


  DEPT         AVG(SALARY)
  ----------   ------------
  Accounting     37200.00
  Sales          48086.25
```

Fig. 8.11. Finding average salaries of specified departments.

In this command, the filter condition first selects the data rows for the employees in the Accounting and Sales departments. These selected rows become the object of the average function; therefore, you must specify the filter condition clause before the GROUP BY clause. Most versions of SQL do not allow you to reverse the two clauses in the statement.

The AVG() function is useful for producing group averages. However, you also can produce group averages with the SUM() and COUNT() functions by dividing the values of the SUM() function by those of the COUNT() function, as shown in figure 8.12.

```
SELECT dept, SUM(salary), COUNT(salary),
       SUM(salary)/COUNT(salary)
   FROM employee
GROUP BY dept;
```

DEPT	SUM(SALARY)	COUNT(SALARY)	SUM(SALARY)/COUNT(SALARY)
Accounting	74400.00	2	37200.00
Corporate	89500.00	1	89500.00
MIS	72000.00	2	36000.00
Personnel	65825.00	2	32912.50
Sales	192345.00	4	48086.25

Fig. 8.12. Displaying averages by using the SUM( ) and COUNT( ) functions.

By expressing the function argument as a numeric expression, you can produce averages that are computed with values of the expression. This capability is useful for computing averages of derived values. For example, if you have in a table information about the prices and costs of the products you sell, you can compute their average profits and profit margins. Figure 8.13 shows the contents of a *product* table, which is used for computing the averages.

STOCK_NO	P_TYPE	P_DESC	P_COST	P_PRICE
HW101	Printer	Epson LQ-1050 printer	650.90	895.00
HW102	Printer	HP LaserJet II printer	1435.00	1950.25
HW201	Monitor	NEC MultiSync monitor	459.00	690.00
HW301	V. board	Paradise VGA board	230.00	345.50
HW401	Computer	IBM PS/2 Model 70/60MB	3250.00	4395.00
HW402	Computer	COMPAQ 386S DeskPro/40MB	2600.00	3790.00
HW403	Computer	Zenith Supersport 286/20	2975.00	4250.50
SW101	Spreadsheet	Lotus 1-2-3 Version 2.01	250.00	330.00
SW201	WP	WordPerfect 5.0	195.00	259.00
SW202	WP	Microsoft Word 5.0	183.50	225.95
SW301	Database	Paradox 3.0	385.75	495.00
SW302	Database	dBASE IV Version 1.0	360.00	450.90

Fig. 8.13. The product table.

To compute the average values of the prices, costs, and profits for these products by product type, you can use the AVG() function in the SELECT command (see fig. 8.14).

```
SELECT p_type, AVG(p_cost), AVG(p_price), AVG(p_price-p_cost)
    FROM product
GROUP BY p_type;
```

P_TYPE	AVG(P_COST)	AVG(P_PRICE)	AVG(P_PRICE-P_COST)
Computer	2941.67	4145.17	1203.50
Database	372.88	472.95	100.08
Monitor	459.00	690.00	231.00
Printer	1042.95	1422.63	379.68
Spreadsheet	250.00	330.00	80.00
V. board	230.00	345.50	115.50
WP	189.25	242.48	53.23

Fig. 8.14. *Profits computed using the AVG() function with derived values.*

If you want to compute the profit margin and express it as a percentage of the price, you can define the profit margin as a numeric expression in the AVG() function argument:

AVG(p_price-p_cost/p_price)*100

If you do not like the long label for describing the profit margin, with versions of SQL you can use a column alias to label the margin. The column alias is enclosed in single quotation marks, as shown in figure 8.15.

```
SELECT p_type,
        AVG((p_price-p_cost)/p_price)*100 'Profit Margin (%)'
    FROM product
GROUP BY by p_type;
```

P_TYPE	Profit Margin (%)
Computer	29.15
Database	21.12
Monitor	33.48
Printer	26.85
Spreadsheet	24.24
V. board	33.43
WP	21.75

Fig. 8.15. *Displaying profit margins.*

You can use the average value as a filter condition in a query operation. For example, if you want to determine how many employees earn salaries greater than the average salary, you can specify *AVG(salary)* in the filter condition.

Figure 8.16 shows the command and its results. This command first computes the average salary with the inner SELECT command in parentheses. The computed average value then becomes the value for evaluating the filter condition in the WHERE clause. Finally, the outer SELECT command selects the data rows that satisfy the filter condition.

```
SELECT l_name, f_name, title, salary
   FROM employee
  WHERE salary>(SELECT AVG(salary)
                  FROM employee);
```

L_NAME	F_NAME	TITLE	SALARY
Smith	James J.	President	89500.00
Nelson	Harry M.	Manager	65000.00
Zeller	Albert K.	Salesman	51345.00
Dixon	Kathy T.	Accountant	45000.00

Fig. 8.16. Employees whose salaries are greater than the average salary.

Using the MAX() Function

The MAX() function returns the largest value from the set of values specified in the numeric expression in the function argument. Like the SUM() and AVG() functions, the MAX() function is used only with numeric expressions and numeric columns. The format of the function is

MAX([DISTINCT] <a numeric expression>)

You can use the MAX() function to find the largest value in a numeric column with or without a filter condition. For example, to find the highest-paid employee in the firm, you issue the following command without using a filter condition:

```
SELECT MAX(salary)
   FROM employee;


MAX(SALARY)
-----------
   89500.00
```

You can use the value returned by the MAX() function to find the data elements corresponding to the largest value. For example, if you want to determine which employee earns the highest salary, you use the value returned by MAX(salary) for the filter condition, as follows:

```
SELECT l_name, f_name, title, salary
   FROM employee
  WHERE salary=(SELECT MAX(salary)
                   FROM employee)
```

L_NAME	F_NAME	TITLE	SALARY
Smith	James J.	President	89500.00

By adding the necessary filter conditions to the command, you can find the largest values from certain rows of data in the table. For example, the following command finds the highest-paid employee who is not a manager or president:

```
SELECT MAX(salary)
   FROM employee
  WHERE NOT(title='President' OR title='Manager');
```

```
MAX(SALARY)
-----------
   51345.00
```

You also can divide the data into selected groups and then find the largest values in these groups by using the MAX() function. For example, if you want to find the highest price for each product type from the *product* table, you can issue the SELECT command shown in figure 8.17.

```
SELECT p_type, MAX(p_price)
   FROM product
GROUP BY p_type;
```

P_TYPE	MAX(P_PRICE)
Computer	4395.00
Database	495.00
Monitor	690.00
Printer	1950.25
Spreadsheet	330.00
V. board	345.50
WP	259.00

Fig. 8.17. Displaying maximum prices from product categories.

If you want to determine which printer is the most expensive, you can use the MAX() function to find the highest printer price. Using this value, you then can find the information about the printer by issuing the following command:

```
SELECT stock_no, p_type, p_desc, p_price
  FROM product
 WHERE p_price=(SELECT MAX(p_price)
                  FROM product
                 WHERE p_type='Printer');
```

STOCK_NO	P_TYPE	P_DESC	P_PRICE
HW102	Printer	HP LaserJet II printer	1950.25

In this command, the inner SELECT command first finds the highest printer price. Using the highest printer price in the filter condition, the outer SELECT command then finds the information about that printer. If more than one printer has the same highest price, the command lists the information about all the printers with this price.

Using the MIN() Function

The MIN() function works in the same way as the MAX() function, but MIN() returns the smallest value from the set of values identified in the numeric expression in the function argument. The format of the function is

MIN([DISTINCT] <a numeric expression>)

For example, the following command enables you to find the lowest price listed in the *product* table:

```
SELECT MIN(p_price)
  FROM product;
```

```
MIN(P_PRICE)
------------
      225.95
```

To find the lowest price for a hardware item in the *product* table, you use a filter condition first to find the hardware items (stock numbers beginning with HW) before applying the MIN() function, as the following example illustrates:

```
SELECT  min(p_price)
  FROM  product
 WHERE  stock_no LIKE 'HW%';
```

```
MIN(P_PRICE)
------------
      345.50
```

If you want to identify the least expensive hardware item, you issue the following command:

```
SELECT  stock_no, p_type, p_desc, p_price
  FROM  product
 WHERE  p_price=(SELECT  MIN(p_price)
                   FROM  product
                  WHERE  stock_no LIKE 'HW%');
```

STOCK_NO	P_TYPE	P_DESC	P_PRICE
HW301	V. board	Paradise VGA board	345.50

Because you can specify a numeric expression as an argument in the MIN() function, you can find the least profitable items in the *product* table by defining the profit as the numeric expression *p_price-p_cost* in the MIN() function, as in figure 8.18.

```
SELECT  stock_no, p_type, p_desc, p_price,
        p_cost, p_price-p_cost
  FROM  product
 WHERE  (p_price-p_cost)=(SELECT  MIN(p_price-p_cost)
                            FROM  product);
```

STOCK_NO	P_TYPE	P_DESC	P_PRICE	P_COST	P_PRICE-P_COST
SW202	WP	Microsoft Word 5.0	225.95	183.50	42.45

Fig. 8.18. *Using a numeric expression as the argument of a MIN() function.*

Similarly, you can find the lowest profits for each product group among the software items in the *product* table by issuing the command shown in figure 8.19.

By combining the MAX() and MIN() functions and calculating the difference of the two functions, you can produce a range value. For example, the command shown in figure 8.20 gives you the salary ranges for each department in the *employee* table.

```
SELECT  p_type, MIN(p_price-p_cost)
   FROM  product
  WHERE  stock_no LIKE 'SW%'
GROUP BY  p_type;
```

```
P_TYPE         MIN(P_PRICE-P_COST)
-----------    -------------------
Database                     90.90
Spreadsheet                  80.00
WP                           42.45
```

Fig. 8.19. *Displaying the lowest prices in software product categories.*

```
SELECT  dept, MAX(salary), MIN(salary), MAX(salary)-MIN(salary)
   FROM  employee
GROUP BY  dept;
```

```
DEPT         MAX(SALARY)   MIN(SALARY)   MAX(SALARY)-MIN(SALARY)
----------   -----------   -----------   -----------------------
Accounting      45000.00      29400.00                  15600.00
Corporate       89500.00      89500.00                      0.00
MIS             44000.00      28000.00                  16000.00
Personnel       38000.00      27825.00                  10175.00
Sales           65000.00      33500.00                  31500.00
```

Fig. 8.20. *Displaying salary ranges according to department.*

Grouping Data by Using the GROUP BY Clause

The previous sections discussed how to use aggregate functions to produce summary statistics. If you do not specify any filter conditions in the SELECT command, all the rows in the table are subject to the aggregate functions. The GROUP BY clause enables you to divide the table rows into several groups and then produce group summary statistics using the aggregate functions.

When properly used, the GROUP BY clause can produce useful summary statistics. However, it must follow certain syntactic and semantic rules, which are discussed in this section. The syntax for the GROUP BY clause in the context of the SELECT statement is

```
   SELECT  <column list>
     FROM  <table name>
   [WHERE  <filter condition>]
 GROUP BY  <column list>;
   [HAVING  <grouping condition>]
 [ORDER BY  <sorting keys>]
```

In the GROUP BY clause, you specify the names of the columns by which you plan to divide your data into groups. You can include one or more aggregate functions in this column list, but you cannot use any expressions containing formulas.

The optional WHERE clause enables you to filter out data rows you do not want to subject to the grouping operation, and you can use the optional HAVING clause to select the groups to be returned by the SELECT command.

When you use the GROUP BY clause to separate data into groups, the returned group values are arranged according to the values in the grouping columns. If you want, you can use the optional ORDER BY clause to arrange the group values in a different order.

To illustrate the grouping operation, this section uses a table named *sweater*, which contains information about the sweaters in stock. It has seven columns describing the following attributes associated with the stock items:

Column Name	Attribute	Column Type
stock_no	Stock number	CHAR(4)
sw_type	Type of material (wool, blend, poly)	CHAR(5)
sw_color	Color (red, navy)	CHAR(4)
sw_size	Size (L, M, S)	CHAR(1)
sw_qty	Quantity in stock	SMALLINT
sw_price	Unit price	DECIMAL(8,2)
sw_cost	Unit cost	DECIMAL(8,2)

Figure 8.21 shows the contents of the *sweater* table.

STOCK_NO	SW_TYPE	SW_COLOR	SW_SIZE	SW_QTY	SW_PRICE	SW_COST
SW01	wool	red	L	5	65.95	45.50
SW02	wool	red	M	3	65.95	45.50
SW03	wool	red	S	4	65.95	45.50
SW04	wool	navy	L	2	62.85	43.00
SW05	wool	navy	M	0	62.85	43.00
SW06	wool	navy	S	3	62.85	43.00
SW07	blend	red	L	8	45.95	32.90
SW08	blend	red	M	3	45.95	32.90
SW09	blend	red	S	0	45.95	32.90
SW10	blend	navy	L	7	48.50	35.50
SW11	blend	navy	M	4	48.50	35.50
SW12	blend	navy	S	2	48.50	35.50
SW13	poly	red	L	0	29.95	19.95
SW14	poly	red	M	1	29.95	19.95
SW15	poly	red	S	3	29.95	19.95
SW16	poly	navy	L	2	25.95	17.90
SW17	poly	navy	M	0	25.95	17.90
SW18	poly	navy	S	5	25.95	17.90

Fig. 8.21. *The* sweater *table.*

Grouping Data without Using Aggregate Functions

The GROUP BY clause is designed mainly for working with aggregate functions. You can use it in a simple SELECT command as well, however. For example, you can find the sweater types in the table by using a SELECT command that includes a GROUP BY clause

Figure 8.22 shows the results of this command, which does not include any aggregate functions. With the GROUP BY clause, the command first divides the data in the *sweater* table into groups according to the distinct values in the *sw_type* column. The command then returns a distinct value from each group, listing three values that represent the sweater types. Note that these values are arranged alphabetically in ascending order.

```
    SELECT  sw_type
      FROM  sweater
  GROUP BY  sw_type;


SW_TYPE
-------
blend
poly
wool
```

Fig. 8.22. *Sweater types displayed using a GROUP BY clause without an aggregate function.*

When no aggregate function is involved, the same effect as the GROUP BY clause can be achieved by using the DISTINCT keyword in the SELECT clause and an ORDER BY clause. The following command produces the same results as the SELECT command that uses the GROUP BY clause:

```
  SELECT  DISTINCT sw_type
    FROM  sweater
ORDER BY  sw_type;
```

Using Subgroups

You also can use the GROUP BY clause to produce subgroups by using multiple columns as the grouping criteria. For example, in the *sweater* table, stock items can first be divided into groups by type. Within each type, the items can be further divided into subgroups by color. The command in figure 8.23 accomplishes this subdivision.

```
    SELECT  sw_type, sw_color
      FROM  sweater
  GROUP BY  sw_type, sw_color;


SW_TYPE  SW_COLOR
-------  --------
blend    navy
blend    red
poly     navy
poly     red
wool     navy
wool     red
```

Fig. 8.23. *Items displayed according to type and color.*

You can have as many levels of subgroups as you want; the only restriction is that the columns you use for grouping also must be included in the items to be selected. For example, if you want to group the data in the *sweater* table by color, type, and size, you must include these three columns in the column list of the SELECT command (see fig. 8.24).

```
SELECT  sw_color, sw_type, sw_size
    FROM  sweater
GROUP BY  sw_color, sw_type, sw_size;
```

```
SW_COLOR SW_TYPE SW_SIZE
------------------------
navy     blend   L
navy     blend   M
navy     blend   S
navy     poly    L
navy     poly    M
navy     poly    S
navy     wool    L
navy     wool    M
navy     wool    S
red      blend   L
red      blend   M
red      blend   S
red      poly    L
red      poly    M
red      poly    S
red      wool    L
red      wool    M
red      wool    S
```

Fig. 8.24. Items displayed according to color, type, and size.

Using the WHERE Clause

By using the appropriate filter conditions in the SELECT command, you can limit the grouping operation to specified data. For example, if you want to find out which sweaters are out of stock, you can issue one of two SELECT statements. The first command identifies individually each out-of-stock item (see fig. 8.25):

```
SELECT stock_no, sw_type, sw_color, sw_size
  FROM sweater
 WHERE sw_qty=0;


STOCK_NO  SW_TYPE  SW_COLOR  SW_SIZE
--------  -------  --------  -------

SW05      wool     navy      M
SW09      blend    red       S
SW13      poly     red       L
SW17      poly     navy      M
```

Fig. 8.25. Displaying out-of-stock items.

you can find similar information for these out-of-stock items by using the GROUP BY clause to arrange them by color (see fig. 8.26).

```
   SELECT sw_color, sw_type, sw_size
     FROM sweater
    WHERE sw_qty=0
 GROUP BY sw_color, sw_type, sw_size;


SW_COLOR  SW_TYPE  SW_SIZE
--------  -------  -------

navy      poly     M
navy      wool     M
red       blend    S
red       poly     L
```

Fig. 8.26. Displaying out-of-stock items according to color.

Grouping Data by Using Aggregate Functions

Although you can use the GROUP BY clause without any aggregate functions in a SELECT command, the clause is mainly designed for working with aggregate functions. The power of the clause can be appreciated fully when you use it to produce useful group summary statistics.

In the previous sections, you have learned how to generate summary statistics (count, sum, average, and maximum and minimum values) from grouped data. This section summarizes the discussion of the GROUP BY clause. In addition, you learn how to use the GROUP BY clause to produce summary statistics from multilevel groups. You also learn how to qualify your groups by using the HAVING clause.

Producing Group Statistics

By specifying the grouping criteria in the GROUP BY clause, you can divide the data into groups. After these groups are formed, you then can apply any aggregate function to the data values in these groups. For example, by using the *sw_type* column as the grouping criterion in the GROUP BY clause, you can divide all the sweaters into three groups (blend, poly, and wool). Using the data entries in these groups, you then can compute the average prices of the items in each group. The following command illustrates:

```
SELECT  sw_type, AVG(sw_price)
   FROM  sweater
GROUP BY  sw_type;


SW_TYPE  AVG(SW_PRICE)
-------  -------------
blend          47.23
poly           27.95
wool           64.40
```

Note that the AVG() function returns a single value for each data group. These returned values are summary statistics obtained from the data values in these groups; they cannot be identified with a single data row. Therefore, all SELECT items in the command must be GROUP BY columns or aggregate functions. For example, including *stock_no* as a value to be returned by the SELECT command is illegal:

```
SELECT  stock_no, sw_type, AVG(sw_price)
   FROM  sweater
GROUP BY  sw_type;
```

Using Subgroups

With the GROUP BY clause, you can form groups within groups. After these subgroups are formed, you can produce summary statistics by using the data elements in these subgroups. To produce summary statistics of subgroups, you specify grouping columns in the GROUP BY clause, separating the grouping columns in the clause with commas, and moving from large groups to smaller groups. For example, if you want to divide all the sweaters in stock into two groups by color (red and navy) and then group each color by size, producing summary statistics from these subgroups, you can issue the command shown in figure 8.27. The command returns the average price and average cost for each subgroup.

```
    SELECT  sw_color, sw_type, AVG(sw_price), AVG(sw_cost)
      FROM  sweater
  GROUP BY  sw_color, sw_type;
```

SW_COLOR	SW_TYPE	AVG(SW_PRICE)	AVG(SW_COST)
navy	blend	48.50	35.50
navy	poly	25.95	17.90
navy	wool	62.85	43.00
red	blend	45.95	32.90
red	poly	29.95	19.95
red	wool	65.95	45.50

Fig. 8.27. *Displaying summary statistics for subgroups.*

You also can produce a summary inventory report showing the average inventory values (by multiplying *sw_qty* with *sw_cost*) for each group by using the command shown in figure 8.28.

```
    SELECT  sw_type, sw_color, AVG(sw_qty),
            AVG(sw_cost), AVG(sw_qty)*AVG(sw_cost)
      FROM  sweater
  GROUP BY  sw_type, sw_color;
```

SW_TYPE	SW_COLOR	AVG(SW_QTY)	AVG(SW_COST)	AVG(SW_QTY)*AVG(SW_COST)
blend	navy	4.33	35.50	153.83
blend	red	3.67	32.90	120.63
poly	navy	2.33	17.90	41.77
poly	red	1.33	19.95	26.60
wool	navy	1.67	43.00	71.67
wool	red	4.00	45.50	182.00

Fig. 8.28. *Displaying average inventory values.*

Using the ORDER BY Clause

When you use the GROUP BY clause to divide data into groups and produce summary statistics, the returned values are not necessarily in the order you want. In this case, you can sort the summary statistics into a different order by using the ORDER BY clause. For example, if you want to sort the sweaters that have been grouped by their colors and types according to average price, you can issue the command shown in figure 8.29.

The ORDER BY clause specifies the sorting order. Because the sorting key in the clause is not a column in the *sweater* table, you must refer to it by its position number in the selected items. (Chapter 7 explains how to specify the ordering keys.) When the command is processed, you get the results shown in figure 8.29.

```
    SELECT  sw_color, sw_type, AVG(sw_price)
      FROM  sweater
  GROUP BY  sw_color, sw_type
  ORDER BY  3;


SW_COLOR  SW_TYPE  AVG(SW_PRICE)
--------  -------  -------------
navy      poly           25.95
red       poly           29.95
red       blend          45.95
navy      blend          48.50
navy      wool           62.85
red       wool           65.95
```

Fig. 8.29. Ordering results according to price.

Note that the items are arranged by average prices in ascending order, not by the values in the *sw_color* column. An important point to remember when you are including the ORDER BY clause with GROUP BY in the SELECT command is that the ORDER BY clause must appear *after* the GROUP BY clause. Otherwise, your command will not be processed.

When you use the ORDER BY clause, values are arranged in ascending order by default. If you want to show the results in descending order, you can add the keyword DESC to the sorting key (see fig. 8.30).

```
    SELECT  sw_color, sw_type, AVG(sw_price)
      FROM  sweater
  GROUP BY  sw_color, sw_type
  ORDER BY  3 DESC;


SW_COLOR  SW_TYPE  AVG(SW_PRICE)
--------  -------  -------------
red       wool           65.95
navy      wool           62.85
navy      blend          48.50
red       blend          45.95
red       poly           29.95
navy      poly           25.95
```

Fig. 8.30. Displaying the items in descending order according to price.

Using the WHERE Clause

In a query operation, you can define filter conditions in the WHERE clause to qualify the data rows to be selected. You also can use filter conditions with the GROUP BY clause to select the data rows on which you want the command to work. The WHERE clause always acts first to screen the data rows before data elements are sorted by the GROUP BY operations. For example, the command in figure 8.31 groups all the out-of-stock items according to their colors and sizes by using sw_qty = 0 as the filter condition.

```
   SELECT  sw_color, sw_size
     FROM  sweater
    WHERE  sw_qty=0
 GROUP BY  sw_color, sw_size;


SW_COLOR  SW_SIZE
--------  -------
navy      M
red       L
red       S
```

Fig. 8.31. Displaying out-of-stock items by color and size.

Using the HAVING Clause

The example in figure 8.31 shows that you can use a WHERE clause to screen the data rows. The filter conditions in the WHERE clause can be a combination of columns and numeric expressions, but you cannot include aggregate functions in the WHERE clause. For example, you cannot issue the following command:

```
   SELECT  sw_type, sw_color, AVG(sw_price)
     FROM  sweater
    WHERE  AVG(sw_price)>35.95
 GROUP BY  sw_type;
```

This command is unacceptable because the data rows are first screened using the filter condition specified in the WHERE clause. At this point, the value for the aggregate function AVG() is unknown, so the data screening process cannot be carried out. The group averages are computed only after the items are divided into groups by the GROUP BY clause. A solution to this problem is to use the HAVING clause to define the filter condition that includes the aggregate value (see fig. 8.32).

```
  SELECT  sw_type, sw_color, AVG(sw_price)
    FROM  sweater
GROUP BY  sw_type, sw_color
  HAVING  AVG(sw_price)>35.95;
```

SW_TYPE	SW_COLOR	AVG(SW_PRICE)
blend	navy	48.50
blend	red	45.95
wool	navy	62.85
wool	red	65.95

Fig. 8.32. *Displaying data using a HAVING clause.*

For example, you can use the HAVING clause in the SELECT command to find the items (grouped by their sizes) that have an average stock level of less than three (see fig. 8.33).

```
  SELECT  sw_size, AVG(sw_qty)
    FROM  sweater
GROUP BY  sw_size
  HAVING  AVG(sw_qty)<3;
```

SW_SIZE	AVG(SW_QTY)
M	1.83
S	2.83

Fig. 8.33. *Grouping by size items that have an average stock level of less than three.*

As with a filter condition in the WHERE clause, you can include logical operators ($=$, $<>$, $>$, $>=$, $<$, $<=$, BETWEEN, and so on) and connectors (AND, OR, NOT) in the HAVING clause to define the group selection conditions. The command is illustrated in figure 8.34.

```
   SELECT sw_type, sw_color, AVG(sw_price), AVG(sw_price-sw_cost)
     FROM sweater
 GROUP BY sw_type, sw_color
   HAVING AVG(sw_price-sw_cost)>13.00
      AND AVG(sw_price)>39.95
 ORDER BY 4 DESC;


 SW_TYPE  SW_COLOR  AVG(SW_PRICE)  AVG(SW_PRICE-SW_COST)
 -------  --------  -------------  ---------------------

 wool     red           65.95              20.45
 wool     navy          62.85              19.85
 blend    red           45.95              13.05
```

Fig. 8.34. Displaying data by using logical operators and connectors in the HAVING clause.

You also can use a value returned from an aggregate function as a conditional value in the HAVING clause (see fig. 8.35).

```
   SELECT sw_type, sw_color, AVG(sw_price-sw_cost)
     FROM sweater
 GROUP BY sw_type, sw_color
   HAVING AVG(sw_price-sw_cost) > (SELECT AVG(sw_price-sw_cost)
                                     FROM sweater);


 SW_TYPE  SW_COLOR  AVG(SW_PRICE-SW_COST)
 -------  --------  ---------------------
 wool     navy             19.85
 wool     red              20.45
```

Fig. 8.35. Displaying data by using a value returned from an aggregate function as a conditional value in the HAVING clause.

This command finds the sweaters (grouped by type and color) with an average profit (price – cost) greater than the overall average profit. When the command is processed, the overall average profit is returned by the inner SELECT command. If you process the inner SELECT command alone, you get the following results:

```
 SELECT AVG(sw_price-sw_cost)
   FROM sweater;


 AVG(SW_PRICE-SW_COST)
 ---------------------
            14.07
```

The returned value (14.07) is then used as the group selection condition in the HAVING clause. At this point, the original SELECT command is equivalent to

```
    SELECT  sw_type, sw_color, AVG(sw_price − sw_cost)
      FROM  sweater
  GROUP BY  sw_type, sw_color
    HAVING  AVG(sw_price − sw_cost)>14.07;
```

You can verify the results from this command by looking at the average profits for each group (see fig. 8.36).

```
    SELECT  sw_type, sw_color, AVG(sw_price-sw_cost)
      FROM  sweater
  GROUP BY  sw_type, sw_color;

SW_TYPE   SW_COLOR   AVG(SW_PRICE-SW_COST)
-------   --------   ---------------------
blend     navy                       13.00
blend     red                        13.05
poly      navy                        8.05
poly      red                        10.00
wool      navy                       19.85
wool      red                        20.45
```

Fig. 8.36. *Displaying the average profits to verify the data displayed in fig. 8.35.*

Note that only the last two groups have average profits greater than the overall profit average of 14.07.

Chapter Summary

This chapter focuses on the aggregate functions of COUNT(), SUM(), AVG(), MAX(), and MIN(). From the examples presented, you have learned how to produce useful summary statistics with these aggregate functions. You can apply these functions to all the rows in a specified column and to certain subsets of these rows by using the WHERE clause. You also can divide your data into groups with the GROUP BY clause before applying the aggregate functions to produce group summary statistics. In addition, you can use the ORDER BY clause to obtain a particular arrangement of the results. Finally, the HAVING clause enables you to select and display only the group statistics that are of interest to you.

All the aggregate functions discussed in this chapter can be applied to data elements in one or more tables. If the data elements are stored in more than one table, you need to join the tables before applying the aggregate function. In the next chapter, you learn how to join your data tables properly.

Joining Data Tables

In the last chapter, you learned how to produce summary statistics by using the aggregate functions. You can apply these functions to data elements in any specified columns. If the specified columns are in different tables, however, before you can apply the aggregate functions, you need to join the tables. In this chapter, you learn how to use the commands and procedures for joining data from several tables. When you have joined various columns from different tables, you can treat the joined columns as if they were from the same table. You can apply all the SQL commands you have learned in the previous chapters.

Reasons for Joining Tables

Joining tables is one of the most important functions provided by a relational query language like SQL. This capability provides an effective means for retrieving and manipulating data from different tables by using a simple command.

As discussed in Chapter 3, when you design a relational database, you should keep your data tables as simple as possible. A simple table is easy to understand and maintain. A good relational database design organizes your data elements logically in tables according to the elements' associations with unique data entities. Therefore, databases normally contain many small tables. In order to manipulate and retrieve information from these tables, you must join them.

In designing your database, you should structure your data tables so that they are flexible enough to accommodate most future data applications. One way to accomplish this goal is to organize your data in several tables, each of which stores information about certain attributes of a data entity. In these tables, you can set up the primary and foreign keys to provide the necessary links between the tables. Then when you need information from more than one table, you can join the tables with the appropriate keys.

263

In addition, to avoid difficulties in data maintenance, you need to split large tables into several smaller tables through the normalization process. A rule governing the fifth normal form requires that if you divide a table into several tables, you must be able to recreate the original table by joining the separate tables. If you want to manage your data efficiently in a relational database, therefore, you must learn how to join data from several tables.

Ways of Joining Tables

In a simple database, you may use only one table for storing your data. In this case, you have no need for the join operation. But most practical databases require several tables for organizing the data elements. With these databases, you most likely will need to retrieve information from more than one table. A major function of joining tables is to combine columns from different tables so that you can retrieve and manipulate information from these columns as if they were in the same table.

Tables can be joined in several different ways. Not every implementation of SQL supports all the join techniques. A common way to join two tables is using the equijoin. In this technique, two tables are linked by a common column. Other types of joins also can be useful. In the following sections, you learn the logic behind these methods of joining tables.

Join Syntax

Although joining tables is one of the most important functions of SQL, no explicit join command is available. Instead, all the join operations are carried out in the context of the SELECT statement. The end result of a join operation is that you can select any column from any of the tables you join in the same statement. You can join as many tables as you want simply by specifying their names in the FROM clause. In the WHERE clause, you can specify the necessary joining condition. The basic format of a SELECT statement for joining two or more tables is

```
SELECT   <column list>
  FROM   <table list>
 WHERE   <joining condition>;
```

In the column list, you identify the names of the columns, separated by commas. In the table list, you specify the names of two or more tables you want to join. You also can define the table aliases in the table list and refer to these tables by their aliases. The joining condition in the WHERE clause specifies conditions for the join; the condition can be described as follows:

WHERE table1.column_name <join operator> table2.column_name

The join operator defines the relationship between the two items you are joining.

The most common join operator is the equal sign (=). Other join operators include

!=, <>	not equal
>	greater than
>=	greater than or equal to
<	less than
<=	less than or equal to
BETWEEN	
LIKE	
NOT	

An example of a SELECT statement for joining two tables is

SELECT   c_title, t_lname, t_rank
  FROM   course, teacher
WHERE   course.t_id = teacher.t_id;

The *course* and *teacher* tables, used in the command, are shown in figure 9.1.

The sample command joins the *course* and *teacher* tables by using a common column named *t_id* (teacher ID). The names of the two tables are specified in the FROM clause. The joining condition in the WHERE clause defines the column for linking the two tables. This command is an example of an equijoin because the rows are linked only when the values in the joining columns in the two tables are equal. The items selected are columns from both tables:

Column Name	Source Table
c_title	course
t_lname	teacher
t_rank	teacher

Course table:

```
C_ID   C_TITLE    C_CREDITS   C_DESC                T_ID
----   --------   ---------   ------------------    ----
C1     ENGL 101          3    English Literature    T2
C1     ENGL 101          3    English Literature    T5
C2     HIST 100          3    American History      T1
C3     MATH 105          5    Calculus I            T3
C4     PHIL 101          3    Philosophy            T4
C5     PHYS 102          5    Physics I             T3
```

Teacher table:

```
T_ID   T_LNAME     T_FNAME      T_RANK            T_OFFICE   T_PHONE
----   --------    ----------   ---------------   -------------------
T1     Franklin    Benjamin     Professor         West 103   235-1234
T2     Hemingway   Ernest M.    Professor         West 301   287-6666
T3     Newton      Isaac        Associate Prof.   East 150   635-1414
T4     Quine       Willard V.   Professor         East 250   636-2626
T5     Shaw        George B.    Assistant Prof.   West 104   235-7878
```

Fig. 9.1. The course *and* teacher *tables.*

If the column names are unique (not common to the tables to be joined), you can specify the column names as they are in the preceding SELECT clause. Otherwise, you need to add the name of the source table in front of the column name, separated by a period (.). To avoid ambiguity, you can always put the table names in front of the column names (see fig. 9.2).

```
SELECT course.c_title, teacher.t_lname, teacher.t_rank
  FROM course, teacher
 WHERE course.t_id=teacher.t_id;
```

```
COURSE.C_TITLE    TEACHER.T_LNAME    TEACHER.T_RANK
---------------   ----------------   ----------------
ENGL 101          Hemingway          Professor
ENGL 101          Shaw               Assistant Prof.
HIST 100          Franklin           Professor
MATH 105          Newton             Associate Prof.
PHIL 101          Quine              Professor
PHYS 102          Newton             Associate Prof.
```

Fig. 9.2. An alternative way of joining tables.

the joining condition, every row in the first table is linked to every row in the second table. The result, in the form of a Cartesian product, is all the possible matches you can make by using every row in each table.

For an illustration of the Cartesian product, look at a sample database that contains two tables: *usa* and *spain*. The *usa* and *spain* tables hold information about tennis players from the United States and Spanish teams, respectively. Each table has three columns describing the attributes of the players:

Column name	*Description*
Player	Name of the player
Skill	Skill level (Advanced, Beginner)
Sex	Gender (Male, Female)

The contents of these two tables are shown in figure 9.5.

```
USA table:


PLAYER  SKILL      SEX
------  --------   ------

Albert  Advanced   Male
Brenda  Beginner   Female
Candy   Advanced   Female
Daniel  Beginner   Male


Spain table:


PLAYER    SKILL      SEX
--------  --------   ------

Amilia    Beginner   Female
Fernando  Advanced   Male
Jose      Beginner   Male
Maria     Advanced   Female
```

Fig. 9.5. *The* usa *and* spain *tables.*

From the *usa* table, note that the team has four members, two advanced and two beginners. Male and female players are equally divided on the team. The Spanish team has the same number of members, with the same breakdown in skill level and gender.

You can join the members in the two tables in several ways, based on the joining condition you define in the WHERE clause. If you do not specify any joining condition in the SELECT command, it returns a Cartesian product representing all the possible matches between all the members in each team. This result can be seen in the command and display in figure 9.6.

```
SELECT *
  FROM usa, spain;
```

USA. PLAYER	USA. SKILL	USA. SEX	SPAIN. PLAYER	SPAIN. SKILL	SPAIN. SEX
Albert	Advanced	Male	Amilia	Beginner	Female
Albert	Advanced	Male	Fernando	Advanced	Male
Albert	Advanced	Male	Jose	Beginner	Male
Albert	Advanced	Male	Maria	Advanced	Female
Brenda	Beginner	Female	Amilia	Beginner	Female
Brenda	Beginner	Female	Fernando	Advanced	Male
Brenda	Beginner	Female	Jose	Beginner	Male
Brenda	Beginner	Female	Maria	Advanced	Female
Candy	Advanced	Female	Amilia	Beginner	Female
Candy	Advanced	Female	Fernando	Advanced	Male
Candy	Advanced	Female	Jose	Beginner	Male
Candy	Advanced	Female	Maria	Advanced	Female
Daniel	Beginner	Male	Amilia	Beginner	Female
Daniel	Beginner	Male	Fernando	Advanced	Male
Daniel	Beginner	Male	Jose	Beginner	Male
Daniel	Beginner	Male	Maria	Advanced	Female

Fig. 9.6. *A Cartesian product produced by omitting a joining condition.*

In your version of SQL, the order used in displaying the results may be different from figure 9.6. Both versions should display the same information, however.

The results represent all the possible single matches you can make by choosing one member from each team, regardless of skill level or gender. Each player on the U.S.A. team is matched with every player on the Spanish team. For example, Albert on the U.S.A. team is linked with Amilia, Fernando, Jose, and Maria on the Spanish team. In other words, each row in the *usa* table is linked with each row in the *spain* table. Because each table contains 4 rows, 16 rows (the product of multiplying 4 by 4) are returned from the join command.

Although the Cartesian product in this example can be used to show all the possible single matches you can play with players from the two teams, the Cartesian product is not useful in most applications. A Cartesian product usually occurs because the joining condition is missing or is specified incorrectly. For example, to join the *course* and *teacher* tables without specifying the joining condition, you issue the following SELECT command:

```
SELECT  *
FROM  course, teacher;
```

The Cartesian product from this command includes all the columns from the *course* and *teacher* tables. (The results take up too much space to show here. Therefore, the command is modified to select only a few columns from these two table so that the results will fit into fig. 9.7.)

```
SELECT c_title, t_lname, t_fname, t_rank
  FROM course, teacher;
C_TITLE    T_LNAME      T_FNAME      T_RANK
--------   ---------    ----------   ----------------
ENGL 101   Franklin     Benjamin     Professor
ENGL 101   Hemingway    Ernest M.    Professor
ENGL 101   Newton       Isaac        Associate Prof.
ENGL 101   Quine        Willard V.   Professor
ENGL 101   Shaw         George B.    Assistant Prof.
ENGL 101   Franklin     Benjamin     Professor
ENGL 101   Hemingway    Ernest M.    Professor
ENGL 101   Newton       Isaac        Associate Prof.
ENGL 101   Quine        Willard V.   Professor
ENGL 101   Shaw         George B.    Assistant Prof.
HIST 100   Franklin     Benjamin     Professor
HIST 100   Hemingway    Ernest M.    Professor
HIST 100   Newton       Isaac        Associate Prof.
HIST 100   Quine        Willard V.   Professor
HIST 100   Shaw         George B.    Assistant Prof.
MATH 105   Franklin     Benjamin     Professor
MATH 105   Hemingway    Ernest M.    Professor
MATH 105   Newton       Isaac        Associate Prof.
MATH 105   Quine        Willard V.   Professor
MATH 105   Shaw         George B.    Assistant Prof.
PHIL 101   Franklin     Benjamin     Professor
PHIL 101   Hemingway    Ernest M.    Professor
PHIL 101   Newton       Isaac        Associate Prof.
PHIL 101   Quine        Willard V.   Professor
PHIL 101   Shaw         George B.    Assistant Prof.
PHYS 102   Franklin     Benjamin     Professor
PHYS 102   Hemingway    Ernest M.    Professor
PHYS 102   Newton       Isaac        Associate Prof.
PHYS 102   Quine        Willard V.   Professor
PHYS 102   Shaw         George B.    Assistant Prof.
```

Fig. 9.7. A Cartesian product producing meaningless results.

From the resulting Cartesian product, you can see that each row in the *course* table is matched with every row in the *teacher* table. Information presented in these rows does not make sense. Because each course is taught by only certain instructors, linking each course with every instructor in the *teacher* table is not meaningful.

Joins Based on Equality

The most common way to join two tables is to use an *equijoin*. The join is based on values in the column common to both tables. The column serves as a joining key. When you are joining two tables, you can define one or more joining conditions in the WHERE clause. You want to link the data rows in the first table to the data rows of the second table only when both rows have the same value in the joining key column.

Single-Column Equijoins

If you look again at the *usa* and *spain* tables, you will note that both tables have *skill* and *sex* columns. Either of these two columns can provide the necessary link between the two tables in an equijoin. For example, you can join the two tables by using the *skill* column as the joining column. When the rows in these two tables have the same values in the *skill* column, the rows are linked. Figure 9.8 shows the SELECT command for joining the two tables by using the *skill* column. (As pointed out previously, different versions of SQL display the same information in a different format or a different order.)

```
SELECT *
  FROM usa, spain
 WHERE usa.skill=spain.skill;
```

USA. PLAYER	USA. SKILL	USA. SEX	SPAIN. PLAYER	SPAIN. SKILL	SPAIN. SEX
Albert	Advanced	Male	Fernando	Advanced	Male
Albert	Advanced	Male	Maria	Advanced	Female
Brenda	Beginner	Female	Amilia	Beginner	Female
Brenda	Beginner	Female	Jose	Beginner	Male
Candy	Advanced	Female	Fernando	Advanced	Male
Candy	Advanced	Female	Maria	Advanced	Female
Daniel	Beginner	Male	Amilia	Beginner	Female
Daniel	Beginner	Male	Jose	Beginner	Male

Fig. 9.8. A single-column equijoin based on the skill *column.*

The equijoin produces all the single matches in which both players are equal in skill level. This result is an example of a simple join based on an equality joining condition.

In the results in figure 9.8, note that the two players in each match may not be the same gender. For example, in the second match, a male player, Albert, plays a female player, Maria. If you want to have both players of the same gender, regardless of their skill levels, you can join the tables by using the *sex* column as the joining key (see fig. 9.9).

```
SELECT *
  FROM usa, spain
 WHERE usa.sex=spain.sex;
```

USA. PLAYER	USA. SKILL	USA. SEX	SPAIN. PLAYER	SPAIN. SKILL	SPAIN. SEX
Albert	Advanced	Male	Fernando	Advanced	Male
Albert	Advanced	Male	Jose	Beginner	Male
Brenda	Beginner	Female	Amilia	Beginner	Female
Brenda	Beginner	Female	Maria	Advanced	Female
Candy	Advanced	Female	Amilia	Beginner	Female
Candy	Advanced	Female	Maria	Advanced	Female
Daniel	Beginner	Male	Fernando	Advanced	Male
Daniel	Beginner	Male	Jose	Beginner	Male

Fig. 9.9. *A single-column equijoin based on the* sex *column.*

The two players in each match are the same gender, but their skill levels may be different.

Multicolumn Equijoins

The two preceding examples use a single column (*skill* or *sex*) in an equijoin for linking the *usa* and *spain* tables. If you want to ensure that the two players in each match are equal in skill and the same in gender, you add another joining condition in the WHERE clause:

```
SELECT *
  FROM usa, spain
 WHERE usa.skill=spain.skill
   AND usa.sex=spain.sex;
```

This condition produces the following results:

USA. PLAYER	USA. SKILL	USA. SEX	SPAIN. PLAYER	SPAIN. SKILL	SPAIN. SEX
Albert	Advanced	Male	Fernando	Advanced	Male
Brenda	Beginner	Female	Amilia	Beginner	Female
Candy	Advanced	Female	Maria	Advanced	Female
Daniel	Beginner	Male	Jose	Beginner	Male

The logical connector AND used to specify more than one joining condition in the statement.

Natural Joins

When you select all the columns from the tables in an equijoin, the joining columns are duplicated in the results. To avoid the duplicate columns, you use a natural join. A *natural join* is obtained by making an equijoin on the joining column of two tables and then removing the duplicate of the joining column. For example, when you make an equijoin between the *usa* and *spain* tables by using the *skill* column as the linking column, the results show the joining column twice (see fig. 9.10).

```
SELECT *
  FROM usa, spain
  WHERE usa.skill=spain.skill;
```

USA. PLAYER	USA. SKILL	USA. SEX	SPAIN. PLAYER	SPAIN. SKILL	SPAIN. SEX
Albert	Advanced	Male	Fernando	Advanced	Male
Albert	Advanced	Male	Maria	Advanced	Female
Brenda	Beginner	Female	Amilia	Beginner	Female
Brenda	Beginner	Female	Jose	Beginner	Male
Candy	Advanced	Female	Fernando	Advanced	Male
Candy	Advanced	Female	Maria	Advanced	Female
Daniel	Beginner	Male	Amilia	Beginner	Female
Daniel	Beginner	Male	Jose	Beginner	Male

Fig. 9.10. A multicolumn equijoin producing redundant data.

This command matches (one at a time) each player on the U.S.A. team with every Spanish player who has the same skill level.

You can see that information appearing in the *usa.skill* and *spain.skill* columns is identical. Because information in the *skill* column of the *spain* table is redundant, you do not need to show the joining columns from both tables.

Instead, you need to select the joining column from only one table by using a natural join. Figure 9.11 shows the command and the results for producing a natural join between the *usa* and *spain* tables.

```
SELECT usa.*, spain.player, spain.sex
  FROM usa, spain
 WHERE usa.skill=spain.skill;
```

USA. PLAYER	USA. SKILL	USA. SEX	SPAIN. PLAYER	SPAIN. SEX
Albert	Advanced	Male	Fernando	Male
Albert	Advanced	Male	Maria	Female
Brenda	Beginner	Female	Amilia	Female
Brenda	Beginner	Female	Jose	Male
Candy	Advanced	Female	Fernando	Male
Candy	Advanced	Female	Maria	Female
Daniel	Beginner	Male	Amilia	Female
Daniel	Beginner	Male	Jose	Male

Fig. 9.11. A multicolumn equijoin producing only needed data.

This command selects all the columns from the *usa* table plus the *player* and *sex* columns from the *spain* table. As a result, you have all the information about the U.S.A. players and the Spanish players. You do not select the *skill* column from the *spain* table because that column has the same information as the *skill* column of the *usa* table.

The results show all the relevant information about the two joined tables. The information in the joining column appears only once in the results.

Joins on Selected Columns

In a natural join, all the columns in the joined tables are returned without duplicating the joining columns. If you do not want to show all the columns, you can specify only the columns you want to see in the list of items to be selected. For example, if you need to know only names of the players in all the single matches with equal skill levels, you issue the command shown in figure 9.12.

```
SELECT usa.skill, usa.player, spain.player
  FROM usa, spain
 WHERE usa.skill=spain.skill;
```

USA. SKILL	USA. PLAYER	SPAIN. PLAYER
Advanced	Albert	Fernando
Advanced	Albert	Maria
Beginner	Brenda	Amilia
Beginner	Brenda	Jose
Advanced	Candy	Fernando
Advanced	Candy	Maria

Fig. 9.12. *Joining selected columns.*

As another example, you can retrieve selected columns from the *course* and *teacher* tables after making an equijoin between the two tables. The SELECT command and results of the equijoin using the *t_id* as the joining column can be issued as follows:

```
SELECT c_id, c_title, y.t_id, t_lname, t_rank
  FROM course x, teacher y
 WHERE x.t_id=y.t_id;
```

C_ID	C_TITLE	Y.T_ID	T_LNAME	T_RANK
C1	ENGL 101	T2	Hemingway	Professor
C1	ENGL 101	T5	Shaw	Assistant Prof.
C2	HIST 100	T1	Franklin	Professor
C3	MATH 105	T3	Newton	Associate Prof.
C4	PHIL 101	T4	Quine	Professor
C5	PHYS 102	T3	Newton	Associate Prof.

The command joins the *course* and *teacher* tables by using the *t_id* column as a joining column. As a result, you can show the names and ranks of the instructors for each course in the *course* table.

Filter Conditions in Joins

When you are joining tables with a SELECT command, the WHERE clause allows you to specify your joining conditions. The same clause also can be used for defining your filter conditions. You can use one or more filter conditions for selecting data rows before or after joining the tables. For example, if you want to produce a list of all the single matches in which both players are on the advanced skill level, you can specify the filter conditions in two different ways.

First, in the WHERE clause you can select the rows from the tables before you join them. Here is the command for doing that:

```
SELECT usa.player, usa.skill, spain.player
  FROM usa, spain
 WHERE usa.skill='Advanced' AND spain.skill='Advanced'
   AND usa.skill=spain.skill;
```

USA.PLAYER	USA.SKILL	SPAIN.PLAYER
Albert	Advanced	Fernando
Albert	Advanced	Maria
Candy	Advanced	Fernando
Candy	Advanced	Maria

When this command is processed, the data rows that satisfy the filter condition (usa.skill = 'Advanced' AND spain.skill = 'Advanced') are selected first. The command ignores all other rows not meeting the filter condition. The two tables then are joined by using the values in the joining column of the selected rows.

A second way to produce the player list is to specify the filter condition after the two tables are joined. You specify the filter condition for selecting the rows after defining your joining condition. Here is the command and results:

```
SELECT usa.player, usa.skill, spain.player
  FROM usa, spain
 WHERE usa.skill=spain.skill
   AND usa.skill='Advanced';
```

USA.PLAYER	USA.SKILL	SPAIN.PLAYER
Albert	Advanced	Fernando
Albert	Advanced	Maria
Candy	Advanced	Fernando
Candy	Advanced	Maria

When this command is processed, all the rows in both tables are considered in the join. After linking the two tables by using the *skill* column as the joining column, the filter condition (usa.skill = 'Advanced') is used to select only the rows that satisfy the filter condition.

The two approaches for specifying the filter conditions produce the same results, but the processing effort required to produce the results may be quite different. The difference depends on several factors. One important factor is the size of the tables and the number of rows satisfying the filter conditions. For example, by qualifying the rows from the tables before joining them, you speed the query if the rows to be selected represent a small subset of the tables. Otherwise, you may not see any significant difference in the retrieval speeds between the two approaches.

These two approaches are used only for illustrating the difference in the order in which the filter conditions are specified and executed. But for practical purposes, the approach you choose does not matter much. Most implementations of SQL determine the most efficient way to execute the command. SQL attempts to produce the results with the best approach for the query.

Joins Based on Inequality

In an equijoin, data rows in the first table are linked with the rows of the second table when the values in the joining columns are equal. Although this method is the most common way of joining tables, in some applications, you may want to join tables when the values in the joining columns are not equal. This join is called a non-equijoin. For example, if you want to produce from the *usa* and *spain* tables all the possible single matches in which the two players are different genders, you can use a non-equijoin. For making the non-equijoin, you specify an inequality (!=) relationship in the joining condition (see fig. 9.13).

The inequality joining condition causes the rows in the *usa* table to be linked to the rows of the *spain* table when the value in the *usa.sex* column is not equal to the value in the *spain.sex* column. As a result, only a male player is coupled with a female player in the match.

From the results, you can see that each player on the U.S.A. team is matched with a player of the opposite sex on the Spanish team because of the inequality joining condition used. But the two players in each match may be of dif-

```
SELECT  usa.player, usa.skill, usa.sex,
        spain.player, spain.skill, spain.sex
  FROM  usa, spain
 WHERE  usa.sex!=spain.sex;
```

USA. PLAYER	USA. SKILL	USA. SEX	SPAIN. PLAYER	SPAIN. SKILL	SPAIN. SEX
Albert	Advanced	Male	Amilia	Beginner	Female
Albert	Advanced	Male	Maria	Advanced	Female
Brenda	Beginner	Female	Fernando	Advanced	Male
Brenda	Beginner	Female	Jose	Beginner	Male
Candy	Advanced	Female	Fernando	Advanced	Male
Candy	Advanced	Female	Jose	Beginner	Male
Daniel	Beginner	Male	Amilia	Beginner	Female
Daniel	Beginner	Male	Maria	Advanced	Female

Fig. 9.13. A non-equijoin.

ferent skill levels. If you want to allow only players with the same skill levels to play in a match, you add a qualifying condition in the WHERE clause:

```
SELECT  usa.player, usa.skill, usa.sex,
        spain.player, spain.skill, spain.sex
  FROM  usa, spain
 WHERE  usa.sex!=spain.sex
   AND  usa.skill=spain.skill;
```

USA. PLAYER	USA. SKILL	USA. SEX	SPAIN. PLAYER	SPAIN. SKILL	SPAIN SEX
Albert	Advanced	Male	Maria	Advanced	Female
Brenda	Beginner	Female	Jose	Beginner	Male
Candy	Advanced	Female	Fernando	Advanced	Male
Daniel	Beginner	Male	Amilia	Beginner	Female

Although non-equijoins are sometime necessary for producing the information for certain applications, non-equijoins are not common. At times, they may produce confusing results. To illustrate, make a non-equijoin between the *teacher* and *course* tables by using the *t_id* as the joining column. The command for making the non-equijoin and the results are illustrated in figure 9.14.

```
SELECT t_lname, t_rank, c_id, c_title
  FROM teacher, course
 WHERE teacher.t_id!=course.t_id;
```

T_LNAME	T_RANK	C_ID	C_TITLE
Franklin	Professor	C1	ENGL 101
Franklin	Professor	C1	ENGL 101
Franklin	Professor	C3	MATH 105
Franklin	Professor	C4	PHIL 101
Franklin	Professor	C5	PHYS 102
Hemingway	Professor	C1	ENGL 101
Hemingway	Professor	C2	HIST 100
Hemingway	Professor	C3	MATH 105
Hemingway	Professor	C4	PHIL 101
Hemingway	Professor	C5	PHYS 102
Newton	Associate Prof.	C1	ENGL 101
Newton	Associate Prof.	C1	ENGL 101
Newton	Associate Prof.	C2	HIST 100
Newton	Associate Prof.	C4	PHIL 101
Quine	Professor	C1	ENGL 101
Quine	Professor	C2	HIST 100
Quine	Professor	C1	ENGL 101
Quine	Professor	C3	MATH 105
Quine	Professor	C5	PHYS 102
Shaw	Assistant Prof.	C1	ENGL 101
Shaw	Assistant Prof.	C2	HIST 100
Shaw	Assistant Prof.	C3	MATH 105
Shaw	Assistant Prof.	C4	PHIL 101
Shaw	Assistant Prof.	C5	PHYS 102

Fig. 9.14. *A non-equijoin producing confusing results.*

The non-equijoin was intended to show all the courses not taught by a given instructor. The intention was met partially. For example, you can see that the four courses linked to instructor Franklin were C1 (ENGL 101), C3 (MATH 103), C4(PHIL 101), and C5(PHYS 102). The course not linked to that instructor was C2 (HIST 100), the course taught by that instructor. If you study the results more carefully, however, you will notice that the course C1 (ENGL 101) is linked to instructor Hemingway. This error occurred because the course is taught jointly by two instructors—Hemingway and Shaw—and the course appears in two rows of the *course* table. A partial solution to the problem is to treat this course separately. To treat the course separately, you can add a filter condition, c_id!='C1' in the WHERE clause so that the course is excluded from the join operation (see fig. 9.15).

```
SELECT t_lname, t_rank, c_id, c_title
  FROM teacher, course
 WHERE c_id!='C1'
   AND teacher.t_id!=course.t_id;
```

T_LNAME	T_RANK	C_ID	C_TITLE
Franklin	Professor	C3	MATH 105
Franklin	Professor	C4	PHIL 101
Franklin	Professor	C5	PHYS 102
Hemingway	Professor	C2	HIST 100
Hemingway	Professor	C3	MATH 105
Hemingway	Professor	C4	PHIL 101
Hemingway	Professor	C5	PHYS 102
Newton	Associate Prof.	C2	HIST 100
Newton	Associate Prof.	C4	PHIL 101
Quine	Professor	C2	HIST 100
Quine	Professor	C3	MATH 105
Quine	Professor	C5	PHYS 102
Shaw	Assistant Prof.	C2	HIST 100
Shaw	Assistant Prof.	C3	MATH 105
Shaw	Assistant Prof.	C4	PHIL 101
Shaw	Assistant Prof.	C5	PHYS 102

Fig. 9.15. *Using a filter condition to avoid confusing results in a non-equijoin.*

You can see that this method is not a satisfactory solution because you need to deal with the information about the excluded course (C1). Unfortunately, no simple solution to this problem exists. You may have to restructure the *course* table so that the non-equijoin will produce the results you want.

Self-Joins

In most applications, you join two or more tables so that you can retrieve information from them with a single SELECT command. In certain instances, you may need to join a table to itself, for example, to match rows within the same table.

To link a table with itself, you repeat the table name in the FROM clause and assign two different aliases to the table name. Then you can treat the two aliases as if they were two different tables and join them accordingly.

In the earlier examples, the rows in the *usa* and *spain* tables are joined to produce single tennis matches. Each match has two players, one from the U.S.A. team and the other from the Spanish team. Suppose, however, that you want to match players from the same team. That is, you want to have single matches made up of players from the same country. To make the matches, you need to join a table with itself. But you have to be careful in defining the joining condition. For example, you cannot allow a player to be matched with himself or herself. So you need to use a filter condition for excluding such cases (see fig. 9.16).

```
SELECT x.player, x.skill, x.sex,
       y.player, y.skill, y.sex
  FROM usa x, usa y
 WHERE x.player!=y.player;
```

X.PLAYER	X.SKILL	X.SEX	Y.PLAYER	Y.SKILL	Y.SEX
Albert	Advanced	Male	Brenda	Beginner	Female
Albert	Advanced	Male	Candy	Advanced	Female
Albert	Advanced	Male	Daniel	Beginner	Male
Brenda	Beginner	Female	Albert	Advanced	Male
Brenda	Beginner	Female	Candy	Advanced	Female
Brenda	Beginner	Female	Daniel	Beginner	Male
Candy	Advanced	Female	Albert	Advanced	Male
Candy	Advanced	Female	Brenda	Beginner	Female
Candy	Advanced	Female	Daniel	Beginner	Male
Daniel	Beginner	Male	Albert	Advanced	Male
Daniel	Beginner	Male	Brenda	Beginner	Female
Daniel	Beginner	Male	Candy	Advanced	Female

Fig. 9.16. Using a filter condition when joining a table to itself.

In this example, aliases *x* and *y* are assigned to the *usa* table. After you assign these aliases, table *usa* is considered to be two different tables. The self-join produces all the matches regardless of the skill level and gender of the players in each match. If you want the players in all the matches to have the same level of skill, you issue the following command:

```
SELECT x.player, x.skill, x.sex,
       y.player, y.skill, y.sex
  FROM usa x, usa y
 WHERE x.player!=y.player
   AND x.skill=y.skill;
```

X.PLAYER	X.SKILL	X.SEX	Y.PLAYER	Y.SKILL	Y.SEX
Albert	Advanced	Male	Candy	Advanced	Female
Brenda	Beginner	Female	Daniel	Beginner	Male
Candy	Advanced	Female	Albert	Advanced	Male
Daniel	Beginner	Male	Brenda	Beginner	Female

This command matches each player in the U.S.A. team with another U.S.A. player with the same skill level. By using a self-join, you can form matches of players from the same team. Similarly, you can have matches with players of the same gender by issuing the commands shown in figures 9.17 and 9.18.

```
SELECT x.player, x.skill, x.sex,
       y.player, y.skill, y.sex
  FROM usa x, usa y
 WHERE x.sex=y.sex;
   AND x.player!=y.player
```

X.PLAYER	X.SKILL	X.SEX	Y.PLAYER	Y.SKILL	Y.SEX
Albert	Advanced	Male	Daniel	Beginner	Male
Brenda	Beginner	Female	Candy	Advanced	Female
Candy	Advanced	Female	Brenda	Beginner	Female
Daniel	Beginner	Male	Albert	Advanced	Male

Fig. 9.17. Matching players of the same gender.

```
SELECT x.*, y.*
  FROM usa x, usa y
 WHERE x.player!=y.player;
```

X.PLAYER	X.SKILL	X.SEX	X.PLAYER	Y.SKILL	Y.SEX
Brenda	Beginner	Female	Brenda	Beginner	Female
Brenda	Beginner	Female	Brenda	Beginner	Female
Brenda	Beginner	Female	Brenda	Beginner	Female
Brenda	Beginner	Female	Brenda	Beginner	Female
Candy	Advanced	Female	Candy	Advanced	Female
Candy	Advanced	Female	Candy	Advanced	Female
Candy	Advanced	Female	Candy	Advanced	Female
Candy	Advanced	Female	Candy	Advanced	Female
Daniel	Beginner	Male	Daniel	Beginner	Male
Daniel	Beginner	Male	Daniel	Beginner	Male
Daniel	Beginner	Male	Daniel	Beginner	Male
Daniel	Beginner	Male	Daniel	Beginner	Male

Fig. 9.18. *Matching players of the same skill level and gender.*

Joins Involving Several Tables

The procedure you use to join two tables also can be used for joining several tables. In order to join several tables in the same statement, you need to define all the links between every pair of tables to be joined. For example, if you need to join tables *a*, *b*, and *c*, you first join tables *a* and *b* and then join tables *b* and *c*.

The tables used to illustrate the procedure for joining more than two tables are *course*, *assign*, *teacher*, *student*, and *class*. The *teacher* table is the same as the one used earlier. For easy reference, the table is repeated in figure 9.19.

Teacher table:

T_ID	T_LNAME	T_FNAME	T_RANK	T_OFFICE	T_PHONE
T1	Franklin	Benjamin	Professor	West 103	235-1234
T2	Hemingway	Ernest M.	Professor	West 301	287-6666
T3	Newton	Isaac	Associate Prof.	East 150	635-1414
T4	Quine	Willard V.	Professor	East 250	636-2626
T5	Shaw	George B.	Assistant Prof.	West 104	235-7878

Fig. 9.19. *The* teacher *table.*

The *course* table has been restructured so that it no longer contains redundant data. Each course appears as one row in that table. The *t_id* column from the original *course* table has been removed. In order to provide the links between courses and teachers, a new table named *assign* has been added to the *school* database. Each row of the *assign* table relates a course with an instructor (see fig. 9.20).

Course table:

C_ID	C_TITLE	C_CREDITS	C_DESC
C1	ENGL 101	3	English Literature
C2	HIST 100	3	American History
C3	MATH 105	5	Calculus I
C4	PHIL 101	3	Philosophy
C5	PHYS 102	5	Physics I

Assign table:

C_ID	T_ID
C1	T2
C1	T5
C2	T1
C3	T3
C4	T4
C5	T3

Fig. 9.20. *The* course *and* assign *tables.*

Information about all the students in the *school* database is stored in the *student* table. The contents of the table is assumed to be as follows:

S_ID	S_LNAME	S_FNAME	S_BDATE	S_SEX	S_HSGPA
S1	Austin	Linda D.	03/08/71	F	3.98
S2	Brown	Nancy J.	05/14/70	F	3.35
S3	Carter	Jack F.	10/10/71	M	2.87
S4	Ford	Harvey P.	06/12/71	M	2.60
S5	Freed	Barbara J.	07/28/69	F	3.15
S6	Gilmore	Danny S.	11/01/70	M	3.86
S7	Jackson	Brad L.	04/15/71	M	2.75
S8	Madison	George G.	08/15/70	M	2.35
S9	Reed	Donna E.	09/26/69	F	2.96
S10	Taylor	Bob K.	02/14/71	M	3.14

For finding information about the courses taken by these students, the *class* table is created. The table provides the links between the *course* and *student* tables. Each row in the *class* table relates a course and a student who is taking that course. The *class* table is given in figure 9.21.

Class table:

C_ID	S_ID
C1	S3
C1	S5
C1	S10
C2	S4
C2	S5
C2	S7
C2	S8
C3	S1
C3	S2
C3	S9
C4	S2
C4	S5
C4	S8
C5	S3
C5	S6
C5	S8
C5	S9

Fig. 9.21. *The* class *table.*

Joining Courses and Instructors

Because the information about the courses and the instructors is stored in two separate tables, to relate these two entities, you need to join these two tables by using the third table, named *assign*. The *assign* table contains information about teaching assignments. The logic of joining these three tables is diagrammed in figure 9.22.

From figure 9.22, you can see that the *course* and *assign* tables are joined by using the *c_id* column as the joining column. When you use equijoins between the two tables, the rows in the *course* table are joined with the rows in the *assign* table when the values in the joining column are the same. In a similar manner, you can use *t_id* as the joining column to link

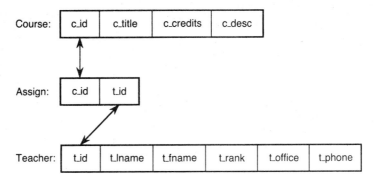

Fig. 9.22. *Joining the* course *and* teacher *tables.*

the rows in the *assign* table with the rows in the *teacher* table with equi-joins. The SELECT command you use to make the equijoins can be issued as follows:

```
SELECT   x.c_id, c_title, z.t_id, z.t_lname, z.t_rank
  FROM   course x, assign y, teacher z
 WHERE   x.c_id = y.c_id
   AND   y.t_id = z.t_id;
```

In the FROM clause, you assign x, y, and z as the table aliases for the *course*, *assign*, and *teacher* tables, respectively. The first part of the WHERE clause, x.c_id = y.c_id, defines the link between the *course* and *assign* tables. The second condition, y.t_id = z.t_id, specifies the joining column between the *assign* and *teacher* tables. The items to be selected from the *course* and *teacher* tables are specified in the SELECT clause. Figure 9.23 shows how these data items are linked between the three tables joined by the SELECT command.

```
Course:                 Assign:        Teacher:

C_ID C_TITLE            C_ID T_ID      T_ID T_LNAME      T_RANK
------------            ---- -----     ---- ---------    -------------
C1    ENGL 101           C1   T2        T1   Franklin     Professor
C2    HIST 100           C1   T5        T2   Hemingway    Professor
C3    MATH 105           C2   T1        T3   Newton       Associate Prof.
C4    PHIL 101           C3   T3        T4   Quine        Professor
C5    PHYS 102           C4   T4        T5   Shaw         Assistant Prof.
                         C5   T3
```

Fig. 9.23. *Linking data rows in the* course, assign, *and* teacher *tables.*

When you process the SELECT command, you get the following results:

C_ID	C_TITLE	T_ID	T_LNAME	T_RANK
C1	ENGL 101	T2	Hemingway	Professor
C1	ENGL 101	T5	Shaw	Assistant Prof.
C2	HIST 100	T1	Franklin	Professor
C3	MATH 105	T3	Newton	Associate Prof.
C4	PHIL 101	T4	Quine	Professor
C5	PHYS 102	T3	Newton	Associate Prof.

By joining the three table with this SELECT command, you can find out the names of the instructors who are teaching the courses. The results show the instructors for all the courses in the *course* table. If you want to know the instructor for a given course, you can add a filter condition to the WHERE clause. The following command, for example, shows you the instructors who are teaching the course ENGL 101:

```
SELECT x.c_id, c_title, z.t_id, z.t_lname, z.t_rank
  FROM course x, assign y, teacher z
 WHERE x.c_id=y.c_id
   AND y.t_id=z.t_id
   AND x.c_title='ENGL 101';
```

C_ID	C_TITLE	T_ID	T_LNAME	T_RANK
C1	ENGL 101	T2	Hemingway	Professor
C1	ENGL 101	T5	Shaw	Assistant Prof.

The results from these two SELECT commands show the course identification numbers as the first column. SQL lists names of the courses, followed by the names of the instructors. You can modify the SELECT command so that you can arrange the results by teacher identification numbers. Here is the SELECT command:

```
SELECT  x.t_id, x.t_lname, z.c_title, z.c_desc
  FROM  teacher x, assign y, course z
 WHERE  x.t_id=y.t_id AND y.c_id=z.c_id;
```

T_ID	T_LNAME	C_TITLE	C_DESC
T1	Franklin	HIST 100	American History
T2	Hemingway	ENGL 101	English Literature
T3	Newton	MATH 105	Calculus I
T3	Newton	PHYS 102	Physics I
T4	Quine	PHIL 101	Philosophy
T5	Shaw	ENGL 101	English Literature

From the results, you can find out the courses each instructor is teaching. If you want to know the course assignments for a given instructor, say Newton, you can specify the necessary filter condition, as in the following statement:

```
SELECT  x.t_id, x.t_lname, z.c_title, z.c_desc
  FROM  teacher x, assign y, course z
 WHERE  x.t_id=y.t_id
   AND  y.c_id=z.c_id
   AND  x.t_lname='Newton';
```

T_ID	T_LNAME	C_TITLE	C_DESC
T3	Newton	MATH 105	Calculus I
T3	Newton	PHYS 102	Physics I

Joining Courses and Students

If you want to find out which students are taking what courses, you can obtain that information by linking the *course* and *student* tables. Because the *class* table contains information that relates courses to students, you need to use *class* to link the *course* and *student* tables. Figure 9.24 shows the common columns you use to link the *course*, *class*, and *class* tables.

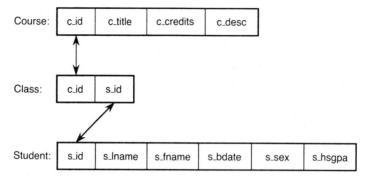

Figure 9.24. *Joining the* course *and* student *tables.*

The SELECT command for joining the three tables can be issued as follows:

> SELECT   x.c_id, x.c_title, z.s_lname, z.s_fname
>   FROM   course x, class y, student z
> WHERE   x.c_id=y.c_id
>   AND   y.s_id=z.s_id;

In this command, the rows in the *course* table are joined with rows in the *class* table when they have the same value in the joining column, *c_id*. The rows in the *class* table are then linked with rows in the *student* table when the rows have the same value in the *s_id* column. Figure 9.25 shows how these rows are joined by using *c_id* and *s_id* as the joining columns in equijoins.

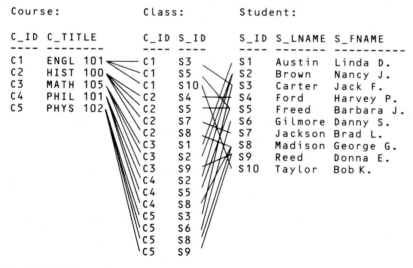

Fig. 9.25. *Joining data rows in the* course, class, *and* student *tables.*

After processing the SELECT command, the program returns the information that is obtained from the *course* and *student* tables (see fig. 9.26).

```
C_ID   C_TITLE    S_LNAME    S_FNAME
----   --------   -------    ----------
C1     ENGL 101   Carter     Jack F.
C1     ENGL 101   Freed      Barbara J.
C1     ENGL 101   Taylor     Bob K.
C2     HIST 100   Ford       Harvey P.
C2     HIST 100   Freed      Barbara J.
C2     HIST 100   Jackson    Brad L.
C2     HIST 100   Madison    George G.
C3     MATH 105   Austin     Linda D.
C3     MATH 105   Brown      Nancy J.
C3     MATH 105   Reed       Donna E.
C4     PHIL 101   Brown      Nancy J.
C4     PHIL 101   Freed      Barbara J.
C4     PHIL 101   Madison    George G.
C5     PHYS 102   Carter     Jack F.
C5     PHYS 102   Gilmore    Danny S.
C5     PHYS 102   Madison    George G.
C5     PHYS 102   Reed       Donna E.
```

Fig. 9.26. *Results of joining the* course *and* student *tables.*

The results are arranged by course identification numbers. From these results, you can find all the students who are taking each course. If you want to know all the students who are taking HIST 100, you add a filter condition to the WHERE clause for specifying the course title:

```
SELECT x.c_id, x.c_title, z.s_lname, z.s_fname
  FROM course x, class y, student z
 WHERE x.c_id=y.c_id
   AND y.s_id=z.s_id
   AND x.c_title='HIST 100';
```

```
C_ID   C_TITLE    S_LNAME    S_FNAME
----   --------   -------    ----------
C2     HIST 100   Ford       Harvey P.
C2     HIST 100   Freed      Barbara J.
C2     HIST 100   Jackson    Brad L.
C2     HIST 100   Madison    George G.
```

If you want to know the courses that are being taken by each student, you can organize the results by student identification. Figure 9.27 shows the command and the results.

```
SELECT  x.s_id, x.s_lname, x.s_fname, z.c_title, z.c_desc
  FROM  student x, class y, course z
 WHERE  x.s_id=y.s_id
   AND  y.c_id=z.c_id;
```

S_ID	LNAME	S_FNAME	C_TITLE	C_DESC
S1	Austin	Linda D.	MATH 105	Calculus I
S2	Brown	Nancy J.	MATH 105	Calculus I
S2	Brown	Nancy J.	PHIL 101	Philosophy
S3	Carter	Jack F.	ENGL 101	English Literature
S3	Carter	Jack F.	PHYS 102	Physics I
S4	Ford	Harvey P.	HIST 100	American History
S5	Freed	Barbara J.	ENGL 101	English Literature
S5	Freed	Barbara J.	HIST 100	American History
S5	Freed	Barbara J.	PHIL 101	Philosophy
S6	Gilmore	Danny S.	PHYS 102	Physics I
S7	Jackson	Brad L.	HIST 100	American History
S8	Madison	George G.	HIST 100	American History
S8	Madison	George G.	PHIL 101	Philosophy
S8	Madison	George G.	PHYS 102	Physics I
S9	Reed	Donna E.	MATH 105	Calculus I
S9	Reed	Donna E.	PHYS 102	Physics I
S10	Taylor	Bob K.	ENGL 101	English Literature

Fig. 9.27. *Organizing results by student ID numbers.*

To find out what classes a given student is taking, you can specify his or her last name in the filter condition. The following command shows all the classes Madison is taking:

```
SELECT  x.s_id, x.s_lname, x.s_fname, z.c_title, z.c_desc
  FROM  student x, class y, course z
 WHERE  x.s_id=y.s_id
   AND  y.c_id=z.c_id
   AND  x.s_lname='Madison';
```

S_ID	LNAME	S_FNAME	C_TITLE	C_DESC
S8	Madison	George G.	HIST 100	American History
S8	Madison	George G.	PHIL 101	Philosophy
S8	Madison	George G.	PHYS 102	Physics I

Joining Students, Courses, and Teachers

Information about courses and students is stored in the *course* and *student* tables, respectively. The *class* table provides the link between the *course* and *student* tables. You can find the courses taken by a student by linking the *student* and *course* tables through the *class* table. But if you need to know the names of the instructors teaching these courses, you need to find the names in the *teacher* table. Therefore, you need to link the *teacher* table with the *course* and *student* tables for that information. This link can be accomplished by using information from the *assign* table to join the *course* and *teacher* tables. Figure 9.28 depicts the links among these five tables.

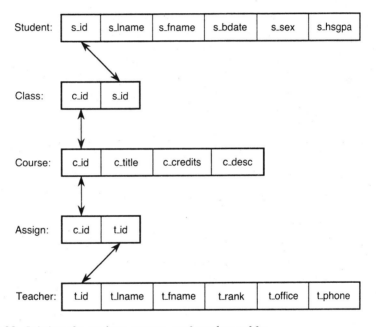

Fig. 9.28. *Joining the* student, course, *and* teacher *tables.*

The SELECT command for joining these tables can be written as follows:

```
SELECT   v.s_id, v.s_lname, x.c_title, x.c_desc,
         z.t_id, z.t_lname
  FROM   student v, class w, course x, assign y, teacher z
 WHERE   v.s_id = w.s_id
   AND   w.c_id = x.c_id
   AND   x.c_id = y.c_id
   AND   y.t_id = z.t_id;
```

In the SELECT statement, the *student* and *class* tables are joined by using the *s_id* column as the joining column. The *c_id* column links the *class* and *course* tables. The information in the *assign* table links the rows between the *course* and *assign* tables. Finally, when you join the *course* and *teacher* tables, you use *t_id* as the joining column. Figure 9.29 diagrams how data rows in these tables are joined.

```
Student:          Class:        Course:              Assign:         Teacher:

S_LNAME S_ID      S_ID C_ID     C_ID C_TITLE         C_ID T_ID       T_ID T_LNAME
------- ----      ---- ----     ---- ---------       ---- ----       ---- ---------
Austin  S1        S3   C1       C1   ENGL   101      C1   T2         T1   Franklin
Brown   S2        S5   C1       C2   HIST   100      C1   T5         T2   Hemingway
Carter  S3        S10  C1       C3   MATH   105      C2   T1         T3   Newton
Ford    S4        S4   C2       C4   PHIL   101      C3   T3         T4   Quine
Freed   S5        S5   C2       C5   PHYS   102      C4   T4         T5   Shaw
Gilmore S6        S7   C2                            C5   T3
Jackson S7        S8   C2
Madison S8        S1   C3
Reed    S9        S2   C3
Taylor  S10       S9   C3
                  S2   C4
                  S5   C4
                  S8   C4
                  S3   C5
                  S6   C5
                  S8   C5
                  S9   C5
```

Fig. 9.29. Joining data rows in the student, course, *and* teacher *tables.*

The results produced by the SELECT command are shown in figure 9.30.

S_ID	S_LNAME	C_TITLE	C_DESC	T_ID	T_LNAME
S1	Austin	MATH 105	Calculus I	T3	Newton
S2	Brown	MATH 105	Calculus I	T3	Newton
S2	Brown	PHIL 101	Philosophy	T4	Quine
S3	Carter	ENGL 101	English Literature	T2	Hemingway
S3	Carter	ENGL 101	English Literature	T5	Shaw
S3	Carter	PHYS 102	Physics I	T3	Newton
S4	Ford	HIST 100	American History	T1	Franklin
S5	Freed	ENGL 101	English Literature	T2	Hemingway
S5	Freed	ENGL 101	English Literature	T5	Shaw
S5	Freed	HIST 100	American History	T1	Franklin
S5	Freed	PHIL 101	Philosophy	T4	Quine
S6	Gilmore	PHYS 102	Physics I	T3	Newton
S7	Jackson	HIST 100	American History	T1	Franklin
S8	Madison	HIST 100	American History	T1	Franklin
S8	Madison	PHIL 101	Philosophy	T4	Quine
S8	Madison	PHYS 102	Physics I	T3	Newton
S9	Reed	MATH 105	Calculus I	T3	Newton
S9	Reed	PHYS 102	Physics I	T3	Newton
S10	Taylor	ENGL 101	English Literature	T2	Hemingway
S10	Taylor	ENGL 101	English Literature	T5	Shaw

Fig. 9.30. *Results of joining the* student, course, *and* teacher *tables.*

From the results, you can see that any student in the *course* table is first linked to the courses he or she is taking by using the information in the *class* table. Each course is then joined with the *teacher* table, showing the names of the instructors. As a result, names of the courses that any student takes can be traced back through these tables. To find the instructors who are teaching the student Freed, you issue the following command:

```
SELECT  v.s_id, v.s_lname, x.c_title, x.c_desc,
        z.t_id, z.t_lname
  FROM  student v, class w, course x, assign y, teacher z
 WHERE  v.s_id=w.s_id
   AND  w.c_id=x.c_id
   AND  x.c_id=y.c_id
   AND  y.t_id=z.t_id
   AND  v.s_lname='Freed';
```

S_ID	S_LNAME	C_TITLE	C_DESC	T_ID	T_LNAME
S5	Freed	ENGL 101	English Literature	T2	Hemingway
S5	Freed	ENGL 101	English Literature	T5	Shaw
S5	Freed	HIST 100	American History	T1	Franklin
S5	Freed	PHIL 101	Philosophy	T4	Quine

The results are arranged by student identification numbers. If you want to arrange your results by instructors so that you can find all the students who are taught by a given instructor, you can issue the command shown in figure 9.31.

```
SELECT v.t_lname, v.t_rank, x.c_title, z.s_lname
  FROM teacher v, assign w, course x, class y, student z
 WHERE v.t_id=w.t_id
   AND w.c_id=x.c_id
   AND x.c_id=y.c_id
   AND y.s_id=z.s_id;
```

T_LNAME	T_RANK	C_TITLE	S_LNAME
Franklin	Professor	HIST 100	Ford
Franklin	Professor	HIST 100	Freed
Franklin	Professor	HIST 100	Jackson
Franklin	Professor	HIST 100	Madison
Hemingway	Professor	ENGL 101	Carter
Hemingway	Professor	ENGL 101	Freed
Hemingway	Professor	ENGL 101	Taylor
Newton	Associate Prof.	MATH 105	Austin
Newton	Associate Prof.	MATH 105	Brown
Newton	Associate Prof.	MATH 105	Reed
Newton	Associate Prof.	PHYS 102	Carter
Newton	Associate Prof.	PHYS 102	Gilmore
Newton	Associate Prof.	PHYS 102	Madison
Newton	Associate Prof.	PHYS 102	Reed
Quine	Professor	PHIL 101	Brown
Quine	Professor	PHIL 101	Freed
Quine	Professor	PHIL 101	Madison
Shaw	Assistant Prof.	ENGL 101	Carter
Shaw	Assistant Prof.	ENGL 101	Freed
Shaw	Assistant Prof.	ENGL 101	Taylor

Fig. 9.31. Finding the students taught by each teacher.

You can add any filter conditions to the WHERE clause for qualifying the results after joining the tables. For example, the statement in figure 9.32 returns information about the students who are being taught by instructors with the rank of Professor.

```
SELECT v.t_lname, v.t_rank, x.c_title, z.s_lname
  FROM teacher v, assign w, course x, class y, student z
 WHERE v.t_id=w.t_id
   AND w.c_id=x.c_id
   AND x.c_id=y.c_id
   AND y.s_id=z.s_id
   AND v.t_rank='Professor';
```

```
T_LNAME     T_RANK      C_TITLE    S_LNAME
---------   ---------   --------   ---------
Franklin    Professor   HIST 100   Ford
Franklin    Professor   HIST 100   Freed
Franklin    Professor   HIST 100   Jackson
Franklin    Professor   HIST 100   Madison
Hemingway   Professor   ENGL 101   Carter
Hemingway   Professor   ENGL 101   Freed
Hemingway   Professor   ENGL 101   Taylor
Quine       Professor   PHIL 101   Brown
Quine       Professor   PHIL 101   Freed
Quine       Professor   PHIL 101   Madison
```

Fig. 9.32. Finding students taught by instructors with rank of Professor.

Similarly, you can find information about the courses and students taught by selected instructors by specifying their last names in a filter condition. The following statement displays the course titles and student names that are being taught by instructors named Franklin and Shaw:

```
SELECT  v.t_lname, v.t_rank, x.c_title, z.s_lname
  FROM  teacher v, assign w, course x, class y, student z
 WHERE  v.t_id=w.t_id
   AND  w.c_id=x.c_id
   AND  x.c_id=y.c_id
   AND  y.s_id=z.s_id
   AND  (v.t_lname='Franklin' OR v.t_lname='Shaw');
```

```
T_LNAME    T_RANK             C_TITLE   S_LNAME
--------   ----------------   --------  -------
Franklin   Professor          HIST 100  Ford
Franklin   Professor          HIST 100  Freed
Franklin   Professor          HIST 100  Jackson
Franklin   Professor          HIST 100  Madison
Shaw       Assistant Prof.    ENGL 101  Carter
Shaw       Assistant Prof.    ENGL 101  Freed
Shaw       Assistant Prof.    ENGL 101  Taylor
```

Lookup Tables for Classifying Data

You gain access to information from multiple tables by using the join operation. After you have joined the tables, you can select from the joined tables the columns that provide the information you need. The actual locations of these columns are irrelevant. They can be treated as if they were from the same table. With the join operation, you can design your database so that you can use lookup tables to classify your data values in other tables.

Determining Grades

A lookup table is usually designed for storing information you use to determine the criteria for classifying your data values. For example, if you want to determine a student's grade by his or her test score, you may set up a lookup table. In the lookup table, you store information about the lower and upper limits for all the appropriate grades. The contents of the lookup table, named *grade*, may look something like figure 9.33.

Grade table:

GRADE	LOW_SCORE	HIGH_SCORE
A	90.00	100.00
B	80.00	89.99
C	60.00	79.99
D	40.00	59.99
F	0.00	39.99

Fig. 9.33. The grade *lookup table.*

In this table, the score range for each grade is stored in one row. For example, if a student's test score is between 90 and 100, he or she is given an A. A student gets a failing grade (or F) if his or her test score is below 40. Information in this table can be used to determine a student's grade by comparing the test score, which may be stored in another table, with the information in the lookup table. In other words, for each test score in a table, you can find the corresponding grade from the lookup table. As an example, assume that two test scores for each of the ten students are stored in the *tests* table. One test score is for the mid-term examination, and the other is for the final examination. The *tests* table is shown in figure 9.34.

Tests table:

S_ID	MID_TERM	FINAL
S1	75	87
S2	65	75
S3	90	95
S4	50	60
S5	82	85
S6	68	70
S7	70	75
S8	92	93
S9	69	74
S10	62	72

Fig. 9.34. The tests *table.*

To determine the grades of the students, based on their mid-term test scores, you use the information from the *grade* table to classify the data values in the *mid-term* column in the *tests* table. In a way, you want to associate the information from the *tests* table with information from the *grade* table. But this procedure is different from joining the two tables because this procedure does not involve a joining column. The SELECT statement for finding the grades for the students can be written as in figure 9.35.

```
SELECT  s_id, mid_term, grade
  FROM  tests, grade
 WHERE  mid_term BETWEEN low_score AND high_score;
```

S_ID	MID_TERM	GRADE
S1	75	C
S2	65	C
S3	90	A
S4	50	D
S5	82	B
S6	68	C
S7	70	C
S8	92	A
S9	69	C
S10	62	C

Fig. 9.35. *Using a lookup table to determine grades.*

When the statement is processed, each score in the *mid-term* column of the *tests* table is compared with the values in the *low-score* and *high-score* columns in the *grade* table. When the score is found to lie between two values in the *grade* table, the letter grade in the *grade* column is returned. From the results, you will note that a grade based on the *mid-term* score was returned with each student identification number in the *tests* table. Of course, if you want to link the student identification numbers with their names, you can join the *tests* and *grade* tables with the *student* table (see fig. 9.36).

```
SELECT  x.s_id, s_lname, s_fname, mid_term, grade
   FROM  student x, tests y, grade z
  WHERE  mid_term BETWEEN low_score AND high_score
    AND  x.s_id=y.s_id;
```

```
S_ID   LNAME     S_FNAME      MID_TERM   GRADE
----   -------   ----------   --------   -----
S1     Austin    Linda D.          75    C
S2     Brown     Nancy J.          65    C
S3     Carter    Jack F.           90    A
S4     Ford      Harvey P.         50    D
S5     Freed     Barbara J.        82    B
S6     Gilmore   Danny S.          68    C
S7     Jackson   Brad L.           70    C
S8     Madison   George G.         92    A
S9     Reed      Donna E.          69    C
S10    Taylor    Bob K.            62    C
```

Fig. 9.36. *Listing grades for each student by name.*

You also can use the information in the *grade* table to determine a student's grade based on a weighted-average test score. The weighted-average test score is computed by assigning different weighting factors to the mid-term and final test scores. For example, you can determine a student's grade by using a weighted average that is comprised of 40 percent of the mid-term test score and 60 percent of the final test score. A weighted-average test score is expressed as a numeric expression, $mid\_term*0.4 + final*0.6$, in the following SELECT statement:

```
SELECT   tests.*, (mid_term*0.4 + final*0.6), grade
  FROM   tests, grade
 WHERE   (mid_term*0.4 + final*0.6)
BETWEEN   low_score AND high_score;
```

This command uses the score range in the *grade* table to assign a letter grade to the weighted-average test score.

When this command is processed, the value of the numeric expression is compared with the values in the *low_score* and *high_score* columns in the *grade* table for determining its grade. The results are shown in figure 9.37.

S_ID	MID_TERM	FINAL	(MID_TERM*0.4+FINAL*0.6)	GRADE
S1	75	87	82.20	B
S2	65	75	71.00	C
S3	90	95	93.00	A
S4	50	60	56.00	D
S5	82	85	83.80	B
S6	68	70	69.20	C
S7	70	75	73.00	C
S8	92	93	92.60	A
S9	69	74	72.00	C
S10	62	72	68.00	C

Fig. 9.37. Using a numeric expression with a lookup table.

Computing Quantity Discounts

A lookup table can be useful for other applications. One application is determining quantity discounts based on sale quantities. For example, you may store information about the discount schedule in a table and then use the information to determine the amount of discount, which is based on the amount of sale. The contents of the discount schedule may look like figure 9.38.

Discount table:

DISC_RATE	LOW_VALUE	HIGH_VALUE
0.00	0.00	99.99
0.10	100.00	199.99
0.15	200.00	299.99
0.20	300.00	4999.99

Fig. 9.38. The discount *table.*

The *discount* table contains three columns describing the discount rates and the relevant ranges for these rates. For example, if the amount of a sale is between $100 and $199.99, the discount rate is 10 percent (.10). Discount rates stored in this table can be used to compute the amounts of discount for the sale values that are stored in a separate table. The contents of the *sale* table may include information about the invoice number, the amount of sale, the sale price, and so on. A sample *sale* table is shown in figure 9.39.

Sale table:

```
INVOICE_NO  QTY_SOLD  UNIT_PRICE
----------  --------  ----------
A1                12      19.95
A2                 5      29.95
A3                 3      89.50
A4                 7      12.95
```

Fig. 9.39. *A sample* sale *table.*

To compute the quantity discount for each sale in the *sale* table, you first find the item's appropriate discount rate from the *discount* table. With the discount rate, you then compute the amount of discount by using the values in the *qty_sold* and *unit_price* columns in the *sale* table. One way to access information in the two tables is to join the tables with the following SELECT statement:

```
SELECT  sale.*, qty_sold*unit_price, disc_rate,
        (qty_sold*unit_price)*disc_rate
  FROM  sale, discount
 WHERE  qty_sold*unit_price
BETWEEN  low_value AND high_value;
```

INVOICE_ NO	QTY_ SOLD	UNIT_ PRICE	QTY_SOLD* UNIT_PRICE	DISC_ RATE	(QTY_SOLD*UNIT_PRICE)* DISC_RATE
A1	12	19.95	239.40	0.15	35.91
A2	5	29.95	149.75	0.10	14.98
A3	3	89.50	268.50	0.15	40.28
A4	7	12.95	90.65	0.00	0.00

The results from this statement show that for each value in the *qty_sold* column of the *sale* table, a discount rate is returned from the *discount* table through the join operation. After the *sale* and *discount* tables are joined, their columns are treated as if they were from the same table.

Chapter Summary

In this chapter, you have learned how you can retrieve and manipulate information stored in several tables by joining these tables. After you have joined the tables, all the columns in the tables can be treated as if they were from the same table. Different kinds of joins are available to link information between two tables. The most common way to link two tables is an equijoin, in which the tables are joined based on equality relationships in the joining conditions. You can join two tables that are not based on equality conditions. You also can do a self-join, in which you link a table to itself.

Although most joins are made by using one or more columns that are common to these tables, you can retrieve and manipulate information from multiple tables without any common joining column. In this chapter, you have seen how you can structure a lookup table, which allows you to use information from one table for classifying data in another table. This capability is a powerful feature of relational databases. In the next chapter, you learn other powerful relational database operations, such as using views and subqueries.

IV

Advanced
Topics

Includes

Advanced Operations
Data Security and Integrity
Interfacing with Other Database Management Systems

10

Advanced Operations

In the first part of this book, you learned the basic concepts and principles of relational databases. In Parts II and III, you were introduced to all the SQL commands and procedures you use to create and maintain relational databases. With these procedures and commands, you also can manipulate the data elements in the database to satisfy the data needs of most database management applications. In this chapter, you learn additional procedures and commands for performing data retrieval and manipulation operations. These procedures and commands are related to the techniques of using subqueries and views.

Not all the new procedures and commands discussed in this chapter are necessarily better or more efficient than the commands and procedures introduced in earlier chapters. Some procedures are just different approaches for getting the same results. For example, most subqueries can be expressed as joins. The choice between the two approaches often depends on your personal preference. In many cases, however, the approaches introduced in this chapter illustrate the flexibility of the SQL language.

Using Subqueries

Subqueries are powerful SQL tools you can use for performing sophisticated database management operations. Basically, subqueries are queries nested within other queries. The results returned from one level of queries are used for the other levels of queries.

As you have seen in earlier chapters, a query is represented by a SELECT statement. In a SELECT statement's WHERE clause, you can specify the filter conditions. In the WHERE clause, you can specify the logical operator and filter value with which you compare the values of an expression. The expression can be made up of one or more columns from one or more tables and the necessary arithmetic operators (+, -, *, /). A subquery usually is represented by a SELECT statement in the place of the filter value.

309

Because of the capability of setting up multiple levels of queries in one SQL statement, the relational database language is called a Structured Query Language (SQL). Properly structured subqueries can give you tremendous power for retrieving and manipulating your data elements with the least amount of effort.

Subquery Syntax

Subqueries are often called nested SELECT statements, although subqueries can be specified in a number of different ways. For most cases, a subquery is often structured within a SELECT statement. You can have several levels of subqueries within a SELECT statement. A simple subquery is specified in the WHERE clause of another query in the following format:

```
SELECT   <column list>
  FROM   <table list>
 WHERE   <expression> <logical operator> (SELECT   <column list>
                                            FROM   <table list>
                                           [WHERE  ........ ]);
```

The SELECT statement in the WHERE clause is a subquery. Because it is nested within the first SELECT statement, the subquery is called an inner query. The first SELECT statement represents the main, or outer, query. The results returned by the inner query, or subquery, are used as filter values for the filter condition in the WHERE clause. Here is an example of a simple subquery:

```
SELECT   l_name, salary*1.15
  FROM   employee
 WHERE   l_name IN (SELECT   l_name
                      FROM   bonus);
```

The IN operator in the filter condition matches the names in the *l_name* column of the *employee* table with the names in the *l_name* column of the *bonus* table.

The subquery is the query nested in the WHERE clause of the main query:

```
SELECT   l_name
  FROM   bonus
```

The last names returned from the *bonus* table are compared with the values of the *l_name* column in the *employee* table of the main, or outer, query.

You can structure many levels of subqueries in one statement. Each subquery is nested within another subquery in the structure shown in figure 10.1.

```
SELECT  ....
  FROM  ....
 WHERE  ....  (SELECT  ....
                 FROM  ....
                WHERE  ....  [(SELECT  ....
                                FROM  ....
                               [WHERE  ....  [(SELECT  ....
                                                ....
                                                ....              )] )] );
```

Fig. 10.1. The basic structure of a query containing multiple subqueries.

Some implementations of SQL have restrictions on the maximum number of subqueries you can specify in the same statement. Nevertheless, most implementations allow enough levels of subqueries for performing most, if not all, the database management applications.

Although most subqueries are set up in the WHERE clause of a SELECT statement, you also can define a query in the WHERE clause of an UPDATE, INSERT INTO, or DELETE statement. Strictly speaking, the query within an UPDATE, INSERT, and DELETE statement is not a subquery because the statement is not a nested SELECT statement. However, the query serves a function similar to that of a subquery. For this discussion, queries in these clauses are treated as subqueries. Figure 10.2 shows some examples of the syntax of these types of subqueries.

```
INSERT  INTO  <table name> (SELECT  <column names>
                             FROM  <table name>
                            [WHERE  <filter condition>]);


UPDATE  <table name>
   SET  <column name> = <data value or expression>
 WHERE  <expression> <logical operator> (SELECT  <column list>
                                          FROM  <table list>
                                         [WHERE  ........ ]);


DELETE  FROM  <table name>
 WHERE  <expression> <logical operator> (SELECT  <column list>
                                          FROM  <table list>
                                         [WHERE  ........ ]);
```

Fig. 10.2. Examples of subqueries in statements other than SELECT statements.

In the first example, the subquery is used to retrieve a set of values from a table. The retrieved values are then inserted into a new table. The second and third examples use a subquery to supply the filter values for the filter condition in the WHERE clause. As a result, only the rows that satisfy the filter conditions will be subject to the UPDATE and DELETE operations. Examples of these subqueries are discussed in the next section.

The Functions of Subqueries

The main function of a subquery is to retrieve information from one or more tables so that the main query can use that information for other data retrieval and manipulation operations. A subquery is most often used for supplying the filter values in the filter condition. You can set up a lookup table to hold information for a subquery. For example, if you want to determine the bonus values for certain employees, you can store their last names in a table named *bonus*. Then to compute the bonus values, you retrieve the names and the salary information from the *employee* table and use a subquery to find the names of the employees deserving the bonuses. The SELECT statement can be issued as

```
SELECT   l_name, salary*1.15
  FROM   employee
 WHERE   l_name IN (SELECT  l_name
                      FROM  bonus);
```

In this example, the *bonus* table is a lookup table. The information in the lookup table determines which rows in the *employee* table are selected for the main query.

You can set up lookup tables to determine which rows are subject to UPDATE and DELETE operations. For example, if you want to change the prices of certain items, you can use the information in the lookup table named *newprice*, which contains the stock numbers for the items that require a price increase. Therefore, you can update the unit prices in the *price* table for the items whose stock numbers appear in the lookup table. The UPDATE statement that uses this subquery and lookup table can be issued as

```
UPDATE   price
   SET   unit_price=unit_price*1.07
 WHERE   stock_no IN (SELECT  stock_no
                        FROM  newprice);
```

In this example, the subquery returns from the *newprice* table the stock numbers of items that require a price change. These stock numbers determine which rows in the *price* table are subject to the UPDATE operation.

Similarly, you can use a lookup table in a subquery to determine which rows should be removed from the table. Here is an example:

```
DELETE   FROM account
              WHERE acct_no IN (SELECT   acct_no
                                FROM   overdue
                                WHERE   past_due>120);
```

In this statement, the rows to be deleted from the *account* table are determined by the account numbers returned by the subquery. The subquery finds from the *overdue* lookup table the account numbers having *past_due* values of more than 120 (days).

Another important function of a subquery is to extract information from one or more tables. The extracted information can be used as data values for the input operation. As a result, with a subquery, you can create new table contents by using information in existing tables. Here is an example:

```
INSERT INTO  names (SELECT  l_name, f_name
                    FROM   employee);
```

In this example, the subquery extracts information from the *l_name* and *f_name* columns of the *employee* table. The extracted values in these columns are used to fill the new *names* table. In this way, you can create a new table from data elements in the *employee* table.

Subqueries versus Joins

Often, you can use a subquery in place of a join for accessing information from more than one table. For example, the following SELECT statement uses a subquery to link information between the *student* and *class* tables:

```
SELECT   s_id, s_lname, s_fname
  FROM   student
WHERE   s_id IN (SELECT  s_id
                 FROM   class
                 WHERE   c_id = 'C4');
```

In this statement, the subquery returns from the *class* table the student identification numbers for students taking the course C4. With the student identification numbers, you can find the students' names from the *student* table. The subquery allows you to join information from the *class* and the *student* tables. The results from the statement look like

```
S_ID  S_LNAME  S_FNAME
----  -------  ----------
S2    Brown    Nancy J.
S5    Freed    Barbara J.
S8    Madison  George G.
```

You can get the same results by joining the two tables with the procedure you learned in Chapter 9. For example, the statement for making an equijoin between the two tables is issued as follows:

```
SELECT   student.s_id, s_lname, s_fname
  FROM   student, class
 WHERE   class.s_id = student.s_id
   AND   class.c_id = 'C4';
```

Although a join may be easier to set up than a subquery, the choice between a join or a subquery is a personal preference in most cases.

Not all the joining operations can be replaced by subqueries, however. Sometimes you cannot get exactly the same information with a join that you can get from a subquery. The differences between using subqueries and using joins are covered in the following sections.

Structuring Simple Subqueries

A simple subquery is one subquery within another query. The simple subquery has a main, or outer, query, which is presented by a SELECT statement. With the main query, you can include all the legitimate clauses needed for manipulating your data in the tables. These clauses may include one or more WHERE, GROUP BY, HAVING, and ORDER BY clauses.

The subquery is specified as another SELECT statement in the WHERE clause of the main query. In the SELECT statement of the subquery, you can include one or more WHERE, GROUP BY, and HAVING clauses, but you cannot use an ORDER BY clause in a subquery. In summary, a simple subquery can be structured as shown in figure 10.3.

In the column lists of the SELECT statements, you can include names of columns, expressions, and aggregate functions. In the WHERE clause of the main query, in addition to defining the subquery, you can specify all the other filter conditions for the main query. These filter conditions are connected with logical connectors (AND, OR, NOT, and so on). Similarly,

```
SELECT   <column list>
  FROM   <table list>
 WHERE   [<filter condition>
    AND]  <expression>  <logical operator>  (SELECT   <column list>
                                               FROM   <table list>
                                              [WHERE   <filter condition>]
                                            [GROUP BY   <column list>]
                                              [HAVING   <grouping condition>])
[GROUP BY   <column list>]
  [HAVING   <grouping condition>]
   [ORDER   <sorting keys>];
```

Fig. 10.3. *Structure of a simple subquery.*

you can specify the necessary filter conditions within the subquery in its WHERE clause.

Evaluating Subqueries

When a SELECT statement that involves a subquery is processed, the SELECT statement of the subquery is evaluated first. The results from the query are used for evaluating the expression in the WHERE clause of the main query. Depending on the logical operator you use in the WHERE clause, the subquery may return one or more data values for the filter condition.

Using the IN Logical Operator

The most useful logical operator for comparing the values returned from a subquery with the value of the expression in the WHERE clause is the IN operator. This operator is used to determine whether the value of the expression matches any of the values returned by the subquery. To understand how SQL processes a subquery, look at a simple subquery:

```
SELECT   l_name, f_name, title, dept
  FROM   employee
 WHERE   l_name IN (SELECT   last_name
                      FROM   payhike);
```

In this example, you want information about employees who are entitled to a pay raise. The last names and the amounts of pay increases (percentages in decimal) of these employees are stored in the *payhike* table (see fig. 10.4).

```
LAST_NAME   INCREASE
---------   --------
Chapman        0.08
Zeller         0.10
Dixon          0.12
Wong           0.15
Duff           0.12
Parker         0.13
```

Fig. 10.4. *The* payhike *table.*

The subquery for finding the last names of the employees who are entitled to a pay raise is

> SELECT   last_name
> FROM   payhike

The values to be returned from the subquery are taken from the *last_name* column of the *payhike* table. The column name in the WHERE clause for the main query is *l_name*. The corresponding columns in the query and subquery may have different names, but the two columns must be of the same type and width.

If you process the subquery as an individual statement, you get the values in the *l_name* column of the *payhike* table:

```
LAST_NAME
---------
Chapman
Zeller
Dixon
Wong
Duff
Parker
```

After the subquery is processed, the returned values are used for evaluating the filter condition in the WHERE clause. At this point, the main query can be interpreted as if it were written as shown in figure 10.5.

```
SELECT  l_name, f_name, title, dept
  FROM  employee
 WHERE  l_name IN ('Chapman','Zeller','Frazer','Wong','Duff','Parker');
```

L_NAME	F_NAME	TITLE	DEPT
Zeller	Albert K.	Salesman	Sales
Chapman	Kirk D.	Salesman	Sales
Frazer	Robert F.	Bookkeeper	Accounting
Wong	Mike J.	Manager	MIS
Duff	Cathy B.	Secretary	Personnel
Parker	Susan C.	Trainee	MIS

Fig. 10.5. The results of the entire query.

Using the NOT IN Logical Operator

In the preceding example, the IN logical operator is used in the WHERE clause for comparing the values in a column with a set of values returned from the subquery. Similarly, you can use the NOT IN logical operator in the WHERE clause. For example, if you want to find the employees who are not entitled to a pay raise, use the SELECT statement with the subquery shown in figure 10.6.

```
SELECT  l_name, f_name, title, dept
  FROM  employee
 WHERE  l_name NOT IN (SELECT  last_name
                         FROM  payhike);
```

L_NAME	F_NAME	TITLE	DEPT
Smith	James J.	President	Corporate
Nelson	Harry M.	Manager	Sales
Baker	Larry A.	Salesman	Sales
Frazer	Robert F.	Bookkeeper	Accounting
King	David G.	Manager	Personnel

Fig. 10.6. Using a subquery with the NOT IN logical operator.

The subquery returns the set of last names in the *payhike* table. The WHERE clause of the main query then uses these last names to filter the rows in the *employee* table and produce the information about employees not listed in the *payhike* table.

Using the EXISTS Logical Operator

You can use the EXISTS logical operator in the WHERE clause for evaluating the values returned from the subquery. Because the EXISTS operator returns only a value representing a true or false state, you use the EXISTS operator as an existence test. For example, you can use EXISTS to determine whether the table listed in the subquery is empty. By specifying the appropriate filter conditions in the subquery, you can use the EXISTS operator to determine whether the table contains any data rows that satisfy certain criteria.

Because EXISTS does not return any actual data, you do not need to specify the data items to be returned from the table in the subquery. Instead, you use the asterisk (*) in the SELECT clause of the subquery. The following is an example:

```
SELECT   *
  FROM   price
WHERE   EXISTS (SELECT  *
                FROM  newprice);
```

When this statement is processed, the subquery returns any data rows currently stored in the *newprice* table. If *newprice* is empty, therefore, no row from the *price* table is selected. In this case, the WHERE clause does not have any effect on the main query, and the main query is interpreted as

```
SELECT   *
  FROM   price;
```

The results are the contents of the *price* table (see fig. 10.7)

```
STOCK_NO  UNIT_PRICE
--------  ----------
HW101        850.50
HW102       1795.00
HW201        590.00
HW301        295.00
HW401       4070.00
HW402       3250.00
HW403       3725.00
SW101        350.00
SW201        275.00
SW202        250.00
SW301        520.00
SW302        490.00
```

Fig. 10.7. *The contents of the* price *table.*

If the *newprice* table has at least one row, every row from the *price* table is selected because a true value is returned from the subquery. To see how the EXISTS logical operator works, assume that the *newprice* table contains the rows of data shown in figure 10.8.

```
STOCK_NO   CHANGE
--------   ------
HW102       0.05
HW301       0.07
HW403       0.10
SW201       0.05
SW301       0.12
```

Fig. 10.8. *The* newprice *table.*

The *newprice* table contains information about the price changes for some of the items whose stock numbers are stored in the *stock_no* column. Values in the *change* column are expressed in decimal values (for percent changes).

You can use the EXISTS logical operator for the subquery to find in the *newprice* table the items requiring price adjustments and then determine the amount of price changes for these items in the main query. The SELECT statement issued and the results are shown in figure 10.9.

```
SELECT stock_no, unit_price, unit_price*1.05
  FROM price
 WHERE EXISTS (SELECT *
                 FROM newprice
                WHERE newprice.stock_no=price.stock_no
                  AND newprice.change=0.05);
STOCK_NO   UNIT_PRICE   UNIT_PRICE*1.05
--------   ----------   ---------------
HW102        1795.00           1884.75
SW201         275.00            288.75
```

Fig. 10.9. *Using the EXISTS logical operator in a subquery.*

The subquery in this statement finds the data rows that satisfy the filter condition of a price change of 0.05 in the *change* column of the *newprice* table. Because two rows in the *newprice* table meet these conditions, the main query is carried out accordingly.

You may notice that this subquery uses data from the main query in its filter condition. For example, in the WHERE clause of the subquery, a reference is made to a column in the *price* table listed in the main query: *price.stock_no*. This concept of a correlated query is presented in a later section.

A subquery with the EXISTS logical operator is just one way to get the results shown in the figure 10.9. You can get the same results by using a join (see fig. 10.10).

```
SELECT  x.stock_no, x.unit_price, x.unit_price*1.05
  FROM  price x, newprice y
 WHERE  x.stock_no=y.stock_no AND y.change=0.05;
X.STOCK_NO  X.UNIT_PRICE  X.UNIT_PRICE*1.05
----------  ------------  -----------------
HW102            1795.00            1884.75
SW201             275.00             288.75
```

Fig. 10.10. Using a join to determine price changes.

In fact, a join may be the preferred approach to the problem because a join is more flexible. Using a subquery, you can process only one price change at a time. For example, if you also need to find the items requiring a 12 percent increase in price adjustment, you need to issue another statement (see fig. 10.11).

```
SELECT  stock_no, unit_price, unit_price*1.12
  FROM  price
 WHERE  EXISTS (SELECT *
                  FROM newprice
                 WHERE newprice.stock_no=price.stock_no
                   AND newprice.change=0.12);
STOCK_NO  UNIT_PRICE  UNIT_PRICE*1.12
--------  ----------  ---------------
SW301         520.00           582.40
```

Fig. 10.11. Issuing a second subquery.

Using a subquery with the EXISTS logical operator, you cannot compute all the price changes in a single statement. You need to use a different statement for each level of price change. This method is not efficient if you need to process all the price adjustments at once. If you use a join operation, you can compute all the price changes with a single statement (see fig. 10.12).

```
SELECT  x.stock_no, x.unit_price,
        y.change, x.unit_price*(1+y.change)
  FROM  price x, newprice y
 WHERE  x.stock_no=y.stock_no;
```

X.STOCK_NO	X.UNIT_PRICE	Y.CHANGE	X.UNIT_PRICE*(1+Y.CHANGE)
HW102	1795.00	0.05	1884.75
HW301	295.00	0.07	315.65
HW403	3725.00	0.10	4097.50
SW201	275.00	0.05	288.75
SW301	520.00	0.12	582.40

Fig. 10.12. *Using a join to compute all price changes with one statement.*

Using Other Logical Operators

In addition to the IN and NOT IN logical operators, in the WHERE clause, you can use any of the following operators:

$=, !=, >, >=, <, <=$

When you are using one of these logical operators in the WHERE clause, the results returned from the subquery must be a single data value. Otherwise, the main query results in an error and is not executed. For example, the following SELECT statement produces an error:

```
SELECT  l_name, f_name, title, dept
  FROM  employee
 WHERE  l_name = (SELECT  last_name
                    FROM  payhike);
```

Because the results returned from the subquery include six last names, evaluating the filter condition is impossible. You cannot compare one value with a set of values. As a result, the query will not be carried out.

Therefore, if you need to use one of these logical operators in the filter condition, you must be familiar with the data elements in the table you are searching with the subquery. You can use these logical operators only if you know that a single data value will be returned by the subquery. For example, if you know that only one employee gets a 15 percent pay increase, you can use the statement shown in figure 10.13 to find the information about this particular employee.

```
SELECT  l_name, f_name, title, dept
  FROM  employee
 WHERE  l_name=(SELECT  last_name
                  FROM  payhike
                 WHERE  increase=.15);


L_NAME   F_NAME   TITLE    DEPT
------   -------  -------  ----
Wong     Mike J.  Manager  MIS
```

Fig. 10.13. Using a subquery to find a single data element.

Eliminating Duplicate Values

When you use a subquery to retrieve values from a table, the subquery may return duplicate values. Because duplicate values provide redundant information for evaluating the filter condition in the WHERE clause of the main query, you may want to eliminate them and retain only the unique values from the subquery. To accomplish that goal, you add the DISTINCT keyword in the subquery SELECT command. For example, if you want to find the students who are taking the C1 or C4 course, you use the following SELECT statement:

```
SELECT   s_id, s_lname, s_fname
  FROM   student
 WHERE   s_id IN (SELECT  DISTINCT s_id
                    FROM   class
                   WHERE   c_id = 'C1'
                      OR   c_id = 'C4');
```

The subquery extracts from the *class* tables the student identification numbers for the students who are taking either the C3 or C4 course. If you process the subquery as an individual statement, you get a list of student identification numbers, which may have duplicate values (see fig. 10.14).

```
SELECT  s_id
  FROM  class
 WHERE  c_id='C1' OR c_id='C4';


S_ID
----
S3
S5
S10
S2
S5
S8
```

Fig. 10.14. *A subquery that returns duplicate values.*

As a result, the main query is equivalent to the following statement:

SELECT   s_id, s_lname, s_fname
  FROM   student
 WHERE   s_id IN ('S3', 'S5', 'S10', 'S2', 'S5', 'S8');

When you evaluate the main query, each value in the *s_id* column of the *student* table is compared with the values in the parentheses following the IN operator. Therefore, you can speed the main query processing if you eliminate any duplicate values in the parentheses. To eliminate the duplicates, you add the DISTINCT keyword in the SELECT statement of the subquery (see fig. 10.15).

```
SELECT DISTINCT s_id
  FROM  class
 WHERE  c_id='C1' OR c_id='C4';
S_ID
----
S10
S2
S3
S5
S8
```

Fig. 10.15. *A subquery producing a set of unique values.*

The final results from processing the main query (including the subquery) with the DISTINCT keyword are shown in figure 10.16.

```
SELECT  s_id, s_lname, s_fname
   FROM  student
  WHERE  s_id IN (SELECT  DISTINCT s_id
                      FROM  class
                     WHERE  c_id='C1' OR c_id='C4');
```

```
S_ID   S_LNAME   S_FNAME
----   -------   ----------
S2     Brown     Nancy J.
S3     Carter    Jack F.
S5     Freed     Barbara J.
S8     Madison   George G.
S10    Taylor    Bob K.
```

Fig. 10.16. *Using the DISTINCT keyword in a subquery to eliminate duplicate values.*

Ordering Data in Subqueries

In a subquery you can sort the selected values before returning them to the main query. However, you cannot use the ORDER BY clause in a subquery. For example, the following SELECT statement is illegal:

```
SELECT   l_name, f_name, title, dept
  FROM   employee
 WHERE   l_name IN ( SELECT   last_name
                       FROM   payhike
                   ORDER BY   last_name);
```

You use the GROUP BY clause to order the data values to be returned by the subquery. That is, the preceding statement can be written as shown in figure 10.17.

The last names sorted by the GROUP BY clause in the subquery, however, did not have an effect in the main query on the order of the values in the *l_name* column. (This condition is true for most versions of SQL.) This problem occurred because the IN logical operator in the WHERE clause of the main query was not concerned with the order of the values in the parentheses. As long as the value of the *l_name* column matches one of the values in the IN parentheses, the filter condition is satisfied. Therefore, to sort the last names, you use the ORDER BY clause in the main query (see fig. 10.18)

```
SELECT  l_name, f_name, title, dept
  FROM  employee
 WHERE  l_name IN ( SELECT  last_name
                      FROM  payhike
                  GROUP BY  last_name);
```

L_NAME	F_NAME	TITLE	DEPT
Zeller	Albert K.	Salesman	Sales
Chapman	Kirk D.	Salesman	Sales
Dixon	Kathy T.	Accountant	Accounting
Wong	Mike J.	Manager	MIS
Duff	Cathy B.	Secretary	Personnel
Parker	Susan C.	Trainee	MIS

Fig. 10.17. Using GROUP BY in the subquery to order data.

```
SELECT  l_name, f_name, title, dept
  FROM  employee
 WHERE  l_name IN ( SELECT  last_name
                      FROM  payhike)
ORDER BY  l_name;
```

L_NAME	F_NAME	TITLE	DEPT
Chapman	Kirk D.	Salesman	Sales
Dixon	Kathy T.	Accountant	Accounting
Duff	Cathy B.	Secretary	Personnel
Parker	Susan C.	Trainee	MIS
Wong	Mike J.	Manager	MIS
Zeller	Albert K.	Salesman	Sales

Fig. 10.18. Ordering data by using ORDER BY in the main query.

Using Aggregate Functions

The list of objects to be selected in a subquery can be the same as the objects in a regular query. These objects can be table columns and expressions made up of columns and arithmetic operators (+, -, *, /). You also can include aggregate functions in the select list. For example, by using the MIN() aggregate function in the subquery, you can find the employee who earns the lowest salary in the firm (see fig. 10.19).

```
SELECT  f_name, l_name, title, dept, salary
   FROM  employee
  WHERE  salary=(SELECT MIN(salary)
                    FROM employee);
```

F_NAME	L_NAME	TITLE	DEPT	SALARY
Cathy B.	Duff	Secretary	Personnel	27825.00

Fig. 10.19. *Using the MIN() function in a subquery.*

The subquery finds and returns the minimum salary from the *employee* table. Notice that the WHERE clause in the main query uses an equality relation for comparing the value in the *salary* column of the *employee* table with the value returned from the subquery. You can use this subquery because it returns only one value.

If you want to find the employees who are earning more than the average salary in the firm, you use the AVG() function in the subquery. The average salary computed in the subquery then is used as a filter value in the WHERE clause of the main query (see fig. 10.20).

```
SELECT  f_name, l_name, title, dept, salary
   FROM  employee
  WHERE  salary>(SELECT AVG(salary)
                    FROM employee);
```

F_NAME	L_NAME	TITLE	DEPT	SALARY
James J.	Smith	President	Corporate	89500.00
Harry M.	Nelson	Manager	Sales	65000.00
Albert K.	Zeller	Salesman	Sales	51345.00
Kathy T.	Dixon	Accountant	Accounting	45000.00

Fig. 10.20. *Using the AVG() aggregate function in a subquery.*

In this example, you can compare each value in the *salary* column with the average value returned from the subquery. This technique is an effective use of a subquery for comparing values in the table with summary statistics computed from that table.

You also can work with group statistics with subqueries. For example, if you want to find the departments whose employees earn an average salary more than the company-wide average salary, you can set up the subquery to provide the information about the company-wide average. The statement can be issued as shown in figure 10.21.

```
    SELECT  dept, AVG(salary)
       FROM  employee
GROUP BY  dept
    HAVING  AVG(salary)>(SELECT  AVG(salary)
                            FROM  employee);


DEPT        AVG(SALARY)
---------   -----------
Corporate     89500.00
Sales         48086.25
```

Fig. 10.21. Using more than one AVG() function in a query and a subquery.

In this example, the subquery returns an overall average salary, which is computed by using all the salary values in the *employee* table. The main query computes the average salaries for each department as a group. Each group average then is compared with the overall average returned from the subquery. Only the group averages that are greater than the overall average are selected and returned by the main query.

To verify the results, you can issue the statement shown in figure 10.22 to see the group averages by department.

```
    SELECT  dept, AVG(salary)
       FROM  employee
GROUP BY  dept;


DEPT        AVG(SALARY)
---------   -----------
Accounting    37200.00
Corporate     89500.00
MIS           36000.00
Personnel     32912.50
Sales         48086.25
```

Fig. 10.22. Verifying results of a query.

The syntax rules require that you use the HAVING CLAUSE when you define the selection criterion for qualifying the group averages. You cannot use the WHERE clause. The following statement is illegal:

```
    SELECT   dept, AVG(salary)
      FROM   employee
  GROUP BY   dept
     WHERE   AVG(salary)>(SELECT  AVG(salary)
                            FROM   employee);
```

Structuring Compound Subqueries

In the preceding examples, you have seen a simple two-level query structure. But you can structure more sophisticated compound subqueries. A compound subquery is a multilevel nested subquery. That is, you can structure a subquery within another subquery, which, in turn, is within another subquery.

As mentioned, SQL theoretically sets no limit on the depth of the subquery structure, although some implementations of SQL do impose limits on the number of subqueries in one statement. Because these limits usually exceed what you need for most data applications, you need not be concerned with these limits for practical purposes.

To see how you can use compound subqueries, assume that you need to find all the courses the instructor named Newton teaches. For finding those courses, you first use a subquery to find the teacher's identification number from the *teacher* table. The subquery, when expressed as an individual SELECT statement, looks like the following:

```
SELECT t_id
  FROM teacher
 WHERE t_lname='Newton';


T_ID
----
T3
```

The teacher's identification number returned from the subquery is T3. With the returned identification number, you can use another subquery to find in the *assign* table the course identification numbers of the courses assigned to T3. The combined subqueries and final results are

```
SELECT c_id
  FROM assign
  WHERE t_id IN (SELECT t_id
                   FROM teacher
                   WHERE t_lname='Newton');


C_ID
----
C3
C5
```

Finally, to find information about these courses, you write the main query. The main query uses the course identification numbers returned from the preceding subquery to find the course titles and descriptions from the *course* table. Figure 10.23 shows the complete SELECT statement for finding information about the courses Newton teaches.

```
SELECT c_id, c_title, c_desc
  FROM course
  WHERE c_id IN (SELECT c_id
                   FROM assign
                   WHERE t_id IN (SELECT t_id
                                    FROM teacher
                                    WHERE t_lname='Newton'));


C_ID  C_TITLE   C_DESC
----  --------  -----------
C3    MATH 105  Calculus I
C5    PHYS 102  Physics I
```

Fig. 10.23. A compound subquery finding the classes taught by Newton.

What happens if you also want to know the names of all the students who are being taught by Newton? To get that information, you need to add more levels of subqueries to the preceding statement. For example, the SELECT statement shown in figure 10.24 produces the list of identification numbers for the students who are taking the courses taught by Newton.

```
SELECT DISTINCT s_id
  FROM class
 WHERE c_id IN
        (SELECT c_id
           FROM course
          WHERE c_id IN
                (SELECT c_id
                   FROM assign
                  WHERE t_id IN
                        (SELECT t_id
                           FROM teacher
                          WHERE t_lname='Newton')));

S_ID
----
S1
S2
S3
S6
S8
S9
```

Fig. 10.24. *A still more complex series of subqueries, producing ID numbers of students taught by Newton.*

You may note that I used the DISTINCT keyword in the top subquery to eliminate duplicate student identification numbers.

If you need to know the names of the students whose identification numbers are returned by the subqueries, you can yet add another query to the statement (see fig. 10.25).

```
SELECT  s_id, s_lname, s_first
   FROM  student
  WHERE  s_id IN
         (SELECT  DISTINCT s_id
             FROM  class
            WHERE  c_id IN
                  (SELECT  c_id
                      FROM  course
                     WHERE  c_id IN
                           (SELECT  c_id
                               FROM  assign
                              WHERE  t_id IN
                                    (SELECT  t_id
                                        FROM  teacher
                                       WHERE  t_lname='Newton'))));
```

```
S_ID   S_LNAME   S_FNAME
----   -------   -------
S1     Austin    Linda D.
S2     Brown     Nancy J.
S3     Carter    Jack F.
S6     Gilmore   Danny S.
S8     Madison   George G.
S9     Reed      Donna E.
```

Fig. 10.25. *A multilevel compound subquery, producing names and ID numbers of students taught by Newton.*

The preceding examples demonstrate how you can structure multilevel compound subqueries for finding the information you need. These compound subqueries also can be expressed as joins and produce identical results. For example, the queries in figure 10.25 can be written as a multiple table join and yield the same results (see fig. 10.26).

```
SELECT DISTINCT v.s_id, v.s_lname, v.s_fname
   FROM student v, class w, course x, assign y, teacher z
  WHERE v.s_id=w.s_id
    AND w.c_id=x.c_id
    AND x.c_id=y.c_id
    AND y.t_id=z.t_id
    AND t_lname='Newton';
```

V.S_ID	V.S_LNAME	V.S_FNAME
S1	Austin	Linda D.
S2	Brown	Nancy J.
S3	Carter	Jack F.
S6	Gilmore	Danny S.
S8	Madison	George G.
S9	Reed	Donna E.

Fig. 10.26. *A multiple table join that produces the same results as the queries in figure 10.25.*

In this multiple table join, the *student*, *class*, *course*, *assign*, and *teacher* tables are joined successively with a set of linking columns. If you have trouble understanding the join, go back to Chapter 9 for review.

The choice between using joins and using subqueries is often a personal preference (except when you are working with aggregate functions); however, you may find that issuing the command as a join is simpler than using multilevel subqueries. With a join, you can display information from all the joined tables; but in the compound subquery structure, you can display only the values of the columns listed in the main query. Therefore, if you need to show data values in some of or all the tables in the operation, you need to use the join. For example, suppose that you want to know information about the instructor Newton and the courses he teaches. You can select those items from the *teacher* and *course* tables in the join (see fig. 10.27).

```
SELECT  v.s_id, v.s_lname, v.s_fname,
        z.t_lname, z.t_fname, x.c_title
  FROM  student v, class w, course x, assign y, teacher z
 WHERE  v.s_id=w.s_id
   AND  w.c_id=x.c_id
   AND  x.c_id=y.c_id
   AND  y.t_id=z.t_id
   AND  t_lname='Newton';
```

V.S_ID	V.S_LNAME	V.S_FNAME	Z.T_LNAME	Z.T_FNAME	X.C_TITLE
S1	Austin	Linda D.	Newton	Isaac	MATH 105
S2	Brown	Nancy J.	Newton	Isaac	MATH 105
S3	Carter	Jack F.	Newton	Isaac	PHYS 102
S6	Gilmore	Danny S.	Newton	Isaac	PHYS 102
S8	Madison	George G.	Newton	Isaac	PHYS 102
S9	Reed	Donna E.	Newton	Isaac	MATH 105
S9	Reed	Donna E.	Newton	Isaac	PHYS 102

Fig. 10.27. Using a join to show information from several tables.

Be sure to note that in order to show the names of the courses a student takes from instructor Newton, you must not use the DISTINCT keyword in the SELECT clause of the join. Otherwise, only one course will be returned.

Structuring Correlated Subqueries

In a regular subquery, the subquery is treated as an independent SELECT statement. Results from the SELECT command in the subquery are passed back as filter values to be evaluated in the WHERE clause of the outer query. The subquery does not need to take information from the outer query in order to process. A correlated subquery is a subquery that uses information from an outer query. In order for a correlated subquery to work, you need to be able to pass data values from the outer query to the subquery. To understand how a correlated subquery works, look at the following example:

```
SELECT   s_id, s_lname, s_fname
  FROM   student
 WHERE   'C1' IN (SELECT  c_id
                    FROM   class
                   WHERE   class.s_id = student.s_id);
```

This command finds the students who are taking the C1 class. Of course, you can issue a different command to get the same results, but this example illustrates the concept of a correlated subquery. Notice that the WHERE clause of the subquery uses a column from the *student* table (*student.s_id*) that also is specified in the outer, or main, query. As a result, the command cannot evaluate the subquery just once as in a regular subquery because the value of the *student.s_id* column changes for each row of the *student* table that the main query evaluates. Therefore, the subquery must be evaluated for each row in the *student* table. That is, when the main query looks at the first row in the *student* table, the value of the *s_id* column (S1) is passed to the subquery. The first time around, the subquery is interpreted as

```
SELECT   c_id
  FROM   class
WHERE    class.s_id = 'S1';
```

The value returned from this subquery is C3. The complete query then is interpreted as

```
SELECT   s_id, s_lname, s_fname
  FROM   student
WHERE    'C1' IN ('C3');
```

Because the value C1 is not the value in the parentheses, the first row of the *student* table is not selected by the main query.

Next, the main query moves on to evaluate the next row in the *student* table. Then the value of S2 is passed to the subquery:

```
SELECT   s_id, s_lname, s_fname
  FROM   student
WHERE    'C1' IN (SELECT   c_id
                    FROM   class
                   WHERE   class.s_id = 'S2');
```

This process continues until the main query has evaluated all the rows in the *student* table. The final results from the complete query are as follows:

```
S_ID   S_LNAME   S_FNAME
----   -------   ----------
S3     Carter    Jack F.
S5     Freed     Barbara J.
S10    Taylor    Bob K.
```

For the same results, you can use a column in the WHERE clause of the main query and specify a filter condition in the subquery for identifying the C1 course (see fig. 10.28).

```
SELECT  s_id, s_lname, s_fname
  FROM  student
WHERE  s_id IN (SELECT  s_id
                        FROM  class
                        WHERE  c_id='C1');


S_ID  S_LNAME  S_FNAME
----  -------  ----------
S3    Carter   Jack F.
S5    Freed    Barbara J.
S10   Taylor   Bob K.
```

Fig. 10.28. *A correlated subquery.*

The query involving the correlated subquery also can be written as a join. Here is the statement for this join:

```
SELECT   student.s_id, s_lname, s_fname
  FROM   student, class
WHERE   student.s_id = class.s_id
   AND   class.c_id = 'C1';
```

For many people, a join is easier to understand than a correlated subquery. But using a correlated subquery is an important concept for passing data from an outer query to a subquery. Although you may not need the procedure often, knowing how to use correlated subqueries can be handy for some applications.

Structuring Subqueries on a Single Table

In Chapter 9, you learned that you can join a table to itself. You also can structure your subqueries so that they refer to data elements in the same table. For example, you can find the other classes taken by students who are taking the C3 course. The statement can be written as follows:

```
SELECT  DISTINCT c_id, c_title, c_desc
  FROM   class
WHERE   s_id IN (SELECT  s_id
                      FROM  class
                      WHERE  c_id = 'C3');
```

In this example, both the main query and the subquery refer to the same *class* table. In the subquery, the program finds the student identification numbers for the students taking the C3 course. You get the following results if you process the subquery independently:

```
SELECT  s_id
  FROM  class
 WHERE  c_id='C3';

S_ID
----
S1
S2
S9
```

After the values are returned from the subquery, the main query will be interpreted as follows:

```
SELECT  DISTINCT c_id
  FROM    class
 WHERE    s_id IN ('S1', 'S2', 'S9');
```

When you process the main query, it finds all the courses taken by these students. Therefore, the query displays the course identification numbers of those courses, including C3, from the *class* table:

```
C_ID
----
C3
C4
C5
```

If you need to know more about these courses, you can find their titles and descriptions by using another query built on the preceding query (see fig. 10.29).

```
SELECT  c_id, c_title, c_desc
  FROM  course
 WHERE  c_id IN (SELECT DISTINCT c_id
                   FROM class
                  WHERE s_id IN (SELECT s_id
                                   FROM class
                                  WHERE c_id='C3'));

C_ID  C_TITLE   C_DESC
----  --------  ----------
C3    MATH 105  Calculus I
C4    PHIL 101  Philosophy
C5    PHYS 102  Physics I
```

Fig. 10.29. Structuring more than one subquery on a single table.

Again, the preceding subqueries also can be expressed as a self-join. You can obtain the same course identification numbers by using the following statement:

```
SELECT DISTINCT x.c_id
  FROM class x, class y
 WHERE x.s_id=y.s_id
   AND y.c_id='C3';

X.C_ID
------
C3
C4
C5
```

If you want to find more information about these courses, you can add the *course* table to the join. The following statement displays the titles and descriptions of these courses:

```
SELECT DISTINCT x.c_id, x.c_title, x.c_desc
  FROM course x, class y, class z
 WHERE x.c_id=y.c_id
   AND y.s_id=z.s_id
   AND z.c_id='C3';

X.C_ID  X.C_TITLE  X.C_DESC
------  ---------  ----------
C3      MATH 105   Calculus I
C4      PHIL 101   Philosophy
C5      PHYS 102   Physics I
```

Updating Data with Subqueries

You can use a subquery to select for the main query the rows whose values need to be changed. As you may recall, the *newprice* table contains information about the price changes for the items whose stock numbers are stored in the table (see fig. 10.30).

```
STOCK_NO  CHANGE
--------  ------
HW102     0.05
HW301     0.07
HW403     0.10
SW201     0.05
SW301     0.12
```

Fig. 10.30. *The* newprice *table.*

You can use the *newprice* table in a subquery for updating those items in the *price* table. Before the update operation, the contents of the *price* table are assumed to be as shown in figure 10.31.

```
SELECT *
  FROM price;


STOCK_NO  UNIT_PRICE
--------  ----------
HW101        850.50
HW102       1795.00
HW201        590.00
HW301        295.00
HW401       4070.00
HW402       3250.00
HW403       3725.00
SW101        350.00
SW201        275.00
SW202        250.00
SW301        582.40
SW302        490.00
```

Fig. 10.31. *The contents of the* price *table before updating.*

The following statement changes the unit prices for some of the items in the main query, by using a subquery:

```
UPDATE   price
   SET   unit_price = unit_price*1.05
 WHERE   stock_no IN (SELECT   stock_no
                        FROM   newprice
                       WHERE   change = 0.05);
```

The subquery returns the stock numbers from the *stock_no* column in the *newprice* table for the items that require a five percent increase in their prices. The returned stock numbers are HW102 and SW201. The SET clause changes the values of the *unit_cost* column accordingly. As a result, the values in the *unit_price* column of the *price* table for these two items are changed accordingly (see fig. 10.32).

```
SELECT *
  FROM price;

STOCK_NO   UNIT_PRICE
--------   ----------
HW101          850.50
HW102         1884.75
HW201          590.00
HW301          295.00
HW401         4070.00
HW402         3250.00
HW403         3725.00
SW101          350.00
SW201          288.75
SW202          250.00
SW301          582.40
SW302          490.00
```

Fig. 10.32. *The contents of the* price *table after updating.*

Deleting Data with Subqueries

You also can use subqueries to select for the main query the data rows you want to delete. To illustrate the deletion operation, assume that the *account* table contains information about current active accounts (see fig. 10.33).

```
Account table:

ACCT_NO   ACCT_NAME              ADDRESS               CITY        STATE   ZIP
-------   --------------------   -------------------   ---------   -----   -----
A-101     Fairwind Travel        3256 Lakeview Dr.     Mesa        AZ      85201
B-101     Evergreen Florists     2658 Broadway         Vancouver   WA      98664
C-101     ACME Construction      1456 S.E. 132nd Ave.  Portland    OR      97204
A-201     B & J Fine Furniture   3567 S.W. Canyon Rd.  Beaverton   OR      97203
A-301     Western Electronic     2478 University Ave.  Seattle     WA      98105
C-201     Ace Office Service     5214 Main Street      Salem       OR      97201
C-301     Lake Grove Bookstore   3456 Salmon Street    Portland    OR      97203
A-202     Johnson & Associates   10345 Riverside Dr.   New York    NY      10038
A-203     Superior Computers     1345 Market Street    San Diego   CA      91355
B-201     National Auto Service  3081 Columbus Ave.    San Jose    CA      90406
```

Fig. 10.33. *The* account *table before overdue accounts are deleted.*

In another table, named *overdue*, you keep track of the number of days each current account is past due. The contents of the overdue account are assumed to be as shown in figure 10.34.

```
ACCT_NO  DAYS_OLD
-------  --------
 A-101        12
 B-101        35
 C-101       190
 A-201        30
 A-301        10
 C-201        60
 C-301        90
 A-202       205
 A-203        45
 B-201        29
```

Fig. 10.34. *The* overdue *table.*

If you want to remove from the *account* table the accounts that have been due for more than 180 days, you can set up a subquery for removing the accounts. In the subquery, you find the account numbers for the accounts you want to delete and then pass those numbers back to the main query. Here is the statement for removing information about these accounts:

```
DELETE FROM   account
        WHERE   acct_no IN (SELECT   acct_no
                              FROM   overdue
                             WHERE   days_old>180);
```

Because two accounts (C-101 and A-202) have values greater than 180 in the *days_old* column in the *overdue* table, two rows of the *account* table are deleted by the statement (see fig. 10.35).

```
SELECT * FROM account
   ORDER BY acct_no;
```

ACCT_NO	ACCT_NAME	ADDRESS	CITY	STATE	ZIP
A-101	Fairwind Travel	3256 Lakeview Dr.	Mesa	AZ	85201
A-201	B & J Fine Furniture	3567 S.W. Canyon Rd.	Beaverton	OR	97203
A-203	Superior Computers	1345 Market Street	San Diego	CA	91355
A-301	Western Electronic	2478 University Ave.	Seattle	WA	98105
B-101	Evergreen Florists	2658 Broadway	Vancouver	WA	98664
B-201	National Auto Service	3081 Columbus Ave.	San Jose	CA	90406
C-201	Ace Office Service	5214 Main Street	Salem	OR	97201
C-301	Lake Grove Bookstore	3456 Salmon Street	Portland	OR	97203

Fig. 10.35. *The* account *table after overdue accounts have been deleted.*

Subqueries on Joined Tables

From the preceding examples, you can see that you can use joins and subqueries interchangeably for many applications. You also can combine joins and subqueries in the same statement (see fig. 10.36).

```
SELECT c_id, c_title, c_desc
   FROM course
 WHERE c_id IN (SELECT x.c_id
                  FROM class x, student y
                 WHERE x.s_id=y.s_id
                   AND y.s_lname='Madison');
```

C_ID	C_TITLE	C_DESC
C2	HIST 100	American History
C4	PHIL 101	Philosophy
C5	PHYS 102	Physics I

Fig. 10.36. *Combining a join and a subquery.*

This statement finds information about the courses taken by the student named Madison. In this example, the subquery is expressed as a equijoin between the *class* and *student* table. If you process the subquery independently, you get the following results:

```
SELECT  x.c_id
  FROM  class x, student y
 WHERE  x.s_id=y.s_id
   AND  y.s_lname='Madison';


X.C_ID
------
C2
C4
C5
```

The course identification numbers retrieved by the equijoin in the subquery are used in the main query for finding the information about these courses. These identification numbers are then used in the filter condition for finding the courses for the main query. The main query then retrieves the information about these courses from the *course* table.

Using Views

Views are one of the powerful tools provided by a relational database language like SQL for examining data. Views allow you to look through a predefined frame, or window, at a subset of the data elements in one or more base tables. As a result, you can organize your data logically in a relational database by the data entities without much concern about the size and number of base tables. By using views, you can retrieve data efficiently from your base tables regardless of how the data elements are grouped into tables.

What Is a View?

A view, often called a virtual table, is created by using data elements from one or more base tables or another view. The term *virtual table* means that for most operations, a view looks and works like a table, but a view is not a real table.

A view does not actually hold data elements. Instead, it stores the definition of the view. The definition has all the information about data elements that make up the view and tells where they are stored. In addition to the names of the columns and base tables for the data elements, the definition contains any formulas and expressions involved.

You can think of a view as a viewing frame for looking at data elements that are stored in the base tables. By defining your viewing frame, you can examine certain data elements in a particular combination. If you change the viewing frame, you can look at different combinations of the data elements from different perspectives.

Advantages and Disadvantages of Views

The most important function of a view is that it allows you to look through a predefined frame at selected data elements in the base tables. The benefits of views can be seen in the areas of data security and data confidentiality. For example, if you want only authorized persons to access certain information in the database, a view is an efficient way to achieve that goal. By creating a view for looking at only the prescribed data elements, you can control data confidentiality.

Similarly, to protect the integrity of your data, you may want to grant to only certain people the right to add and modify data. By using views, you can let other people look at the data without risking unauthorized modifications on the data.

Views are a shortcut for repeated data retrieval and query operations. In managing your data, you need to find specific information from certain base tables. For this information, you issue the appropriate SELECT statement for the data query operation. If you need to repeat the same data query operation, you have to reissue the statement. This process can be tedious if the statement is complicated and you repeat it often. In this case, a view is a nice shortcut. By defining the data query as a view, you can repeat the query operation by issuing the simple command for the view.

Views provide an economical way to organize your data logically. When you design a relational database, you should try to group your data according to the data entities involved. But for some applications, you may want to regroup your data elements in a different way in order to facilitate the data manipulation process. For this purpose, you can group these data elements in a view. You then can manipulate your data elements in the view as if they were organized in a base table. Because a view does not actually contain the data elements, it is an economical way to organize your data elements.

Although views provide many benefits for managing a relational database, they do have some disadvantages. First, views take more time to process. For example, if you create a view for performing a data query with a SELECT statement, processing the view takes longer than processing the query independently. This difference occurs because the view contains only the definition of the query, not the results of the query. Therefore, when you issue the command for processing the view, the program needs first to interpret the definition of the view and then to carry out the query operation accordingly. Each time you process the view, it must regenerate the results of the query.

Another problem with using views is that certain operations are not available for working with views. Many restrictions are imposed on updating views. For example, when the view is created in a certain way (with certain keywords), you cannot update the view. These problems are discussed in the following sections.

Finally, although you can use views as shortcuts for repeated data retrieval and manipulation operations, views do take up memory, or storage, space.

In summary, views require additional processing time and take up extra memory space. However, these disadvantages are usually not significant when you consider the benefits of using views. When views are properly created and maintained, they save you a great deal of work reissuing the same statements over and over.

Creating Views

You create a view by selecting data elements from tables in the database. These data elements can be columns of data in one or more base tables. You also can use arithmetic expressions for combining these data elements for the view. Although a view looks like a table when its contents are displayed, the view does not contain actual data columns. Therefore, you need not define a table structure for a view.

View Syntax

A view is created by using the CREATE VIEW command in the following format:

```
CREATE VIEW  <view name> [(<column list>)]
        AS  SELECT   <column list>
            FROM    <table list>
          [WHERE   <filter condition>]
            [WITH CHECK OPTION];
```

Views are assigned names according to the same conventions as table names. You cannot use an existing table name for a view. The column list for the view is optional. If you do not specify the column names, the names of the selected columns are used, provided they are not in the form of expressions. Here is an example:

```
CREATE VIEW title
      AS SELECT ss_no, title, l_name, f_name
         FROM employee;
```

```
view TITLE created
```

This statement creates a view named *title* with data elements in the *title*, *l_name*, and *f_name* columns from the *employee* table. In this example, columns in the view will have the same names as the columns selected from the *employee* table. These column names are used for displaying the results of processing the view.

Displaying Views

You display a view the same way you display the contents of a table. You use the asterisk for showing the results produced by the view. For example, if you want to display the view named *title*, created in the preceding example, you can issue the SELECT command shown in figure 10.37.

```
SELECT *
  FROM title;
```

SS_NO	TITLE	L_NAME	F_NAME
123-45-6789	President	Smith	James J.
634-56-7890	Manager	Nelson	Harry M.
445-67-8801	Salesman	Zeller	Albert K.
562-87-8800	Salesman	Chapman	Kirk D.
404-22-4568	Salesman	Baker	Larry A.
256-09-5555	Accountant	Dixon	Kathy T.
458-90-3456	Bookkeeper	Frazer	Robert F.
777-34-6543	Manager	King	David G.
100-45-8021	Manager	Wong	Mike J.
303-25-7777	Secretary	Duff	Cathy B.
909-10-8910	Trainee	Parker	Susan C.

Fig. 10.37. *Displaying the view named* title.

You can perform any query operation on the view just as if it were a base table. The following statement, for example, finds the managers from the *title* view by adding the appropriate filter conditions:

```
SELECT title, l_name, f_name
  FROM title
 WHERE title='Manager';
```

```
TITLE     L_NAME   F_NAME
-------   ------   --------
Manager   Nelson   Harry M.
Manager   King     David G.
Manager   Wong     Mike J.
```

Naming View Columns

The names of the view's columns may be different from the names of the columns selected from the table, in order to provide better descriptions of the information. To create different column names in the view, you define the view's column names in parentheses following the view name. If you define the view's columns, you must include all the columns in the definition. The column names defined in the view must match in number and order the selected columns from the base table. Figure 10.38 shows an example.

```
CREATE VIEW dept (department, last_name, first_name)
        AS SELECT dept, l_name, f_name
            FROM employee;
```

View DEPT created

```
SELECT *
  FROM dept;
```

DEPARTMENT	LAST_NAME	FIRST_NAME
Corporate	Smith	James J.
Sales	Nelson	Harry M.
Sales	Zeller	Albert K.
Sales	Chapman	Kirk D.
Sales	Baker	Larry A.
Accounting	Dixon	Kathy T.
Accounting	Frazer	Robert F.
Personnel	King	David G.
MIS	Wong	Mike J.
Personnel	Duff	Cathy B.
MIS	Parker	Susan C.

Fig. 10.38. Creating a view with column names different from column names in the base table.

You must name your view columns if these columns result from expressions in the selection list from the base table. For example, if you compute the monthly salary from the base table for use as a column in the view, you must assign a column name for the computed value. Figure 10.39 shows the statement for creating such a view.

```
CREATE VIEW monthly (soc_sec_no, month_pay)
        AS SELECT ss_no, salary/12
            FROM employee;
```

View MONTHLY created

```
SELECT *
  FROM monthly;
```

SOC_SEC_NO	MONTH_PAY
123-45-6789	7458.33
634-56-7890	5416.67
445-67-8801	4278.75
562-87-8800	3541.67
404-22-4568	2791.67
256-09-5555	3750.00
458-90-3456	2450.00
777-34-6543	3166.67
100-45-8021	3666.67
303-25-7777	2318.75
909-10-8910	2333.33

Fig. 10.39. Using a mathematical expression to create a column in a view.

Using Selected Rows from Base Tables

You can add any legal filter conditions to the WHERE clause in the SELECT statement for the base table. For example, the view in figure 10.40 is created for viewing the names and salaries of the employees with high annual salaries.

```
CREATE VIEW hisalary (last_name, first_name, job_title, salary)
        AS SELECT l_name, f_name, title, salary
            FROM employee
            WHERE salary>50000;
```

View HISALARY created

```
SELECT *
  FROM hisalary;
```

LAST_NAME	FIRST_NAME	JOB_TITLE	SALARY
Smith	James J.	President	89500.00
Nelson	Harry M.	Manager	65000.00
Zeller	Albert K.	Salesman	51345.00

Fig. 10.40. *Displaying selected rows of a view.*

Using WITH CHECK OPTION

As you will learn later, you can change the data elements associated with a view by using the UPDATE or INSERT command on the view. In order to ensure that the data elements will satisfy the conditions defined in the view, you can use the WITH CHECK OPTION clause when you create the view. Here is an example:

```
CREATE VIEW  hisalary (last_name, first_name, job_title, salary)
        AS  SELECT  l_name, f_name, title, salary
            FROM  employee
            WHERE  salary>50000
            WITH  CHECK OPTION;
```

When the view is created including the WITH CHECK OPTION clause, if you attempt to add information to the view about a new employee with a salary of less than $50,000, the program displays an error message and does not let you add that data. You will learn more than the operations of adding and changing data with a view in a later section.

Using Grouped Data

You can create a view by using grouped data from one or more base tables. You can add the necessary GROUP BY clause in the SELECT statement for the base tables. For example, the statement shown in figure 10.41 creates a view displaying the average salaries for all the departments in a firm.

```
CREATE VIEW deptavg (department, avg_salary)
      AS SELECT dept, AVG(salary)
            FROM employee GROUP BY dept;
```

View DEPTAVG created

```
SELECT *
  FROM deptavg;
```

DEPARTMENT	AVG_SALARY
Accounting	37200.00
Corporate	89500.00
MIS	36000.00
Personnel	32912.50
Sales	48086.25

Fig. 10.41. Grouped data in a view.

This command creates a view for displaying average salaries for each department. The values in the *salary* column of the *employee* table are grouped before the average values are computed.

Using Joined Tables

You can create a view for retrieving information from several tables that are linked by the join operation. In the SELECT statement, define the join the same way you define a join for linking tables. Here is an example:

```
CREATE VIEW   classlst  (course, student)
         AS   SELECT  c_title, s_lname
               FROM  course x, class y, student z
               WHERE  x.c_id = y.c_id AND y.s_id = z.s_id;
```

View CLASSLST created

In the SELECT statement for creating the view, three tables are joined by using the *c_id* and *s_id* columns as joining keys. The results represented by the view show the class list containing names of the courses and the students who are taking these courses (see fig. 10.42).

This view shows the students for each class in the database. Information displayed by the view is retrieved from the data produced by joining the *course*, *class*, and *student* tables.

```
SELECT *
  FROM classlst;

COURSE      STUDENT
--------    -------
ENGL 101    Carter
ENGL 101    Freed
ENGL 101    Taylor
HIST 100    Ford
HIST 100    Freed
HIST 100    Jackson
HIST 100    Madison
MATH 105    Austin
MATH 105    Brown
MATH 105    Reed
PHIL 101    Brown
PHIL 101    Freed
PHIL 101    Madison
PHYS 102    Carter
PHYS 102    Gilmore
PHYS 102    Madison
PHYS 102    Reed
```

Fig. 10.42. *A view created from joined tables.*

Joining Views with Base Tables

Although views do not contain actual data, they can be joined with base tables as if the views were base tables. Before performing the join operation, data produced by the view command is generated. The results are used in the join as if they were the contents of a base table. For example, the view in figure 10.43 is created by joining the *employee* base table with an existing view named *monthly*.

```
CREATE VIEW wage (last_name, first_name, job_title, month_pay)
     AS SELECT x.l_name, x.f_name, x.title, y.month_pay
        FROM employee x, monthly y
       WHERE x.ss_no=y.soc_sec_no
         AND (x.title!='President'
         AND x.title!='Manager');

View WAGE created

SELECT *
  FROM wage;

LAST_NAME   FIRST_NAME   JOB_TITLE    MONTH_PAY
----------  -----------  -----------  ----------
Zeller      Albert K.    Salesman       4278.75
Chapman     Kirk D.      Salesman       3541.67
Baker       Larry A.     Salesman       2791.67
Dixon       Kathy T.     Accountant     3750.00
Frazer      Robert F.    Bookkeeper     2450.00
Duff        Cathy B.     Secretary      2318.75
Parker      Susan C.     Trainee        2333.33
```

Fig. 10.43. *Joining a view with a base table.*

Joining Views with Other Views

As with base tables, you can join two or more views for a query operation. You also can create a view by using information produced by one or more existing views. The views are joined by using the same procedure as for joining base tables. The statement in figure 10.44, for example, creates a view by joining two views named *title* and *monthly*.

```
CREATE VIEW execpay (last_name, first_name, job_title, month_pay)
       AS SELECT x.l_name, x.f_name, x.title, y.month_pay
          FROM title x, monthly y
         WHERE x.ss_no=y.soc_sec_no
           AND (x.title='Manager' OR x.title='President');
```

View EXECPAY created

```
SELECT *
  FROM execpay;
```

LAST_NAME	FIRST_NAME	JOB_TITLE	MONTH_PAY
Wong	Mike J.	Manager	3666.67
Smith	James J.	President	7458.33
Nelson	Harry M.	Manager	5416.67
King	David G.	Manager	3166.67

Fig. 10.44. Joining two views to create another view.

Deleting Views

Any view can be deleted from the database by using the DROP VIEW command in the following format:

DROP VIEW <view name>;

For example, if you want to remove the view named *dept*, you issue the following command:

DROP VIEW dept;

Modifying View Definitions

You cannot change the definition in a view without recreating it. No command allows you to add or delete columns defined in the view. If you need to select different columns in the view, you need to reissue the CREATE VIEW command defining the new view. Before you reissue the CREATE VIEW command, delete the existing view by using the DROP VIEW command. You cannot have two or more views with the same view name. Neither can you assign an existing table name to a new view.

Modifying Data through Views

Except for some restrictions, discussed in the following section, you can modify the data represented by most views by using the INSERT INTO, UPDATE, and DELETE commands, provided that the view is based on only one table. When you perform an insert, delete, or update operation on the view, not only are the results of the view changed, the base table from which the view values are retrieved also is changed. If the view contains only certain columns of the base table, only values of these columns in the base table are changed. In some versions of SQL, NOT NULL columns in the base table must be included in the view if inserts are to be done.

Restrictions on Modifying Views

You cannot modify the data elements introduced by a view if the view is created with one or more of the following conditions:

❑ The view includes the DISTINCT keyword in the SELECT list.

❑ The view includes a GROUP BY or HAVING clause.

❑ The SELECT list contains any expression or formula.

❑ The SELECT list contains any aggregate function.

❑ The view is created by using joined tables.

❑ The view is created with one or more other views.

These restrictions may not apply to every implementation of SQL. You need to experiment with your version of SQL to find out its restrictions on modifying views. If your views do not violate any of the listed restrictions, you should not have any problem using views for modifying your data elements.

Adding Data through Views

You can add data to the base table by using an existing view. Use the INSERT INTO command. When you insert data into a view, the contents of the base table corresponding to the columns selected by the view are changed accordingly. For example, the following statement adds a new set of values to the view named *title*:

```
INSERT INTO  title
        VALUES  ('Chairman', 'Bush', 'George J.');
```

After processing, this command adds the values to the base table named *employee*, from which the *title* view was created. As a result, after the insert operation, the contents of the base table contain the inserted data values (see fig. 10.45).

```
SELECT *
  FROM employee;
```

SS_NO	L_NAME	F_NAME	TITLE	DEPT	SALARY
123-45-6789	Smith	James J.	President	Corporate	89500
634-56-7890	Nelson	Harry M.	Manager	Sales	65000
445-67-8801	Zeller	Albert K.	Salesman	Sales	51345
562-87-8800	Chapman	Kirk D.	Salesman	Sales	42500
404-22-4568	Baker	Larry A.	Salesman	Sales	33500
256-09-5555	Dixon	Kathy T.	Accountant	Accounting	45000
458-90-3456	Frazer	Robert F.	Bookkeeper	Accounting	29400
777-34-6543	King	David G.	Manager	Personnel	38000
100-45-8021	Wong	Mike J.	Manager	MIS	44000
303-25-7777	Duff	Cathy B.	Secretary	Personnel	27825
909-10-9010	Parker	Susan C.	Trainee	MIS	28000
	Bush	George J.	Chairman		

Fig. 10.45. *Base table with data added through a view.*

Note that in the inserted row only selected columns contain values because the view was created using only these columns from the base table. The insert operation on the view affects only those columns. When you use the view to display the information, the view shows the added information (see fig. 10.46).

```
SELECT  *
  FROM  title;

SS_NO         TITLE        L_NAME    F_NAME
-----------   ----------   -------   ----------
123-45-6789   President    Smith     James J.
634-56-7890   Manager      Nelson    Harry M.
445-67-8801   Salesman     Zeller    Albert K.
562-87-8800   Salesman     Chapman   Kirk D.
404-22-4568   Salesman     Baker     Larry A.
256-09-5555   Accountant   Dixon     Kathy T.
458-90-3456   Bookkeeper   Frazer    Robert F.
777-34-6543   Manager      King      David G.
100-45-8021   Manager      Wong      Mike J.
303-25-7777   Secretary    Duff      Cathy B.
909-10-8910   Trainee      Parker    Susan C.
              Chairman     Bush      George J.
```

Fig. 10.46. *The view with inserted information.*

If you need to fill in the rest of columns with values, you use the UPDATE operation on the base table itself. For example, you can fill in the social security number for the new employee by using the UPDATE command as follows:

```
UPDATE  employee
    SET  ss_no = '999-99-9999'
  WHERE  title = 'Chairman';
```

Updating Data through Views

You can change the contents of a base table by changing a view with the UPDATE command. The update operation you make through the view changes the data in the base table from which the view was created. Here is an example:

```
UPDATE  title
    SET  title = 'CEO'
  WHERE  title = 'Chairman';
```

This statement changes the title from Chairman to CEO in the *employee* table by updating the view named *title*. The effects of the update operation are reflected in the changed values in the *title* column of the *employee* base table. The contents of the *employee* table after the update operation look like figure 10.47.

```
SELECT *
  FROM employee;
```

SS_NO	L_NAME	F_NAME	TITLE	DEPT	SALARY
123-45-6789	Smith	James J.	President	Corporate	89500
634-56-7890	Nelson	Harry M.	Manager	Sales	65000
445-67-8801	Zeller	Albert K.	Salesman	Sales	51345
562-87-8800	Chapman	Kirk D.	Salesman	Sales	42500
404-22-4568	Baker	Larry A.	Salesman	Sales	33500
256-09-5555	Dixon	Kathy T.	Accountant	Accounting	45000
458-90-3456	Frazer	Robert F.	Bookkeeper	Accounting	29400
777-34-6543	King	David G.	Manager	Personnel	38000
100-45-8021	Wong	Mike J.	Manager	MIS	44000
303-25-7777	Duff	Cathy B.	Secretary	Personnel	27825
909-10-9010	Parker	Susan C.	Trainee	MIS	28000
999-99-9999	Bush	George J.	CEO		

Fig. 10.47. *Table updated by updating a view.*

Deleting Data through Views

You can use views to delete data from the base table from which the view is created. When you delete a row in the view, the corresponding row in the base table is deleted even though the view selected only certain columns of the row from the base table. Here is an example:

```
DELETE FROM  title
        WHERE  title = 'CEO';
```

Although the *title* view selected only the *l_name*, *f_name*, and *title* columns from the base table, when you delete the row in the view, the whole corresponding row in the base table is eliminated. The contents of the *employee* table no longer contain the row deleted from the view even though the row may have contained values (for example the social security number), which were not in the view (see fig. 10.48).

```
SELECT *
  FROM employee;
```

SS_NO	L_NAME	F_NAME	TITLE	DEPT	SALARY
123-45-6789	Smith	James J.	President	Corporate	89500
634-56-7890	Nelson	Harry M.	Manager	Sales	65000
445-67-8801	Zeller	Albert K.	Salesman	Sales	51345
562-87-8800	Chapman	Kirk D.	Salesman	Sales	42500
404-22-4568	Baker	Larry A.	Salesman	Sales	33500
256-09-5555	Dixon	Kathy T.	Accountant	Accounting	45000
458-90-3456	Frazer	Robert F.	Bookkeeper	Accounting	29400
777-34-6543	King	David G.	Manager	Personnel	38000
100-45-8021	Wong	Mike J.	Manager	MIS	44000
303-25-7777	Duff	Cathy B.	Secretary	Personnel	27825
909-10-9010	Parker	Susan C.	Trainee	MIS	28000

Fig. 10.48. The employee *table after a row has been deleted through the view.*

Applications of Views

As you can see in the preceding examples, views allow you to look through a predetermined view frame, or format, at any combination of data elements in the database. You can use views to ensure data confidentiality by limiting data access to only authorized persons. You also can create different views for different people who need to look at the information in different formats and combinations. If you frequently need to repeat certain data retrieval and data query operations, you can set up views for carrying out these operations efficiently.

Data Confidentiality

Data confidentiality is one of the most important considerations in a database management operation. You want to allow only authorized persons to gain access to the sensitive information in the database. Views provide efficient tools for that purpose. By granting authorized persons the appropriate data accessing right, you can control the access of any base table or view. The procedures for granting these access rights are the subject of the next chapter.

For example, the *employee* table contains some payroll information that you may not want every employee to see. To keep unauthorized persons from gaining access to the salary information, you set up a view excluding those columns of data in the *employee* tables. You then can allow employees to perform query operations only on the view, not on the entire *employee* table (see fig. 10.49).

```
CREATE VIEW personal (soc_sec_no, last_name, first_name,
                    job_title, department)
         AS SELECT ss_no, l_name, f_name, title, dept
            FROM employee;
```

View PERSONAL created

```
  SELECT *
    FROM personal
ORDER BY department, last_name;
```

SOC_SEC_NO	LAST_NAME	FIRST_NAME	JOB_TITLE	DEPARTMENT
256-09-5555	Dixon	Kathy T.	Accountant	Accounting
458-90-3456	Frazer	Robert F.	Bookkeeper	Accounting
123-45-6789	Smith	James J.	President	Corporate
909-10-8910	Parker	Susan C.	Trainee	MIS
100-45-8021	Wong	Mike J.	Manager	MIS
303-25-7777	Duff	Cathy B.	Secretary	Personnel
777-34-6543	King	David G.	Manager	Personnel
404-22-4568	Baker	Larry A.	Salesman	Sales
562-87-8800	Chapman	Kirk D.	Salesman	Sales
634-56-7890	Nelson	Harry M.	Manager	Sales
445-67-8801	Zeller	Albert K.	Salesman	Sales

Fig. 10.49. A view denying access to confidential columns in a base table.

Data Security and Integrity

Besides maintaining data confidentiality, you need to ensure the security and integrity of the information in your database. You should not let unauthorized persons make changes to the contents of your base tables. For example, if you store all the salary information in the *payroll* base table, you may grant permission to certain people to view the information in the base table. But for security reasons, you should allow only payroll people to make any changes to the contents of the table. Therefore, you can create a view for certain authorized persons and grant them the right to perform the update, insert, and delete operations on that view. The statement shown in figure 10.50 creates a view named *salary*, which contains the columns to which certain authorized people can make changes.

```
CREATE VIEW salary (soc_sec_no, last_name, salary, exemptions)
       AS SELECT ss_no, last_name, salary, exemptions
     FROM payroll;

View SALARY created

SELECT *
  FROM salary;


SOC_SEC_NO    LAST_NAME    SALARY   EXEMPTIONS
-----------   ---------   --------  ----------
123-45-6789   Smith       89500.00           3
634-56-7890   Nelson      65000.00           2
445-67-8801   Zeller      51345.00           4
562-87-8800   Chapman     42500.00           2
404-22-4568   Baker       30500.00           1
256-09-5555   Dixon       45000.00           3
458-90-3456   Frazer      29400.00           3
777-34-6543   King        38000.00           2
100-45-8021   Wong        44000.00           2
303-25-7777   Duff        27825.00           2
909-10-8910   Parker      28000.00           1
```

Fig. 10.50. *A view allowing limited access to payroll information.*

After setting up the view, you can grant data modification rights to authorized persons so that they can make the necessary changes to the payroll information. As you will learn in the next chapter, you can grant any user one or more of the insert, update, and delete rights for data modification by using the view.

Performing Repetitive Data Queries

One of the most important functions in managing your data is finding information by using a data query operation. You perform a data query operation by issuing the appropriate SELECT statement. For example, if you want to find the managers of each department in the firm, you issue the following data query statement:

```
SELECT   dept, l_name, f_name
  FROM   employee
WHERE    title = 'Manager'
```

Each time you need the same information, you have to reissue the same statement. A shortcut is to create a view for performing the data query. You create the view with the following statement:

```
CREATE VIEW depthead (department, last_name, first_name)
        AS SELECT dept, l_name, f_name
            FROM employee
            WHERE title='Manager'
```

```
View DEPTHEAD created
```

After the view is created, whenever you need information about the managers, you issue the simple command activating the view:

```
SELECT *
  FROM depthead;
```

DEPARTMENT	LAST_NAME	FIRST_NAME
Sales	Nelson	Harry M.
Personnel	King	David G.
MIS	Wong	Mike J.

To find in the *school* database, the names of students who are taking a given course, you create a view with the name of the course. You create the view for displaying names of the students who are taking the course ENGL 101 (C1) by joining all the related tables:

```
CREATE VIEW engl101 (last_name, first_name, hs_gpa)
        AS SELECT s_lname, s_fname, s_hsgpa
            FROM student x, class y
            WHERE x.s_id=y.s_id AND c_id='C1';
```

```
View ENGL101 created
```

You then use the view as a shortcut for displaying the information when you need it by issuing the following simple command:

```
SELECT *
  FROM engl101;
```

LAST_NAME	FIRST_NAME	HS_GPA
Carter	Jack F.	2.87
Freed	Barbara J.	3.15
Taylor	Bob K.	3.14

Similarly, to find the students who are taking a group of related courses, you can create a view for displaying the information. The statement in figure 10.51, for example, uses a view to display the names of students who are taking the courses MATH 101 and PHYS 102.

```
CREATE VIEW science (course, last_name, first_name, hs_gpa)
      AS SELECT  c_title, s_lname, s_fname, s_hsgpa
           FROM  student x, class y, course z
          WHERE  x.s_id=y.s_id
            AND  y.c_id=z.c_id
            AND  (c_title='MATH 105' OR c_title='PHYS 102');


View SCIENCE created

  SELECT  *
    FROM  science
ORDER BY  course;


COURSE     LAST_NAME   FIRST_NAME   HS_GPA
--------   ---------   ----------   ------

MATH 105   Austin      Linda D.      3.98
MATH 105   Brown       Nancy J.      3.35
MATH 105   Reed        Donna E.      2.96
PHYS 102   Carter      Jack F.       2.87
PHYS 102   Gilmore     Danny S.      3.86
PHYS 102   Madison     George G.     2.35
PHYS 102   Reed        Donna E.      2.96
```

Fig. 10.51. *A view displaying names of students taking related courses.*

Chapter Summary

In this chapter, you have learned additional approaches to managing your data. Subqueries allow you to perform complex data queries by using nested SELECT statements. When properly constructed, subqueries can be powerful tools for performing data retrieval and query operations on your database. From the examples in this chapter, you have seen that many subqueries can be expressed as joins. The choice between subqueries and joins often depends on your personal preference. The concepts you have learned about subqueries should help you better appreciate the power of a relational database management language.

Views are another powerful SQL tool for managing your database more efficiently. Besides using views as shortcuts for performing repetitive data queries, you can use views to ensure the confidentiality and security for your data. By granting users the appropriate rights to certain restricted views, you can effectively address the problems of data confidentiality, security, and integrity. In the next chapter, you learn about the procedures for granting different levels of privileges and rights to data access.

11

Data Security and Integrity

In the last chapter, you learned how you can use views to limit access to subsets of the data elements in a database. This method is an effective way to address the issues of data security and data integrity. In order to use views for solving the problems of data security, however, you must be able to restrict access to views by granting users the appropriate privileges and rights.

You have other approaches to the problems of maintaining the security and integrity of your data. These approaches involve granting privileges authorizing specified users to perform designated database management operations on base tables. You also can deny unauthorized people access to any views or base tables by revoking privileges. This chapter discusses how SQL handles these operations. Unfortunately, not many versions of SQL implement the same procedures and provide the same set of commands for dealing with these issues. Although I use actual examples from some versions of SQL to illustrate these procedures, the emphasis of this chapter's discussion is on concept rather than practice.

Data Security

Data security is of the utmost importance in data management. Besides preserving the confidentiality of your data, you need to make sure that only authorized personnel perform data maintenance. If you are working with a single-user system, controlling the security of the information in your database is relatively easy. By allowing only the authorized person to use the computer system and gain access to the database, you can effectively maintain the confidentiality and integrity of the data.

The issue of maintaining data security plays a vital role in a multiuser database management system. A major advantage of using a multiuser system is that it allows more than one user to view or work with the same database.

That is, at the same time, two or more users may be looking at the same set of data objects. For example, you can designate more than one data entry person for handling the data entry and modification operations. Because a number of people can access the database, several issues deserve careful consideration:

❏ Authorized users who need certain information must be permitted to retrieve and manipulate it in the properly assigned operations.

❏ Unauthorized persons must be denied access to any information in your database.

❏ Only designated data entry personnel should carry out data maintenance.

❏ You need to be able to limit certain users' access to subsets of the data elements.

❏ You need to decide how to handle the situation when authorized users need to view certain data elements while those data elements are being modified.

❏ You have to devise a system to ensure that no more than one person can edit the same data elements at the same time.

Creators of relational database systems choose from among several approaches to handle the data security problem. Significant variations exist among different implementations of SQL in the solutions to this problem. Not only do the approaches differ in concept, they provide different procedures and commands for handling the problem.

Setting Up Password Protection

A common approach to the data security problem is to institute a password protection system. In this system, each legitimate user is given a unique user name and a secret password. Before the user is allowed to get on the computer system or gain access to the database, his or her user name and password are checked. As a result, only authorized users can retrieve and manipulate the data in your database.

Depending on the sophistication of your system and the desired level of protection, you can choose different types of password protection procedures. For example, if your computer system is structured as a multiuser local area network (LAN), you can set up a log-in procedure so that all users are checked for their passwords before they are allowed on the computer system. This precaution, done at the operating system level, represents the first line of defense against unauthorized users. When you turn on your workstation or terminal, you are asked for your user name and password. Only after entering the correct user name and password are you allowed to issue any system commands.

Because not all users authorized at the system level are also authorized to access data in your database management system, some database management systems set up another password protection scheme for further screening the users. The checking of user name and password at this level is done after you issue the command at the operating system. For example, suppose that you are running SQL*Plus in Oracle's RDBMS under the MS-DOS operating system. First, you issue the following command at the DOS prompt:

    ORACLE

Next, you issue the following command:

    SQLPLUS

Then you are prompted to enter your user name and password before you can run SQL*Plus.

Any database management system allows two different types of users: system administrators and database users. These users are identified by their privileges. A system administrator has all the privileges for managing the database. The system administrator "owns" certain system tables and data dictionary tables. He or she has the right to assign user names and passwords to other users. Database users are the end users of the information in the database.

System Administrators

The system administrator is set up when the database management system is first installed. At that time, the system also assigns names and passwords to the system administrators. For example, when you install the Oracle RDBMS system, SQL*Plus, the installation process automatically creates two system administrators: SYS and SYSTEM. Both SYS and SYSTEM have all the database administration privileges assigned by the Oracle RDBMS. The administrators own different sets of system tables. SYS owns the data dictionary tables, which are maintained by the system, and SYSTEM owns different data dictionary views (created from tables). SYSTEM is used for performing all the system administration functions, including assigning passwords to new users. Because most of the functions of SYS are performed by SQL*Plus itself, you rarely have to use SYS.

At the time of system installation, system administrators also are given predefined passwords. For example, when you install SQL*Plus, the Oracle RDBMS, the passwords MANAGER and CHANGE_ON_INSTALL are assigned, respectively, to the SYSTEM and SYS users. After you have installed the system, you can change the predefined passwords. If you want to change the password for SYS from CHANGE_ON_INSTALL, you first log on to SQL*Plus by issuing the following command at the system (DOS) prompt:

SQLPLUS SYS/CHANGE_ON_INSTALL

This command allows you to enter SQL*Plus by using the predefined password for the SYS. When you are in SQL (indicated by the appearance of the SQL> prompt), you can assign a new password with the following command:

GRANT CONNECT TO SYS
    IDENTIFIED BY <new password>;

To change the password for SYSTEM, you first need to connect to SYSTEM by entering the current password (MANAGER) in the following command, at the SQL prompt:

CONNECT SYSTEM/MANAGER

Then you can specify your new password by issuing the following command at the SQL prompt:

GRANT CONNECT TO SYSTEM
    IDENTIFIED BY <new password>;

Database Users

The other type of users are those who perform the database management functions: creating, retrieving, and manipulating data. These users own the data objects (base tables, views, and so on) they create. The system administrator must assign each user a user name, or ID, and a password before he or she can become a legitimate user. For example, when you are in Oracle's RDBMS, the SYSTEM administrator enables you to add a new user ID and password with the following statement:

ADDUSER SYSTEM <current password for SYSTEM>

In response to this command, you are prompted for a new user ID and password (see fig. 11.1).

After a user is given a unique user ID and password, he or she is allowed to enter SQL*Plus and perform the authorized operations. For example, after you have been given a user ID and password, you can enter SQL*Plus, the Oracle RDBMS, by issuing the following command at the system prompt:

SQLPLUS <your user ID>/<your password>

```
C:\>ADDUSER SYSTEM My Password

C:\>ECHO OFF

Enter value for new_user name: NEWUSER
Enter value for new_password: NEWPASSWORD

Grant succeeded.

C:\>
```

Fig. 11.1. *Adding a new user to the Oracle RDBMS.*

Restricting Data Access

Another approach to solving the data security problem is to grant data access rights to authorized persons according to their data needs and designated functions. For example, to protect the confidentiality and security of payroll information, you should allow only authorized persons in the payroll department to access payroll information. Because this information may be stored in different parts of the database, you need to allow the authorized persons access to various parts of the database. These persons should be allowed to retrieve data from certain data rows or data columns from one or more tables in the database. With this option, only a selected subset of the information in the database is available to certain authorized users.

Using views is an effective way for ensuring that only authorized persons can gain access to the information to which they are entitled. A view can consist of information from one or more tables. You can use a view to display all the data objects you want to provide for a given user. These data objects can be data rows or data columns from a number of joined tables. Therefore, by granting a user permission to use the view, you have complete control of the type of information that user needs and can use.

Granting Privileges

When a user creates a base table, he or she is the owner of that data object. The owner automatically has the privileges of retrieving and manipulating data in the table. He or she can add new data to the table, change the contents of the table, delete data from the table, and so on. A user who does not own the table, however, may or may not perform certain operations on that table. What one can do with or to the table depends on the privileges that have been granted to that user. Therefore, by granting the appropriate privileges to authorized persons, you can control the security and confidentiality of your data elements.

Privileges are explicit to the specific data object and operation. For example, if you want a certain user to be able to view information in a given table, you need to grant that user the right to perform the SELECT operations on that table. Usually, only owners can grant permission to access their data objects. A user then can be granted the right to grant privileges to other users for the data objects on which he or she has privileges.

The GRANT statement is an SQL statement you use explicitly to specify the privileges you grant to another user. In the statement, you need to specify the types of privileges, the data objects involved, and the recipient; you also can specify whether this user has the right to pass the privileges on to other users.

Although minor variations exist among different SQL implementations with respect to the syntax rules of the GRANT statement, most versions follow this format:

```
GRANT  (ALL|<privilege list>)
    ON  (<data objects>)
    TO  (PUBLIC|<user list>)
        [WITH GRANT OPTION];
```

The simplest GRANT statement grants all the privileges to a base table to every user in the system:

```
GRANT  ALL
    ON  employee
    TO  PUBLIC;
```

The effect of this GRANT statement is that every user (PUBLIC) can perform all data retrieval and manipulation operations on the base table named *employee*.

Privileges are defined as the types of data management operations you can carry out on the data object. The types of privileges you can grant relate to the data object involved. If you are giving permission to access a base table, you can grant privileges for these operations: SELECT, UPDATE, INSERT, DELETE, ALTER, and INDEX. If the data object is a view, you can grant privileges only for these operations: SELECT, UPDATE, INSERT, and DELETE. For example, if you want to allow users to view but not to modify the contents of the *employee* table, you grant them only the SELECT privilege:

```
GRANT  SELECT
    ON  employee
    TO  PUBLIC;
```

You can grant privileges to some of or all the columns in a base table or a view. If you are granting the users permission to work on only certain columns, you must specify the names of these columns in parentheses in the ON clause in the following format:

ON <table name|view name> [(<column list>]

For example, if you want to restrict users from viewing financial (*salary*) data in the *employee* table, you specify the columns that contain nonfinancial information:

```
GRANT  SELECT
     ON  employee (L_name, f_name, title, dept)
     TO  PUBLIC;
```

All the data objects must be from one table or one view. That is, you cannot join tables in the GRANT statement. If you need to grant users permission to access a combination of data columns from several base tables, you must create a view displaying that information. You then can grant the appropriate privileges to the view.

The recipients can be some of or all the users who have been given user IDs and passwords. If you use PUBLIC as the recipient of the privilege, however, you include yourself. That is, if you grant to PUBLIC limited privileges to the base table you own, you may limit your own privileges to that table after the GRANT statement is processed. If you accidentally make that mistake, you can reissue the appropriate GRANT statement to give yourself additional privileges.

If you are granting privileges to certain users, their names or IDs can be specified in the TO clause. For example, the following command grants privileges to John and Kirk so that they can view and modify the data in a view named *monthly* (for viewing monthly salary information in the *employee* base table):

```
GRANT  SELECT, INSERT, UPDATE, DELETE,
     ON  monthly
     TO  John, Kirk;
```

Granting privileges does not constitute transfer of ownership; privileges merely allow the users to perform the specified operations on the tables and views. However, by using the WITH GRANT OPTION clause, you can allow users to grant their privileges to other users. For example, suppose that you also want to grant the privileges specified in last statement to Kathy in a way that she can pass the privileges to her assistant, Doris. To accomplish that purpose, you use the WITH GRANT OPTION clause in the following GRANT statement:

GRANT   SELECT, INSERT, UPDATE, DELETE,
    ON   monthly
    TO   Kathy
       WITH GRANT OPTION;

Kathy then can issue the following command for giving Doris some of the privileges (just SELECT and INSERT) she has:

GRANT   SELECT, INSERT
    ON   monthly
    TO   Doris;

The order of the GRANT commands is important. The most recently issued GRANT statement supersedes all the statements issued earlier. This factor is especially important when statements conflict.

Keeping Track of Privileges

In most SQL implementations, information about all the privileges that have been granted is kept in a system table. The name of the table may vary among different versions of SQL. In Oracle, for example, the table holding the information about privileges granted to users is called SYSTABAUTH. This table contains information about all the privileges that have been granted to existing base tables and views. Table 11.1 shows the contents of SYSTABAUTH.

Table 11.1
Contents of SYSTABAUTH

Column Name	Information
Grantor	Name of grantor of the privileges
Grantee	Name of recipient of the privileges
Creator	Name of the table owner
Tname	Table name
Timestamp	Creation or granting date
A	Granting status for ALTER operation
D	Granting status for DELETE operation
N	Granting status for INDEX operation
I	Granting status for INSERT operation
S	Granting status for SELECT operation
U	Granting status for UPDATE operation

For example, to find all the privileges that have been granted by Susan, issue the following statement:

```
SELECT   grantee, tname, creator,a,d,n,i,s,u
  FROM   SYSTABAUTH
 WHERE   creator = 'Susan';
```

The results may look like figure 11.2. The value G in one of the last six columns indicates that the particular operation has been granted to the creator.

```
GRANTEE   GRANTOR   TNAME      CREATOR   A   D   N   I   S   U
-------   -------   --------   -------   -   -   -   -   -   -
PUBLIC    SUSAN     EMPLOYEE   SUSAN                         G
ROBERT    SUSAN     EMPLOYEE   SUSAN     G   G   G   G   G   G
KATHY     SUSAN     MONTHLY    SUSAN                     G   G   G
KATHY     DORIS     MONTHLY    SUSAN                     G   G
.....
.....
```

Fig. 11.2. *Finding privileges granted by a specific user.*

Revoking Privileges

Privileges granted to any user can be revoked by the REVOKE statement. For instance, you can use this statement to keep an ex-employee from gaining access to company information after his or her employment has ended. Similarly, when the job responsibilities of an employee change, you need to reassign different data access privileges to that employee.

Although the REVOKE statement may differ slightly among different SQL implementations, the format for a REVOKE statement in most versions is as follows:

```
REVOKE   (ALL|<privilege list>)
    ON   (<data objects>)
  FROM   (PUBLIC|<user list>);
```

You can revoke all or some of the privileges that have been previously granted to one or more users on selected data objects. For example, you can use the following statement to revoke all the privileges that have been granted to an ex-employee (named Kirk) on the *employee* base table:

```
REVOKE   ALL
    ON   employee
  FROM   Kirk;
```

Similarly, you can revoke some of the privileges that have been granted to certain employees as their job responsibilities change. The following statement revokes from John the INSERT and UPDATE privileges on the view named *monthly*:

    REVOKE INSERT, UPDATE
        ON monthly
      FROM John;

Another use of the REVOKE command provides an alternative for specifying a long list of privileges. For example, you can give a user most of the privileges on most of the columns of a base table in two ways. One is to use the GRANT statement to list all the privileges and data objects in the statement. This statement may be long and tedious. An alternative is to grant the user every privilege on every column of the table and then use the REVOKE statement to revoke a few privileges and columns from the user. For example, to allow John to perform all data management operations except deletion on the *employee* table, you successively issue the following two commands:

    GRANT ALL
       ON employee
       TO John;

    REVOKE DELETE
        ON employee
      FROM John;

Locking Data

Locking data is another way to solve some of the problems related to data security and integrity. Locking data prevents unauthorized persons from making changes to the data elements another user is modifying. This precaution is essential in a multiuser system in which more than one user can gain simultaneous access to the same data in the database. For example, when you are entering new data into an existing base table, you may want to lock the base table until the data entry operation has been completed. By locking the base table, you keep other users from changing the table contents before the new items are entered into the table. Similar protection is required when you are modifying the data elements in the database. You need to keep other users from making changes to the data elements while they are being modified.

Locking operations usually do not prevent other users from viewing the data objects if the users are the owners or they have been granted the SELECT privilege. If you want to keep users from looking at the contents of a base table, you need to revoke the SELECT privilege.

Depending on the data objects to which you intend to keep users from making changes, you can lock some of or all data elements in the base table.

Types of Locks

Different types of locks are available. These lock types vary among different SQL implementations. Most versions, however, support two basic types of locks: share locks and exclusive locks. Other versions of SQL provide additional mechanisms for locking data. For example, in addition to share and exclusive locks, Oracle's SQL*Plus also supports share update and table definition locks.

SQL places some locks automatically while certain commands are being processed. For example, when you issue the UPDATE command, the table being updated is locked to keep other users from editing the same table. You also can place various types of locks on your data objects by issuing the appropriate lock commands. Through these locks, you gain better control of certain subsets of your data elements.

Share Lock

Share lock is a common way to lock a table during nonmodification operations. By using a share lock, you let other users view the data in the locked table, but you do not allow them to modify any data in that table. For example, when you are performing a series of the query operations on a table, you want to keep other users from changing the data in the table until your query operations are completed. More than one user can place a share lock on the same table at the same time.

Exclusive Lock

An exclusive lock works the same way as a share lock. An exclusive lock allows other users to view the data in the locked table but not to change data. An exclusive lock differs from a share lock because an exclusive lock does not permit another user to place any type of lock on the locked table. Whoever first places an exclusive lock on a table has all the data modification (insert, update, and delete) rights on the table. No other user can change any data elements in that table until the exclusive lock is released. An exclusive lock is appropriate when you intend to make extensive modifications to the table.

Share Update Lock

A share update lock, which may not be supported by every SQL implementation, is designed for locking selected rows of a table. While the rows are locked, other users cannot make any changes to any values in these rows. Other users can view the locked rows and can modify data in other rows. You place a share update lock on selected rows before you begin making modifications to the values in these rows with the UPDATE operation. The share update lock reserves those rows for the update. Remember, however, that as soon as you issue the UPDATE command for modifying these rows, the whole table will be locked until the update operation is completed.

Table Definition Lock

A table definition lock prevents more than one user from changing the structure of a base table. SQL places a table definition lock automatically while a user is defining the table structure with a CREATE TABLE, ALTER TABLE, or DROP TABLE statement. Until the operation is completed, the table is locked to every other user in a multiuser system.

Locking Tables

Most database management systems provide mechanisms for locking a table in part or in whole. The SQL statement for specifying the type of lock to place on one or more base tables is LOCK TABLE. The type of lock is defined by specifying the MODE in the statement:

```
LOCK TABLE   <table list>
        IN   <EXCLUSIVE|SHARE|SHARE UPDATE> MODE [NOWAIT];
```

For example, to place an exclusive lock on the *employee* table, you issue the following statement:

```
LOCK TABLE   employee
        IN   EXCLUSIVE MODE;
```

Similarly, you place a share lock on the *parts* and *stock* tables with the following command:

```
LOCK TABLE   parts, stock
        IN   SHARE MODE;
```

If another user's use of a locked table prevents you from placing the requested type of lock on that table with the LOCK TABLE statement, the statement waits until the other user finishes using the table; then the statement is processed. You can add the NOWAIT keyword to the LOCK TABLE command for checking to see whether you can place your lock on the table:

```
LOCK TABLE   employee
     IN    SHARE UPDATE MODE NOWAIT;
```

If the statement cannot establish the type of lock you want to place on the table, you are informed accordingly. For example, if the *employee* table has been placed in an exclusive lock, you are told that fact when you issue the preceding statement. The statement proceeds when the exclusive lock is removed.

Locking Selected Rows

Besides locking an entire table, you also can lock certain rows in the table so that other users can use data only in other rows of that table. To lock specific rows, you use the FOR UPDATE OF clause in a SELECT statement. The format of the statement is as follows:

```
     SELECT   <column list>
       FROM   <table name>
      WHERE   <filter condition>
FOR UPDATE OF   <column list>;
```

For example, if you want to change the titles of all the managers to directors and increase their salaries by 10 percent, you may want to issue the UPDATE command for accomplishing the changes. Before you issue the UPDATE command, you want to lock the data rows containing information about the managers so that other users cannot modify the values in these rows. To lock the selected rows, you issue the following SELECT statement with the FOR UPDATE OF clause:

```
     SELECT   title, salary
       FROM   employee
      WHERE   title = 'Manager'
FOR UPDATE OF   title, salary;
```

This statement locks the selected rows defined by the WHERE clause. No other user is allowed to modify the values in the *title* and *salary* columns of these rows until you have finished updating the rows.

To change these data values, you issue the UPDATE command:

```
UPDATE  employee
    SET  title = 'Director', salary = salary*1.1
  WHERE  title = 'Manager';
```

While the UPDATE *employee* statement is being processed, the entire contents of the *employee* table are locked. After the update operation is completed, or committed, the whole table is free for use by other users.

If you want to lock the whole row of data while you are modifying a column in that row, you select all the columns in the table. The following example locks the row that contains information about the president in the *employee* table:

```
       SELECT   *
         FROM   employee
        WHERE   title = 'President'
 FOR UPDATE OF   salary;
```

Unlocking Data

The main purpose of locking data is to let you modify your data objects without interference from other users. After you have placed a lock on your data objects, the lock stays in effect until you have completed the data modification operations. The commands for modifying your data elements include the INSERT, UPDATE, and DELETE statements. In many versions of SQL, the data modification operations are not completed until you issue the COMMIT command. Therefore, the locked data is released for use by other users only after you have committed your data changes. If you use the ROLLBACK command, provided by some SQL implementations for restoring your data to prior data changes, the locked data is released when you issue the ROLLBACK command.

Data Integrity

Another important issue in database management is data integrity. Data integrity concerns the accuracy and consistency of the data elements in your database. A good database management system should provide automatic mechanisms for maintaining the integrity of the data. Unfortunately, few versions of SQL provide sufficient tools for maintaining data integrity. Instead, you need to develop your own procedures and programming codes for checking the accuracy of the data elements and for maintaining their consistency.

The issue of data integrity can be addressed on different levels. At the data entry level, all the data elements to be entered into your database must be accurate and entered correctly. This requirement means that the data elements must be free from recording and measurement errors. For example, you must not misspell an employee's name, title, and so forth. For quantitative data, you must make sure that the value is represented with the correct number of digits, having the right precision. The responsibility for maintaining this level of data accuracy belongs to the users themselves. The database management system has no way of knowing the correctness of the data values.

When you create a table, you define the table structure, specifying the type of data elements to be stored in a given column. The data values you enter into the column must be the correct type. For example, you can enter a character string only into a character column, not into a numeric column. If the system supports a date value, you can enter a date only into a date column even though the date is represented by a character string. For checking the data accuracy in this respect, most SQL implementations provide an automatic check as the data elements are entered into a table. Values with incorrect data types are rejected automatically. Some implementations also check the length of a character string before it is entered into a character column. If the character string exceeds the width of the column, the program may prompt you for truncating the string to fit the column before entering the character string into the table.

Data Validity Check

Data accuracy also means that data elements entered into a table must be within the valid data domain. That is, an accurate data element must be represented correctly and its values must be within the valid range. For example, if you store an employee's identification number by using his or her social security number, the number must be represented by a valid format, such as 123-45-6789. These numbers must be in groups of nine-digit numbers with or without hyphens. Each digit must be a numeral from 0 to 9.

Similarly, if for withholding income tax purposes, you store the number of exemptions for an employee in a table column, the exemption value must not be negative. In a account balance column of a table, however, the value can be negative or positive.

Some database management systems provide mechanisms that automatically check for the validity of the data elements as they are entered. Unfortunately, most SQL implementations do not provide an automatic data validity check. Instead, you need to issue the appropriate commands for checking your data. One way to perform a data validity check is by using a lookup table. For example, if you want to check the validity of a state abbreviation (CA for California, WA for Washington, and so on), you can set up a lookup table named *states*. In the lookup table, you store the valid state abbreviation codes in a column named *state*. You then can check the data values with the values in the lookup table to determine whether the values are valid. The following statement checks all the values in the *state* column in the *account* table against the values in the lookup table named *states*:

```
SELECT   acct_no, state
  FROM   account, states
WHERE    state NOT IN (SELECT   state
                         FROM   states);
```

When you process this statement, the accounts with invalid state codes are displayed. You then can make the necessary corrections.

Entity Integrity

Another important issue of data integrity is related to the primary key in a base table. A primary key provides a unique identification of the values in a row. These values, in turn, represent the characteristics that are associated with a data entity. For example, in the *course* table, the course identification (*c_id*) column can be used as a primary key because the *c_id* column can identify uniquely the information associated with a specific course. A primary key also provides a vital link between two tables. As a result, the primary key must not be a null value or be left blank. One solution to the problem is to add the NOT NULL clause to the column definition when the table is created (see fig. 11.3).

```
CREATE TABLE course
            (c_id        char(2) NOT NULL,
             c_title     char(8),
             c_credits   smallint,
             c_desc      char(20));

SELECT *
  FROM course;

C_ID  C_TITLE   C_CREDITS  C_DESC
----  --------  ---------  --------------------
C1    ENGL 101          3  English Literature I
C2    HIST 100          3  American History
C3    MATH 105          5  Calculus I
C4    PHIL 101          3  Philosophy
C5    PHYS 102          5  Physics I
```

Fig. 11.3. Using the NOT NULL statement.

Referential Integrity

A powerful feature of a relational database management system is that you can access information stored in several tables by joining these tables. The link between the tables is made by using a primary key in one table and a foreign key in the other. As a result, for each distinct non-null foreign key value in a relational table, you must have a matching primary key value in the other table.

For example, suppose that you need to join the *assign* (course assignment) table with the *instructor* table by using the *t_id* column as the linking column. In the *teacher* table, the *t_id* column is the primary key, identifying each teacher. The same column is considered a foreign key in the *assign* table. Therefore, for each teacher's identification number in the *assign* table, you must find a matching value in the *t_id* column in the *teacher* table. As a result, for all the instructors assigned to a given course, you will be able to find information about each of these instructors. Figure 11.4 depicts the links between the two tables through the *t_id* columns.

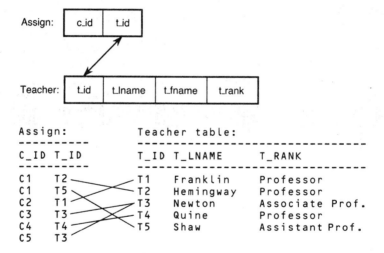

Fig. 11.4. Joining the assign *and* teacher *tables.*

The statement for linking these tables is

```
SELECT   x.c_id, y.t_id, y.t_lname, y.t_rank
  FROM   assign x, teacher y
 WHERE   x.t_id = y.t_id;
```

If you have no problem with data integrity, you will get results that look like figure 11.5.

X.C_ID	Y.T_ID	Y.T_LNAME	Y.T_RANK
C1	T2	Hemingway	Professor
C1	T5	Shaw	Assistant Prof.
C2	T1	Franklin	Professor
C3	T3	Newton	Associate Prof.
C4	T4	Quine	Professor
C5	T3	Newton	Associate Prof.

Fig. 11.5. *Linking tables with primary and foreign keys.*

A serious problem arises when a table has in a foreign key a value that is not matched in a primary key of another table. A correct link cannot be made with a missing value in a primary key. This error is a violation of the principle of referential integrity and may happen in a number of ways. The problem may occur because the value in the foreign key is incorrectly entered or modified. The solution to this problem is to correct the value in the foreign key. Another reason for the violation is that the value in the primary key has been deleted, intentionally or unintentionally, without updating the corresponding values in the foreign key.

You have several approaches to ensure the referential integrity of your data. First, when you modify or delete a value in a primary key, you also must delete the matching values in all the foreign keys. For example, if one teacher resigns from the school and is no longer teaching any of the courses assigned to him, you remove his name from the *teacher* table. When you remove the teacher's name, you also must delete the corresponding identification numbers in the *t_id* columns in all the other tables that use that column as a foreign key. Similarly, if you change a teacher's identification number in the primary key in the *teacher* table, you also must change the identification numbers in the foreign columns of other tables. This approach is called a cascade approach.

Another approach to ensure referential integrity is to keep users from changing the value in a primary key if one or more matching values exist in the foreign keys of other tables. You first must change the matching values in the foreign keys before you can modify the value in the primary key. The same requirement applies when you attempt to delete a value in the primary key. You are not allowed to delete the value unless no matching value exists in the foreign keys in other tables.

Finally, you can approach the problem of referential integrity in still another way. Before you change or delete the value in a primary key, you change its matching values to null values in the foreign keys.

These approaches are necessary to maintain the referential integrity of the data so that your data manipulation operations can be carried out logically and successfully. Unfortunately, few SQL implementations provide mechanisms for maintaining referential integrity automatically. Instead, you need to write the necessary program code for performing these tasks. These program codes are discussed in Chapter 12.

Because of the importance of this issue, however, some SQL implementations are beginning to address it. For example, some versions of SQL provide a trigger mechanism for controlling referential integrity. A trigger is represented by a set of SQL commands or statements describing the operations to be carried out when you attempt to modify the data values in a given column or table. When these data values are modified, the trigger is processed automatically so that all other related data is updated accordingly in order to maintain the referential integrity.

Chapter Summary

This chapter presents the two most important issues associated with relational database management. The issue of data security deals with the requirements for maintaining the confidentiality and security of the data elements in your database. You must provide the mechanism for ensuring that only authorized persons are given the appropriate permission for data access. This chapter discusses granting privileges and locking data as means of addressing the data security issue.

The issue of data integrity means that the data values you enter into a table must be accurate and correct in type and size. They must be free from measurement error and fall within the valid range. Before data elements are used in data retrieval and manipulation operations, these data elements must be validated if you want to ensure accuracy. This chapter also discusses the necessity of maintaining the entity and referential integrity of your data elements so that you can perform all the operations provided by a relational database system.

Unfortunately, most approaches for automatically controlling the entity and referential integrity are not supported by most SQL implementations. You need to maintain data integrity by issuing the appropriate SQL commands. This requirement can be done by incorporating a collection of these commands into a program so that the procedure can be carried out when it is needed. In the next chapter, among other things, you learn some aspects of how to incorporate a set of SQL statements into a program that can be written in a regular computer program language.

12

Interfacing with Other Database Management Systems

At this point, you have learned sufficient standard SQL statements and procedures for managing your data in a relational database. You can create the necessary base tables and views to organize and maintain your data elements. You can use the query operation to find the information you need, and you can manipulate the data in the ways you desire. Unfortunately, the standard version of SQL does not provide adequate mechanisms for performing some important operations required for an efficient system. The lack of form generators and report generators is one example. As a result, you need to find ways to supplement the standard SQL commands and procedures in order to design and develop an efficient and effective relational database. This goal can be accomplished in several ways.

One approach to the problem is to allow other database management systems access to the databases created in SQL so that you can use the tools provided by these systems. This method involves interfacing the SQL database with the other database management system. The other approach is to embed SQL statements in a procedural programming language or another database language. By incorporating your SQL commands into another language, you can write the necessary code for performing additional data management operations. You learn about these approaches in this chapter.

Needs for Interfacing

SQL is a powerful language for managing data in a relational model. As the name implies, however, SQL is a structured query language. The focus of the language is on providing powerful commands to perform data query operations. You can find information quickly and effortlessly by using the SELECT statement. With the join operation, you can retrieve information from two or more base tables or views. But SQL is inadequate for performing other opera-

385

tions required by a user-friendly database management system. For example, if you need to add new data elements to a base table, you must add them one row at a time by using the INSERT statement. The procedure is tedious and time-consuming. SQL does not provide the procedures or commands with which you can design a data entry screen to be used by someone without special training in the language. The data entry person must know SQL.

Similarly, SQL does not provide adequate commands or procedures for designing sophisticated reports. Although you can display your query results with the SELECT command, the format of these results is restricted. The results are listed in a tabular form in data columns. You have little flexibility in defining your own formats. In standard SQL, for example, you have no way to display a title with the results or to define more descriptive column labels. It is very difficult, if not impossible, to show summary statistics with a listing of data elements by using the SELECT statement.

As you learned from the preceding chapter, most versions of SQL do not provide the mechanisms for validating your data elements as they are entered into the database. For example, in the INSERT statement, you cannot specify the valid ranges for a numeric value. INSERT does not provide the clause with which you can tell whether a character string is in the right format or case. When you enter a date value, the program has no way of checking that the value is a valid date.

One reason that SQL lacks these capabilities is that the language was developed to rely on other means for providing these capabilities. The language is designed so that SQL commands can be incorporated into procedural programming languages (like COBOL, C, and others) and the features not available in SQL can be provided by your own programs written in one of these languages.

Because SQL is designed as an interactive relational database language, the commands usually are issued one at a time at the prompt. This approach can be restrictive for many data management applications. Not only do you need to monitor the results from each statement, you may not be able to pass the results from one statement to another. Even though some implementations of SQL allow you to process a set of SQL commands in a batch, this method is not efficient if you have a large set of commands. A preferred approach is to embed your SQL commands in a procedural programming language. As a result, the bridge between SQL and the procedural programming language plays an important role in using SQL for managing your data.

If you choose not to incorporate your SQL commands into your own programs, you need to rely on other systems to provide additional tools for performing the operations that cannot be carried out with standard SQL commands. Fortunately, some database management systems do provide powerful features you can use to perform the operations for which SQL is inadequate. Many systems have easy-to-use form generators and report generators so that you can design sophisticated data entry forms and reports with little effort. Some of these systems also allow you to define the parameters for validating your data before it is accepted and entered into the database. In order to use these features, you need to build a bridge between the SQL databases and the database management systems.

Interacting with Database Management Systems

Currently, you can choose among many commercial database management systems for managing your data. Most of these systems manage data elements that are organized in a relational data model. The two database management systems featured in this book are Oracle's RDBMS and dBASE IV. Both systems allow you to use their versions of SQL to create, maintain, and manipulate your data in the databases. In addition, both systems offer additional features with which you can supplement the SQL commands for other data management operations.

Besides supporting its version of SQL, dBASE IV provides another means for managing your databases. dBASE IV offers the dBASE programming language and a pull-down menu system for performing data management functions. In addition, dBASE IV gives you a form generator for designing custom data entry forms and a report generator for creating report forms. Similarly, Oracle's RDBMS offers a set of SQL commands that are not part of the standard version of the language. Oracle also provides the SQL*FormsDesigner and SQL*ReportWriter for designing and developing your data entry forms and reports in a manner similar to dBASE IV's.

You can exchange data among databases that are created in different systems. For example, when you are in dBASE, you can design the entry form for entering data into SQL tables. Similarly, you can create a database file and move it to an SQL database so that you can use SQL commands to manipulate the data.

Accessing SQL Tables

One important link between SQL and another database management system is sharing data elements in a database created in either system. For example, after you create the *parts* base table in the SQL database, you can allow another database system to access the data elements in that table. As a result, you can perform on these data elements all the data manipulation operations available in another system. The procedure for exchanging data differs among different database management systems. You need to consult the system's reference manual for details. I am using dBASE to illustrate this procedure.

In dBASE IV, you can use all the tables created either in the regular dBASE mode or in SQL mode. When you are in dBASE mode, you can open an SQL table. Similarly, you can convert a dBASE *.dbf* file to an SQL table so that you can use it in SQL mode.

Before you can access these tables, you need to know where they are stored. When you create SQL base tables in dBASE IV's SQL, all the tables are kept in a separate subdirectory. For example, all the base tables created for this book are stored in C:\DBASE\SQLBOOK. You can use these base tables when you are in the regular dBASE mode. To move from SQL mode to dBASE mode, however, you need to issue the following command at the SQL prompt:

```
SQL. SET SQL OFF
```

(The SQL prompt has been set by issuing the SET SQL ON command at the dot prompt or by specifying COMMAND = SET SQL ON in the CONFIG.DB configuration file.)

In response to this command, you return to the dot prompt. When you are in the regular dBASE mode, you may be assigned to a different default subdirectory. Therefore, to access your SQL tables, you need first to switch to the appropriate subdirectory. Issue the RUN CD (change directory) command at the dot prompt:

```
. RUN CD   C:\DBASE\SQLBOOK
```

RUN is the command for issuing a DOS command at the dot prompt. The preceding command changes your current subdirectory to the specified subdirectory: C:\DBASE\SQLBOOK, where all the SQL tables are located.

Viewing SQL Tables

After you are in the correct subdirectory, you can issue a dBASE command to access an SQL table. For example, if you have created the *parts* base table in SQL, you can view its contents at the dot prompt by issuing the LIST dBASE command. Figure 12.1 shows the commands and the contents of the base table named *parts* in the dBASE mode.

```
SQL. SET SQL OFF
. RUN CD C:\DBASE\SQLBOOK
```

```
. USE PARTS
. LIST
Record#  STOCK_NO  PART_TYPE    DSCRIPTION                UNIT_COST
      1  HW101     Printer      Epson LQ-1050 printer        650.90
      2  HW102     Printer      HP LaserJet II printer      1435.00
      3  HW201     Monitor      NEC multisync monitor        459.00
      4  HW301     V. board     Paradise VGA board           230.00
      5  HW401     Computer     IBM PS/2 Model 70/60MB      3250.00
      6  HW402     Computer     COMPAQ 386S DeskPro/40MB    2600.00
      7  HW403     Computer     Zenith Supersport 286/20    2975.00
      8  SW101     Spreadsheet  Lotus 1-2-3 Version 2.01     289.00
      9  SW201     WP           WordPerfect 5.0              195.00
     10  SW202     WP           Microsoft Word 5.0           183.50
     11  SW301     Database     Paradox 3.0                  385.75
     12  SW302     Database     dBASE IV Version 1.0         360.00
```

Fig. 12.1. *An SQL table displayed in dBASE IV.*

At this point, you can access data elements in the SQL table. You can add new data rows to the table and modify existing values. You can manipulate the table's data elements by using dBASE commands. You cannot modify the table structure, however. You cannot add a new column to the base table or delete or modify an existing column.

Adding New Data to SQL Tables

When you are in dBASE mode, you can add a new data row to the SQL table by using either the APPEND command or the BROWSE operation. Figure 12.2 shows the data entry screen (with filled data values) for adding a new row to the *parts* table by issuing the APPEND command at the dot prompt.

```
Record No    13
STOCK_NO   HW302
PART_TYPE  V. board
DSCRIPTION NEC G-1 video board
UNIT_COST       359.95
```

Fig. 12.2. *The data entry screen for adding a row to a table.*

You also can add a new row to the end of the *parts* table by issuing the BROWSE command at the dot prompt. In response to the command, you go to the end of the table and insert the data row.

Designing Custom Data Entry Forms

Because dBASE provides an easy-to-use form generator, you can use dBASE to design a data entry form. The form can be used for entering new data into the table. You invoke the form generator by using the dot-prompt command or by selecting the menu option from the Control Center. Figure 12.3 shows a sample data entry form for the *parts* table.

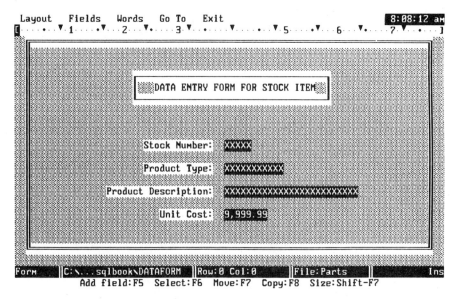

Fig. 12.3. *A sample data entry form.*

After the form is created, you can use it to enter data into the table. Figure 12.4 shows the new data to be appended to the table as it is displayed in the custom data form (named DATAFORM).

Figure 12.5 shows the table contents after the last row of data has been added to the table.

A similar capability is provided by Oracle's SQL*FormsDesigner for developing a custom data entry form. Refer to the SQL*Forms manual for details.

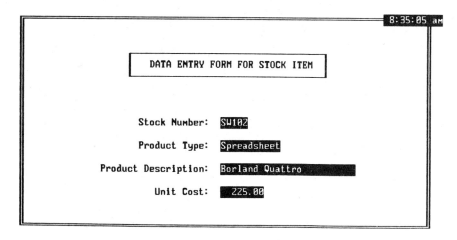

Fig. 12.4. *Data to be added to the* parts *table.*

STOCK_NO	PART_TYPE	DSCRIPTION	UNIT_COST
HW101	Printer	Epson LQ-1050 printer	650.90
HW102	Printer	HP LaserJet II printer	1435.00
HW201	Monitor	NEC multisync monitor	459.00
HW301	V. board	Paradise VGA board	230.00
HW401	Computer	IBM PS/2 Model 70/60MB	3250.00
HW402	Computer	COMPAQ 386S DeskPro/40MB	2600.00
HW403	Computer	Zenith Supersport 286/20	2975.00
SW101	Spreadsheet	Lotus 1-2-3 Version 2.01	289.00
SW201	WP	WordPerfect 5.0	195.00
SW202	WP	Microsoft Word 5.0	183.50
SW301	Database	Paradox 3.0	385.75
SW302	Database	dBASE IV Version 1.0	360.00
HW302	V. board	NEC G-1 video board	359.90
SW102	Spreadsheet	Borland Quattro	225.00

Records   Fields   Go To   Exit   8:03:12 am

Browse   C:\dbase\sqlbook\PARTS   Rec 14/14   File

View and edit fields

Fig. 12.5. *The* parts *table after a new row has been added.*

Editing Data in SQL Tables

You can change data in any row in the SQL table by using the EDIT command. You can find the data row to be edited either by using the filter condition (FOR) in the EDIT command or by going to the specific row (called record in dBASE) with the GOTO command. For example, if you need to edit the price of stock item #SW101, you issue the following command at the dot prompt:

. EDIT FOR STOCK_NO = 'SW101'

If you already know the row, or record, number (for example, record #8), you can issue the following command:

. GOTO 8
. EDIT

In either case, the data in that row, or record, is displayed for modification. At this point, you can begin making the necessary changes to the data elements in that row, or record. Figure 12.6 shows the row, or record, to be edited.

```
Record No      8
STOCK_NO    SW101
PART_TYPE   Spreadsheet
DSCRIPTION  Lotus 1-2-3 Version 2.01
UNIT_COST      289.00
```

Fig. 12.6. *Viewing a row, or record, in the* parts *table.*

You can use the data entry form created earlier for displaying your data to be modified. To use DATAFORM, you can choose the form from the Control Center in order to display the data. If you are at the dot prompt, you can issue the following commands for editing a record with the data entry form:

. USE PARTS
. SET FORMAT TO DATAFORM
. EDIT

In response to the EDIT command, the data elements to be modified are displayed in the data entry form, as shown in figure 12.7. You now can make the necessary modifications.

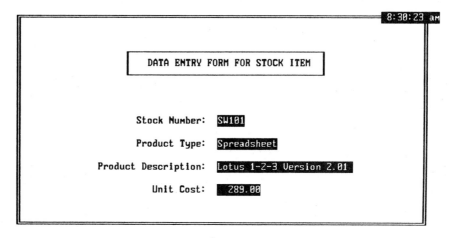

Fig. 12.7. *Displaying a row to be edited in the data entry form.*

Retrieving and Manipulating Data in SQL Tables

You can retrieve and manipulate data elements in the SQL table in the same way you work with data tables created in dBASE mode. Besides performing simple query operations on the table, you can use dBASE commands to obtain results that cannot be achieved easily with SQL commands. Figure 12.8 shows the commands used to compute total costs by product type and save the results to a new file.

```
. USE PARTS
. INDEX ON PART_TYPE TO BYTYPE
   100% indexed          14 Records indexed
. TOTAL ON PART_TYPE TO TOTALS
      14 records totaled
       7 records generated
. USE TOTALS
. LIST PART_TYPE, UNIT_COST
Record#  PART_TYPE   UNIT_COST
      1  Computer      8825.00
      2  Database       745.75
      3  Monitor        459.00
      4  Printer       2085.90
      5  Spreadsheet    514.00
      6  V. board       589.95
      7  WP             378.50
```

Fig. 12.8. *Using dBASE commands to display computed results.*

In figure 12.8, note that you can index the base table according to the values in the *part_type* column. When you issue the TOTAL ON...TO command, group totals are computed by using the unit costs of each product type (*part_type*). Results in the form of group totals are saved to a dBASE file named *totals.dbf*.

Copying SQL Tables in dBASE

When you are using SQL in dBASE IV, making a copy of an existing SQL table requires several steps because SQL has no command for making a copy of an existing table. For example, to make a duplicate copy of the *parts* base table, you need first to create a new table structure. Then you insert the data into the new table from the existing table.

You can accomplish the same copy in dBASE mode. The following command makes a copy of the *parts* table and names the copy *products*:

```
. COPY FILE PARTS.DBF TO PRODUCTS.DBF
```

When you create an SQL table, dBASE IV also creates its corresponding database file (with the *.dbf* file extension). As a result, you can make a copy of the database file. Another way to make a copy of the *parts* table is to use the COPY TO command as follows:

```
. USE PARTS
. COPY TO PRODUCTS
```

Figure 12.9 shows the results of this command.

In either case, you get a duplicate copy of the *parts* table with a different name. But the duplicate table is in dBASE IV database file format (*.dbf*). You cannot use the duplicate table when you return to the SQL prompt until you convert the file to a base table.

```
. USE PARTS
. COPY TO PRODUCTS
  14 records copied
. USE PRODUCTS
. LIST
```

Record#	STOCK_NO	PART_TYPE	DSCRIPTION	UNIT_COST
1	HW101	Printer	Epson LQ-1050 printer	650.90
2	HW102	Printer	HP LaserJet II printer	1435.00
3	HW201	Monitor	NEC MultiSync monitor	459.00
4	HW301	V. board	Paradise VGA board	230.00
5	HW401	Computer	IBM PS/2 Model 70/60MB	3250.00
6	HW402	Computer	COMPAQ 386S DeskPro/40MB	2600.00
7	HW403	Computer	Zenith Supersport 286/20	2975.00
8	SW101	Spreadsheet	Lotus 1-2-3 Version 2.01	289.00
9	SW201	WP	WordPerfect 5.0	195.00
10	SW202	WP	Microsoft Word 5.0	183.50
11	SW301	Database	Paradox 3.0	385.75
12	SW302	Database	dBASE IV Version 1.0	360.00
13	HW303	V. board	NEC G-1 video board	359.95
14	SW102	Spreadsheet	Borland Quattro	225.00

Fig. 12.9. *Copying an SQL table in dBASE mode.*

Converting dBASE Database Files to Base Tables

If you want to use a dBASE database (*.dbf*) file in the SQL mode, you need first to convert the file to a base table with the DBDEFINE command. The command is issued at the SQL prompt as follows:

SQL. DBDEFINE   <name of .dbf file>;

For example, if you want to convert to an SQL base table the *products.dbf* file you created earlier (as a copy of the *parts* base table), you issue the following command:

SQL. DBDEFINE products;

The process is shown in figure 12.10.

```
SQL. DBDEFINE products;
Table(s) DBDEFINEd:
PRODUCTS

DBDEFINE successful


SQL. SELECT * FROM products;
    STOCK_NO PART_TYPE    DSCRIPTION               UNIT_COST
    HW101    Printer      Epson LQ-1050 printer       650.90
    HW102    Printer      HP LaserJet II printer     1435.00
    HW201    Monitor      NEC MultiSync monitor       459.00
    HW301    V. board     Paradise VGA board          230.00
    HW401    Computer     IBM PS/2 Model 70/60MB     3250.00
    HW402    Computer     COMPAQ 386S DeskPro/40MB   2600.00
    HW403    Computer     Zenith Supersport 286/20   2975.00
    SW101    Spreadsheet  Lotus 1-2-3 Version 2.01    289.00
    SW201    WP           Word Perfect 5.0            195.00
    SW202    WP           Microsoft Word 5.0          183.50
    SW301    Database     Paradox 3.0                 385.75
    SW302    Database     dBASE IV Version 1.0        360.00
    HW303    V. board     NEC G-1 video board         359.95
    SW102    Spreadsheet  Borland Quattro             225.00
```

Fig. 12.10. *Converting a dBASE database file to an SQL table.*

Deleting Data

When you are in dBASE mode, you can delete data from an SQL base table by using the DELETE command. You can delete one or more rows (records) of data from the base table by defining the record range for the data rows. You also can delete a set of rows by using a filter condition. Two examples are

```
. USE accounts
. DELETE FOR recno() <=3


. DELETE FOR state =  'CA' AND balance >2500
. PACK
```

The first command deletes the first three rows, or records, from the base table. The second command removes those accounts in the state of CA (California) that have a balance greater than $2,500.

Producing Reports

Because the standard version of SQL lacks the commands for producing sophisticated reports, you have to rely on other means for generating your reports. Most database management systems provide means for designing and producing good reports. For instance, you may use a report painter or report writer for designing the report forms. Then you use the report form to produce the reports with the data elements in the database. An alternative is to write a set of commands in a database language (such as dBASE) or in a procedural programming language (such as C or COBOL) for producing the reports.

Using a Report Generator

dBASE IV provides a report generator for designing and producing your reports. To design a custom report form, you select the appropriate menu option from the Control Center or issue the necessary dot-prompt command to invoke the design screen. In response to the selection of the menu option or the dot-prompt command, you are provided a report form design screen. You specify the report title and column headings on the screen for your report. Figure 12.11 shows an example of a custom report form.

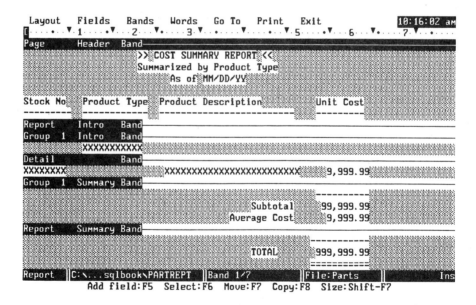

Fig. 12.11. *A custom report form.*

In figure 12.11, note that the report form is designed for displaying unit costs of all the stock items in the *parts* table. In addition, the costs are grouped by product type to produce subtotals and average costs for these groups.

You use the custom report form by choosing the appropriate menu options from the Control Center or by issuing the required dBASE commands at the dot prompt. However, before you use the report form on the data in the *parts* table, you need to sort the data by product type. This sort is done by the index operation. The dBASE commands for producing a report with the report form (named PARTREPT) are

- USE PARTS
- INDEX ON PART_TYPE TO BYTYPE
  100% indexed   14 Records indexed
- REPORT FORM PARTREPT

Figure 12.12 shows the cost summary report produced by using the report form with the data elements stored in the SQL table named *parts*.

>> COST SUMMARY REPORT <<
Summarized by Product Type
As of 12/31/89

Stock No	Product Type	Product Description	Unit Cost
-------------	--------------------	---------------------------------	-------------
	Computer		
HW401		IBM PS/2 Model 70/60MB	3,250.00
HW402		COMPAQ 386S DeskPro/40MB	2,600.00
HW403		Zenith Supersport 286/20	2,975.00

		Subtotal	8,825.00
		Average Cost	2,941.67
	Database		
SW301		Paradox 3.0	385.75
SW302		dBASE IV Version 1.0	360.00

		Subtotal	745.75
		Average Cost	372.88
	Monitor		
HW201		NEC MultiSync monitor	459.00

		Subtotal	459.00
		Average Cost	459.00

	Printer		
HW101		Epson LQ-1050 printer	650.90
HW102		HP LaserJet II printer	1,435.00

		Subtotal	2,085.90
		Average Cost	1,042.95
	Spreadsheet		
SW101		Lotus 1-2-3 Version 2.01	289.00
SW102		Borland Quattro	225.00

		Subtotal	514.00
		Average Cost	257.00
	V. board		
HW301		Paradise VGA board	230.00
HW302		NEC G-1 video board	359.95

		Subtotal	589.95
		Average Cost	294.98
	WP		
SW201		WordPerfect 5.0	195.00
SW202		Microsoft Word 5.0	183.50

		Subtotal	378.50
		Average Cost	189.25

		TOTAL	13,598.10
			= = = =

Fig. 12.12. *The COST SUMMARY REPORT.*

When you are using Oracle's RDBMS, you can use the SQL*ReportWriter to design a custom report form and produce a similar report. The procedure for producing the report is parallel to the procedure used by dBASE. You also can produce basic reports by using some SQL commands implemented by Oracle's SQL*Plus. These commands are not a subset of the standard SQL commands and not all of them are available in other implementations of SQL.

Building Basic Reports with SQL*Plus Commands

If you need to produce reports that follow a simple, basic format, you can issue a sequential set of commands provided by SQL*Plus. These reports can be in tabular form with a report title and with or without summary statistics, such as totals and averages.

The process of producing the report involves the following operations:

❑ Setting page size

❑ Specifying the report title and footnote

❑ Defining column headings and formatting column values

❑ Defining group breaks

❑ Computing summary statistics

❑ Selecting the (ordered) data elements to be displayed

Each operation is carried out by one or more SQL*Plus commands. The sequence in which the commands are carried out is not important because the commands' effects are cumulative. That is, you can define the column headings before specifying the report title or vice versa. However, the column headings and title are displayed only when you display the data elements that make up the report body.

Setting Page Size

Before producing the actual report, you may want to set the size of the pages of the report. This step involves determining the page length and top margin. The command to set the page length in number of lines is

SET PAGESIZE   <number of lines>;

For example, if you want to produce a report up to 66 lines long on each page, you issue the following command:

```
SQL> SET PAGESIZE 66;
```

To define the top margin, use the SET NEWPAGE command in the following format:

SET NEWPAGE <top margin>;

If you want to begin displaying the first line of the report at the fifth line from the top, you issue the following command:

```
SQL> SET NEWPAGE 5;
```

If you set the top margin as 0 (SET NEWPAGE 0), the program will issue a form feed before printing the first line of your report on the top of the page. A form feed causes most printers to advance to the next page.

Specifying Report Titles

The command provided by SQL*Plus for placing a report title at the top of a report page is the TTITLE statement with optional clauses for determining the location of the title. The format of the TTITLE statement is

TTITLE [CENTER|LEFT|RIGHT] [COL<n>] '<report title>' [SKIP<n>];

The CENTER, LEFT, or RIGHT clause is used, respectively, to center, left-align, or right-align the report title. The COL keyword followed by an integer works like a Tab key on a typewriter, allowing you to begin displaying the title from a specified column location. For example, COL20 begins displaying the title at the 20th column. The SKIP clause enables you to skip a number of lines. For example, if you want to have three blank lines after the report title, you specify SKIP3 after the report title. The following statement places a page title on a cost summary report:

```
SQL> TTITLE LEFT COL20 'COST SUMMARY REPORT' -
> SKIP LEFT COL22 'As of 12/31/89' SKIP LEFT ' ';
```

This statement places the first line of the report title *COST SUMMARY REPORT* at the top of the page, beginning at the 20th column from the left margin. After printing the first line, the program skips the next line and displays the second line, *As of 12/31/89*, beginning at the 22nd column from the left. Then the program skips the next line, displaying a blank line. The hyphen (-) is used for extending the statement to the next SQL line if necessary. When you type the hyphen and press the Return or Enter key, a new line appears with the > sign, so that you can continue typing the rest of the command.

You can add a report title or footnote at the bottom of a report page by using the BTITLE command. The command follows the same format as TTITLE:

BTITLE [CENTER|LEFT|RIGHT] [COL<n>] '<report title>' [SKIP<n>];

For example, the following statement places a footnote at the bottom of the report:

```
SQL> BTITLE CENTER 'Report Date: January 15, 1990';
```

If you want to see how the report title will look, you can display the contents of the base table by using the following command:

```
SQL>    SELECT *
  2        FROM parts
  3    ORDER BY item_type;
```

The SELECT command displays the contents of the *parts* table. You use the ORDER BY command to arrange the results by product type. The results produced by this command and by the command for defining the report title are shown in figure 12.13.

```
                      COST SUMMARY REPORT
                        As of 12/31/89


    STOCK   PART_TYPE     DSCRIPTION                   UNIT_COST
    -----   ----------    ------------------------     ----------
    HW401   Computer      IBM PS/2 Model 70/60MB        3250.00
    HW403   Computer      Zenith Supersport 286/20      2975.00
    HW402   Computer      COMPAQ 386S DeskPro/40MB      2600.00
    SW301   Database      Paradox 3.0                    385.75
    SW302   Database      dBASE IV Version 1.0           360.00
    HW201   Monitor       NEC MultiSync monitor          459.00
    HW101   Printer       Epson LQ-1050 printer          628.50
    HW102   Printer       HP LaserJet II printer        1435.00
    SW101   Spreadsheet   Lotus 1-2-3 Version 2.01       250.00
    SW102   Spreadsheet   Borland Quattro                225.00
    HW301   V. Board      Paradise VGA board             230.00
    HW302   V. Board      NEC G-1 video board            359.95
    SW201   WP            WordPerfect 5.0                195.00
    SW202   WP            Microsoft Word 5.0             183.50
                  Report Date: January 15, 1990


    14 records selected.
```

Fig. 12.13. *A report with top and bottom titles.*

Defining Column Headings

When you are using the SELECT statement to display data elements in a column, the column is usually labeled with the column name. In some versions of SQL (SQL*Plus, for example), if the column width defined in the table structure is narrower than the data value, the column name is truncated in the column heading. Look at figure 12.13, which is produced by SQL*Plus; the first column is labeled as STOCK even though the column is defined as *stock_no* in the base table structure. This truncation occurs because the column width is defined as CHAR(5). In order to have a more descriptive column heading, SQL*Plus provides the COLUMN command. The format of the COLUMN command is

COLUMN <column name> HEADING '<heading>' [FORMAT <format>];

The optional FORMAT clause defines the format in which the data value is to be reported. If the data value is a character string, you can define the column width as A<n> where *n* is the number of characters:

```
SQL> COLUMN stock_no HEADING 'Stock No' FORMAT A10;
```

This statement labels the data values of the *stock_no* column as *Stock No* in the report. The FORMAT A10 sets the report column width as 10 characters. The following three statements define the headings for the other three columns of the report:

```
SQL> COLUMN part_type HEADING 'Product Type' FORMAT A15;
SQL> COLUMN dscription HEADING 'Product Description';
SQL> COLUMN unit_cost HEADING 'Unit Cost' FORMAT 9,999.99;
```

In the last statement, FORMAT 9,999.99 defines the format for a numeric value. As a result, the values in the Unit Cost column will be displayed in a conventional business form with commas separating every three digits. Figure 12.14 shows the effects of the COLUMN, TTITLE, and BTITLE commands.

```
                    COST SUMMARY REPORT
                     As of 12/31/89


Stock No  Product Type  Product Description      Unit Cost
--------  ------------  -------------------      ---------
HW401     Computer      IBM PS/2 Model 70/60MB   3,250.00
HW403     Computer      Zenith Supersport 286/20 2,975.00
HW402     Computer      COMPAQ 386S DeskPro/40MB  2,600.00
SW301     Database      Paradox 3.0                385.75
SW302     Database      dBASE IV Version 1.0       360.00
HW201     Monitor       NEC MultiSync monitor      459.00
HW101     Printer       Epson LQ-1050 printer      628.50
HW102     Printer       HP LaserJet II printer   1,435.00
SW101     Spreadsheet   Lotus 1-2-3 Version 2.01   250.00
SW102     Spreadsheet   Borland Quattro            225.00
HW301     V. Board      Paradise VGA board         230.00
HW302     V. Board      NEC G-1 video board        359.95
SW201     WP            WordPerfect 5.0            195.00
SW202     WP            Microsoft Word 5.0         183.50
                  Report Date: January 15, 1990


14 records selected.
```

Fig. 12.14. *A report with custom column headings.*

Grouping Data

You can group your data elements by the values in a specific column. For example, in the cost summary report shown in figure 12.14, you may want to break down the unit costs by product type. You can use the BREAK ON command to group the data values. The BREAK ON command uses the following syntax:

BREAK ON   <grouping column> [SKIP<n>];

To break the data elements into groups by product type, you specify *part_type* as the grouping column in the BREAK ON statement:

```
SQL> BREAK ON part_type SKIP;
```

The SKIP clause is used to place a blank line after each group for easy reading. Because the command places a break after each group, you need to arrange your data elements by using the ORDER BY clause in the SELECT command:

```
SQL>   SELECT *
  2      FROM parts
  3   ORDER BY part_type;
```

The results of the group breaks can be seen in figure 12.15.

Displaying Summary Statistics

After dividing your data into groups, you can compute and display group summary statistics by using the COMPUTE statement. The format for the COMPUTE statement is

COMPUTE   <summary statistics>
    OF   <column to be summarized>
    ON   <grouping column>;

For example, if you want to compute subtotals for the groups shown in the cost summary report in figure 12.15, you issue the following statement:

```
SQL> COMPUTE SUM OF unit_cost ON part_type;
```

```
                        COST SUMMARY REPORT
                          As of 12/31/89

      Stock No   Product Type      Product Description        Unit Cost
      --------   ----------------  -------------------------  ---------
      HW401      Computer          IBM PS/2 Model 70/60MB     3,250.00
      HW403                        Zenith Supersport 286/20   2,975.00
      HW402                        COMPAQ 386S DeskPro/40MB    2,600.00

      SW301      Database          Paradox 3.0                  385.75
      SW302                        dBASE IV Version 1.0         360.00

      HW201      Monitor           NEC MultiSync monitor        459.00

      HW101      Printer           Epson LQ-1050 printer        628.50
      HW102                        HP LaserJet II printer     1,435.00

      SW101      Spreadsheet       Lotus 1-2-3 Version 2.01     250.00
      SW102                        Borland Quattro              225.00

      HW301      V. Board          Paradise VGA board           230.00
      HW302                        NEC G-1 video board          359.95

      SW201      WP                WordPerfect 5.0              195.00
      SW202      WP                Microsoft Word 5.0           183.50
                        Report Date: January 15, 1990

      14 records selected.
```

Fig. 12.15. *Showing group breaks in a report.*

Figure 12.16 shows the subtotals produced by this command for the groups of data by product type.

```
                    COST SUMMARY REPORT
                     As of 12/31/89


  Stock No  Product Type    Product Description       Unit Cost
  --------  ----------------  ----------------------    ---------

  HW401     Computer        IBM PS/2 Model 70/60MB     3,250.00
  HW403                     Zenith Supersport 286/20   2,975.00
  HW402                     COMPAQ 386S DeskPro/40MB    2,600.00
            ***************                            ----------
            sum                                        8,825.00


  SW301     Database        Paradox 3.0                  385.75
  SW302                     dBASE IV Version 1.0         360.00
            ***************                            ----------
            sum                                          745.75


  HW201     Monitor         NEC MultiSync monitor        459.00
            ***************                            ----------
            sum                                          459.00


  HW101     Printer         Epson LQ-1050 printer        628.50
  HW102                     HP LaserJet II printer     1,435.00
            ***************                            ----------
            sum                                        2,063.50


  SW101     Spreadsheet     Lotus 1-2-3 Version 2.01     250.00
  SW102                     Borland Quattro              225.00
            ***************                            ----------
            sum                                          475.00


  HW301     V. Board        Paradise VGA board           230.00
  HW302                     NEC G-1 video board          359.95
            ***************                            ----------
            sum                                          589.95


  SW201     WP              WordPerfect 5.0              195.00
  SW202                     Microsoft Word 5.0           183.50
            ***************                            ----------
            sum                                          378.50
                 Report Date: January 15, 1990


  14 records selected.
```

Fig. 12.16. Showing summary statistics in a report.

In addition to computing the totals with the SUM keyword, you can use other keywords in the statement to calculate and display other summary statistics. These keywords are

Keyword	Summary Statistics
COUNT	Number of rows in the group
MAX	Maximum value in the column
MIN	Minimum value in the column
AVG	Average (mean) value in the column
STD	Standard deviation of the values
VAR	Variance of the values

Effects of the COMPUTE statements are cumulative. One COMPUTE statement does not replace another issued earlier. As a result, you can display more than one summary statistic in the same report by issuing more COMPUTE statements.

Processing Command Files

When you issue SQL commands, you usually type one command at a time. After waiting for the results of that command, you issue another command. In some systems, however, if you need to issue a command that has been issued earlier, you can recall it without re-entering it. The way to reissue a command varies among different database management systems.

When you are using Oracle's SQL*Plus, only the latest command is retained until the next command is issued. To reissue the last command entered, you type *run* at the SQL prompt. The latest command is reissued and processed. If you anticipate a later use of the command, you must save it to a command file before issuing the next command. After a command is saved, you can recall it at any time for processing. To save the latest command issued, you use the SAVE command as follows:

SAVE   <name of command file>;

For example, after creating the *employee* base table, you can save the CREATE TABLE command in a command file, named *createdb.sql* (see fig. 12.17). You can issue the command later to recreate the table, or you can recall the command and modify it for recreating another base table.

```
SQL> CREATE TABLE employee
    2              (ss_no      CHAR(11),
    3               l_name     CHAR(7),
    4               f_name     CHAR(10),
    5               title      CHAR(10),
    6               dept       CHAR(10),
    7               salary     DECIMAL(8,2));

Table created.

SQL> SAVE createdb
Wrote file createdb
```

Fig. 12.17. Saving a command in a command file.

If you later need to recreate the same table, you can reissue the command by using the command file you saved. You issue the GET command to invoke the command file:

GET   <name of command file>;

After invoking the command file, you then issue the RUN command to process the command (see fig. 12.18).

In this example, the *employee* table is recreated by invoking the *createdb* command file for reissuing the CREATE TABLE command. However, you have to drop the existing *employee* table before you can recreate it.

This approach is one way to borrow an existing table structure for another table. You can use the GET command to recall an existing CREATE TABLE command and then modify the statement as needed for another table. For the procedure to modify an SQL*Plus command, consult the SQL*Plus reference manual.

In SQL*Plus, you can save only one command in a command file. If you want to save a set of commands for later processing, you need to embed the commands in a program written in one of the procedural programming languages, such as the C language.

If you are using dBASE IV, you have different ways to recall and process one or more commands. As you issue your commands at the SQL prompt, some recently entered commands you entered in dBASE are stored temporarily in a buffer (a working storage area). You can specify the number of commands retained. Later when you need to find one of these commands, from the SQL prompt, you repeatedly press the up-arrow or down-arrow key. Each time you press the up- or down-arrow key, a previously entered command is displayed at the SQL prompt. When you find the command you want, you press the Return or Enter key to process the command.

```
SQL> DROP TABLE employee;

Table dropped.

SQL> GET createdb
  1   CREATE TABLE employee
  2               (ss_no      CHAR(11),
  3                l_name     CHAR(7),
  4                f_name     CHAR(10),
  5                title      CHAR(10),
  6                dept       CHAR(10),
  7*               salary     DECIMAL(8,2))

SQL> RUN
  1   CREATE TABLE employee
  2               (ss_no      CHAR(11),
  3                l_name     CHAR(7),
  4                f_name     CHAR(10),
  5                title      CHAR(10),
  6                dept       CHAR(10),
  7*               salary     DECIMAL(8,2))

Table created.
```

Fig. 12.18. Processing a command file.

You also can store a set of SQL commands in a command file with *.prs* as the file extension. You need to invoke the text editor by issuing the MODIFY COMMAND (MODI COMM) command at either the dBASE dot prompt or the SQL prompt:

MODIFY COMMAND   <filename.prs>

Because this MODIFY COMMAND is a dBASE command, not an SQL command, you must not end the statement with a semicolon. After you finish typing the commands, you press the Ctrl-End key combination to save the commands to a *.prs* file.

For example, you can write the set of SQL commands for creating the *employee* base table and save the set as *createdb.prs*. The command for invoking the text editor for creating the command file is

```
SQL. MODIFY COMMAND CREATEDB.PRS
```

The command file contains the lists of commands for creating the *employee* base table, as shown in figure 12.19.

```
***************************************************
*** CREATEDB.PRS, Creating employee base table ***
***************************************************
SET TALK OFF

*** Create base table structure ***
CREATE TABLE employee
              (ss_no     CHAR(11),
               l_name    CHAR(7),
               f_name    CHAR(10),
               title     CHAR(10),
               dept      CHAR(10),
               salary    DECIMAL(8,2));

*** Add data values to the base table ***
INSERT INTO employee
      VALUES ('123-45-6789', 'Smith', 'James J.', 'President',
              'Corporate', 89500.00);
INSERT INTO employee
      VALUES ('634-56-7890', 'Nelson', 'Harry M.', 'Manager',
              'Sales', 65000);
INSERT INTO employee
      VALUES ('445-67-8801', 'Zeller', 'Albert K.', 'Salesman'
              'Sales', 48900);
INSERT INTO employee
      VALUES ('562-87-8800', 'Chapman', 'Kirk D.', 'Salesman'
              'Sales', 42500);
INSERT INTO employee
      VALUES ('404-22-4568', 'Baker', 'Larry A.', 'Clerk',
              'Sales', 30500);
INSERT INTO employee
      VALUES ('256-09-5555', 'Dixon', 'Kathy T.', 'Accountant',
              'Accounting', 45000);
INSERT INTO employee
      VALUES ('458-90-3456', 'Frazer', 'Robert F.', 'Bookkeeper',
              'Accounting', 280000);
INSERT INTO employee
      VALUES ('777-34-6543', 'King', 'David G.', 'Manager',
              'Personnel', 38000);
```

```
INSERT INTO employee
    VALUES ('100-45-8021', 'Wong', 'Mike J.', 'Manager',
            'MIS',44000);
INSERT INTO employee
    VALUES ('303-25-7777', 'Duff', 'Cathy B.', 'Secretary',
            'Personnel', 26500);
RETURN
```

Fig. 12.19. *A command file for creating a base table.*

To process the command file, you issue the DO command at the dBASE dot prompt or the SQL prompt:

DO   <name of .prs file>

For example, to create the *employee* base table, you issue the following command:

```
SQL> DO CREATEDB.PRS
```

Remember, do not end the command with a semicolon because the command is not an SQL command.

Embedding SQL Commands

As mentioned earlier, SQL is designed mainly as a query language, you need to rely on other means to perform other data management functions efficiently. You have seen some of these approaches. Another way is to combine SQL commands with commands provided by other database management languages or regular procedural programming languages. In this section, I explain how to combine SQL commands with commands provided by the dBASE language. Later, you will see examples of embedding SQL commands in a program written in the C language.

Embedding SQL Commands in dBASE Programs

dBASE has its own language, which you can use to write a program for performing data management operations. Due to the limited scope of this book, I do not discuss in detail all the aspects of dBASE programming. Instead, I show examples of how to embed SQL commands in a dBASE program so that you can perform some of the data management functions that cannot be done by SQL commands alone.

Combining SQL commands with dBASE commands is a simple matter. You can mix them in the same program. dBASE uses different sets of keywords and commands for SQL and dBASE. dBASE can tell an SQL statement from a dBASE command by its unique keyword. For example, if you use SELECT, the program knows that SELECT is an SQL command. Similarly, a statement that begins with the word EDIT is a dBASE command, and so on. However, you must assign a *.prs* extension to the command file for the program containing both SQL and dBASE commands.

Passing Values with Memory Variables

In order to pass data values between SQL commands and dBASE commands, you need to use memory variables. Memory variables are temporary memory locations for holding data values. Memory variables can be used throughout the program. To see how you can exchange data between SQL commands and dBASE commands, look at the program shown in figure 12.20.

```
*****************************************************************
***  FINDDATA.PRS, Finding a stock item by its stock no.  ***
*****************************************************************

   SET TALK OFF
   CLEAR

   STORE 'Y' TO mFind_Data

   DO WHILE mFind_Data = 'Y'

     *** Initialize variables ***

     CLEAR
     STORE SPACE(5) TO mStock_No
     STORE SPACE(12) TO mPart_Type
     STORE SPACE(25) TO mPart_Desc
     STORE 0 TO mUnit_Cost

     *** Get stock number ***
     @3,1 TO 5,32 DOUBLE
     @4,5 SAY "Enter Stock Number: " GET mStock_No PICTURE "XXXXX"
     READ
```

```
*** Find it in the base table ***
SELECT stock_no, part_type, dscription, unit_cost
  INTO mStock_no, mPart_Type, mPart_Desc, mUnit_Cost
  FROM parts
 WHERE stock_no = mStock_No;

*** Check for successful data query ***
IF SQLCODE <>0
  @20,10 SAY;
  "No such stock no! Do you want to find another item (Y/N) ?";
  GET mFind_Data
  READ
  LOOP
ENDIF

*** Display the results ***
@8,10 TO 18,70
@10,15 SAY "Stock No. ................ " + mStock_No
@12,15 SAY "Product Type ............ " + mPart_Type
@14,15 SAY "Product Description ..... " + mPart_Desc
@16,15 SAY "Unit Cost ............... "
@16,41 SAY mUnit_Cost PICTURE "9,999.99"

@20,15 SAY "Would you like to find another item (Y/N)? ";
  GET mFind_Data
READ
ENDDO
RETURN
```

Fig. 12.20. *Using memory variables in a program.*

This program finds a row of data in the *parts* base table by the stock number. The program uses five memory variables: *mFind_Data*, *mStock_No*, *mPart_Type*, *mPart_Desc*, and *mUnit_Cost*. The *mFind_Data* variable is used to determine whether to continue the data search process. When the value is assigned a Y value, the data search process continues. Otherwise, the program is terminated.

The memory variable *mStock_No* is used to store the stock number entered at the prompt:

```
*** Get stock number ***
@3,1 TO 5,32 DOUBLE
@4,5 SAY "Enter Stock Number: " GET mStock_No PICTURE "XXXXX"
READ
```

The value in the *mStock_No* is used in the WHERE clause of the SELECT command to find the data rows. The other variables—*mPart_Type*, *mPart_Desc*, and *mUnit_Cost*—are used to hold data values returned from the SQL SELECT command.

```
*** Find it in the base table ***
SELECT stock_no, part_type, dscription, unit_cost
  INTO mStock_no, mPart_Type, mPart_Desc, mUnit_Cost
  FROM parts
 WHERE stock_no = mStock_No;
```

The variable *SQLCODE* is used for indicating whether the SELECT command returns any results. If the SELECT command finds any data row in the base table, *SQLCODE* is set to zero. Therefore, you check to see whether *SQLCODE* is zero with the following commands:

```
IF SQLCODE <>0
  @20,10 SAY;
  "No such stock no! Do you want to find another item (Y/N) ?";
  GET mFind_Data
  READ
  LOOP
ENDIF
```

If *SQLCODE* is zero, the program repeats the loop and prompts for another *stock_no*. If the SELECT command finds a data row with an entry in *stock_no* (SQLCODE = 0), the program displays the results with descriptive labels:

```
*** Display the results ***
@8,10 TO 18,70
@10,15 SAY "Stock No. ............... " + mStock_No
@12,15 SAY "Product Type ............ " + mPart_Type
@14,15 SAY "Product Description ..... " + mPart_Desc
@16,15 SAY "Unit Cost ............... "
@16,41 SAY mUnit_Cost PICTURE "9,999.99"

@20,15 SAY "Do you like to find another item (Y/N)? ";
    GET mFind_Data
  READ
ENDDO
RETURN
```

When you process the program, you are prompted for a stock number. After you enter the stock number for the item you want, the program finds the data row for that item and displays the data elements (see fig. 12.21).

```
┌──────────────────────────────────────┐
│ ┌──────────────────────────────────┐ │
│ │  Enter Stock Number:  [HW102]    │ │
│ └──────────────────────────────────┘ │
└──────────────────────────────────────┘
```

```
┌──────────────────────────────────────────────────┐
│                                                    │
│   Stock No. .............. HW102                   │
│                                                    │
│   Product Type ........... Printer                 │
│                                                    │
│   Product Description ..... HP LaserJet II printer │
│                                                    │
│   Unit Cost .............. 1,435.00                │
│                                                    │
└──────────────────────────────────────────────────┘
```

```
Do you like to find another item (Y/N)?  [Y]
```

Fig. 12.21. *Finding an item by its stock number.*

Designing Custom Data Entry Forms

You can use dBASE commands to design a data entry form and then use it to add new data to an SQL base table. Figure 12.22 shows a program for creating a custom data entry form for inserting new data into the *parts* table.

```
***********************************************************
*** ADDDATA.PRS, Adding a row of data to an SQL table  ***
***********************************************************
  SET TALK OFF

*** Clear screen ***
  CLEAR

*** Draw boxes, label columns on the data entry form  ***
  @3,2  TO 21,77 DOUBLE
  @6,22 TO 8,58
  @7,26  SAY "DATA ENTRY FORM FOR STOCK ITEM"
  @11,24 SAY "Stock Number:"
  @13,24 SAY "Product Type:"
  @15,17 SAY "Product Description:"
  @17,27 SAY "Unit Cost:"

*** Initial memory variable  ***
  STORE 'Y' TO mAdd_Data
```

(continued)

```
***  Get data values  ***
  DO WHILE mAdd_Data = 'Y'
    STORE SPACE(5) TO mStock_No
    STORE SPACE(11) TO mPart_Type
    STORE SPACE(25) TO mPart_Desc
    STORE 0 TO mUnit_Cost
    @11,39  GET mStock_No PICTURE "XXXXX"
    @13,39 GET mPart_Type PICTURE "XXXXXXXXXXX"
    @15,39 GET mPart_Desc PICTURE "XXXXXXXXXXXXXXXXXXXXXXXXX"
    @17,39 GET mUnit_Cost PICTURE "9,999.99"
    READ

    ***  Insert data values to the SQL base table  ***
    INSERT INTO parts
        VALUES (mStock_No, mPart_Type, mPart_Desc, mUnit_Cost);
    ***  Exit test  ***
    @19,15 SAY "These data values have been added to Parts table."
    @20,17 SAY "Add another data row to the base table (Y/N)?";
      GET mAdd_Data
    READ
    CLEAR GETS
    @19,15 CLEAR TO 20 [19] ,75
    @20,15 CLEAR TO 21 [20] ,75
  ENDDO
  RETURN
```

***Fig. 12.22.** A program that creates a custom data entry form for inserting data into a table.*

In this program, several memory variables are used to pass values between the dBASE commands and the SQL commands. The data entry form is created by using the dBASE commands for drawing the necessary boxes and placing the column labels on the form. When you process the program, the data entry form is displayed as shown in figure 12.23.

You fill in the necessary data values on the form. After entering the data values, you press the Return or Enter key to insert them into the base table. In response, you are asked whether you want to insert another row of data (see fig. 12.24). If you answer yes, the program repeats the data entry process. Otherwise, the program terminates.

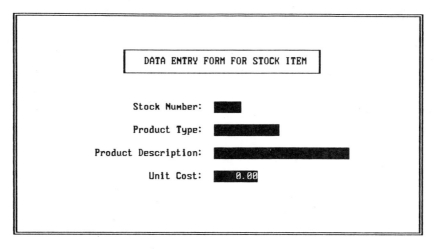

Fig. 12.23. *A custom data entry form.*

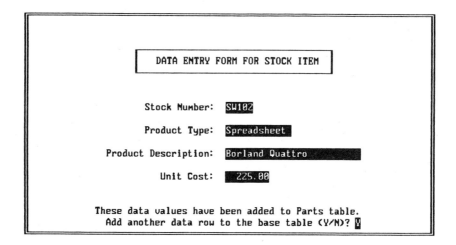

Fig. 12.24. *Inserting a data row into the* parts *table.*

Using Cursor

From the *finddata.prs* example in figure 12.20, note that the SELECT command returns only one set of values to the memory variables. The memory variables store values from one data row found by the SELECT command. What happens if SELECT returns several data rows? Fortunately, a way to retain these results exists. You need to use a cursor. In this context, *cursor* does not refer to the blinking dash or square you see on your computer screen. A cursor is temporary memory space reserved for holding these results.

Before you can use a cursor for holding the results from a SELECT operation, you need to declare the cursor and give it a name. Use the following command:

DECLARE CURSOR <cursor name> FOR
SELECT .... ;

The cursor is invoked by issuing the OPEN cursor command:

OPEN <cursor name>;

In response to this command, the SELECT statement is carried out and the results are stored in the cursor. The number of rows is stored in a memory variable named SQLCNT.

After that, you can retrieve sequentially each data row stored in the cursor. To see how a cursor works, look at the example in figure 12.25.

```
**************************************************
***  CURSOR.PRS, Using cursor for displaying data  ***
**************************************************
  SET TALK OFF
  CLEAR

  STORE 'Y' TO mFind_Data
  STORE ' ' TO mHit_a_Key

  DO WHILE mFind_Data = 'Y'

    *** Get stock number ***
    CLEAR
    STORE SPACE(5) TO mStock_No
    STORE SPACE(11) TO mPart_Type
    STORE SPACE(25) TO mPart_Desc
    STORE O TO mUnit_Cost

    *** Get product type ***
    @3,1 TO 5,42 DOUBLE
    @4,5 SAY "Enter Product Type: ";
      GET mPart_Type PICTURE "XXXXXXXXXXX"
    READ

    *** Define cursor ***
    DECLARE mItems CURSOR FOR
```

```
        SELECT stock_no, part_type, dscription, unit_cost
          FROM parts
         WHERE part_type= mPart_Type;

        *** Open cursor
        OPEN mItems;

        *** Check for successful data query ***
        IF SQLCODE <>0
          @20,10 SAY;
          "No such product type! Do you want to find another type (Y/N) ?";
          GET mFind_Data
          READ
          LOOP
        ENDIF

        *** Data found ***
        STORE SQLCNT TO mRows
        DO WHILE mRows > 0
          FETCH mItems INTO mStock_No, mPart_Type, mPart_Desc, mUnit_Cost;
          *** Display one row of data found ***
          @8,10 TO 18,70
          @10,15 SAY "Stock No. ............... " + mStock_No
          @12,15 SAY "Product Type ............ " + mPart_Type
          @14,15 SAY "Product Description ..... " + mPart_Desc
          @16,15 SAY "Unit Cost ............... "
          @16,41 SAY mUnit_Cost PICTURE "9,999.99"
          mRows = mRows - 1
          @20,20 SAY "Press any key to see next stock item"
          WAIT " " TO mHit_a_Key
        ENDDO

@20,10 SAY "No more data! Would you like to find another product type (Y/N)? ";
        GET mFind_Data

      READ
    ENDDO

  ***Close the cursor***
    CLOSE mITEMS
    RETURN
```

Fig. 12.25. *Using a cursor to store data.*

This example finds all the data rows belonging to a given product type. The first part of the program gets the information about the product type (*part_type*) you are looking for. Then, you declare a cursor named *mItems*, for holding the results from the SELECT command:

```
*** Define cursor ***
DECLARE mItems CURSOR FOR
SELECT stock_no, part_type, dscription, unit_cost
  FROM parts
 WHERE part_type= mPart_Type;


*** Open cursor
OPEN mItems;
```

When the OPEN *mItems* command is processed, the SELECT statement is carried out. The data rows found by the SELECT statement are held in the cursor. At the same time, the row count is saved in the memory variable *SQLCNT*. Next, you display the data one row at a time with a program loop:

```
*** Data found ***
STORE SQLCNT TO mRows
DO WHILE mRows > 0
   FETCH mItems INTO mStock_No, mPart_Type, mPart_Desc, mUnit_Cost;
   *** Display one row of data found ***
   @8,10 TO 18,70
   @10,15 SAY "Stock No. ................ " + mStock_No
   @12,15 SAY "Product Type ............ " + mPart_Type
   @14,15 SAY "Product Description ..... " + mPart_Desc
   @16,15 SAY "Unit Cost ............... "
   @16,41 SAY mUnit_Cost PICTURE "9,999.99"
   mRows = mRows - 1
   @20,20 SAY "Press any key to see next stock item"
   WAIT " " TO mHit_a_Key
ENDDO
```

When you execute the program, you are prompted for a product type. After you enter the product type you want, the program finds all the data rows belonging to that product type. The program then displays the first row of data on the screen, followed by a prompt asking you to press a key to see the next data row (see fig. 12.26).

In response to any key you press, you display the next data row until no more data rows are left. You then are asked whether to find another product type (see fig. 12.27).

```
 Enter Product Type:  Spreadsheet
```

```
     Stock No. ..............  SW101

     Product Type ...........  Spreadsheet

     Product Description .....  Lotus 1-2-3 version 2.01

     Unit Cost ..............    289.00
```

Press any key to see next stock item

Fig. 12.26. Displaying the first row of data found.

```
 Enter Product Type:  Spreadsheet
```

```
     Stock No. ..............  SW102

     Product Type ...........  Spreadsheet

     Product Description .....  Borland Quattro

     Unit Cost ..............    225.00
```

No more data! Do you like to find another product type (Y/N)? Y

Fig. 12.27. The prompt for finding another product type.

After retrieving the data you need to close the cursor so that the cursor may be used for later query operations. The statement for closing the cursor is

CLOSE   <cursor name>

as in

CLOSE mITEMS

Embedding SQL Commands in a C Program

Another way to enhance the power of your SQL commands is to incorporate them into a program written in the C programming language. By combining the features provided by the C language and the query power of SQL, you can develop an efficient database management system.

C is a powerful programming language. It requires a great deal of programming skill and experience in order to use the language effectively. Detailed discussions on programming in C are beyond the scope of this book. If you are a C programmer, you can see how you can embed SQL commands in a C program with the examples presented later. Otherwise, you may skip this section or refer to the C reference manual for details.

The C Precompiler

Like other computer programs, a C program is a listing of commands that satisfy the syntax and semantic rules dictated by the language. Before the computer can process these commands, however, they have to be translated into a code that can be understood by the computer. Without being too technical, this process of translation can be called compilation. The translation takes two steps. First, the C program is converted to an object code (with .*obj* as the file extension) by using a program called a C compiler. The object code is made into an executable file (with an .*exe* file extension) by using a linker. The linker links the object code file with other files that are required by the C language. You then can process the program by typing the executable file name at the operating system prompt (such as C>).

Because the C compiler recognizes only C commands, if your program contains SQL commands, the computer may have trouble understanding them. Therefore, before you can compile your program, you need to translate the SQL commands to their equivalent C commands. This translation is done by a C precompiler. Because of the different versions of C languages, you need different C precompilers to scan the code and translate the commands to the appropriate C commands. In general, the SQL implementor provides its own C precompiler. For example, Oracle's SQL*Plus has the Pro*C precompiler. You can use the precompiler with the Microsoft C programming language or the Lattice C language.

If you are using the Pro*C precompiler to process a C program consisting of embedded SQL commands, here are the steps you take:

1. Use a text editor to write the program with the embedded SQL commands.

2. Use the Pro*C precompiler to generate a regular C program.

3. Generate the object code file with the C compiler of your choice (Microsoft C or Lattice C).

4. Use the linker provided by the C language to make an executable file of the program.

5. Run the executable file at the operating system prompt.

To see how SQL commands are embedded in a C program, look at the example in figure 12.28.

```
/* CREATEDB.PC Creating the employee base table and printing contents */
#include <stdio.h>
int i:

/* Declare host variables */

EXEC SQL BEGIN DECLARE SECTION;
        VARCHAR user_name[20];
        VARCHAR pass_word[20];
        char    essno[11];
        char    elname[7];
        char    efname[10];
        char    etitle[10];
        char    edept[10];
        float   esalary;
EXEC SQL END DECLARE SECTION;

/* Setting up communication area */

EXEC SQL INCLUDE SQLCA;
main()
{

/* Assign user's name and password */

strcpy(user_name.arr, "SYSTEM");
user_name.len = strlen(user_name.arr);
strcpy(pass_word.arr, "LARRY");
pass_word.len = strlen(pass_word.arr);

/* Log on to Oracle */

EXEC SQL CONNECT :user_name IDENTIFIED BY :pass_word;

/* Create employee table structure */
```

(continued)

```
EXEC SQL CREATE TABLE employee
                    (ss_no      CHAR(11),
                     l_name     CHAR(7),
                     f_name     CHAR(10),
                     title      CHAR(10),
                     dept       CHAR(10),
                     salary     DECIMAL(8,2));

EXEC SQL INSERT INTO employee
            VALUES ('123-45-6789', 'Smith', 'James J.',
                    'President', 'Corporate', 89500.00);
EXEC SQL INSERT INTO employee
            VALUES ('634-56-7890', 'Nelson', 'Harry M.',
                    'Manager', 'Sales', 65000);
EXEC SQL INSERT INTO employee
            VALUES ('445-67-8801', 'Zeller', 'Albert K.',
                    'Salesman', 'Sales', 48900);
EXEC SQL INSERT INTO employee
            VALUES ('562-87-8800', 'Chapman', 'Kirk D.',
                    'Salesman', 'Sales', 42500);
EXEC SQL INSERT INTO employee
            VALUES ('404-22-4568', 'Baker', 'Larry A.',
                    'Clerk', 'Sales', 30500);
EXEC SQL INSERT INTO employee
            VALUES ('256-09-5555', 'Dixon', 'Kathy T.',
                    'Accountant', 'Accounting', 45000);
EXEC SQL INSERT INTO employee
            VALUES ('458-90-3456', 'Frazer', 'Robert F.',
                    'Bookkeeper', 'Accounting', 280000);
EXEC SQL INSERT INTO employee
            VALUES ('777-34-6543', 'King', 'David G.',
                    'Manager', 'Personnel', 38000);
EXEC SQL INSERT INTO employee
            VALUES ('100-45-8021', 'Wong', 'Mike J.',
                    'Manager', 'MIS', 44000);
EXEC SQL INSERT INTO employee
            VALUES ('303-25-7777', 'Duff', 'Cathy B.',
                    'Secretary', 'Personnel', 26500);

/* Display table contents */
/* Declare cursor        */
```

```
    EXEC SQL DECLARE CURSOR emplist CURSOR FOR
                        SELECT ss_no, l_name, f_name, title, dept, salary
                        FROM employee;

/* Open cursor */

EXEC SQL OPEN emplist;

/* Display column labels */

printf("soc. sec. # Last Name First Name Title      Dept        Salary\n");
printf("----------- ---------- ----------- ----------- ----------- -----------\n");
  for(i=1; i <=10; i++)
  {
    EXEC SQL FETCH emplist
                INTO :essno, :elname, :efname, :etitle, :edept, esalary;
                printf("%.12s %.10s    %.10s %.10s %.10s %8.2f \n",
                essno, elname, efname, etitle, edept, esalary);
  }

/* Print termination message */

printf("EMPLOYEE table has been created.\n");

/* Close the cursor */

EXEC SQL CLOSE emplist;

/* Commit work and exit the system */

EXEC SQL COMMIT WORK RELEASE;
return;
  }
```

Fig. 12.28. *Embedding SQL commands in a C program.*

Identifying SQL Commands

When you embed SQL commands in your C program, you need to identify each command by the EXEC SQL keyword. This keyword should appear before the SQL command itself. For example, if you want to place a CREATE TABLE command in the C program, you begin the statement with the EXEC SQL keyword:

```
/* Create employee table structure */
EXEC SQL CREATE TABLE employee
                    (ss_no     CHAR(11),
                     l_name    CHAR(7),
                     f_name    CHAR(10),
                     title     CHAR(10),
                     dept      CHAR(10),
                     salary    DECIMAL(8,2));
```

Using Host Variables

Like memory variables in dBASE, host variables are used to pass values between C commands and SQL commands. Host variables can be declared by using C commands. Host variables also can be declared between the EXEC SQL BEGIN DECLARE SECTION and the EXEC SQL END DECLARE SECTION statements:

```
EXEC SQL BEGIN DECLARE SECTION;
        VARCHAR user_name[20];
        VARCHAR pass_word[20];
        char    essno[11];
        char    elname[7];
        char    efname[10];
        char    etitle[10];
        char    edept[10];
        float   esalary;
EXEC SQL END DECLARE SECTION;
```

Because each host variable is used for holding a string of characters, the host variable is declared as a single-array. Two of these variables are used for holding the user's name and password.

When you refer to a host variable in an SQL command, place a colon in front of the variable name. Here is an example:

```
EXEC SQL FETCH emplist INTO
                :essno, :elname, :efname, :etitle,
                :edept, esalary;
```

This command gets a data row from the cursor and stores the data values in the set of corresponding host variables.

Logging On to the System

After the C program is compiled and made into an executable file, the C program is executed at the operating system level. Therefore, you need to provide the commands for logging on to the Oracle system. These commands enter the name and password of the user:

```
/* Assign user's name and password */

strcpy(user_name.arr, "SYSTEM");
user_name.len = strlen(user_name.arr);
strcpy(pass_word.arr, "LARRY");
pass_word.len = strlen(pass_word.arr);

/* Log on to Oracle */

EXEC SQL CONNECT :user_name IDENTIFIED BY :pass_word;
```

Using Cursor

You can declare a cursor like the cursor used in the dBASE program. You declare the cursor for storing the results from a query operation performed by an SQL command. Use the DECLARE CURSOR command:

```
/* Declare cursor        */

EXEC SQL DECLARE CURSOR emplist CURSOR FOR
                   SELECT ss_no, l_name, f_name, title, dept, salary
                   FROM employee;
```

To invoke the SELECT statement in this statement, you need to open the cursor with the following command:

```
/* Open cursor */

EXEC SQL OPEN emplist;
```

In response to this command, the query operation is carried out, and the results are held in the cursor. When you need to access the results, you issue the FETCH CURSOR command to retrieve one row at a time:

```
EXEC SQL FETCH emplist
                   INTO :essno, :elname, :efname, :etitle, :edept, esalary;
                   printf("%.12s %.10s    %.10s %.10s %.10s %8.2f \n",
                   essno, elname, efname, etitle, edept, esalary);
```

When you execute the program, you get results like those shown in figure 12.29.

```
C:\>e:

E:\ORACLE5\PRO\C>createdb
SOC. SEC. #   LAST NAME   FIRST NAME   TITLE        DEPT        SALARY
-----------   ---------   ----------   ----------   --------    --------
123-45-6789   Smith       James J.     President    Corporate   89500.00
634-56-7890   Nelson      Harry M.     Manager      Sales       65000.00
445-67-8801   Zeller      Albert K.    Salesman     Sales       48900.00
562-87-8800   Chapman     Kirk D.      Salesman     Sales       42500.00
404-22-4568   Baker       Larry A.     Clerk        Sales       30500.00
256-09-5555   Dixon       Kathy T.     Accountant   Accounting  45000.00
458-90-3456   Frazer      Robert F.    Bookkeeper   Accounting  28000.00
777-43-6543   King        David G.     Manager      Personnel   38000.00
100-45-8021   Wong        Mike J.      Manager      MIS         44000.00
303-25-7777   Duff        Cathy B.     Secretary    Personnel   26500.00
EMPLOYEE table has been created.

E:\ORACLE5\PRO\C>
```

Fig. 12.29. Table created by embedding SQL commands in a C program.

Chapter Summary

In this chapter, you have learned different approaches you can take to supplement the standard SQL language for performing your database management functions. By using a form generator and a report writer provided by a database system, you can design and develop sophisticated data entry forms and reports. In addition, you have learned how to cause SQL to interact with other programming languages. The language can be a database language like dBASE or a regular procedural programming language like C. When you combine the SQL query commands with these form generators and report generators, you can design a powerful database management system.

This chapter concludes the discussion of how to use SQL, the relational database language, to design and develop your databases. Due to the limited scope of this book, I have covered only the standard version of the language. Many implementations of the SQL are now available. Many additional features beyond the standard SQL have been implemented by different versions of the language. You need to study your version's reference manual carefully so that you can take advantage of these added features.

Summary of Legitimate Data Types

I. Summary of data types in commercial implementations of SQL

Data Type	DB2	ORACLE	INGRES	DB4SQL	SYBASE
Character					
CHAR(n)	X	X	X	X	X
VARCHAR(n)	X	X	X		X
LONG		X			
Number					
Integer					
INTEGER	X	X		X	
INT					X
I			X		
SMALLINT	X	X		X	X
TINYINT					X
Decimal					
DECIMAL(m,n)	X			X	
FLOAT(m,n)				X	
FLOAT	X	X			X
F			X		
NUMBER		X			
NUMBER(n)		X			
NUMBER(m,n)		X			
NUMERIC(m)				X	
MONEY		X	X		X
Binary number					
RAW		X			
LONGRAW		X			

429

	SQL Implementation				
Data Type	*DB2*	*ORACLE*	*INGRES*	*DB4SQL*	*SYBASE*
Date/Time					
DATE	X	X	X		
DATETIME				X	
Logical					
LOGICAL			X		
BIT				X	

II. Legitimate data types for commercial versions of SQL

DB2 SQL

Data Type	*Notes*
CHAR(n)	A fixed-length character string, where $0 < n < 255$ Example: CHAR(10)
VARCHAR(n)	A variable-length character string Example: VARCHAR(20)
INTEGER	A 32-bit (including sign) binary integer
SMALLINT	A 16-bit (including sign) binary integer
DECIMAL(m,n)	A decimal value with m digits (including sign) and n decimal places, where $0 < m < 16, n < m$ Example: DECIMAL(8,2)
FLOAT	A double-precision floating decimal

*ORACLE's SQL*Plus*

Data Type	*Notes*
CHAR(n)	A fixed-length character string, where $0 < n < 240$ Example: CHAR(10)
VARCHAR(n)	A variable-length character string, where $0 < n < 240$ Example: VARCHAR(20)
LONG	A variable-length character string up to 65,535 characters Limited to one per table
NUMBER	A number (with or without a decimal point) containing up to 40 significant digits
NUMBER(n)	A number (with or without a decimal point) with up to n digits of precision, where $0 < n < 42$ Example: NUMBER(5)

Data Type	Notes
NUMBER(m,n)	A decimal value with m digits and n decimal places, where $0 < m < 42$ and $n < m$ Example: NUMBER(8,2)
DECIMAL(m)	A decimal value with m digits, where $0 < m < 42$ Example: DECIMAL(12)
FLOAT	A floating number containing up to 40 significant digits, treated as NUMBER
INTEGER	An integer containing up to 40 significant digits, treated as NUMBER
SMALLINT	An integer containing up to 40 significant digits, treated as NUMBER
RAW(n)	A binary value of n bytes, where $0 < n < 240$
LONGRAW	A binary value in hexadecimal notation
DATE	A date value between January 1, 4712 B.C. and December 31, 4712 A.D.

SYBASE's SQL

Data Type	Notes
CHAR(n)	A fixed-length character string, where $0 < n < 255$ Example: CHAR(10)
VARCHAR(n)	A variable-length character string Example: VARCHAR(20)
INTEGER	A 32-bit (including sign) binary integer
SMALLINT	A 16-bit (including sign) binary integer
DECIMAL(m,n)	A decimal value with m digits (including sign) and n decimal places, where $0 < m < 16$, $n < m$ Example: DECIMAL(8,2)
FLOAT	A double-precision floating decimal

INGRES's SQL

Data Type	Notes
CHAR(n)	A fixed-length character string, where $0 < n < 255$ Example: CHAR(10)
VARCHAR(n)	A variable-length character string, where $0 < n < 2,000$ Example: VARCHAR(20)

Data Type	Notes
I1, I2, I4	A binary integer of 1, 2, and 4 bytes long, respectively
F4, F8	A floating-point number of 4 and 8 bytes long, respectively
MONEY	A monetary value up to 16 digits long with 2 decimal places
DATE	A date, time, and time interval value Sample values: "10/10/90", "8:30:10 am", "07-Jul-1991 12:00 pm", "5 years 10 months 3 days 50 minutes"

dBASE IV's SQL

Data Type	Notes
CHAR(n)	A fixed-length character string, where $0 < n < 255$ Example: CHAR(10)
INTEGER	An integer up to 11 digits (including sign)
SMALLINT	An integer up to 6 digits (including sign)
DECIMAL(m,n)	A decimal values with m digits (including sign) and n decimal places, where $0 < m < 20$, $n < m$ Example: DECIMAL(8,2)
NUMERIC(m,n)	A decimal values with m digits (including sign) and n decimal places, where $0 < m < 21$, $n < m - 1$ Example: DECIMAL(8,2)
FLOAT(m,n)	A floating decimal value with m digits and n decimal places Example: FLOAT(6,2)
DATE	A date value in the format of mm/dd/yy Example: 07/04/90
LOGICAL	A single-character logical value of T or F

Base Tables and Views

In this appendix, you find contents of the base tables and views used in this book. The contents of these tables and views may be slightly different in various parts of the book because of changes made in some chapters.

Base Tables

Base tables are listed in alphabetical order.

Assign Table:

```
CREATE TABLE  assign
            (c_id      CHAR(2),
             t_id      CHAR(2));
SELECT  *
 FROM  assign;
```

C_ID	T_ID
C1	T2
C1	T5
C2	T1
C3	T3
C4	T4
C5	T3

Account Table:

```
CREATE TABLE  account
            (acct_no        CHAR(5),
             acct_name      CHAR(25),
             address        CHAR(15),
             city           CHAR(10),
             state          CHAR(2),
             zip            CHAR(5));
```

```
SELECT  *
  FROM  account;
```

ACCT_NO	ACCT_NAME	ADDRESS	CITY	STATE	ZIP
A-101	Fairwind Travel	3256 Lakeview Dr.	Mesa	AZ	85201
B-101	Evergreen Florists	2658 Broadway	Vancouver	WA	98664
C-101	ACME Construction	1456 S.E. 132nd Ave.	Portland	OR	97204
A-201	B & J Fine Furniture	3567 S.W. Canyon Rd.	Beaverton	OR	97203
A-301	Western Electronic	2478 University Ave.	Seattle	WA	98105
C-201	Ace Office Service	5214 Main Street	Salem	OR	97201
C-301	Lake Grove Bookstore	3456 Salmon Street	Portland	OR	97203
A-202	Johnson & Associates	10345 Riverside Dr.	New York	NY	10038
A-203	Superior Computers	1345 Market Street	San Diego	CA	91355
B-201	National Auto Service	3081 Columbus Ave.	San Jose	CA	90406

Bonus Table:

```
CREATE TABLE  bonus
              (l_name    CHAR(7));
SELECT  *
  FROM  bonus;
```

L_NAME
Zeller
Frazer
Duff

Class Table:

```
CREATE TABLE class
              (c_id CHAR(2),
               s_id CHAR(3));
```

```
SELECT  *
  FROM  CLASS;
C_ID    S_ID
————    ————
C1      S3
C1      S5
C1      S10
C2      S4
C2      S5
C2      S7
C2      S8
C3      S1
C3      S2
C3      S9
C4      S2
C4      S5
C4      S8
C5      S3
C5      S8
C5      S9
```

Course Table:

```
CREATE TABLE course
              (c_id       CHAR(2),
               c_title    CHAR(8),
               c_credits  SMALLINT,
               c_desc     CHAR(20));
SELECT  *
  FROM  course;
```

C_ID	C_TITLE	C_CREDITS	C_DESC
C1	ENGL 101	3	English Literature I
C2	HIST 100	3	American History
C3	MATH 105	5	Calculus I
C4	PHIL 101	3	Philosophy
C5	PHYS 102	5	Physics I

Discount Table:

```
CREATE TABLE discount
              (disc_rate   DECIMAL(6,2),
               low_value   DECIMAL(8,2),
               high_value  DECIMAL(8,2));
```

```
SELECT  *
FROM  discount;
```

DISC_RATE	LOW_VALUE	HIGH_VALUE
0.00	0.00	99.99
0.10	100.00	199.99
0.15	200.00	299.99
0.20	300.00	4999.99

Employee Table:

```
CREATE TABLE employee
        (ss_no       CHAR(11),
         Lname       CHAR(7),
         f_name      CHAR(10),
         title       CHAR(10),
         dept        CHAR(10),
         salary      DECIMAL(8,2));
```

```
SELECT  *
FROM  employee;
```

SS_NO	L_NAME	F_NAME	TITLE	DEPT	SALARY
123-45-6789	Smith	James J.	President	Corporate	89500.00
634-56-7890	Nelson	Harry M.	Manager	Sales	65000.00
445-67-8801	Zeller	Albert K.	Salesman	Sales	51345.00
562-87-8800	Chapman	Kirk D.	Salesman	Sales	42500.00
404-22-4568	Baker	Larry A.	Salesman	Sales	33500.00
256-09-5555	Dixon	Kathy T.	Accountant	Accounting	45000.00
458-90-3456	Frazer	Robert F.	Bookkeeper	Accounting	29400.00
777-34-6543	King	David G.	Manager	Personnel	38000.00
100-45-8021	Wong	Mike J.	Manager	MIS	44000.00
303-25-7777	Duff	Cathy B.	Secretary	Personnel	27825.00
909-10-8910	Parker	Susan C.	Trainee	MIS	28000.00

Grade Table:

```
CREATE TABLE grade
        (grade         CHAR(1),
         low_score     DECIMAL(8,2),
         high_score    DECIMAL(8,2));
```

```
SELECT  *
FROM  grade;
```

GRADE	LOW_SCORE	HIGH_SCORE
A	90.00	100.00
B	80.00	89.99
C	60.00	79.99
D	40.00	59.99
F	0.00	39.99

Hwstock Table:

```
CREATE TABLE hwstock
            (stock_no    CHAR(5),
             item        CHAR(25)
             qty         SMALLINT,
             unit_cost   DECIMAL(8,2));
```

```
SELECT  *
 FROM  hwstock;
```

STOCK_NO	ITEM	QTY	UNIT_COST
HW101	Epson LQ-1050 printer	8	628.50
HW102	HP LaserJet II printer	2	1435.00
HW201	NEC MultiSync monitor	4	459.00
HW301	Paradise VGA board	6	230.00
HW401	IBM PS/2 Model 70/60MB	3	3250.00
HW402	COMPAQ 386S DeskPro/40MB	4	2600.00
HW403	Zenith Supersport 286/20	3	2975.00

Managers Table:

```
CREATE TABLE managers
            (ss_no    CHAR(11),
             l_name   CHAR(7),
             f_name   CHAR(10),
             title    CHAR(10),
             dept     CHAR(10),
             salary   DECIMAL(8,2));
```

```
SELECT  *
 FROM  managers;
```

SS_NO	L_NAME	F_NAME	TITLE	DEPT	SALARY
634-56-7890	Nelson	Harry M.	Manager	Sales	65000.00
777-34-6543	King	David G.	Manager	Personnel	38000.00
100-45-8021	Wong	Mike J.	Manager	MIS	44000.00

Newprice Table:

```
CREATE TABLE newprice
            (stock_no      CHAR(5),
             change        DECIMAL(6,2));
```

```
SELECT  *
 FROM  newprice;
```

STOCK_NO	CHANGE
HW102	0.05
HW301	0.07
HW403	0.10
SW201	0.05
SW301	0.12

Overdue Table:

```
CREATE TABLE overdue
            (acct_no      CHAR(5),
             days_old     SMALLINT);
```

```
SELECT  *
 FROM  overdue;
```

ACCT_NO	DAYS_OLD
A-101	12
B-101	35
C-101	190
A-201	30
A-301	10
C-201	60
C-301	90
A-202	205
A-202	45
B-201	29

Payroll Table:

```
CREATE TABLE payroll
            (ss_no         CHAR(11),
             first_name    CHAR(10),
             last_name     CHAR(7),
             salary        DECIMAL(8,2),
             month_pay     DECIMAL(8,2),
             exemptions    SMALLINT);
```

```
SELECT  *
 FROM   payroll;
```

SS_NO	FIRST_NAME	LAST_NAME	SALARY	MONTH_PAY	EXEMPTIONS
123-45-6789	James J.	Smith	89500.00	7458.33	3
634-56-7890	Harry M.	Nelson	65000.00	5416.67	2
445-67-8801	Albert K.	Zeller	51345.00	4278.75	4
562-87-8800	Kirk D.	Chapman	42500.00	3541.67	2
404-22-4568	Larry A	Baker	30500.00	2541.67	1
256-09-5555	Kathy T.	Dixon	45000.00	3750.00	3
458-90-3456	Robert F.	Frazer	29400.00	2450.00	3
777-34-6543	David G.	King	38000.00	3166.67	2
100-45-8021	Mike J.	Wong	44000.00	3666.67	2
303-25-7777	Cathy B.	Duff	27825.00	2318.75	2
909-10-8910	Susan C.	Parker	28000.00	2333.33	1

Parts Table:

```
CREATE TABLE parts
            (stock_no    CHAR(5),
             part_type   CHAR(11),
             dscription  CHAR(25),
             unit_cost   DECIMAL(8,2));
```

```
SELECT  *
 FROM   parts;
```

STOCK_NO	PART_TYPE	DSCRIPTION	UNIT_COST
HW101	Printer	Epson LQ-1050 printer	628.50
HW102	Printer	HP LaserJet II printer	1435.00
HW201	Monitor	NEC MultiSync monitor	459.00
HW301	V. board	Paradise VGA board	230.00
HW401	Computer	IBM PS/2 Model 70/60MB	3250.00
HW402	Computer	COMPAQ 386S DeskPro/40MB	2600.00
HW403	Computer	Zenith Supersport 286/20	2975.00
SW101	Spreadsheet	Lotus 1-2-3 Version 2.01	250.50
SW201	WP	WordPerfect 5.0	195.00
SW202	WP	Microsoft Word 5.0	183.50
SW301	Database	Paradox 3.0	385.75
SW302	Database	dBASE IV Version 1.0	360.00

Price Table:

```
CREATE TABLE price
            (stock_no    CHAR(5)
             unit_price  DECIMAL(8,2));
```

```
SELECT  *
 FROM  price;
```

STOCK_NO	UNIT_PRICE
HW101	850.50
HW102	1795.00
HW201	590.00
HW301	295.00
HW401	4070.00
HW402	3250.00
HW403	3725.00
SW101	350.00
SW201	275.00
SW202	250.00
SW301	520.00
SW302	490.00

Sale Table:

```
CREATE TABLE sale
            (invoice_no  CHAR(2),
             qty_sold    SMALLINT,
             unit_price  DECIMAL(8,2));
```

```
SELECT  *
 FROM  sale;
```

INVOICE_NO	QTY_SOL	UNIT_PRICE
A1	12	19.95
A2	5	29.95
A3	3	89.50
A4	7	12.95

Spain Table:

```
CREATE TABLE spain
            (player  CHAR(8),
             skill   CHAR(8),
             sex     CHAR(6));
```

```
SELECT  *
 FROM  spain;
```

PLAYER	SKILL	SEX
Amilia	Beginner	Female
Fernando	Advanced	Male
Jose	Beginner	Male
Maria	Advanced	Female

Staff Table:

```
CREATE TABLE staff
         (ss_no      CHAR(11),
          l_name     CHAR(7),
          f_name     CHAR(10),
          title      CHAR(10),
          dept       CHAR(10),
          salary     DECIMAL(8,2));
```

```
SELECT  *
 FROM  staff;
```

SS_NO	L_NAME	F_NAME	TITLE	DEPT	SALARY
123-45-6789	Smith	James J.	President	Corporate	89500.00
634-56-7890	Nelson	Harry M.	Manager	Sales	65000.00
445-67-8801	Zeller	Albert K.	Salesman	Sales	51345.00
562-87-8800	Chapman	Kirk D.	Salesman	Sales	42500.00
404-22-4568	Baker	Larry A.	Salesman	Sales	33500.00
256-09-5555	Dixon	Kathy T.	Accountant	Accounting	45000.00
458-90-3456	Frazer	Robert F.	Bookkeeper	Accounting	29400.00
777-34-6543	King	David G.	Manager	Personnel	38000.00
100-45-8021	Wong	Mike J.	Manager	MIS	44000.00
303-25-7777	Duff	Cathy B.	Secretary	Personnel	27825.00
909-10-8910	Parker	Susan C.	Trainee	MIS	28000.00

Stock Table:

```
CREATE TABLE stock
         (stock_no    CHAR(5)
          on_hand     SMALLINT,
          reorder     SMALLINT,
          vendor_id   CHAR(2));
```

```
SELECT  *
 FROM  stock;
```

STOCK_NO	ON_HAND	REORDER	VENDOR_NO
HW101	8	3	V1
HW102	2	1	V1
HW201	4	2	V2
HW301	6	3	V2
HW401	3	2	V3
HW402	4	5	V3
HW403	3	1	V3
SW101	10	3	V4
SW201	7	4	V4
SW202	3	2	V5
SW301	3	1	V5
SW302	3	1	V5

Student Table:

```
CREATE TABLE student  (s_id     CHAR(3),
                        s_lname  CHAR(7),
                        s_fname  CHAR(10),
                        s_bdate  DATE,
                        s_sex    CHAR(1),
                        s_hsgpa  DECIMAL(6,2));
```

```
SELECT  *
 FROM  student;
```

S_ID	S_LNAME	S_FNAME	S_BDATE	S_SEX	S_HSGPA
S1	Austin	Linda D.	03/08/71	F	3.98
S2	Brown	Nancy J.	05/14/70	F	3.35
S3	Carter	Jack F.	10/10/71	M	2.87
S4	Ford	Harvey P.	06/12/71	M	2.60
S5	Freed	Barbara J.	07/28/69	F	3.15
S6	Gilmore	Danny S.	11/01/70	M	3.86
S7	Jackson	Brad L.	04/15/71	M	2.75
S8	Madison	George G.	08/15/70	M	2.35
S9	Reed	Donna E.	09/26/69	F	2.96
S10	Taylor	Bob K.	02/14/71	M	3.14

Sweater Table:

```
CREATE TABLE sweater
            (stock_no   CHAR(4),
             sw_type    CHAR(5),
             sw_color   CHAR(4),
             sw_size    CHAR(1),
             sw_qty     SMALLINT,
             sw_price   DECIMAL(8,2),
             sw_cost    DECIMAL(8,2));
```

```
SELECT *
FROM   sweater;
```

STOCK_NO	SW_TYPE	SW_COLOR	SW_SIZE	SW_QTY	SW_PRICE	SW_COST
SW01	wool	red	L	5	65.95	45.50
SW02	wool	red	M	3	65.95	45.50
SW03	wool	red	S	4	65.95	45.50
SW04	wool	navy	L	2	62.85	43.00
SW05	wool	navy	M	0	62.85	43.00
SW06	wool	navy	S	3	62.85	43.00
SW07	blend	red	L	8	45.95	32.90
SW08	blend	red	M	3	45.95	32.90
SW09	blend	red	S	0	45.95	32.90
SW10	blend	navy	L	7	48.50	35.50
SW11	blend	navy	M	4	48.50	35.50
SW12	blend	navy	S	2	48.50	35.50
SW13	poly	red	L	0	29.95	19.95
SW14	poly	red	M	1	29.95	19.95
SW15	poly	red	S	3	29.95	19.95
SW16	poly	navy	L	2	25.95	17.90
SW17	poly	navy	M	0	25.95	17.90
SW18	poly	navy	S	5	25.95	17.90

Teacher Table:

```
CREATE TABLE teacher
            (t_id       CHAR(2),
             t_lname    CHAR(10),
             t_fname    CHAR(10)
             t_rank     CHAR(15),
             t_office   CHAR(8),
             t_phone    CHAR(8));
```

```
SELECT  *
 FROM  teacher;
```

T_ID	T_LNAME	T_FNAME	T_RANK	T_OFFICE	T_PHONE
T1	Franklin	Benjamin	Professor	West 103	235-1234
T2	Hemingway	Ernest M.	Professor	West 301	287-6666
T3	Newton	Isaac	Associate Prof.	East 150	635-1414
T4	Quine	Willard V.	Professor	East 250	636-2626
T5	Shakspeare	George B.	Assistant Prof.	West 104	235-7878

Tests Table:

```
CREATE TABLE tests
              (s_id       CHAR(3),
               mid_term   SMALLINT,
               final      SMALLINT);
SELECT  *
 FROM  tests;
```

S_ID	MID_TERM	FINAL
S1	75	87
S2	65	75
S3	90	95
S4	50	60
S5	82	85
S6	68	70
S7	70	75
S8	92	93
S9	69	74
S10	62	72

Usa Table:

```
CREATE TABLE usa
              (player   CHAR(8),
               skill    CHAR(8),
               sex      CHAR(6));
```

```
SELECT  *
 FROM  usa;
```

PLAYER	SKILL	SEX
Albert	Advanced	Male
Brenda	Beginner	Female
Candy	Advanced	Female
Daniel	Beginner	Male

Vendors Table:

```
CREATE TABLE vendors
           (vendor_id   CHAR(2),
            name        CHAR(10),
            address     CHAR(13),
            city        CHAR(8),
            state       CHAR(2),
            zip         CHAR(5),
            phone_no    CHAR(12));
SELECT  *
 FROM  vendor;
```

VENDOR_ID	NAME	ADDRESS	CITY	STATE	ZIP	PHONE_NO
V1	Micromart	100 Main St.	Seattle	WA	98105	800-123-4567
V2	CompuPlus	2120 Oak Ave.	Portland	OR	97202	503-555-9999
V3	PC Ware	750 Grand Ave.	Austin	TX	78727	800-666-4444
V4	CompuSoft	101 Fifth Ave.	New York	NY	10120	212-333-5555
V5	PC Source	200 Front St.	San Jose	CA	94930	415-777-8888

Views

Views are listed in alphabetical order.

Classlst View:

```
CREATE VIEW    classlst  (course, student)
        AS  SELECT  c_title, s_lname
            FROM  course x, class y, student z
            WHERE  x.c_id = y.c_id AND y.s_id = z.s_id;
```

```
SELECT  *
 FROM  classlst;
```

COURSE	STUDENT
ENGL 101	Carter
ENGL 101	Freed
ENGL 101	Taylor
HIST 100	Ford
HIST 100	Freed
HIST 100	Jackson
HIST 100	Madison
MATH 105	Austin
MATH 105	Brown
MATH 105	Reed
PHIL 101	Brown
PHIL 101	Freed
PHIL 101	Madison
PHYS 102	Carter
PHYS 102	Gilmore
PHYS 102	Madison
PHYS 102	Reed

Dept View:

```
CREATE VIEW  dept (department, last_name, first_name)
        AS  SELECT  dept, l_name, f_name
            FROM  employee;
```

```
SELECT  *
 FROM  dept;
```

DEPARTMENT	LAST_NAME	FIRST_NAME
Corporate	Smith	James J.
Sales	Nelson	Harry M.
Sales	Zeller	Albert K.
Sales	Chapman	Kirk D.
Sales	Baker	Larry A.
Accounting	Dixon	Kathy T.
Accounting	Frazer	Robert F.
Personnel	King	David G.
MIS	Wong	Mike J.
Personnel	Duff	Cathy B.
MIS	Parker	Susan C.

Deptavg View:

    CREATE VIEW   deptavg (department, avg_salary)
              AS   SELECT   dept, AVG(salary)
                   FROM   employee GROUP BY dept;

    SELECT *
     FROM deptavg;

DEPARTMENT	AVG_SALARY
Accounting	37200.00
Corporate	89500.00
MIS	36000.00
Personnel	32912.50
Sales	48086.25

Depthead View:

    CREATE VIEW   depthead (department, last_name, first_name)
              AS   SELECT   dept, l_name, f_name
                   FROM   employee
                   WHERE   title = 'Manager'

    SELECT *
     FROM depthead;

DEPARTMENT	LAST_NAME	FIRST_NAME
Sales	Nelson	Harry M.
Personnel	King	David G.
MIS	Wong	Mike J.

Engl101 View:

    CREATE VIEW   engl101 (last_name, first_name, hs_gpa)
              AS   SELECT   s_lname, s_fname, s_hsgpa
                   FROM   student x, class y
                   WHERE   x.s_id = y.s_id AND c_id = 'C1';

    SELECT *
     FROM engl101;

LAST_NAME	FIRST_NAME	HS_GPA
Carter	Jack F.	2.87
Freed	Barbara J.	3.15
Taylor	Bob K.	3.14

Execpay View:

```
CREATE VIEW   execpay (last_name, first_name, job_title, month_pay)
         AS  SELECT  x.l_name, x.f_name, x.title, y.month_pay
             FROM   title x, monthly y
             WHERE  x.ss_no = y.soc_sec_no
             AND   (x.title = 'Manager' OR x.title = 'President');
```

```
SELECT  *
 FROM  execpay;
```

LAST_NAME	FIRST_NAME	JOB_TITLE	MONTH_PAY
Wong	Mike J.	Manager	3666.67
Smith	James J.	President	7458.33
Nelson	Harry M.	Manager	5416.67
King	David G.	Manager	3166.67

Hisalary View:

```
CREATE VIEW  hisalary (last_name, first_name, job_title, salary)
        AS  SELECT  l_name, f_name, title, salary
            FROM   employee
            WHERE  salary>50000;
```

```
SELECT  *
 FROM  hisalary;
```

LAST_NAME	FIRST_NAME	JOB_TITLE	SALARY
Smith	James J.	President	89500.00
Nelson	Harry M.	Manager	65000.00
Zeller	Albert K.	Salesman	51345.00

Monthly View:

```
CREATE VIEW  monthly (soc_sec_no, month_pay)
        AS  SELECT  ss_no, salary/12
            FROM   employee;
```

```
SELECT  *
FROM   monthly;
```

SOC_SEC_N0	MONTH_PAY
123-45-6789	7458.33
634-56-7890	5416.67
445-67-8801	4278.75
562-87-8800	3541.67
404-22-4568	2791.67
256-09-5555	3750.00
458-90-3456	2450.00
777-34-6543	3166.67
100-45-8021	3666.67
303-25-7777	2318.75
909-10-8910	2333.33

Personal View:

```
CREATE VIEW personal  (soc_sec_no, last_name, first_name,
                          job_title, department)
       AS  SELECT  ss_no, l_name, f_name, title, dept
            FROM   employee;
```

```
SELECT  *
 FROM   personal
ORDER BY  department, last_name;
```

SOC_SEC_NO	LAST_NAME	FIRST_NAME	JOB_TITLE	DEPARTMENT
256-09-5555	Dixon	Kathy T.	Accountant	Accounting
458-90-3456	Frazer	Robert F.	Bookkeeper	Accounting
123-45-6789	Smith	James J.	President	Corporate
909-10-8910	Parker	Susan C.	Trainee	MIS
100-45-8021	Wong	Mike J.	Manager	MIS
303-25-7777	Duff	Cathy B.	Secretary	Personnel
777-34-6543	King	David G.	Manager	Personnel
404-22-4568	Baker	Larry A.	Salesman	Sales
562-87-8800	Chapman	Kirk D.	Salesman	Sales
634-56-7890	Nelson	Harry M.	Manager	Sales
445-67-8801	Zeller	Albert K.	Salesman	Sales

Salary View:

```
CREATE VIEW salary (soc_sec_no, last_name, salary, exemptions)
       AS  SELECT  ss_no, last_name, salary, exemptions
            FROM   payroll;
```

```
SELECT  *
  FROM  salary;
```

SOC_SEC_NO	LAST_NAME	SALARY	EXEMPTIONS
123-45-6789	Smith	89500.00	3
634-56-7890	Nelson	65000.00	2
445-67-8801	Zeller	51345.00	4
562-87-8800	Chapman	42500.00	2
404-22-4568	Baker	30500.00	1
256-09-5555	Dixon	45000.00	3
458-90-3456	Frazer	29400.00	3
777-34-6543	King	38000.00	2
100-45-8021	Wong	44000.00	2
303-25-7777	Duff	27825.00	2
909-10-8910	Parker	28000.00	1

Science View:

```
CREATE VIEW  science (course, last_name, first_name, hs_gpa)
         AS  SELECT  c_title, s_lname, s_fname, s_hsgpa
             FROM  student x, class y, course z
             WHERE  x.s_id = y.s_id
               AND  y.c_id = z.c_id
               AND  (c_title = 'MATH 105' OR c_title = 'PHYS 102');
```

```
SELECT  *
  FROM  science
ORDER BY
course;
```

COURSE	LAST_NAME	FIRST_NAME	HS_GPA
MATH 105	Austin	Linda D.	3.98
MATH 105	Brown	Nancy J.	3.35
MATH 105	Reed	Donna E.	2.96
PHYS 102	Carter	Jack F.	2.87
PHYS 102	Gilmore	Danny S.	3.86
PHYS 102	Madison	George G.	2.35
PHYS 102	Reed	Donna E.	2.96

Title View:

```
CREATE VIEW  title
         AS  SELECT  ss_no, title, l_name, f_name
             FROM  employee;
```

```
SELECT  *
FROM  title;
```

SS_NO	TITLE	L_NAME	F_NAME
123-45-6789	President	Smith	James J.
634-56-7890	Manager	Nelson	Harry M.
445-67-8801	Salesman	Zeller	Albert K.
562-87-8800	Salesman	Chapman	Kirk D.
404-22-4568	Salesman	Baker	Larry A.
256-09-5555	Accountant	Dixon	Kathy T.
458-90-3456	Bookkeeper	Frazer	Robert F.
777-34-6543	Manager	King	David G.
100-45-8021	Manager	Wong	Mike J.
303-25-7777	Secretary	Duff	Cathy B.
909-10-8910	Trainee	Parker	Susan C.

Wage View:

```
CREATE VIEW  wage (last_name, first_name, job_title, month_pay)
        AS  SELECT  x.l_name, x.f_name, x.title, y.month_pay
            FROM  employee x, monthly y
            WHERE  x.ss_no = y.soc_sec_no
            AND  (x.title! = 'President'
                  AND x.title! = 'Manager');
```

```
SELECT  *
FROM  wage;
```

LAST_NAME	FIRST_NAME	JOB_TITLE	MONTH_PAY
Zeller	Albert K.	Salesman	4278.75
Chapman	Kirk D.	Salesman	3541.67
Baker	Larry A.	Salesman	2791.67
Dixon	Kathy T.	Accountant	3750.00
Frazer	Robert F.	Bookkeeper	2450.00
Duff	Cathy B.	Secretary	2318.75
Parker	Susan C.	Trainee	2333.33

Summary of SQL Commands

This appendix presents the standard SQL commands that have been covered in this book; it does not exhaust all the SQL commands currently supported by the different versions of SQL. The commands given here are legal for most commercial implementations of SQL. However, the format of some of these commands and the format used to display the results may vary among different implementations. You need to experiment with these commands in the version of SQL you are using to determine their legality and their output formats.

```
ALTER TABLE  <table name>
        ADD (<column name> <data type> [,
              <column name> <data type> ...]);
```

Example:

```
ALTER TABLE  employee
        ADD (children    SMALLINT,
             area_code   CHAR(3),
             phone_no    CHAR(8));
```

```
CREATE [UNIQUE] INDEX  <index name>
              ON  <table name>
                   (<column name> [ASC|DESC] [,
                    <column name> [ASC|DESC] ...]);
```

Examples:

```
CREATE INDEX  bylast
        ON  employee (L_name);
```

```
CREATE UNIQUE INDEX  manager
                ON  employee
                     (title DESC, salary);
```

```
CREATE TABLE  <table name>
                (<column name>  <data type>  [NOT NULL] [,
                 <column name>  <data type>  [NOT NULL]...]);
```

Example:

```
CREATE TABLE  employee
                (ss_no        CHAR(11) NOT NULL,
                 l_name       CHAR(7),
                 f_name       CHAR(10),
                 title        CHAR(10),
                 dept         CHAR(10),
                 salary       DECIMAL(8,2),
                 exemptions   SMALLINT);
```

```
CREATE VIEW  <view name>  [(<column name>, <column name> ...)]
        AS  <SELECT statement>
            [WITH CHECK OPTION];
```

Examples:

```
CREATE VIEW  salary (soc_sec_no, last_name, salary)
        AS  SELECT ss_no, l_name, salary
            FROM  employee;
```

```
CREATE VIEW  monthly (soc_sec_no, month_pay)
        AS  SELECT ss_no, salary/12
            FROM  employee;
```

```
CREATE VIEW  deptavg (department, avg_salary)
        AS  SELECT dept, AVG(salary)
        FROM  employee GROUP BY dept;
```

```
CREATE VIEW  science (course, last_name, first_name, hs_gpa)
        AS  SELECT c_title, s_lname, s_fname, s_hsgpa
            FROM  student x, class y, course z
            WHERE x.s_id = y.s_id
              AND y.c_id = z.c_id
              AND (c_title = 'MATH 105' OR c_title = 'PHYS
                   102');
```

```
DECLARE  <cursor name>  CURSOR
                        FOR <SELECT statement>
                        [FOR UPDATE OF <column list>];
```

Examples:

DECLARE emplist CURSOR
                   FOR SELECT *
                         FROM employee;

DECLARE partlist CURSOR
                   FOR SELECT stock_no
                       FROM parts
                   FOR UPDATE OF stock_no;

DELETE FROM <table name>
     [WHERE <filter condition>];

Examples:

DELETE FROM temptble;

DELETE FROM staff
          WHERE dept = 'Sales'
              OR dept = 'Accounting';

DROP INDEX <index name>;

Example:

DROP INDEX bylast;

DROP TABLE <table name>;

Example:

DROP TABLE staff;

DROP VIEW <view name>;

Example:

DROP VIEW deptavg;

FETCH <cursor>
 INTO <variable list>;

Example:

DECLARE emplist CURSOR

      FOR SELECT *
            FROM employee;

....

....

OPEN emplist

....

....

FETCH emplist
INTO :ess_no, :elname, :efname, :etitle, :edept, :salary;

....

GRANT ALL [PRIVILEGES]|<privilege list>
    ON [TABLE] <table list>
    TO PUBLIC|<user list>
    [WITH GRANT OPTION];

Examples:

GRANT ALL PRIVILEGES ON account
    TO John;

GRANT INSERT ON parts
  TO PUBLIC;

GRANT SELECT
  ON payroll
  TO Mike, Jim
  WITH GRANT OPTION;

GRANT SELECT, INSERT, UPDATE, DELETE
  ON employee
  TO Susan;

INSERT INTO <table name>
    [(<column list>]
  VALUES (<value list>)|<SELECT statement>;

Examples:

INSERT INTO employee
    VALUES ('123-45-6789', 'Smith', 'James J.',
        'President', 'Corporate', 89500);

INSERT INTO employee (ss_no, l_name, f_name, title)
    VALUES ('909-10-8910', 'Parker', 'Susan', 'Trainee');

INSERT INTO staff
      SELECT *
      FROM employee;

```
            INSERT INTO  roster (first_name, last_name)
                    SELECT f_name, l_name
                    FROM  employee;

OPEN  <cursor name>;

    Example:

    DECLARE emplist CURSOR
        FOR SELECT *
                FROM  employee;

    ....
    ....
    OPEN  emplist

REVOKE ALL  [PRIVILEGES]|<privilege list
        ON  [TABLE]  <table list>
        FROM  PUBLIC|<user list>;

    Examples:

    REVOKE ALL  PRIVILEGES
            FROM  John;

    REVOKE  DELETE
        ON  employee
        FROM  PUBLIC;

    REMOVE  UPDATE, INSERT
        ON  payroll, staff
        FROM  Susan, Mike:

ROLLBACK [WORK];

    Examples:

    ROLLBACK;

    ROLLBACK WORK;


    SELECT  <data objects>
    FROM  <table list>
    [WHERE  <filter condition>]
    [GROUP  <column list>]
        BY
    [HAVING  <grouping condition>]
[ORDER BY  <sorting key>];
```

Examples:

```
SELECT *
  FROM employee;

SELECT *
  FROM employee
 WHERE f_name LIKE 'John%';

SELECT l_name, f_name, salary, salary/12
  FROM employee
 WHERE title != 'Manager'
   AND salary BETWEEN 25000 AND 35000;

SELECT l_name, f_name, dept, salary
  FROM employee
 WHERE title = 'Manager'
ORDER BY salary;

SELECT x.l_name, x.f_name, x.title, y.month_pay
  FROM title x, monthly y
 WHERE x.ss_no = y.soc_sec_no
   AND (x.title = 'Manager' OR x.title = 'President');

SELECT dept, AVG(salary)
  FROM employee
 WHERE dept = 'MIS' OR dept = 'Sales'
GROUP BY dept;

SELECT sw_type, sw_color, AVG(sw_price)
  FROM sweater
GROUP BY sw_type, sw_color
HAVING AVG(sw_price) > 35.95;

SELECT s_id, s_lname, s_fname
  FROM student
 WHERE s_id IN (SELECT DISTINCT s_id
                  FROM class
                 WHERE c_id = 'C1' OR c_id = 'C4');

SELECT f_name, l_name, title, dept, salary
  FROM employee
 WHERE salary = (SELECT MIN(salary)
          salary = (SEFROM employee);
```

```
    SELECT  DISTINCT s_id
     FROM  class
    WHERE  c_id IN
            (SELECT c_id
              FROM  course
             WHERE  c_id IN
                    (SELECT c_id
                      FROM  assign
                     WHERE  t_id IN
                            (SELECT t_id
                              FROM  teacher
                             WHERE  t_lname = 'Newton')));

    INSERT INTO  managers
        SELECT  ss_no, l_name, f_name, title, dept, salary
         FROM  employee
        WHERE  title = 'Manager';

UPDATE  <table name>
   SET  <column name> = <expression> [,
        <column name> = <expression> ...]
[WHERE  <filter condition>];
```

Examples:

```
UPDATE  parts
   SET  unit_cost = 650.9
WHERE  stock_no = 'HW101';

UPDATE  parts
   SET  unit_cost = unit_cost*1.05
WHERE  stock_no LIKE 'SW%';

UPDATE  employee
   SET  dept = 'MIS', Title = 'Programmer'
WHERE  l_name = 'Parker';
```

INDEX

461

D

More Computer Knowledge from Que

Lotus Software Titles

1-2-3 Database Techniques	24.95
1-2-3 Release 2.2 Business Applications	39.95
1-2-3 Release 2.2 Quick Reference	7.95
1-2-3 Release 2.2 QuickStart	19.95
1-2-3 Release 2.2 Workbook and Disk	29.95
1-2-3 Release 3 Business Applications	39.95
1-2-3 Release 3 Quick Reference	7.95
1-2-3 Release 3 QuickStart	19.95
1-2-3 Release 3 Workbook and Disk	29.95
1-2-3 Tips, Tricks, and Traps, 3rd Edition	22.95
Upgrading to 1-2-3 Release 3	14.95
Using 1-2-3, Special Edition	24.95
Using 1-2-3 Release 2.2, Special Edition	24.95
Using 1-2-3 Release 3	24.95
Using Lotus Magellan	21.95
Using Symphony, 2nd Edition	26.95

Database Titles

dBASE III Plus Applications Library	24.95
dBASE III Plus Handbook, 2nd Edition	24.95
dBASE III Plus Tips, Tricks, and Traps	21.95
dBASE III Plus Workbook and Disk	29.95
dBASE IV Applications Library, 2nd Edition	39.95
dBASE IV Handbook, 3rd Edition	23.95
dBASE IV Programming Techniques	24.95
dBASE IV QueCards	21.95
dBASE IV Quick Reference	7.95
dBASE IV QuickStart	19.95
dBASE IV Tips, Tricks, and Traps, 2nd Edition	21.95
dBASE IV Workbook and Disk	29.95
dBXL and Quicksilver Programming: Beyond dBASE	24.95
R:BASE User's Guide, 3rd Edition	22.95
Using Clipper	24.95
Using DataEase	22.95
Using Reflex	19.95
Using Paradox 3	24.95

Applications Software Titles

AutoCAD Advanced Techniques	34.95
AutoCAD Quick Reference	7.95
AutoCAD Sourcebook	24.95
Excel Business Applications: IBM Version	39.95
Introduction to Business Software	14.95
PC Tools Quick Reference	7.95
Smart Tips, Tricks, and Traps	24.95
Using AutoCAD, 2nd Edition	29.95
Using Computers in Business	24.95
Using DacEasy	21.95

Using Dollars and Sense: IBM Version, 2nd Edition	19.95
Using Enable/OA	23.95
Using Excel: IBM Version	24.95
Using Generic CADD	24.95
Using Harvard Project Manager	24.95
Using Managing Your Money, 2nd Edition	19.95
Using Microsoft Works: IBM Version	21.95
Using PROCOMM PLUS	19.95
Using Q&A, 2nd Edition	21.95
Using Quattro	21.95
Using Quicken	19.95
Using Smart	22.95
Using SmartWare II	24.95
Using SuperCalc5, 2nd Edition	22.95

Word Processing and Desktop Publishing Titles

DisplayWrite QuickStart	19.95
Harvard Graphics Quick Reference	7.95
Microsoft Word 5 Quick Reference	7.95
Microsoft Word 5 Tips, Tricks, and Traps: IBM Version	19.95
Using DisplayWrite 4, 2nd Edition	19.95
Using Freelance Plus	24.95
Using Harvard Graphics	24.95
Using Microsoft Word 5: IBM Version	21.95
Using MultiMate Advantage, 2nd Edition	19.95
Using PageMaker: IBM Version, 2nd Edition	24.95
Using PFS: First Choice	22.95
Using PFS: First Publisher	22.95
Using Professional Write	19.95
Using Sprint	21.95
Using Ventura Publisher, 2nd Edition	24.95
Using WordPerfect, 3rd Edition	21.95
Using WordPerfect 5	24.95
Using WordStar, 2nd Edition	21.95
Ventura Publisher Techniques and Applications	22.95
Ventura Publisher Tips, Tricks, and Traps	24.95
WordPerfect Macro Library	21.95
WordPerfect Power Techniques	21.95
WordPerfect QueCards	21.95
WordPerfect Quick Reference	7.95
WordPerfect QuickStart	21.95
WordPerfect Tips, Tricks, and Traps, 2nd Edition	21.95
WordPerfect 5 Workbook and Disk	29.95

Macintosh/Apple II Titles

The Big Mac Book	27.95
Excel QuickStart	19.95
Excel Tips, Tricks, and Traps	22.95
Using AppleWorks, 3rd Edition	21.95
Using AppleWorks GS	21.95
Using dBASE Mac	19.95
Using Dollars and Sense: Macintosh Version	19.95
Using Excel: Macintosh Verson	22.95
Using FullWrite Professional	21.95

Using HyperCard:	24.95
Using Microsoft Word 4: Macintosh Version	21.95
Using Microsoft Works: Macintosh Version, 2nd Edition	21.95
Using PageMaker: Macintosh Version	24.95
Using WordPerfect: Macintosh Version	19.95

Hardware and Systems Titles

DOS Tips, Tricks, and Traps	22.95
DOS Workbook and Disk	29.95
Hard Disk Quick Reference	7.95
IBM PS/2 Handbook	21.95
Managing Your Hard Disk, 2nd Edition	22.95
MS-DOS Quick Reference	7.95
MS-DOS QuickStart	21.95
MS-DOS User's Guide, Special Edition	29.95
Networking Personal Computers, 3rd Edition	22.95
Norton Utilities Quick Reference	7.95
The Printer Bible	24.95
Understanding UNIX: A Conceptual Guide, 2nd Edition	21.95
Upgrading and Repairing PCs	27.95
Using DOS	22.95
Using Microsoft Windows	19.95
Using Novell NetWare	24.95
Using OS/2	23.95
Using PC DOS, 3rd Edition	22.95

Programming and Technical Titles

Assembly Language Quick Reference	7.95
C Programmer's Toolkit	39.95
C Programming Guide, 3rd Edition	24.95
C Quick Reference	7.95
DOS and BIOS Functions Quick Reference	7.95
DOS Programmer's Reference, 2nd Edition	27.95
Power Graphics Programming	24.95
QuickBASIC Advanced Techniques	21.95
QuickBASIC Programmer's Toolkit	39.95
QuickBASIC Quick Reference	7.95
SQL Programmer's Guide	29.95
Turbo C Programming	22.95
Turbo Pascal Advanced Techniques	22.95
Turbo Pascal Programmer's Toolkit	39.95
Turbo Pascal Quick Reference	7.95
Using Assembly Language	24.95
Using QuickBASIC 4	19.95
Using Turbo Pascal	21.95

For more information, call

1-800-428-5331

All prices subject to change without notice. Prices and charges are for domestic orders only. Non-U.S. prices might be higher.

Networking Personal Computers, 3rd Edition

by Michael Durr and Mark Gibbs

The most in-depth coverage of local area networks! Learn LAN standards, LAN hardware, LAN installation, and practical solutions to common LAN problems. The text also covers networking IBM-compatible PCs with Macintosh machines.

$22.95 USA
Order #955
0-88022-417-7
400 pp.

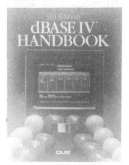

dBASE IV Handbook, 3rd Edition

by George T. Chou, Ph.D.

A complete introduction to dBASE IV functions! Beginning users will progress systematically from basic database concepts to advanced dBASE features, and experienced dBASE users will appreciate the information on the new features of dBASE IV. Includes Quick Start tutorials.

$23.95 USA
Order #852
0-88022-380-4
785 pp.

Using Novell NetWare

by Bill Lawrence

An inside look at the leading local network sofware. NetWare users will appreciate this thorough guide to installation, network management, and advanced NetWare topics.

Order #1013
$24.95 USA
0-88022-466-5, 400 pp.

Using DOS

Developed by Que Corporation

The most helpful DOS book available! Que's *Using DOS* teaches the essential commands and functions of DOS Versions 3 and 4—in an easy-to-understand format that helps users manage and organize their files effectively. Includes a handy **Command Reference**.

Order #1035
$22.95 USA
0-88022-497-5, 550 pp.